D0340453

p.22

ROOSEVELT TO REAGAN

ROOSEVELT
TO
REAGAN

*A Reporter's Encounters with
Nine Presidents*

HEDLEY DONOVAN

A Cornelia & Michael Bessie Book

HARPER & ROW, PUBLISHERS, New York
*Cambridge, Philadelphia, San Francisco, London
Mexico City, São Paulo, Singapore, Sydney*

Acknowledgment is made for permission to reprint material which appeared in some-what different form in the following publications:

American Heritage: Excerpts from "The Lincoln Cabinet," December 1984.
Fortune: Excerpts from "Reagan's First Two Hundred Days," Sept. 21, 1981; "A Vacuum in Leadership," March 22, 1982; "Reagan's Make-or-Break Year," March 7, 1983; "How the White House Reads the Press," Dec. 20, 1980;. Copyright © 1980, 1981, 1982, 1983 Time Inc. Reprinted by permission of *Fortune.*
Time: Excerpts from "Fluctuation on the Presidential Exchange," Nov. 9, 1981; "Job Specs for the Oval Office," Dec. 13, 1982; Copyright © 1981, 1982 Time Inc.
Washington Star: Excerpt from Sunday Magazine section, April 26, 1981. Reprinted by permission of the *Washington Post.*

FIRST EDITION

Designer: Sidney Feinberg

The text of this book was set in 10-point Gael. It was composed by Haddon Craftsmen, Inc., Scranton, Pennsylvania, and printed and bound by Haddon Craftsmen.

Library of Congress Cataloging in Publication Data

Donovan, Hedley.
  Roosevelt to Reagan: a reporter's encounters with nine presidents.

  "A Cornelia & Michael Bessie book."
  Includes index.
  1. Presidents—United States—Biography. 2. United
States—Politics and government—1933-1945. 3. United
States—Politics and government—1945-   .
4. Donovan, Hedley. 5. Journalists—United States—
Biography. I. Title.
E176.1.D69   1985   973'.09'92   84-48592
ISBN 0-06-039042-5

85 86 87 88 10 9 8 7 6 5 4 3 2 1

To Dorothy
and our children,
Peter, Helen, Mark

Contents

Acknowledgments

I wish to acknowledge my indebtedness to the Washington *Post,* for introducing me to Franklin Roosevelt and Senator Harry Truman, and to Time Incorporated, for putting me in touch with the succeeding Presidents, from Eisenhower through Reagan. I owe special thanks to Jimmy Carter, my very good-natured employer during a difficult year of his life.

I am indebted to *Time* and *Fortune* for permission to reprint material from articles I wrote for those publications during 1980–83. These articles were written while I was a Time Inc. consultant, a happy arrangement first set up for me by Andrew Heiskell, then Chairman of the Board, and generously continued by J. Richard Munro, president, and Henry Grunwald, my successor as Editor in Chief. Much of Chapter 18 originally appeared as a *Fortune* article. Chapter 20 is drawn in part from three articles on the Reagan Administration I wrote for *Fortune.* Two essays I wrote for *Time* have been expanded into Chapters 21 and 22 of the present book. Parts of Chapter 17 were first used in lectures at Duke University and at the University of Virginia, and were then published in *The Virginia Papers on the Presidency,* and also in the *Washington Star.*

My somewhat permissive editors for these articles were William Rukeyser and Richard Armstrong of *Fortune;* Ronald Kriss, Edward Jamieson, Jason McManus and Ray Cave of *Time;* and Murray Gart of the *Star.* My indispensable collaborators from the reporter/researcher staffs were Ford Worthy, Anna Cifelli, Claire Makin and Louis Richman of *Fortune,* and Anne Hopkins and Melissa Ludtke of *Time.* Dorothy Ferenbaugh was my research assistant while I was Editor in Chief of

Time Inc.; my articles and speeches of those years, some quoted in this book, benefited greatly from her reporting and her scrutiny.

I owe a large debt to the many colleagues and friends who reviewed parts of this book in manuscript form or gave me comments on the chapters that started out as magazine articles. Ralph Graves, former Editorial Director of Time Inc., gave me excellent advice on many matters, including how to find a publisher. Strobe Talbott, *Time*'s diplomatic correspondent through four administrations, now *Time* Bureau Chief in Washington, lugged the manuscript around on airplanes, told me he was going to be absolutely candid, and I think was. Talbott's three predecessors as *Time* Washington Bureau chiefs, Robert Ajemian, Hugh Sidey and John Steele, astute President-watchers all, Ike through Reagan, gave me very valuable insights and criticism.

For perceptive comments on Chapter 22, I am indebted to Richard Neustadt, Jonathan Moore and Joseph Nye of Harvard; Henry Graff of Columbia; Kenneth Thompson, University of Virginia; William Leuchtenberg, University of North Carolina; Gerhard Loewenberg, University of Iowa; Stephen Hess, of the Brookings Institution; Alexander Heard, former chancellor of Vanderbilt University; James Billington, Director of the Woodrow Wilson Center for International Scholars in Washington; and R. Gordon Hoxie, president of the Center for The Study of the Presidency.

Captain Gary Sick, formerly of the Navy and the National Security Council, author of the forthcoming history of the Iranian revolution *All Fall Down* (Random House, 1985), was kind enough to review my account of the Iranian hostage crisis.

Brenda Reger, Director of the Office of Information Policy and Security Review, National Security Council, reviewed the manuscript for possible breaches of classification, found it generally sanitary and while she was at it, caught a couple of non-classified mistakes.

For their wisdom and their generosity with their time, I am deeply grateful to all those cited here. For such oversights and misjudgments as may remain in the book, I am of course responsible.

Finally, I am grateful to my editor and publisher, Simon Michael Bessie, for encouraging this venture and for strengthening the manuscript in many ways; Beena Kamlani of Harper & Row, my patient and vigilant text editor; Eileen Chiu Graham, formerly of *Time*, my wonderfully bright and resourceful research assistant; Carol Rinzler, of Cahill, Gordon and Reindel, my lawyer and agent, herself an author and skillful editor; and not least, Gertrude Lanz and Lynnette Williams, who heroically translated this work from Donovan handwriting into clean typescript. When people used to ask me if I had a word processor, I would say, "No, something better."

A Note on Attribution:

Presidential speeches, statements, messages, press conference comments are quoted from *Public Papers of the Presidents of the United States* (Washington: Office of the Federal Register), a series which now covers all the Presidencies from Hoover through the third year of Reagan, except for Roosevelt, who is covered in *Public Papers and Addresses of Franklin D. Roosevelt,* ed. S. Rosenman (New York: Harper & Brothers, 1938–1950).

Where Presidents or other individuals are quoted without attribution to a published source, the remark was made in a personal conversation or interview with the author.

Foreword

This book is an essay about the modern American Presidents, as encountered by a reporter who once thought of being a history professor.

Since I didn't become a professor, this book is not scholarship but journalism, highly personal and impressionistic journalism at that. The text is opinion, recollection, and firsthand observation. An opinionated approach to the Presidency is surely an "entitlement" (nontaxable) for a citizen who has lived under thirteen Presidents, seen eleven of them, and known nine of them.

The modern Presidency, by consensus of the scholars and the people who have worked in the White House, begins with Franklin Roosevelt. Nine men have held the office. In one way or another, I have "covered" each of them and had some personal acquaintance with each, slight in some instances, rather close in others.

As a newspaper reporter, I worked four years in a fascinating time and place, New Deal Washington. For six months or so before Pearl Harbor, and six weeks or so after, I was covering the FDR White House for the Washington *Post.* On the shoestring *Post* of that era a healthy young man was encouraged to treat the White House and State Department as one beat (State was then just across the street), and I did.

Out of the Navy four years later, I went to work for Time Incorporated. I could recite my Time Inc. jobs by presidential administrations. (I once could name all the kings of England in order.) I was a writer and editor for *Fortune* during the Truman years, managing editor of *Fortune* during the Eisenhower Administration, editorial director, then Editor in Chief of Time Inc. from Jack Kennedy through Jimmy Carter. As candidates, these politicians all came to meals with the senior Time Inc. editors. (They also ate, of course, with the *New York Times,* Washington *Post, Newsweek,* etc.) For the Editor in Chief of Time Inc. it is an important part of his work to know the President, and if possible understand him, and it is one of the President's minor chores to know the Editor in Chief.

For nearly forty years, then, I was looking at Presidents from the perspective, and with the access, of a reporter and editor. Quite suddenly, just a few weeks after retiring from Time Inc., I was offered almost unlimited access to a President and the perspective of a White House insider. I accepted the absorbing and frustrating adventure, late in Jimmy Carter's Administration, of working for a year as Senior Adviser to the President.

This book tells of that inside year with one President, and of the other Presidents I have known from the outside. I hope the two vantage points yield some useful triangulations. Both influence my concluding reflections on "Job Specs for the Oval Office."

These sketches of the modern Presidents do not purport to be "objective" but they are not colored by any partisan commitment. As a journalist I enjoyed equal access to Democratic and Republican Presidents. When Jimmy Carter asked me to come to work for him in the summer of 1979, I told him I had just barely voted for him in 1976 and I wasn't necessarily going to vote for him in November 1980. I am a card-carrying independent, of conservative leanings. And I am an old history major (minor: political science) with a lifelong fascination with the greatest political office in the world.

The first President I ever saw was Calvin Coolidge. He had come to Scandinavian Minnesota in 1925 to take part in a Norse-American celebration. School was let out in Minneapolis, and the children could watch the presidential motorcade move along a stately residential street called Park Avenue, Cal periodically lifting his tall silk hat. That evening I reported to my parents that I hadn't realized the President had such reddish hair.

In 1981, still President-watching, I think I made one of the first close-in sightings, during an interview in the Century Plaza Hotel in Los Angeles, of a few strands of gray in Ronald Reagan's full, gleaming head of auburn hair. He has earned a few more since.

As a schoolboy I had on my desk at home a little painted wooden figure of Lincoln, a present from an aunt. In family dinner table conversations, Lincoln ranked not too far behind Jesus Christ and somewhat ahead of George Washington. My mother included among Lincoln's many virtues that he had not had as many advantages as Washington. Even as late as 1981, I felt a shiver of horror, as the *New York Times* meant me to, on seeing in a *Times* subhead* that President Reagan might appoint a "Lincoln Foe" as head of the National Endowment for the Humanities. This was a Texas historian, Melvin Bradford, who had written unfavorably of Lincoln's broad construction of the Constitution. Reagan eventually appointed William Bennett, Director of the National Humanities Center in North Carolina. Bill is a conservative all right, but so far as I know, not a Lincoln foe.

Just as I was finishing this book, I received an invitation from Byron Dobell, editor of *American Heritage,* to join some sixty scholars, journalists, public officials in naming "the one scene or incident in American history you would have liked to witness." Immersed as I was in Presidents, and the appraisal of Presidents, I wrote:

> I would choose to be at one of the cabinet meetings of early 1865, as the Civil War was ending, when Abraham Lincoln, out of all the strange and glorious forces within him, had totally matured as a statesman-saint. An especially revealing meeting must have been the one at which Lincoln talked of an appropriation of four hundred million dollars, an immense sum for the time, to help the South recover. Though Lincoln had assumed virtually dictatorial authority over the conduct of the war, he did listen to his cabinet, even invited them to vote, and then from time to time outvoted them. "Seven no and one aye, the ayes have it," was his legendary summation of the powers of the President vis-à-vis his cabinet. But the Lincoln cabinet meetings were far from the perfunctory sessions of the recent Presidencies. Lincoln's cabinet dissuaded him from proposing his magnanimous Reconstruction grant. They felt the Congress wasn't ready. Lincoln made it clear he would set aside the idea only temporarily. The dialogue must have illuminated the ways in which Lincoln, at the height of his powers, could strike the balance between "practical politics" and longer-range purpose and vision. I would like to have listened.†

Along with my little painted figure of Lincoln, another schoolboy treasure was a kind of memorial certificate, black-bordered, elegantly printed on heavy paper, issued at the time of Theodore Roosevelt's death. My father had saved it a few years, then gave it to me. He was not in fact a great T.R. admirer (and had voted for William Howard Taft and the Republican regulars in 1912, against the Roosevelt insurgency). In later years, during long and affectionate arguments with my boss Henry Luce, who revered Teddy Roosevelt, I used to enjoy citing my

---

*October 22, 1981.
†"I wish I'd Been There." *American Heritage,* December 1984.

father's orthodox views. Luce still described himself, somewhat quaintly in the 1950s and 1960s, as a Bull Mooser. He thought of me as generally more "liberal" than he was, and for some reason found it odd to have to think of himself as more liberal than my father. I in fact admired almost everything about T.R. except the streak of juvenile jingoism. What an extraordinarily gifted man—surely our most versatile President since Thomas Jefferson.

Those, as I was growing up, were the mythic Presidents, Lincoln and Washington, then Teddy Roosevelt, then Woodrow Wilson (for the beautiful language, the idealism, and for winning a war) and Thomas Jefferson, whom one of my high school teachers accurately called a great man but not a great President. Do high school students care today about the old Presidents? I hope so.

For me today it is not a flippancy to say that the mythic Presidents are those I didn't know personally. Those are the first thirty-one— disastrous, mediocre, good, and great—versus the recent nine. Awesome and grand as the living office still is, there is an undeniable difference between Presidents studied in books and Presidents known in the flesh.

President No. 31 was Herbert Hoover. I never knew him but saw him give a campaign speech in St. Paul in 1932. It was not electrifying. I was for him, however. It was not just that I had grown up in a Republican family, but my father was a mining engineer, as Hoover was, and years before Hoover ran, he was often cited at our dinner table as the best-qualified man in the country for the Presidency. Some Democrats of that day thought so too (not that many of them turned up at our table). In 1928 I won my first election bet, Hoover against Al Smith, one dollar, with a Catholic friend at school.

In 1932, age seventeen, I even wrote a metropolitan newspaper editorial attacking Hoover's probable opponent, Franklin Roosevelt. I was a sophomore at the University of Minnesota, quite a radical campus in those Depression days, and I was an editorial writer for the student newspaper, the *Minnesota Daily.* I wrote an editorial unfriendly to Roosevelt and, at least by implication, indicating that Hoover should be reelected. The editor of the *Minnesota Daily,* Phil Potter, later to be a distinguished correspondent of the Baltimore *Sun,* told me my editorial was really too partisan to print in a student paper supported by state tax funds. I happened to mention this to my father, and he mentioned it to the editor of the old Minneapolis *Journal,* whom he sometimes saw on the streetcar riding downtown. The editor of the *Journal* said he'd like to see this piece I'd written, and the very next day he printed it, as his lead editorial, without changing a word. For some days afterward I kept expecting a check for $5, or possibly even $10, but nothing ever came. Apparently the Minneapolis *Journal* felt it was simply the duty of all ablebodied citizens to write editorials denouncing the Democrats.

When Hoover was defeated, my grandmother Mollie Knox Dougan was especially indignant. Since she knew no one who had voted for Roosevelt, she suspected the Democrats might have stolen the election. Even more dangerous than the Democrats were Minnesota's home-grown radicals, the Farmer Laborites (later merged with the Democrats to become the DFL of Hubert Humphrey and Walter Mondale). My grandmother once claimed that by brandishing her cane she had driven off a young man attempting to leave Farmer-Labor campaign literature on our front porch.

I would have liked to be President. In one of our conversational rambles through everything under sun, I was deploring with Harry Luce the fashionable cliché that the Presidency was an impossible job, how can anybody possibly want it, etc., etc. "I wouldn't mind having a shot at it," Luce said. "How about you?" I had to admit I wouldn't mind either. At the time Eisenhower was President, Luce as Editor in Chief had been running Time Inc. for about thirty years, and was occasionally restless. I had been managing editor of *Fortune* for two or three years and was not especially restless. Luce once briefly considered, and was considered for, a try at a Republican nomination for senator from Connecticut. That is a lot closer than I ever came to elective office.

I do like to think of the President as my employee. This is not just sour grapes. The Founding Fathers thought of the President as the servant of the people, the chief clerk for their common business, which business was of course quite limited in those days. The public business and the President's powers have grown stupendously, but there is still relevance in the early republican doctrine of the citizen-king. The Founders, better grounded in the classics than our modern Presidents, would cite Cicero, who said his greatest pride, to the end of his life, would be *Civis romanus sum,* "I am a Roman citizen."

In a commencement speech in 1968, in the last year of the Lyndon Johnson Administration, I ventured to tell the seniors of the University of Rochester they were entering into a lifetime "contract" with the President of the United States. I politely noted that one or two of them might hold the job some day but in all honesty I had to add, "Maybe none of you will get there; most people don't." I went on:

But all of us here have a working relationship with the President, and he has a considerable bearing, to say the least, on our careers and lives. By the actuarial tables, you should probably deal with eight or ten Presidents in your adult lifetime. I have had five Presidents since I was twenty-one; I hope I'm good for three or four more. [So it has turned out.]

The job description, as they would say in the Business School, is a formidable one. And that brings us to a deepening paradox in our American system. We have been getting more and more dependent, as a nation, on a strong Presidency, at the same time we have been becoming a more and more broadly democratic society. There has been a vast diffusion of education and influence, and a multiplication of decision-making places, throughout our society. We now have the staggering number of 33 million people in this country who have had some college education—an absolutely extraordinary number in any historical terms. [That was the number in 1968 —it is now 52 million.] More and more people have enough education, enough income, and enough leisure to assert some voice in how things go, in their community, or their company, or somewhere in the huge American network of organizations. In these ways, our democracy is constantly getting more democratic.

Yet at the same time, the growing complexity of the problems we face at home and abroad, and the heavy emotional content of these problems, make the moral leadership of the President more and more often the crucial factor. Or putting it negatively: If we don't have real moral authority in the Presidency, more things can go wrong, and more seriously wrong, than ever before . . . Our American system has come to require an almost mystical union: you will lead Presidents no less than being led by them.

I had been invited to give the Rochester speech by Chancellor Allen Wallis. Wallis, an old friend from Minnesota days, generally liked my speech except for one passage where I failed to assert fervently enough that a President needn't always be *doing* something. In 1982, Wallis became Under Secretary of State for Economic Affairs in the Reagan Administration.

I still believe strongly in the concept of a compact between the citizen and his servant the President. But we the employers have been asking both too little and too much of Presidents. We may be getting the Presidents we deserve, but we have not been getting the Presidents we need. So toward the end of this book, I ask how we could arrange matters so as to deserve better.

December 1984
New York

PART I

"The President Is Calling"

1

———◆———

Gray Hair Preferred

One steamy Friday in July 1979, I had flown down from New York to a board of directors meeting of the Washington *Evening Star.**
The *Star* was faithfully observing President Carter's request that air conditioning be set no lower than 78 degrees. The *Star* board met in an interior room, and two of the directors were smoking cigars (I was one), which did not improve the air quality. When I got home that afternoon, to Sands Point, Long Island, I subsided into my swimming pool, and congratulated myself on not working in Washington.

The phone rang. Normally I let it ring when I'm in the pool; it will have stopped by the time I can get to it. This time I went to answer because I thought it might be my daughter Helen in Boston, who was hoping to get down to Sands Point for a weekend visit with me and her brother Mark. It turned out to be a White House operator, and then I was talking to Jimmy Carter.

"Hey, how are you, Hedley?"

"Well, I'm in my swimming pool. [Approximately true.] So I'm feeling great."

He was sorry to disturb me, but could I come down and talk with him? Of course; would Monday be convenient? Well, he had been hoping for a couple of days sooner, i.e., tomorrow, Saturday. I explained that I had been planning a weekend with two of my children, and didn't like to break in on that. We settled for Monday.

*Time Inc. bought the Washington *Star* in 1978, and had to close it down in 1981, after losing about $85 million, pretax. We found the competition from the Washington *Post,* my old alma mater, overpowering.

3

The President had just conducted his week-long "retreat" at Camp David, conferring in relays with 134 distinguished private citizens on what ailed the country (and by inference, his own standing in the polls, down to a sickly approval rating of 29 percent). He had come down from the mountain to deliver his "crisis of confidence" speech, had fired almost half his Cabinet, hadn't yet replaced them all, and had announced there would also be changes in the White House staff.

I knew that a number of his Camp David visitors had urged him to broaden the White House staff: to bring in one or more non-Georgians "with gray hair" acquired in business or the professions, familiar with public affairs but not directly of the political world. I saw one or two newspaper stories where I was "among those mentioned." At the *Star* board meeting, in fact, Murray Gart, the editor of the paper, had asked, "Have you heard from the President?" When I said no, he said, "You will."

The President's summons made for an unsettled weekend. I had retired only a few weeks earlier after thirty-four years with Time Incorporated, fifteen of them in the richly privileged job of Editor in Chief. I had come through a painful year. My wife Dorothy had died the previous summer after a long and harrowing illness. The prospect of retirement, not too inviting for most executives, is especially difficult when you have held one of those jobs you should really pay to do. And it was especially hard to face alone. Post-retirement travels, hobbies, indulgences that are great fun to think about as a couple, turn empty. But old friends began to think up things for me to do. By spring there had been a warming variety of board invitations, consulting propositions, writing offers, teaching offers. It seemed I could be as busy as I wanted to be, or possibly more so. I was beginning to feel a little comfortable with my retirement portfolio.

Washington, even apart from the July climate, did not have great appeal. Of course when I imagined myself President, as I had done now and then, I usually compared very favorably with the incumbent (a view shared by my mother and one or two others). There were only three or four offices in Washington that would have tempted me at all, and they seemed quite solidly occupied in July 1979. I could think of several Cabinet posts that sounded dreary, and countless assistant secretaryships that would be even less fun. But from many years back I had

been taught that except for compelling personal reasons, or unbreaka-
ble commitments in another position, a citizen does not refuse the
President of the United States. Just retired, I felt defenseless. I spent
much of the weekend thinking up not personal excuses but excellent
reasons why the President himself, after further reflection, should conclude he didn't want me in his Administration after all.

When we met in the Oval Office, I told the President I had really
been quite spoiled by my previous job. I had no boss, except for an
indulgent Time Inc. Board of Directors, who could theoretically fire me
but never showed any tendency to do so. I could speak out on any
subject, write what I felt like, assign articles to others whose views were
congenial to me. I couldn't imagine having to worry about various
layers of federal officialdom, or a hundred senators, before opening my
mouth.

This would be no problem, the President said. He wanted me to fill
a new position on the White House staff, Senior Adviser. I would be
responsible only to the President, and he thought he was quite easy to
work for. So far as he knew, nobody had quit because they found him
difficult to work for. Hamilton Jordan, de facto chief of staff from early
in the Administration, had just been formally designated as such, but I
would not be reporting through him. I would have direct access to the
President, and as much of it as I wanted. I wouldn't have any fixed
operating responsibilities, but the President and I would have a running
dialogue on the substance of national policy—foreign and domestic—
and would be totally candid with each other about people and strategies
in all areas. This would be a great service to him, but more important,
the country. He would feel free to tell me things he didn't tell anyone
else. (During my year with him, he did occasionally preface some confidence by saying: "I haven't even told Rosalynn this.")

I hoped my journalistic background hadn't led to any notion that
I should be his private PR consultant or "image" expert. I was not
interested in second-guessing Jody Powell or Jerry Rafshoon. No, no,
that wasn't the idea at all. Of course, he and I would often be discussing
public opinion, but that is part of the substance of policy choices.

I reminded the President that I am a political independent and said
I didn't want to be involved in the coming presidential campaign.
When I told him I had just barely voted for him in 1976, I did not repeat
the formulation I used when friends asked me at the time how I liked
the election returns. "Perfect," I used to say. "I just barely voted for

him, and he just barely won." I did, however, tell the President how I finally decided on my vote on the Sunday evening before the election. I had taken my wife that afternoon to New York Hospital, where she was to have surgery the next morning. She was a strong Carter supporter. Since she wouldn't be able to vote, I told her that if I decided I was for Ford, I would refrain from voting. She and I would be "paired." If I decided in favor of Carter, I would drive out on Tuesday to our polling place on Long Island, and Carter would at least get one vote out of the family. So alone in our New York apartment that Sunday evening, to try to take my mind off my wife's ordeal, I spent some hours plowing through a pile of political speeches and campaign materials I had been saving. In the end I probably voted the vested interest of a journalist: I thought a Carter Administration would be more *interesting* than four more years of Jerry Ford. The President, so I heard later, liked my telling him the story so frankly, repeated it to others, and also added that he preferred Dorothy's judgment to mine.

When I told the President I wasn't necessarily committed to supporting him in November 1980, he may have been a little taken aback but his response was gentle: he hoped he would have earned my vote by then. He added: "I'm running—to the last delegate." This would have been a front-page story in July 1979. It was rather widely assumed in Washington that summer that the Democratic nomination was Ted Kennedy's for the asking, and there was even speculation that Carter might quit rather than take a beating.

But why in the world did President Carter want Hedley Donovan, with all his crotchety stipulations, in a White House role of such intimacy and trust? Journalists are not Carter's favorite breed of people, nor are card-carrying political independents. He had always been wary, furthermore, of the "Northeastern Establishment," which for better or worse had become my home territory.

It seemed that two good friends of mine, Washington lawyers and old government hands, Sol Linowitz and Clark Clifford, had been among the Camp David communicants who urged the President to bring me onto his staff. When the President tried out my name on others at Camp David, he was really amazed—"this may seen undiplomatic of me to say"—at the depth of the approval. He had once tried to get Charlie Kirbo to come up from Atlanta and take a full-time White House staff position, but Charlie didn't want to live in Washington, and now in any case it probably wouldn't be wise to bring in another Georgian. Carter had tremendous affection for Hamilton Jordan and Jody

Powell, and trust in their political judgment, but that was a different relationship—he was almost like a father or much older brother to them. He needed a Senior Adviser of great maturity, experience, and stability, and he was convinced I was the best person in the country for the job. I said if he would give me a little time I bet I could think of some better people. No, nobody else was even mentioned at Camp David, and he hadn't even thought about anybody else. It is never easy to contradict the President of the United States, and he is especially convincing when he is saying flattering things about you.

Could I have a couple of days to think about it? Certainly—but what was my feeling about it right now? I was greatly honored, and would consider it very seriously.

2

Name-Dropping

I had known Jimmy Carter from the early 1970s, and seen him perhaps eight or ten times over those years. When reporters interviewing me after my appointment said they understood I was an "old friend" or "close friend" of the President's, I felt it was presumptuous to agree. But it seemed somehow standoffish to say, Well, no, we are simply acquaintances. I never did hit on just the right description. Some people who knew him much better than I said he had no real friends. But he does have great friendliness. His particular mix of modesty, warmth, and courtesy could be completely winning.

I first met Carter when *Time* was considering a cover story on one or all of the new southern governors elected in 1970. He came to lunch with some of our editors on the forty-seventh floor of the Time & Life Building, was suitably admiring of our mid-Manhattan view, and lived up to our Atlanta news bureau's argument that he was very quotable, represented something new in the Deep South, and was a politician from whom more might be heard. In later years Carter often said the *Time* cover story* gave him his first national prominence and helped start him on his way.

It was written by a woman, B. J. Phillips, who had originally known Carter while she was a reporter on the Atlanta *Constitution*. Her first encounter with Carter was only a month or two after he had been beaten for governor in 1966. She found him speaking to about fifteen people at a Kiwanis lunch, and he told her after his speech exactly what he was going to do during the next three years and where it would lead,

*May 31, 1971.

which is where it did lead, and that in the meantime he was accepting any invitations to any audiences of whatever size.

When Jimmy came to the *Time* lunch, I was delighted that as he entered the room and saw B. J. Phillips, he went over at once and gave her a loud kiss. This was before social kissing reached the epidemic proportions we know today, and I thought it promised remarkable empathy between our writer and the cover subject. I subsequently saw Jimmy kiss thousands of women at White House parties, and on TV at political rallies, and admired his inexhaustible enthusiasm.

Carter came back to the Time & Life Building for other meetings and meals, and I also began to see something of him as a fellow member of the Trilateral Commission. This was a worthy and then obscure organization, later "controversial" because various kook outfits attacked it as a hidden government serving communism, or Zionism, or Wall Street imperialism, or some combination thereof. It was and is a useful organization, originally formed by David Rockefeller to try to bring Japan into the private and informal communication channels that linked the North American and European business, academic, and political communities. The U.S. members, along with Carter, included Fritz Mondale, Harold Brown, Zbigniew Brzezinski, Cyrus Vance, Mike Blumenthal. Also George Bush and John Anderson.

Jimmy Carter was an assiduous attender of Trilateral Commission meetings and often said, as he was starting to run for President, and before the commission began to attract zany attacks, that it was one of the places where he learned something about foreign policy. More significant, it was where he got well acquainted with Vance and Brzezinski.

Carter's most memorable performance at any Trilateral meeting came at an event in Washington. Secretary of State Kissinger was giving a dinner for the commission, and after his talk he invited questions. The first came from a former British Cabinet minister, rather drunk unfortunately, who had a complicated and interminable question. When the man finally sat down to everyone's relief, Jimmy Carter got up instantly, and very mischievously, for a fellow not noted for mischief, asked would Secretary Kissinger please restate the question. When the room quieted down, Kissinger gave a brilliant extemporaneous performance. Without in any way putting down the British politician, he did restate the question, organizing it, as I recall, into three parts, and yet it was still recognizable as having something to do with what the questioner had said. Then Kissinger proceeded to answer his own question with unassailable clarity and logic.

Partly through the Trilateral connection, and also no doubt because of the circulation figures of the Time Inc. publications, my wife and I were invited to spend a weekend with the Carters while he was Governor of Georgia. (I later read the prophetic memo in which Hamilton Jordan outlined all the steps by which Carter could parlay the governorship into the Presidency, including a recommendation that he invite important publishers and editors and TV people to visit the Mansion in Atlanta while he was still governor.) One of the first people we met in the Governor's Mansion was a black woman, convicted of manslaughter, who was on parole in custody of the governor. She was Amy's governess. It was interesting to hear from Carter that George Wallace also had paroled convicts working at the Governor's Mansion in Alabama.

Later in the afternoon the Governor gave us a cocktail party of a special kind. He said it was against his policy to serve liquor in the Mansion, but a friend of his who lived down the road had very kindly agreed to make his house available for a party. In a nice way the governor made it plain that he was giving the party, that he was paying for the liquor. Several people later to become famous were there, among them Charles Kirbo and Andrew Young. About half the people at the party were black.

In conversation in his car, in his office at the Mansion, and at the Capitol, Carter talked more about energy than anything else. This was in December 1973, at the time of the Arab oil embargo and the first wave of concern in this country about an energy shortage. Carter took it very seriously. I foresaw the easing off of the situation the next year, which he didn't, but he was more perceptive about the middle-range problem. (I think I had it right for the longer range.)

His interest in energy led us into a colorful episode on a highway outside Atlanta. Carter and his legislature had just installed a 55-mile-an-hour limit, and as we were driving back toward Atlanta from a day of factory-gate politicking, a car passed us going at least 65. Jimmy told his driver to catch up and nose the speeder over to the side of the road. He said he was going over to talk with the fellow; I decided to go along and listen. He was very quiet and gentle and said, "I'm Jimmy Carter." The man said, "Oh, yes, Governor." Carter said, "You know we've just put in a fifty-five-mile-an-hour limit here in the state, and I certainly wish you'd cooperate with us." The man said, "Governor, I'm sorry, I didn't realize I was going over fifty-five, but I certainly appreciate your calling it to my attention." Jimmy said, "Well, I'd certainly appreciate your cooperation in the future." The man said, "Well, thank you, Governor." Jimmy said, "Thank you, sir." They went on and on, thank-yous and good nights, a marvelous southern exchange, and I wasn't sure they could ever break it off.

When I wrote Carter to congratulate him after he was elected President, I said, "From now on, for name-dropping purposes, I'm going to claim that I once helped you make a citizen's arrest." He wrote back very promptly, with a great put-down. He said, "And to think for name-dropping purposes, I used to tell my staff I knew you."

3

———◆———

Horowitz and the *Titanic*

Early in the Carter Administration, I gave a talk to some of the Time Inc. staff on my impressions of the new President. He had been in office fifty days, and I gave him a very mixed report card. I made only one prediction—"Carter will remain for us journalistically a somewhat elusive man . . . The gentleness, softness of voice and manner, compassion, alongside the very cool steely ambition, a certain degree of arrogance, a degree of vindictiveness—these things are not necessarily contradictory, but we don't usually think of them as going together. One of his staff people told one of our reporters, 'Jimmy is his own Haldeman.' A pretty rough quote. And yet also interesting that a staff member very close to him would feel perfectly secure in saying that. . . . All of these contrasts and paradoxes startle and will continue to startle us. It will be a long time before we dare think we have him really figured out. He will keep journalism good and busy."

Just twenty minutes before I was to go to the Time Inc. auditorium to deliver these remarks, I had a phone call from Secretary of State Cyrus Vance. He and the President wanted me to be an ambassador. I was then only two years short of retirement; the post was an important country that fascinated my wife and me; she would have been a superb ambassador's wife (better than I as an ambassador). It was odd to have this tempting presidential offer pending while I stood up before several hundred journalists, in a perfectly open meeting, to give my not overly flattering appraisal of the President. My wife and I spent a happy weekend thinking what a wonderful experience that embassy might be. She was game; I was worried about getting very far away from her doctors. I didn't want to give that to Dorothy as a reason for declining, however, or to anyone else lest it somehow get back to her. I told Dorothy—and Cy Vance—I owed Time Inc. more work on my "succession" scenario, and it wouldn't be right to leave just then. Not counting a vague feeler from Lyndon Johnson, this was the first time I had ever been offered a major presidential appointment. Dorothy and I agreed, after our weekend of vicarious diplomacy: "It was nice to have been asked."

Now in 1979, I was being asked again, same President, very different job. With Carter's permission, I consulted a few close friends in government and out. One of them suggested it would be prudent to find out whether Hamilton Jordan understood my independent access to the President in the same way it had been described to me. Hamilton did (and there was never any difficulty on this point). The most engaging advice came from the generally sober and high-minded Fritz Mondale, whose lively private wit includes a nice tough-pol act. Said the Vice-President, "Come on now, you've been sitting up there in New York being judicious for thirty years. Cut out all this integrity shit. Come on down into the hog wallow with the rest of us. The first week will be a shock, but then it's a lot of fun."

Somewhere in my career as a Time Inc. executive I got into the fussy habit of setting down on a piece of paper the pros and cons of a difficult decision. I have read that Richard Nixon liked to do the same thing, though so far as I know I developed the habit quite independently.

I still have the jottings I made after my visit to the Oval Office. I listed under "Minus":

• *Inconvenient.* A reference to the fact that I would want to keep my New York apartment and Long Island house but would have to set up some sort of quarters in Washington, a cumbersome way for a bachelor to live.

• *$$.* Grubby of me to mention. I made a guess (quite accurate) at income forgone and expenses added if I went to Washington for a year. As it turned out, a greater cost was inattention to various financial matters, though even if I had been in New York and paying attention I might not have been smart enough to make the right decisions.

• *Horowitz.* This was a reference to the curious fact that the President, for all his stress on our having known each other for some years and the urgency of his plea that I now join his staff, had never asked to see me during his first two and a half years in office. I had been invited along with two or three hundred others to a delightful Vladimir Horowitz recital one Sunday afternoon in the East Room, and that was it.

• *Trudi point.* Trudi Lanz, my superb secretary and friend of many years, noted that people of hitherto high reputation often seemed to get muddied up if they went to Washington. Did I need that at this point in my life?

• *Titanic?* was the other notation on the Minus list. But I wasn't really much concerned with the then low state of the President's political fortunes. I would not have wanted to stay into a second term even if he were reelected, which seemed very unlikely in midsummer 1979, and he in no way dangled any such possibility.

Under "Plus" I listed:

• *Maybe do a little for country?*
• *Excitement of something different.*
• *Kick myself.* Meaning kick myself around the block the rest of my life if I didn't give it a try.
• *Chance to see Govt. from inside.* And what could be more inside than the Oval Office, where Jimmy Carter had just put his appeal to me, where as an awestruck young reporter I had once covered the press conferences of Franklin Roosevelt?

PART II

"The Champ": Seen Then and Now

4

Franklin Roosevelt

A wave of cheering yesterday rolled up Pennsylvania Avenue at 6 miles an hour, pacing President Roosevelt's triumphant trip from Union Station to the White House.

"The Champ," wearing his weather-beaten campaign hat and the most famous smile in America, was back on the job . . .

"My old friends of Washington . . . [he said at the station] You all know how much Henry Wallace [the Vice-President-elect] and I like farm life, but of all the cities in the world we'd rather live in Washington than any other place . . ."

Thus Hedley Donovan, age twenty-six, in the Washington *Post* of November 7, 1940, two days after FDR's election to a third term. As a cub reporter in 1938 and 1939, I had been given occasional chances to cover President Roosevelt when he was being "local," dedicating buildings, welcoming the king and queen of England, lighting Christmas trees. Then through much of 1940–41, I was assigned to Capitol Hill, where the biggest stories arose out of World War II and the fateful struggles between the isolationists and an increasingly "interventionist" Roosevelt Administration. Through the key senators and congressmen, and the Administration's spokesmen and agents on the Hill, a journalist was exposed almost daily to the mind and methods of Franklin Roosevelt. Finally, in the autumn and winter days before and after Pearl Harbor, I was covering the White House itself, and in forty or more press conferences saw the man close up in some of the most demanding hours of his life.

17

In those quaint pre-TV days, there were seldom more than forty or fifty of us at the press conference as compared with 250 or so today. We stood only two deep in a semicircle in the Oval Office, and the President presided from behind his curio-cluttered desk. There was a Tuesday afternoon press conference, so the news would break for the morning papers, and a Friday morning conference for "the evenings." The conference would last about half an hour, at least one Camel cigarette's worth, sometimes two (for the President, not the press). There were seldom more than two or three women present; one regular was a great favorite of the President's, May Craig, representing some resolutely Republican Maine papers, and he would always recognize May for a question.

Roosevelt knew how skillful he was at the press conference, and this of course is why he held so many of them; 998 in twelve-plus years, or roughly eighty a year. (Nixon averaged about seven full-dress press conferences a year, Carter about fifteen, Reagan about seven in his first term, though Carter occasionally and Reagan frequently met with smaller groups of journalists in other settings.)

It may be questioned whether Roosevelt, for all his virtuosity and zest in sparring with the correspondents, would have had as much success with the relentlessly skeptical White House press corps of the 1970s and 1980s. FDR was dealing with journalists basically respectful toward American institutions, especially the Presidency, and conventionally patriotic. I include in this characterization the mildly cynical *Front Page* types.

The cynics joined in applauding Winston Churchill, guest at a memorable press conference two weeks after Pearl Harbor, when he stood on a chair in the Oval Office and gave the V-sign. I saw him at the old Foundry Methodist Church on Sixteenth Street and heard Franklin Roosevelt's stage whisper to Eleanor as they approached their pew, "No, the Prime Minister next." I saw Roosevelt and Churchill at George Washington's grave at Mount Vernon on New Year's Day 1942. Neither man spoke. Churchill laid a wreath of iris and chrysanthemums on the tomb, then permitted himself a mischievous smile at the press, to let us know he savored the historical overtones.

Journalists were far less self-important then than now. Editorial writers and columnists might write harsh things about FDR, but the White House reporters in no sense imagined themselves co-stars with the President in a Washington morality play. A large majority of them were personally sympathetic to Roosevelt's policies, whatever their publishers may have thought, and few indeed were immune to the famous charm. I was greatly flattered one day, standing in my customary place at one end of the semicircle, near the big globe, to receive a large wink from the President as he delivered some transparent piece of humbug. FDR loved to make the reporter a fellow conspirator: you-know-and-I-know-you-know this is just a bit of flimflam.

Yet no reasonably alert political reporter could fail to see behind the charm and surface warmth, the schoolboy humor, the easy style of the country gentleman, a personality of deep subtleties and complexity. "No man who gets to be President," writes George Reedy, one of Lyndon Johnson's press secretaries, "is going to be easy to read." The supremely presidential Franklin Roosevelt was at least as complicated as any of our other modern Presidents. Perhaps it would be a three-way tie with Lyndon Johnson and Richard Nixon, of both of whom more later.

FDR could brilliantly oversimplify. His best-remembered single statement, "The only thing we have to fear is fear itself," is patently absurd—and was probably excellent tonic for a country whose banking system had collapsed. But in the early and middle stages of decision making, before it was time to simplify and oversimplify, Roosevelt could be impenetrable. Rexford Tugwell, one of the early New Deal brain trusters, wrote: "No one could tell what he was *thinking*, to say nothing of what he was *feeling*."* He clearly relished being hard to figure out. He liked secrets, and had a few. He was often devious for good reason, but could also be devious just for the fun of it. General Douglas MacArthur, who despised him, said Roosevelt "would never tell the truth when a lie would serve him just as well."† This was a considerable slander. But FDR unquestionably did enjoy manipulation and maneuver for their own sake, all part of the great game of politics and power.

He was also a man of deep convictions and dedication and unquenchable idealism. He was firm and serene in his religious faith, and had a decent sense of privacy about it—it is impossible to imagine him at a congressional prayer breakfast. He was impatient with the abstract or theoretical, in no sense profound, but spacious in vision, for America and ultimately all the nations. He believed, if not in the perfectibility of man, in a rather spectacular improvement in man's behavior, world-

*Tugwell, *The Democratic Roosevelt* (Garden City: Doubleday, 1957), p. 66.
†William Manchester, *American Caesar: Douglas MacArthur 1880–1964* (Boston: Little Brown and Company, 1978) p. 240.

wide. For him the "Four Freedoms" (freedom of speech, worship, freedom from want, fear) was not just wartime sloganeering. Roosevelt genuinely believed that something approximating the four freedoms was attainable everywhere. For humanity to achieve freedom from fear would of course require that all those who cause fear in others should turn benign, and that people who are fearful without reason should become braver. Roosevelt's co-signer of the Atlantic Charter, Churchill, saw no harm in such dreams, but would have settled for crushing the "Naahzis" and Hitler's "utensil" Mussolini.

The Consummate Campaigner

The devious politician and the farsighted statesman were totally intermingled in the Roosevelt of the third-term campaign. It was clear by late spring of 1940 that he would run again. (He may have decided long before.) He was entitled to be tired after two terms but wasn't. He gloried in the office, and though he was a traditionalist in many matters, the breaking of the two-term tradition must have been an exciting challenge in itself. He was also entirely persuaded that he was the best man to lead the country through the perilous times ahead. France had fallen in June; Britain stood alone against Hitler; the Japanese were increasingly aggressive in the Pacific.

A huge majority of the delegates to the 1940 convention in Chicago were committed to Roosevelt. All he needed was to say he was running, and after the unavoidable speeches and demonstrations, he would have been nominated as fast as the roll call could be run off. But he insisted on "releasing" his delegates to go for any candidate of their choice. (Vice-President Jack Garner and Postmaster General Jim Farley, both disaffected with FDR, were both running, feebly.) Duly released, the convention then "drafted" Roosevelt.

I was there in Chicago as "color" reporter on the Washington *Post* team, as this charade was played out. There was plenty of color for me, including the famous "voice from the sewer" (the Democratic machine's superintendent of sewers, on a P.A. from the basement of the stadium), demanding "We Want Roosevelt!" This set the scene for the painful humbuggery of Roosevelt's acceptance speech:

"Lying awake, as I have on many nights, I have asked myself whether I have the right, as commander in chief of the Army and Navy to call men and women to serve their country or to train themselves to serve, and at the same time decline to serve my country in my own personal capacity, if I am called upon to do so by the people of my country. . . . In the face of an overriding public danger, no individual retains . . . the right of personal choice, which free men enjoy in times of peace." He had made other, private plans for himself, "but my conscience would not let me turn my back on a call to service."

Being highly eligible myself for the other draft, the nonpresidential one (Selective Service would be enacted two months later), I couldn't grieve too much for FDR's lost private plans. In many young reporters of that era, certainly in myself, there was a tension a little like the one inside Roosevelt himself, between high-mindedness and a sophisticated savoring of the craft and wiles of politics. I was assigned to cover Roosevelt's first openly political speech of the 1940 campaign, in the Philadelphia Convention Hall in October, and it was a joy to watch the master at work. For some minutes he went through a solemn recitation of his hopes that the campaign could be kept on a high plane; because of the gravity of the international situation he had intended to stay in Washington; but finally the misrepresentations by his opponent (never named, but he was Wendell Willkie) had grown so outrageous they must be directly rebutted. Long pause, the lugubrious expression slowly fading, a confident grin spreading, the great head tilting back: "I will not pretend that I find this an unpleasant duty. I am an old campaigner, and I love a good fight!" Twenty thousand of the faithful went crazy.

In the club car on our way back to Washington that night, General Edwin "Pa" Watson, the President's military aide, summed it up: "God, how I'd love to see that man play Hamlet." Roosevelt once told Orson Welles: "There are only two great actors in America—you are the other one."*

I had a hard time deciding how to vote. The hokum, when I wasn't admiring it technically, bothered me. So did the third term. So did his Supreme Court packing plan of 1937 and the somewhat leftist drift of the New Deal in Roosevelt's second term. But in the end I agreed with him that he was better equipped than Wendell Willkie to cope with the dangerous world around us. I don't regret that vote today.

In 1944, I voted for him with no heart searching. I thought he was far better qualified than Tom Dewey to finish the war and negotiate in the postwar. In a letter saying he would accept the fourth-term nomination, the "good soldier" motif appeared again. "All that is within me cries to go back to my home on the Hudson River." This time it could

*Quoted in John Gunther, *Roosevelt in Retrospect* (New York: Harper & Brothers, 1950), p. 62.

have been true. He couldn't have known how little time he had left, but he knew his health was failing. In the present age of candor about the health of Presidents and candidates, it is doubtful that he would have been allowed to run or would have dared to try. Even by the codes of 1944, one must conclude that he was dishonest to offer himself again, or else his ego was now so towering that he felt a part of his old strength for any part of four years was better than anything the Republicans— or indeed his own party—could offer.

A Vast Stage

With all the flaws, I believe he was a great President. He acted in six immense arenas of statecraft, more than any other President in our history. This was partly because of the exceptional times, the Depression and World War II, partly because he was in office so long, but also because of his far-ranging interests, his optimism, and his huge vitality.

1) In one arena, Roosevelt was fighting the Depression. This indeed was what he was primarily elected to do in 1932, and it was here, ironically, that he achieved the least. There were some 13 million unemployed when he took office, and there were still about 9 million seven years later.* Gross national product, national income, and corporate profits were all far healthier in 1940 than in the devastation of 1932–33, but still much short of anything that could be called prosperity.

It was the fall of France in June of 1940, the gearing up of the American defense program, and the startup of the draft that finally brought the beginning of the end of the Depression.† And after Pearl Harbor, the country moved into a war economy of full employment, production at capacity and beyond, soaring GNP and national income, and shortages and rationing.

A few days after his first inauguration, a friend told Roosevelt that if he pulled the country out of the economic disaster, he would be remembered as the greatest President, but if he failed, as the worst. "If I fail," said FDR, "I shall be the last."‡ He did not succeed—nor entirely fail—and we have had eight Presidents since.

*Measurements of unemployment were even more inexact then than now. By some reckonings, there were 14–15 million out of work in the winter of 1932–33—more than a quarter of the labor force—and 10 million still jobless in the spring of 1940.

†Arthur Schlesinger, Jr., masterful and fond historian of the New Deal, is able to get unemployment down to 5 million "by 1940"—by using the year-end figure after the defense program was taking hold.

‡Roy Peel and Thomas Donnelly, *The 1932 Campaign: An Analysis* (New York: Farrar & Rinehart, Inc., 1935), p. 213.

There is no question that Roosevelt's vigor and ebullience fortified the national morale in a black hour. He made the Depression more bearable to millions. He was *doing* things about it—dozens of things a week, it often seemed. It can be argued that his breezy ad hoc-ism at times actually impeded economic recovery. But his very willingness to experiment, to drop ideas that didn't work and try something else, had a powerful popular appeal. Somebody was finally in charge.

Did he "save us from Revolution," Fascist or Marxist? Admiring biographers, historians, and journalists have often argued that he did, and that many capitalists were simply too dense and bitter to see that he had saved their own show. Indeed in recent years, Roosevelt has been criticized for just that, by the Marxist school of "revisionist" historians. No young revisionist, but an elderly Social Democrat, Irving Howe, has written: "The major cause of socialist decline could be put in one word: Roosevelt. That canny politician, half savior and half confidence man, ruined us."*

My unprovable view is that we were not on the edge of a revolution of the left or right. Ours is a very stable system and society, as we have been proving for a long time. Of the four major democracies that endured the Depression, only the youngest and most fragile, Germany, succumbed to totalitarianism. Neither Britain nor France, despite utterly uninspiring leaders, went Fascist or Marxist. In our election of 1932, despite the breadlines and despair, the dour and seemingly inert Herbert Hoover was able to take 39.7 percent of the popular vote. Norman Thomas, a not very wild-eyed Socialist, got only 2.2 percent; William Foster, the Communist, got 0.4 percent. Franklin Roosevelt, whose "program" was essentially optimism and vigor (one of his few specifics was a balanced budget), won 57.4 percent. Not exactly a prerevolutionary landscape.

In the mid-1930s, amidst the demagoguery of Louisiana Senator Huey Long and the radio priest Charles Coughlin, it was briefly possible to discern lineaments of a fascism with an American accent. But much of what was was being spouted was really the old agrarian populism of the South and Middle West, and the old suspicion of the eastern "interests" (including a whiff of nativist anti-Semitism owing nothing to Hitler). Roosevelt worried a good deal about Huey Long running as a third-party candidate in 1936—not that he was going to lead the country into fascism, but that he might divert enough votes from FDR to give the White House back to the Republicans. The Kingfish died be-

A Margin of Hope: An Intellectual Biography (New York: Harcourt Brace Jovanovich, 1982), p. 32.

fore this could be tested. Instead, William Lemke, a North Dakota congressman, ran as an independent in 1936, and with the support of Father Coughlin and miscellaneous charlatans, he got fewer than a million votes. Despite the stubborn persistence of the Depression, Roosevelt won his famous landslide: 523 electoral votes versus 8 for Alf Landon. "As Maine goes, so goes Vermont."

2) The second great arena of the Roosevelt Presidency was social and economic reform. To be sure, Roosevelt would not have sharply distinguished his role as reformer from his role as Depression fighter. The New Deal stood for both. But today we can see that these were two quite different arenas. However limited FDR's success in combating the Depression, until he was saved by the war, his reforms had an immense influence throughout the postwar. In sum, these reforms were the end of laissez-faire and the beginnings of a welfare state.

During most of Roosevelt's first term, I was a student at Oxford. Looking at my country from England, I saw FDR as a kind of Whig grandee, carrying out reforms that Britain had accepted years earlier. In Germany, social security went back to Bismarck and the 1880s.

It seemed to me then, and does now, that the New Deal helped make America a far more humane society than it had been. The whole apparatus of safety nets, floors, entitlements, and subsidies was extended and overextended in subsequent administrations, especially under Lyndon Johnson and under that anti-hero of all good Democrats, Richard Nixon. FDR would have been amazed at some of it. Still, even with the later excesses (which are not irrevocable), the welfare state that FDR founded is a social and moral advance over sink-or-swim.

In his moving and perceptive essay on FDR, *A Centenary Remembrance,* the journalist Joseph Alsop (distant kin to both Franklin and Eleanor) suggests that the combined impact of all the domestic reforms was to "include the excluded." He notes that the America Roosevelt was born into in 1882, even the America of 1932, was "an entirely White Anglo-Saxon Protestant nation by any practical test."* Today, though harsh disadvantages still face blacks and Hispanics, the children and grandchildren of the "ethnics" of southern and eastern Europe, in their tens of millions, enjoy full citizenship.

The New Deal sought to give some help, after the event, so to speak, to individuals bruised or disadvantaged by the economic system. The New Deal also intervened directly in the system. This was done through

*New York: Viking, 1982, p. 11.

the new agencies regulating the securities business, banking, communications, public utilities, and perhaps most significant, labor relations, with union organizing being powerfully stimulated. There was large-scale help for farmers and those who lend and sell to them, to house builders and buyers and those who lend to them. The Tennessee Valley Authority did not become the model for other regional authorities that some New Dealers dreamed of, but stands as a successful one-shot. The Reconstruction Finance Corporation (started under Hoover, greatly expanded under FDR) bailed out some sick businesses. It was all far short of a planned economy, but it brought in the federal government as a major force in American enterprise.

The New Deal reforms, though they didn't end the Great Depression of the 1930s, may well have helped prevent depressions since. They help smooth out the business cycle by sustaining purchasing power during recessions. They are an implicit guarantee that panic, as per 1873, 1893, 1907, 1932–33, is no longer allowed.

Nathan Miller, in his excellent new biography of FDR, does not argue whether Roosevelt saved us from communism or fascism. He says Roosevelt made his own revolution, "one of the few successful gradualist revolutions in history."*

3) Roosevelt was the founder of the modern Presidency, the focus of authority and initiative in a greatly extended and centralized government. The office was fashioned by the extraordinary needs of a nation in a fifteen-year crisis—the Depression and World War II—and by Roosevelt's own political skills and zest for power.

FDR was not a deep thinker about the Presidency as an institution. His philosophical concept of the office, as Richard Neustadt of Harvard has written, was simply himself as President.† He never said anything about the office as pithy as his cousin Theodore's famous definition: a bully pulpit. He had little of the analytical power (and none of the scholarly inclination) that Woodrow Wilson brought to his studies of the American political system.

Roosevelt did, however, appoint the President's Committee on Administrative Management, headed by Louis Brownlow of the University of Chicago, to make the first modern study of the office. The committee, reporting in 1937, said, "The President needs help."‡ The report

FDR: An Intimate History (Garden City: Doubleday, 1983), p. 343.
†*Presidential Power* (New York: John Wiley and Sons, 1960) p. 162.
‡*Administrative Management in the Government of the United States* (Washington: U.S. Government Printing Office, 1937).

led to legislation in 1939 establishing the Executive Office of the President, incorporating the Bureau of the Budget (previously a small office in the Treasury Department) as the President's major management tool. The President was also authorized to appoint administrative assistants. Roosevelt did, and said they should have a passion for anonymity.

Roosevelt himself was scarcely a model administrator. In his third term, as he aged, he became a poor listener, much given to monologue. He made some excellent appointments and knew how to get the best out of good people. But he also kept a good many mediocrities and eccentrics in office. He enjoyed pitting one official against another, figuring they would eventually have to come to him for the decisions. His fondness for piling agencies on top of agencies and appointing special troubleshooters, roving ambassadors, deputy Presidents, etc., cluttered the organization chart, especially during World War II. But the institutionalization of the Presidency had begun.

Truman and Eisenhower, crisper administrators than Roosevelt and less manipulative, carried out further institutionalizing, especially through the creation of the National Security Council. The Bureau of the Budget (it became the Office of Management and Budget under Nixon) waxed in influence. FDR's administrative assistants were the forerunners of the powerful White House staffs of the Nixon, Carter, and Reagan years, not always marked by a passion for anonymity.

4) Roosevelt redrew the political map of the United States. The transformation was not from a basically Republican country to a basically Democratic country, as was sometimes said. It was from a basically Republican country to a country making up its mind from election to election.

The Republicans have won six presidential elections since FDR's death, the Democrats four. Four of the elections were extremely close (three Democratic victories, one Republican), and three were landslides with the winner taking roughly 60 percent of the popular vote (one Democrat, two Republicans).

Against the post-Roosevelt Republican tilt in presidential elections, the Democrats have held almost continuous majorities in both houses of Congress. But FDR himself had lost working control of Congress in the mid-term elections of his second term. Since 1938, more often than not, the House has been dominated by a coalition of Republicans and conservative Democrats. Even when the Senate was somewhat more liberal (not the case since 1981), the result has been an essentially centrist Congress, dealing with generally centrist Presidents. Even Reagan had to accommodate to the centrists in his first term, and even after his personal triumph in November 1984, may need to do some more accommodating.

Roosevelt and the Depression did work a mighty change in our politics. Since the Civil War there had been only two Democratic Presidents, one of them (Wilson) elected only because of a flukish split in the Republican Party. Ever since Roosevelt put together his New Deal coalition, our national elections have been up for grabs.

5) The next arena in which the Roosevelt Presidency was played out was the vastest of all, World War II. Here Roosevelt becomes one of the truly commanding figures of our century.

The twenty-seven months from the outbreak of war in Europe to the Japanese attack on Pearl Harbor were an unremitting test of his skills as a domestic political leader and his grasp of worldwide diplomacy and strategy. For a time he genuinely believed the U.S. could and should stay out of the war, then after the fall of France he began to doubt that Britain could survive without large-scale U.S. help. By late 1940, he had probably concluded we should go to war, if need be, to save Britain.

In this view he was much ahead of public opinion, still predominantly isolationist. He let "interventionist" senators, private citizens, newspapers and magazines move out in front, his own position masked until he was ready to move Congress and the public one step further toward commitment to defeat of the Axis. His timing was unerring. He eventually carried every "defense" proposal he put to Congress (on some he bypassed Congress), some by very narrow margins that would not have been there a few months or weeks earlier. If he made misrepresentations, as I believe he did, I think the danger justified the deception.

In the end, of course, Pearl Harbor, followed by Hitler's somewhat mystifying initiative in declaring war on the U.S., mooted the isolationist-interventionist debate (except in a weird postwar reincarnation, in which FDR was accused of plotting Pearl Harbor to get us into the war). But Roosevelt's interventionist moves in 1940–41 had helped sustain the British, and had put the U.S. in a better state of preparedness than if we had imagined the war would never touch us. Even at that, we suffered cruel losses to the U-boats in the Atlantic in 1942, a debacle almost as grievous as Pearl Harbor.

Once we were all the way in, Roosevelt was a magnificent war leader. There is no evidence he ever entertained a fleeting doubt about the ultimate victory of the Allies. He knew none of the melancholia of another great war President, Abraham Lincoln, but then he was not running a brothers' war. FDR radiated a calm and righteous confidence. This quality was worth many divisions at a time before we had raised the flesh-and-blood divisions, and especially in the dark hours of Pearl Harbor and Bataan. Winston Churchill of course was Roosevelt's full equal in courage and pertinacity, and vastly superior in martial eloquence. But Churchill's irascibility and meddlesomeness could rattle his commanders. Roosevelt, surprisingly for a man with a lively interest in military matters, especially naval, didn't try to tell his admirals and generals how to fight the war. He picked first-rate commanders and generally came in only on the highest-level decisions. Though he was well aware of Douglas MacArthur's low opinion of him (and in turn thought the melodramatic general one of the most dangerous men in the country), he respected MacArthur's military talents and gave him a great command.

Three quasi-political criticisms of Roosevelt's war leadership must be dealt with. The forcible relocation and internment of the West Coast Japanese, citizens as well as aliens, is now perceived as a gross injustice. With hindsight, we can be ashamed. It was not such an outlandish idea, however, in the immediate aftermath of Pearl Harbor. In the early weeks of the war a Japanese submarine surfaced off Santa Barbara and fired some shells at California. Were there others out there, landing parties, local fifth columnists? I can remember a moment during a briefing by Secretary Cordell Hull in the old State Department Building on the Sunday afternoon of Pearl Harbor, when reporters and officials could distinctly hear some distant explosions. We stared at each other: An air raid? Sabotage? An enemy sub up the Potomac? Some patriot letting off fireworks?

Then there is the painful charge that Roosevelt was fully aware of the extent of the Holocaust, and could have saved many Jews by ordering the bombing of the death camps in Poland and the rail lines leading there. The view of the War and State departments—and Roosevelt did not overrule them—was that the sooner the war ended the better for all the conquered peoples of Europe, including the Jews, and bombing should be concentrated on targets that supported the German war effort. From postwar evidence it would appear that the "Final Solution" had become more heavily dependent on a few camps, especially Auschwitz, than the U.S. government assumed, that these could not necessarily have been replaced at once by other means of murder, that a bombing of the Polish camps and supporting rail lines, while killing some Jews, could well have saved more. But this is hindsight; for Roosevelt to have known all this and been indifferent would have been monstrously out of character.

There is finally the theory that Roosevelt needlessly prolonged the war by insisting on "unconditional surrender." I think there is merit to this. Roosevelt was intent on suppressing any "stab in the back" psychology in postwar Germany. The German military must know it had been thoroughly and totally beaten, so they could not claim as they did after World War I that they had been betrayed by the civilian government, which had been taken in by Woodrow Wilson's "conditions." Roosevelt was perhaps doing what the generals are so often accused of, fighting the last war. By 1944, many of the high German military would have been willing to negotiate with the West. It was the "civilians"— Hitler, Goebbels, Himmler—who were the bitter-enders. And the war went on, all the way to the Führerbunker in Berlin.

Harry Truman modified the unconditional surrender doctrine when it came Japan's turn. He offered a "condition": the Japanese could keep their emperor. Even Hiroshima and Nagasaki might not have shaken the Japanese military in their intent to die fighting for the emperor on the home islands. But when the emperor himself said it was all over, it was, at great saving in human life, Japanese and American.

6) But the haunting question of the wisdom of "unconditional surrender" in Europe relates not only to Roosevelt's role as a war leader but to his role as a statesman peering into the postwar. In this last of the great arenas given him, he did not have long to act. But as victory drew closer in 1944 and early 1945, much of his thought was devoted to the postwar world. He was not notably farsighted.

Unconditional surrender was a key element in the American and British relationship with the Soviets. Any remote whiff of "separate peace" talk in the West—or in the German anti-Nazi resistance— aroused livid suspicion in the Kremlin. The Soviets felt the Western Allies had delayed outrageously in opening a Second Front in France —in part because "certain circles" wanted to see another year of German-Soviet bloodletting on the eastern front. If there were to be any relaxation of "unconditional surrender," the Soviets could readily imagine that the "conditions" would include some language pertinent to Germany's eastern frontiers, to the nationality of the forces that would accept the surrender of German military, and to the character of a postwar German military. In short, in the Soviet view, the offering of "conditions" to Germany would be a formula for continuation, or early renewal, of a Soviet-German war, while the West sat back and watched.

But there was a mirror image. Stalin and the Nazis, after all, had done business only yesterday. It was the nonaggression pact with Stalin, on August 23, 1939, that freed Hitler to start World War II nine days later. What if they got together again, to let Germany and the West fight it out for a while? Unlikely, after all the horror and savagery of the war in the East, but not impossible. So Roosevelt thought unconditional surrender was a good West-East deal with the Soviets as well as a healthy restraint on the postwar Germany.

In the world of sheer might-have-been one can speculate that a peace negotiated in the summer of 1944—after the Normandy invasion had earned the West its credentials vis-à-vis the Soviets as well as Germany—could have led to a better postwar. George Kennan, in more militant days, said the U.S. and Britain should have turned much tougher with the Soviets as soon as the Normandy landings were secure.

FDR underestimated—not totally but seriously—the gulf between the Soviet world and ours, between himself and Stalin as "politicians." He knew Stalin was tough all right, and hard to read—but so was he, and proud of it. He didn't really understand that Stalin was from another planet.

Roosevelt committed no egregious "give-away" at Yalta. The Red Army in February 1945 was holding most of the territory the summiteers were talking about. Only two months before his death, Roosevelt did a valiant job in the Yalta negotiations, especially on Poland. But the language worked out for the communiqué meant much less to Stalin than to Roosevelt. Churchill understood this.

There are a few cables and conversations in the last few weeks of Roosevelt's life that show him starting to get tougher with Stalin. This is a sad and unimportant footnote, because if there was any good time to get tough during the war—and it's not clear there was—the time was, as the young George Kennan said, the summer of 1944.

Our World War II leverage with the Soviets disappeared after the German surrender. At Potsdam, Truman kept in force our handsome bribe to the Soviets to come into the Pacific war, not anticipating that the atomic bomb, and his own good sense in letting the emperor stay, would make Soviet participation unnecessary and indeed dangerous.

Flaws and All

I have tried to identify six great and separate arenas in which Franklin Roosevelt was privileged—the right word, I think, because no other President entered so many, and you wouldn't want to be President unless you liked arenas—to act. He seized or created some of the arenas. Some, like World War II, demanded his attendance.

I have judged him unsatisfactory (I reintroduce the metaphor of the President as my employee) as a thinker about the postwar, and as a solver of the Depression of the 1930s. I credit him with a large role in creating the modern Presidency—a good and necessary thing in our system in these times; with redrawing the political map of America—important, whether you like the new geography or not; and with the social and economic reform that is the enduring New Deal idea. And finally, he was superb as our leader in World War II, which was almost but not quite the sure thing he always made it seem.

The America of FDR is a faraway country, and in some ways he seems a very old-fashioned figure. Not yet being able to think of myself as old, I am astonished that I should have chatted with Franklin Roosevelt in the East Room of the White House at a coming-out dance for Joan Morgenthau, the daughter of Henry. Here at one of the most ridiculed rituals of old-line "society," our affable host was the same politician who could scourge the "economic royalists" and "princes of privilege"; our hostess the earnest and dowdy Eleanor, settlement-house worker on a national scale; and the father of the debutante was the Secretary of the Treasury, Dutchess County gentleman farmer and solemn foil for FDR wit (as in "Henry the Morgue").

When I arrived in Washington as a junior reporter late in the first year of FDR's second term, he had just taken his historic defeat on the Supreme Court packing bill. Still overreaching, probably because of his spectacular victory in the 1936 election, he tried to purge selected conservative Democrats in the mid-term elections of 1938. He was soundly beaten again. The fact that FDR was no longer sweeping everything before him lent a special excitement and drama to the Washington of the late 1930s. The fervent young lawyers and economists I knew in New Deal agencies were still dedicated; the skeptics and critics were becoming bolder.

There were fierce Roosevelt-haters "out there" in the country, and

I frequently encountered them on trips to New York and the Middle West. Though FDR with his sarcasm and scorn had in fact cultivated the hatred, it took such poisonous form that I was revolted. In arguments with doctors, bankers, grain brokers, and even a relative or two, I sometimes found myself defending "that man in the White House" more completely than I really thought he deserved.

In the years since, there have been times when his deceits and hypocrisies seem to intrude heavily on my recollections of Roosevelt. It was not edifying to learn in 1983 that FDR also did some taping in the Oval Office. In one taped conversation in 1940, he suggested some word-of-mouth smearing of Wendell Willkie with rumors that the Republican candidate was having an affair, even as he trotted out his wife Edith for campaign appearances. In the light of all that we now know about Roosevelt's own marriage, this was very shabby stuff.

As each new Presidency has unfolded, in the years since 1945, I find new perspectives on the Roosevelt Presidency. Some of his successors have had some admirable personal qualities that he lacked. Several were more effective in some areas of presidential responsibility than he was. But none by his performance has forced me to revise the judgment that Roosevelt, all in all, was a great President.

PART III

Presidents
of the West

5

---◆---

Harry Truman

The United States came out of World War II with more power—military, economic, political—than all the rest of the world put together. From 1945 until the mid-1960s, Presidents of the United States operated from a position of fabulous strength.

We were the only major belligerent undamaged at home, and our whole economy had been vastly invigorated and expanded by the war. Thanks in part to our own generosity in the rebuilding of Western Europe and Japan, the margin of our economic superiority gradually declined, but as late as 1960, the gross national product of the United States was still 33 percent of world GNP, including the Communist bloc.

After VJ-Day, we set about dismantling our military strength with reckless speed. But the mobilization potential was there, and the world knew it. We kept a formidable Navy, respectable air power, and a long lead in nuclear strength.

Those glory days of American power vis-à-vis the rest of the world were, for the most part, a time of national consensus on foreign policy, and general domestic tranquillity—marred by the early postwar strike epidemics and in the early 1950s by the Joe McCarthy ugliness. Vigorous economic growth, punctuated by a few relatively mild recessions, was delivering a steady increase in living standards. It was less difficult being President of the West in those days than being President of the United States from the mid-1960s on.

So I argue that the Truman, Eisenhower, and Kennedy Presidencies, for all the differences in the politics and style of the three men, are essentially one era. I realize this thesis may offend in considerable

35

numbers the keepers of the Kennedy flame, Ike's longtime fans and recent "discoverers," and the stout partisans of Give-'Em-Hell Harry Truman.

☈

"I'm not big enough for the job. I'm not big enough." George Aiken, former senator from Vermont, recalled these words of Harry Truman's the day FDR died. Truman, as Aiken told the Boston *Globe,* "held on to me and wept."[*]

I first met Harry Truman, junior senator from Missouri, in 1939. Over the next two years I interviewed him perhaps a dozen times, in the lobby off the Senate floor or in the old Senate Office Building. He had been so thoroughly labeled as a protégé of Kansas City's corrupt Boss Pendergast that I was surprised, naively perhaps, at his considerable dignity and straightforward style. He was affable with the press, without overdoing it. He was at least one or two circles removed from the Senate's inner Club, but was a well-regarded first-termer, industrious and a dependable down-the-line supporter of the Administration.

In 1940, when he was up for reelection to the Senate, Truman overcame the substantial handicap that his friend Tom Pendergast was now in jail; he resisted efforts by Roosevelt himself to replace him with another Democrat, Lloyd Stark, and then beat his Republican opponent in November. The Senate and the press decided this was a pretty scrappy fellow, though he was still mild-mannered in those days, even a little bland on the surface. The cocky, belligerent persona did not come into full flower until after the 1948 presidential election, which convinced him he was indeed Give-'Em-Hell Harry.

But Truman never totally forgave Roosevelt for trying to dump him in 1940, and he was not flattered by the offhanded way in which FDR in 1944 put him in line to be President. In a diary entry in 1949, the year after he beat New York Governor Tom Dewey, Truman exulted: "I'm forced on the Democratic ticket as VP by the man who thought Stark was tops—and I'm the President and in my own right."[†] To FDR in 1944, and to the Democratic convention, Truman's principal virtue was that he was not Henry Wallace, too leftist to be renominated for Vice-President, or "Assistant President" Jimmy Byrnes of South Caro-

[*]July 10, 1983.
[†]Harry Truman, *Off the Record,* ed. Robert H. Ferrell (New York: Harper & Row, 1980), p. 168.

lina, unacceptable to labor and the northern liberals. It was not the first or last time a presidential candidate would choose his running mate simply by the criterion of who will hurt the ticket least, but it is still not very flattering to the No. 2.

Truman's one positive credential, which made him an important Senator in his second term and even a national figure, was his leadership of the "Truman Committee" to investigate the efficiency of defense production. I covered some of his briefings on the early work of the committee in 1941, and like other reporters, and many of his witnesses, was impressed by a thoroughness and fairness not always shown by chairmen of showcase investigative committees.

I heard him promise his investigations would never become the affliction to the Administration that the Senate Committee on the Conduct of the War had been to Abraham Lincoln. He reminded the press that General Robert E. Lee had said that committee was worth two divisions to him. This was my first exposure to Truman's lively awareness of American history, the strongest, I think, of any of our modern Presidents. The runners-up would be John Kennedy, who genuinely liked to read, and FDR, who had a heavy bias toward naval history.

The Truman Committee continued through World War II, never became an asset to our enemies, and doubtless saved the taxpayers some money. Truman himself thought the total might be $15 billion. (A substantial sum in those days.)

An Uncommon Common Man

I next saw Truman as President, at press conferences in the ornate old Treaty Room of the Executive Office Building. I admired his incisive (if often abrasive) answers. Counter to the interests of my profession, I admired his ability to say "Yes" or "No" or "No Comment," and break it off right there—a rare talent among our modern Presidents. Eisenhower had a particularly hard time stopping: "It would not really be appropriate to discuss at this time . . . But I will say this . . . ," etc., etc.

I also noticed at these press conferences that Truman had come to look like the President. The office doesn't always have that effect on an incongruous occupant. But Truman, perhaps because he had looked so gray and inconspicuous as a Senator, now seemed a little taller, ruddy and ramrod-straight, glowing with health and authority. The eyes were lively, the flat voice had taken on some force and vibrancy (though it remained deadly monotonous in prepared speeches). He could still be delightfully unpretentious—callers at the White House were "the customers," Mrs. Truman was "The Boss."

He had continued for some months after Roosevelt's death to say there were a million men in the country better qualified to be President. (This was before the days of women's lib.) But the number soon dwindled to a list of about two: General George Marshall, whom he revered but considered too aloof for politics, and General Dwight Eisenhower, whom he assumed for a time to be a Democrat. The short list definitely did not include Governor Dewey, or Senator Robert Taft of Ohio, or Governor Earl Warren of California. A good many prominent Democrats also failed to make the list, including Senator Estes Kefauver ("Cowfever") of Tennessee, a contender for the 1952 nomination, and Senator William Fulbright ("Halfbright") of Arkansas, a Rhodes Scholar ("overeducated") who had the temerity to point out after the Republican sweep of the 1946 congressional elections that if this were Britain, the leader of the defeated party would have to resign. Truman took the sensible position that this was not Britain.

Even as Truman grew in confidence that he could handle the Presidency, he looked on the office with reverence, and on himself as the tenant and trustee. It was a detachment utterly unlike FDR's wholehearted mingling of office and self. Richard Neustadt of Harvard, who worked in the Truman White House (also Kennedy's), puts it this way: Truman felt "the Presidency was just temporarily occupying his body. And he was a temporary visitor in the Presidency."

Clark Clifford, Truman's wise and versatile White House counsel, recalls the President telling him of a prayer he had learned as a young man and repeated every day since. In State of the Union addresses, inaugurals, etc., presidential communications to the Deity become a matter of public record. The private petitions may be more revealing. This was Truman's:

"O Almighty and Everlasting God, Creator of Heaven, Earth and the Universe:

"Help me to be, to think, to act what is right because it is right; make me truthful, honest, and honorable in all things; make me intellectually honest for the sake of right and honor and without thought of reward to me. Give me the ability to be charitable, forgiving, and patient with my fellow men; help me to understand their motives and their shortcomings even as Thou understandest mine."

Harry Truman is the classic example of "growing in the office," which is not to underrate what he brought to the office—courage, incisiveness, the insistence on taking responsibility, self-discipline, and yet along with these military virtues (he was an exemplary captain in field artillery, and always proud of his service in 1918), the somewhat surprising quality of a free-roaming imagination. There was a sweet touch of the small-town small-boy Middle Western bookworm, his eyes too bad for baseball, who had read endlessly in American history. He could respond very fast to spacious ideas like the Marshall Plan or NATO. Frank Pace, Director of the Budget at thirty-seven, then Secretary of the Army, one of Truman's many first-rate appointments, says Truman drew a "wonderful sense of inspiration from *being President.*"

In 1952 it was doubtful that Truman thought Adlai Stevenson better qualified than he to be President, but he may have figured Stevenson had a better chance of being elected. Truman also had an honorable reluctance to violate the spirit of the Twenty-second Amendment. Since it took effect while he was in office, technically it did not apply to him, but its intent was that there should be no more three-term Presidents. Truman had served his own term and all but three months of Roosevelt's last term.

All through his Presidency, Truman would call the White House a "prison," "the Big White Jail," etc. He affected a view of the Presidency as a kind of martyrdom, but he clearly thrived on it, despite turbulence and crisis and two periods of humiliatingly low approval ratings in the Gallup Poll—32 percent in 1946 and 23 percent in 1951. (Nixon, just a few days before he had to quit, still had 24 percent.)

I knew Truman's Washington pretty well, as a writer and editor for *Fortune,* frequently assigned to Washington stories, by Managing Editor Ralph D. Paine Jr., who took a trusting view of my *Post* and Navy credentials. I interviewed most of the Cabinet and the military leadership of those years—Dean Acheson and Robert Lovett; Generals Marshall and Omar Bradley; Admiral Forrest Sherman; James Forrestal, the first Secretary of Defense; various Secretaries of the Treasury, Labor, Commerce; three chairmen of the Federal Reserve Board; Stuart Symington, chairman of the National Security Resources Board; Mayor Mike diSalle of Toledo, hapless price "stabilizer" of the Korean War period; "Electric Charlie" Wilson of the Office of Defense Mobilization (the former president of General Electric, as distinct from "Engine Charlie" Wilson of General Motors, later to be Eisenhower's Secretary of Defense).

Some of what I wrote and edited about the Truman Presidency, in the *Fortune* of 1946–53, still reads well to me, I must confess. At least a few items are downright embarrassing. I didn't write, but allowed to be printed (in February 1952): "The precise shading of mediocrity to be assigned to him may well occupy the historians for many years."

Today I would rank Truman somewhere in the Good to Very Good category of Presidents. He has devout admirers, to be sure, who award the accolade Near Great, and even speculate that someday the "Near" will be dropped off. In a poll of professional historians taken by Arthur Schlesinger, Sr., in 1962, published by *Life,* Truman ranked No. 8 in "greatness" out of thirty-one Presidents rated at the time. He was No. 8 out of thirty-nine, in a Chicago *Tribune* poll of historians and political scientists taken in 1982. (Lincoln, Washington, and Franklin Roosevelt were 1, 2, 3 in both polls.)

Robert Donovan, a journalist turned scholar who spent ten years on his authoritative history of the Truman Administration,* is too prudent to play the ratings game. On the afternoon he became President, Harry Truman, writes Donovan, was a "gregarious, popular, highly experienced, methodical politician . . . conscientious about detail, accustomed to the needs for compromise . . . candid within the limits of a devious profession, endowed with an unpretentious but strong character, a clear and retentive mind . . . a large measure of common sense and self-reliance."† Summing up the Truman Presidency, Donovan says: "In the tormented epoch that began in 1914, no President has emerged from the office as a saint or a hero. Surely, for many reasons, good and bad, for his serious mistakes as well as for his wise decisions, not to mention his vintage American character, Truman's was a most extraordinary Presidency."‡

Yes. To get the least attractive aspect of the Truman Presidency out of the way first, I was repelled at the time, and still am today, by the incorrigibly partisan reflexes of the man. I know vigorous political parties make our system run, and to have vigorous parties, we have to have vigorous partisans—believers and workers. But there are lines that have to be drawn between normal debating license and the rhetoric and tactics that escalate into something vicious and inflammatory. Truman could be shameless. He could say (acceptance speech, 1948): "The people know that the Democratic Party is the people's party and the Republican Party is the party of special interests and it always will be." Period, paragraph. How much of this junk Truman believed himself I

*Volume I, *Conflict and Crisis,* W. W. Norton, 1977; Volume II, *Tumultuous Years,* W. W. Norton, 1982
†Robert Donovan, *Conflict and Crisis,* (New York: W. W. Norton, 1977), p. xv.
‡*Ibid.,* p. 409.

was not then sure and still am not. He did have a genuine populist distrust of Big Business.

The President's partisanship was powerfully fortified—not that it needed to be—by the inflexibly partisan, highly intelligent, and beautifully organized Charles S. Murphy. In the last few years of the Truman Presidency, Murphy was the most influential member of the White House staff. When he died in 1983, James Sundquist of the Brookings Institution, also an alumnus of the Truman Administration, wrote in the Washington *Post** that Murphy was the last truly anonymous White House aide ("perhaps the first as well"), and like Truman, he "just *knew* Republicans were bad for the country."

The pettiness and vindictiveness were always there, even as Truman was being the statesman, sometimes magnificently, on the world stage. On into his fifth, sixth, and seventh years as "leader of the free world" there was something stubbornly small-bore about him. In most of his major appointments he showed an excellent eye for talent and character. But he could stoutly protect, far beyond their merits, foolish or tainted appointees, honoring the code of the machine even within the White House. He could engage in a gross constitutional impropriety by chatting with an old congressional friend, Fred Vinson, now Chief Justice by his appointment, as to whether a presidential seizure of the steel industry would be upheld by the Supreme Court.

In a strictly partisan reflex, he could take a kind of anti-anti-Communist stance when the Republicans first went to work on the issue of subversives in Washington. He could hastily accept a reporter's phrasing about the Alger Hiss case—yes, it was a "red herring"—and still operate a stern system of "loyalty boards" for scrutinizing charges against federal employees. He was about as utterly instinctively anti-Communist as any politician in the country, and he brought on himself the charge of coddling Communists in government out of sheer belligerence against Republicans. Perhaps I too was being petty, but I thought at the time there was some justice in Truman's discomfort on the issue of domestic "Reds."

In the first twelve to eighteen months of Truman's Presidency, the adjustment from a war economy to a peace economy was chaotic, as it probably would have been under any President of either party. Even as this turbulent transition agitated the country, beset by strikes and shortages, Truman began developing his ambitious "Fair Deal," extensions and enlargements of the New Deal. These proposals got almost

*September 1, 1983.

nowhere with Congress; they were too bold and expensive for many of his own party as well as the Republicans.

To understand Truman, said his old friend Charles Ross, one of his press secretaries, "Always look for the obvious explanation."* After looking for the obvious, however, it was sometimes necessary to consider other possibilities. As Truman more and more aggressively identified himself with the Democratic liberal wing, it was never entirely clear how much he wanted his Fair Deal proposals on their merits and how much as "issues."

In the mid-1960s, long after leaving office, he had the satisfaction of seeing some of these proposals become law, under the rubric of Lyndon Johnson's "Great Society." More of the Fair Deal became law in the 1970s. The feisty politician can also be interpreted as a visionary.

The Courage to Decide

Seen from the 1980s, the immense achievement of the Truman Administration was to create the conditions in which a free, prosperous, and defensible Western Europe could rise from the rubble of World War II. Here Truman worked in an arena as vast and dangerous as any that Franklin Roosevelt bestrode. "I make American foreign policy," Truman said. Some of his crucial decisions came to seem obvious enough—after they were successful. They took foresight, faith, and high courage at the time they were made.

In the Middle East and Western Europe, from the showdown over Iran in the first postwar winter, Truman firmly opposed Soviet expansionism wherever he had a chance of making his policy stick. He declared the "Truman Doctrine," protecting Turkey and Greece; launched the Marshall Plan; ordered the 1948–49 airlift which finally broke the Soviet blockade of Berlin. The United States took the initiative in forming NATO, with Britain and France created the independent West German state and incorporated it into the Atlantic defense system.

Truman was much less successful in his encounter with Asia. Did he "lose China"? For all his power, he could not have been the supreme arbiter of the civil war in China, and our subsequent experience in a far smaller place, Viet Nam, imposes a certain humility about American ability to shape Asia. There is still a valid historical question whether we might have done more to help a non-Communist China save itself. We

*Fortune, February 1952, p. 74.

did send Chiang Kai-shek and the Nationalists $2 billion in military and economic aid, but we also accorded to the Chinese Communist Party and army a kind of legitimacy we were denying to European Communists seeking to overthrow legitimate governments. Mao came out of World War II with de facto control of much of northwest China; he was soon master of Manchuria, courtesy of the Soviets, and rapidly moving south. Truman's envoys kept pressing the Nationalists to "recognize" the Communists and bring them into a coalition government, which would have interested the Communists only as an alternative route to total power. They stuck to the military route. As they completed their conquest of the mainland, one U.S. congressman, a Pacific war veteran, said: "What our young men had saved, our diplomats and our President have frittered away." This was the intemperate judgment of John F. Kennedy. The Nationalists may in fact have been beyond saving, but we didn't try intelligently enough then to be sure even today.

If the Communists had not taken over China, there probably would have been no Korean War, and probably no U.S. debacle in Indochina. The fact that Communist China today is anti-Soviet—to our great benefit—does not make the earlier might-have-beens irrelevant.

Another question that can still haunt us is whether Truman Administration statements that seemed to leave South Korea outside our defense perimeter encouraged the North Korean Communist regime in its attack of June 25, 1950. Once that aggression was launched, Truman responded instantly. He grasped at once the danger to our position in Japan, and hence in the whole Western Pacific. He was protecting not only South Korea but the historic miracle—political and economic—that was being achieved in Japan. In the conversion of our Japanese enemy into a prosperous, peaceful, democratic ally, great renown will always go to Douglas MacArthur, but Truman deserves it too, for fully supporting his difficult proconsul.

In his response to the Communist attack on South Korea, Truman also believed he was defending our European allies. He now saw Stalin as a tyrant no less monstrous than Hitler, more cautious but powerfully tempted by the wealth and weakness of Western Europe. If Korea was the opening shot in a two-front Communist offensive, Stalin and Europe must be left in no doubt that the U.S. stood by its friends.

Truman could make up his mind fast and stick to his decision—a great quality in a President, though not without its dangerous side. As commander in chief in the closing chapter of World War II, Truman had not hesitated to order the atomic bomb dropped on Hiroshima and

Nagasaki. He did not agonize over the decision in 1950 to build the H-bomb. To the end of his long life—he died at eighty-eight in 1972— he never expressed the slightest doubt that these were the right decisions.

He did not flinch from the painful decisions that came at him incessantly during the desperate early weeks of the Korean War. He did neglect to line up formal legislative support, which in those days could have been had for the asking, and this imperiousness embittered his relations with Congress, none too good anyway. But first there were the weeks of euphoria, following MacArthur's brilliant landing at Inchon, then desperate days again when the Chinese counterattacked MacArthur's dangerously overextended deployment in North Korea and drove his forces deep into the South again. We eventually settled for a truce line very close to the prewar border, the dream of unifying South and North in a free Korea totally shattered.

Korea was a victory, however, in the sense that we had been able and willing at heavy cost to prevent a small and distant ally from being overrun. There was a larger victory. After several years of foolhardy economizing in the defense budgets, Korea finally pointed the Truman Administration toward defense budgets more in keeping with our commitments. The starving of defense in 1947–50, following the headlong demobilization of the armed forces in 1945–46 (Army strength dropped from 8.2 million to 1.5 million in one year), was very popular, it must be said, with public and congressional opinion. Truman had a horror of budget deficits, and one of the ways to pay for bigger social programs was by cutting military spending. Despite the Korean War, there was no increase in the national debt during his Administration. But if one of the attributes of presidential greatness is the capacity to lead public opinion (even deviously, as per FDR) toward necessary discomforts, Truman as organizer of our pre-Korea defense program does not get good marks.

In one exemplary act of wartime leadership, Truman did defy public opinion. This was the firing of General MacArthur for insubordination. I recall a disagreeable Time Inc. lunch at which I was the only defender of Truman's action among various *Time, Life,* and *Fortune* editors. Henry Luce was a fervent admirer of MacArthur, had a generally low opinion of Truman, and thought the firing an outrage. One of the *Fortune* editors much senior to me was assigned to write our editorial on the subject, but I had some kibitzing rights. Two of my words got into print. In the course of an overwhelmingly anti-Truman, pro-

MacArthur editorial (May 1951), running a thousand words or so, the first reference to the firing is followed by the phrase "however necessary."

I was better pleased with some of my own language in the *Fortune* of January 1952:

A Californian named Robert Carney now commands the greatest striking power in the Mediterranean world, the seat of the classic empires of Alexander and Caesar Augustus. Admiral Carney directs all NATO forces in Southern Europe and the U.S. sixth fleet.

In northern and western Europe, the old realms of Charlemagne and Napoleon, extraordinary military and political influence is held by a Kansas man, Dwight David Eisenhower.

In Korea, the bridge and battlefield of half a dozen historic Oriental imperialisms, the largest Western army ever lodged on the Asiatic mainland is led by Matthew Ridgway, from Virginia.

All these officers are answerable, of course, to a native of Independence, Missouri. If the President of the U.S. were ever tempted to think of himself as Emperor Harry the First—there is no evidence that he has been—he could look about the world with considerable personal satisfaction.

Truman's line-drawing in the Middle East, Mediterranean, Central Europe, and finally Northeast Asia, and his decisions on the bombs, A and H, have given him a sorry place in revisionist treatment of the Cold War. Non-Marxist revisionists see him as a shortsighted provincial blunderer, as much responsible for the Cold War as Stalin. The Marxist revisionists cast him in a more sinister light, and would assign him—and the United States, on up to the present day—the principal blame.

Truman, for a man with a notoriously short fuse, had a therapeutic if indiscreet habit of firing off unmailable letters—not always unmailed —and vitriolic private memos to his files.* Most of this material has now surfaced, as well as the voluble interviews, free-swinging and often factually careless, as he reminisced in his eighties, that he gave the novelist Merle Miller (*Plain Speaking,* Berkley Publishing, 1973). From this salty and sometimes vastly misleading stuff, Truman emerges as a dangerous crackpot. The leftish journalist Pete Hamill can write a whole humorless column taking one of Truman's silliest private memos at full face value and pronouncing: "He was a nasty little man and a

---

*The Almighty had not entirely acceded to His servant Harry's request (p. 38) that he be rendered "charitable, forgiving, and patient with my fellow men."

terrible President."* Hamill is partway right on one point: Truman was in some ways a little man. He did not totally transcend his limitations. He remains to me an enormously moving example of what a politician can sometimes rise to, and of the capacity within our government, and the whole American polity, to sustain a President.

Harry Truman was indeed President of the West. Britain and France remained considerable powers, still empires for a few more years. But it was midway through the Truman Presidency, on my first postwar trip to Europe, that I began to hear from Englishmen, Germans, Italians, even Frenchmen, "You know, he's our President, too." It was not that they were yielding up any of their own sovereignty. It was more an appeal to Americans to temper their own sense of sovereignty with an understanding that the whole West, morally speaking, has a "vote" here.

*Charlotte Observer, April 23, 1982.

6

Dwight Eisenhower

Ike would have run about as well in Devon and Normandy as he did in Kansas. He came to office not as an obscure accidental President but as a world figure who almost as an afterthought had mastered American politics at his first try. He was not only the victor of VE-Day and the first Allied commander of the postwar defenses of Western Europe, he inherited the serious defense buildup that had finally begun in the last Truman years. And the American economy, after the early postwar turbulence and the distortions of Korea, was ready to perform prodigies.

Indeed the economy was already booming during the last two years of the Truman Administration, an awkward circumstance for the Republicans. After I watched them gathered in the Chicago Stockyards Auditorium to pick their 1952 ticket, I wrote in *Fortune** that the boom was a fact the Republicans "resolutely, repeatedly refused to face. It was left to a Catholic priest, offering the invocation . . . to puncture most of the oratory of the speakers who followed him to the Republican rostrum during that noisy week. He did so with no partisan intent; he simply spoke the simple truth:

" 'O God,' said the Archbishop of Chicago, Samuel Cardinal Stritch, '. . . Thou has given us abundant resources. Our farmlands render us bounteous harvests . . . Our industries are the marvel of the whole world . . . Our commerce at home and abroad prospers. Our standard of living has no comparison in all history . . .'

"And in the press gallery one irreverent listener murmured, 'Does the Cardinal know which convention this is?' " (In the previous sentence, I am afraid I was quoting myself.)

It was a glorious week, if you loved the sounds and smells of politics,

*August 1952.

the sudden glimpses of a strategy working or failing. You could still take the Twentieth Century Limited to Chicago, and see Herbert Hoover, now a respected Elder, light up a long cigar in the dining car; the stockyards were still the stockyards; there were still bosses and brokers; and a nominating convention was still a real event where a political party arrived at a decision, not a pageant put on for television. There was genuine suspense about the outcome.

Amidst all the excesses of Republican oratory, a keynote speech by Douglas MacArthur was the most florid and foolish of all. It was too much even for the delegates, and ruined what little chance MacArthur had—he had come to Chicago openly "available."

I was strongly persuaded, not by the keynoter, that the Democrats should be turned out. Twenty years seemed long enough. And Eisenhower's convention victory over Senator Robert Taft, still somewhat isolationist ("damned isolationist," Ike said), seemed to ensure that a Republican Administration would take a responsible course in world affairs. Eisenhower, in part because of the years when nobody was sure whether he was a Republican or a Democrat, was perceived as more "moderate" than Taft in domestic policy. In fact, though much less partisan than Taft, he was essentially more conservative; he later confided in his diary that he found some of Taft's positions "leftish."*

I had such high hopes for an Eisenhower Presidency that I even put in some volunteer hours with the Citizens for Eisenhower Committee in Port Washington, my Long Island suburb. After that one lapse, I decided for the rest of my career I would feel more comfortable, as an editor and avowed political independent, if I let others do the campaigning. I would confine my political advocacy to print. Having reclaimed my virginity, I later drew up rather puritanical rules covering the conditions under which Time Inc. people could take part in national campaigns.

In 1952, however, Time Inc. was deep into the Eisenhower campaign, in weightier precincts than Port Washington, Long Island. Henry Luce, very much a power in the eastern liberal wing of Republicanism, had been among those who persuaded Ike to run; *Time* was vigorously pro-Ike and anti-Taft, then vigorously pro-Ike and anti-Stevenson. Two gifted Time Inc. people were put on leave and loaned to the Republican campaign as speech writers: Emmet Hughes, foreign correspondent, and C. D. Jackson, publisher of *Fortune*.

I was dismayed by several episodes in Ike's campaign. He made an unpleasantly blatant bid for the farm vote in a speech at Kasson, Min-

*Diaries, p. 269.

nesota, at a time when Stevenson was courageously telling some audiences, notably an American Legion convention, things they didn't want to hear. In Indianapolis, Ike appeared on a platform with, and was embraced by, Senator William Jenner, a demagogue who had called George Marshall "a living lie." It is not always easy to evade a senator's embrace, and Eisenhower set out to undo the damage. As he went on to Wisconsin, he told Emmet Hughes to write up a paragraph in praise of Marshall, whom Eisenhower deeply admired and to whom he was, after all, enormously indebted. The praise was duly written, but then Ike was persuaded by Republican leaders in Wisconsin to drop it from his speeches. He permitted further senatorial embraces, these by Joseph McCarthy, who had called Marshall a traitor. The dropping of the paragraph was shameful in itself, but also raised some doubt in my mind as to whether Ike as President might at first be too easily shoved around by political hacks and mountebanks of his own party.

After the 1952 election, Harry Luce stopped off at my office one morning, said he was on his way to call on Eisenhower at the Commodore Hotel, and did I have any advice for the President-elect? I said, "Be President." Luce was puzzled. I said, "You know—one of the kings of England—his mother told him, 'Be King.'" (It was Princess Augusta, to George III, possibly not a felicitous precedent.) Luce mused that Eisenhower would ask him if there was any job he wanted, and Luce would have to say there was only one, and he wouldn't be good at it. Luce would not have suffered congressional committees gladly. He was delighted with Eisenhower's choice for State, John Foster Dulles, a fellow Presbyterian and old friend.

I was given a chance to offer more detailed advice. C. D. Jackson, about to join the White House staff, asked me for a memo he could take to sessions on the cruiser *Helena,* where some of the new Administration were meeting with Eisenhower on his return from keeping his campaign promise: "I shall go to Korea." Over a weekend, I unburdened myself of six thousand words or so—under thirty-five Roman numeral headings—an editorial writer's heaven. Then I frugally recast the memo as an editorial for the next issue of *Fortune,* "The State of the Union," January 1953. I had of course asked Jackson's permission before adapting it for print and was a little disappointed at how readily it was given, suggesting that my memo had not become a red-hot paper on Ike's desk.

Twenty-eight years later, while working in Jimmy Carter's White House, I dug out my old memo. I sent an excerpt to Carter, venturing that one of my 1952 ideas might still be of some interest in 1980:

Right now the Eisenhower Administration can re-examine everything in sight, with the greatest of zest. It will not be so much fun six months from now, or a year from now. But the new Administration must find the will and the means to re-examine its own policies as searchingly as it is now studying the Democrats' performance. Not just because this Administration will inevitably make some mistakes, starting January 21st, but also because policies that are fine for 1953 may be ruinous for 1954.

I had suggested in my old memo the appointment of small policy audit committees, composed of private citizens, who would periodically examine the Administration's performance in foreign policy, fiscal policy, etc.

They would be expected to think in a special way: i.e., to pretend that they were the advance men for a "new Administration" coming into office next August, or February 1954, or whenever, that no existing policy is sacred, that there is no need to make policy fit the hasty thing the President said at his press conference last Tuesday, no need to protect the foolish directive that went out last month over the Secretary's signature, etc. This is one way the Administration could keep itself new.

Finally—whatever system of self-inspection and self-criticism is devised, the product must reach the President himself. The isolation of the Presidency has not been a peculiarly Democratic failing . . . It would seem to be an attribute of the power of the modern Presidency and the size of the modern Government, to be overcome only by the greatest determination and steadiest self-scrutiny on the part of the President himself.

My 1952 memo doubtless impressed me more than it did Carter. But it led me to make some further suggestions which, as related in Chapter 15, led the President in 1980 to assign me to an auditing of U.S. foreign policy.

A Surge of Revisionism

Because of the immense personal assets Eisenhower brought to the office, I believed he might grow into a great President. He did not. But I would today rate him at least as high as Truman, indeed a little higher.

The professional raters of Presidents have been mainly scholars and journalists of Democratic sympathies. In the 1950s, the academics were powerfully attracted by the eloquence, wit, and grace of Adlai Stevenson. He talked like an intellectual— and knew how to handle the Cook County machine!

Democratic intellectuals could never quite forgive Ike for beating Adlai, twice. They also tended to be suspicious of a military man in civilian office. They believed in the FDR model of an "activist" President, and Ike visibly did not. They were generally scornful of his Presidency and remained so for some years after he left office. In the 1962 Schlesinger poll of seventy-five historians, Eisenhower was ranked among the most ineffective of our Presidents—No. 22 out of the thirty-one being rated at the time. He stood just above Andrew Johnson, the only President ever impeached and tied with Chester A. Arthur. ("Chet Arthur, President of the United States?" cried one New York politician on hearing of President James Garfield's death. "Good God!")

Revisionism began to take hold about fifteen years ago. By 1981, in a poll of more than eight hundred historians conducted by Robert K. Murray and Tim H. Blessing, Eisenhower had advanced to No. 11. In 1982, the historians and political scientists polled by the Chicago *Tribune* ranked Eisenhower as the ninth-best President out of thirty-nine.*

I am not a newly minted revisionist about Eisenhower. Nor am I amazed at the recent "discovery" by academics and journalists that Eisenhower could express himself very cogently on paper. During his Presidency, I had seen some of his private letters and memoranda; he wrote forcefully, and frequently. The rambling style of his press conference responses was not so different from the way many people, even journalists, talk extemporaneously (I cringe to read a verbatim transcript of my own remarks in a Q and A session). Some of the muddle was deliberate. Talking with Press Secretary James Hagerty about a sensitive question likely to come up at a press conference, he would boast, "By the time I get through, they won't know what I said."† I once published two pieces of Eisenhower syntax and two by Kennedy, on more or less timeless aspects of farm policy, disarmament, etc., and defied the readers of *Time* to guess which President said which. Answers upside down in small type; if some readers got a perfect score, it was sheer luck.‡

I believed during Eisenhower's Administration that he was a very good President, and I still think so. I didn't think then, and I don't think now, that he rose to his full potential, unlike Truman, who rose to his and, one might say, exceeded it.

*The Journal of American History, Vol. 70, No. 3, December 1983.
†Dwight D. Eisenhower, *Mandate for Change* (New York: Doubleday, 1963), p. 478.
‡January 26, 1962.

In appraising Eisenhower's Presidency today, it is necessary first to understand the man as a politician. Ike was a brilliant politician who liked to think himself above "politics." I need not have worried that the pols would push him around, but his disdain for certain levels of politics and politicians contained a kind of insensitivity and self-righteousness. In the odious hugging scenes with a McCarthy or a Jenner, he could think: Nobody can really imagine that Dwight Eisenhower has anything in common with these rascals, this is just something that happens in a campaign.

The Eisenhower political skills were first sharpened in the small peacetime army of the 1920s and 1930s. In a democratic army the ability to lead requires at least a measure of popularity, the liking and respect of peers and subordinates. Ike had this in abundance, along with ample brains, energy, ambition. He had the organizing ability that depends so heavily on understanding the human resources and limitations within a command, and how to motivate people. He had diplomatic talents and a sharp sense of who was important—rank not an infallible guide—or might become so. In World War II, all this came together in a supreme exercise in politico-military management, carrying rival services, sovereign governments, and assorted prima donnas, military and civilian, to a common victory.

After the liberation of France in 1944, when he began being talked about for President, until the spring of 1952, when he finally agreed to go for it, Ike's letters and diary record a running debate with himself about the propriety and wisdom of entering politics. Over and over he insists he has no desire to be President, and he is vexed that so many people think he is just playing hard to get. ("That's the way to play it, Ike," MacArthur told him one day in Tokyo.*) Eisenhower had a deep belief in the political purity of the U.S. Army, "the finest organization in government," immaculately subordinate to civil authority.† A President of either party should be able to assume the total loyalty of the military and promote and assign commanders without having to think about an officer's political affiliation or ambitions. Would he be "letting the Army down" by running for President? Ike finally persuaded himself that he was being drafted, and was responding to a national necessity to save the two-party system and with it the republic.

Here, as with FDR in 1940, it is hard to disentangle personal drives from patriotic dedication. FDR, of course, had been a professional poli-

*Manchester, *American Caesar,* p. 309.
†*The Eisenhower Diaries,* edited by Robert H. Ferrell (New York: W. W. Norton & Co., 1981), pp. 169–70.

tician since age twenty-eight, and he vastly relished the top job in the business. Ike had already had a job about as big as President, in his view. He didn't need the Presidency—but he betrayed no doubt that he could handle it. The office had indeed sought the man, though the man began to help out, strenuously, in the last weeks before the convention. His competitive instincts were now aroused; to the distress of his handlers, who were trying to preserve the draft image, he told John Steele, then with the United Press, later with *Time*, "I'm going to fight like hell for the nomination." The Democrats thereupon drafted the reluctant Adlai Stevenson, with very little exertion on his part. Some historians say there has been no totally unsolicited draft since George Washington was summoned. These two 1952 nominations came close enough, rare phenomena not witnessed since.

In his appeal to the American voter in the decade of the 1950s, Ike was of course the most successful politician of either party. Once in office, he was shrewd enough to understand the political uses of seeming not to be a politician. He husbanded his popularity, like a military commander holding back his reserves. He could be quite inscrutable in a genial way—a talent going back to junior officer days (he was one of the best bridge and poker players in the Army). Frank Waldrop, editor of the old Washington *Times-Herald*, saw a good deal of Eisenhower over the years, starting when Ike was a major sitting in a little War Department office next to Chief of Staff MacArthur. Waldrop has an acute perception:

> Ike fooled a great many people for a long time about his total nature. MacArthur's limitation lay in the fact that he could not conceal himself while taking the measure of an opponent. Eisenhower slipped very seldom at that profound art.
>
> Along toward the close of his presidential career, he had lunch with a detachment of heavy thinkers from the Washington press corps. One of them said, never thinking how condescending it sounded, that he hoped the President didn't think they'd been too hard on him in their published estimates of his performance.
>
> Said Ike, unmasked at last: "What could *you* do to *me?*" He didn't elaborate, but after all, what were a few reporters to a man who had endured Montgomery . . . and beaten Hitler?*

Eisenhower had as much self-confidence as FDR, without the imperious manner. He was a man of natural reserve strengthened by the years of military command and a strong sense of presidential dignity.

*Frank C. Waldrop, *The Washingtonian,* December 1981, p. 97.

The irresistible grin and the general modesty of his style were decep-tive. Underneath, there was a very cool customer. I used to shock Democratic friends by arguing that Adlai Stevenson was basically friendlier than Ike but not as smart.

Eisenhower didn't mind having some of his Cabinet function as heavies (Reagan has the same instinct, FDR had it in spades). Dulles, Engine Charlie Wilson at Defense, and Agriculture Secretary Ezra Benson—the James Watt of his day—all served. Press Secretary Jim Hagerty recalled occasions when he had said to Eisenhower, "If I go to that press conference and say what you want me to say, I'll get hell."* With that, Ike would smile, get up and walk around the desk, pat Jim on the back, and say, "My boy, better you than me."

Jim Hagerty, by general agreement, was the best of the modern press secretaries. And presidential press secretary, with the tremen-dous amplification of all our communications channels, has become one of the major offices in our political system. I would argue that Presidents and public have been well served by most of these officials for some fifty years, starting with the first White House press secretary I knew, Steve Early, under FDR.

Hagerty advised the press there would be times he couldn't tell them the whole story, but whatever he did tell them would be true. It was. He understood Eisenhower's views and reflexes and could speak for him with confidence. His job was less difficult, however, than some of his successors'. TV was beginning to matter, but it had not yet dou-bled (at the least) the work load of the press office. And Hagerty had an immensely popular President to represent.

Lyndon Johnson consumed six press secretaries, of whom two, George Reedy and Bill Moyers, were outstanding. Jody Powell, of whom more later, was another very capable spokesman for a troubled Administration. Jim Brady, disabled by John Hinckley's bullet, might have been one of the best—a highly likable man with a nice touch with the press and the beginnings of a sound rapport with his President.

The Hidden Hand

Eisenhower was content to be seen as a passive, even lazy President —Professor Fred Greenstein of Princeton has called it "the Hidden-Hand Presidency."† After leaving the White House, Ike was bitter that

*Gordon Hoxie, ed., *The White House: Organization and Operations* (New York: Center for the Study of the Presidency, 1971), p.4.
†New York: Basic Books, 1982.

his Presidency was not more highly rated in the polls, but it was his own management technique that had in part concealed his accomplishments.

The accomplishments greatly outweighed the failures. This is the balance as I would strike it today:

Just by getting elected, Ike did invigorate the two-party system. But today I would doubt that it was in any danger of extinction in 1952. As we have seen, it is a pretty tough old system. The Republicans could endure a debacle in 1964 and win the White House four years later; the Democrats endured a debacle in 1972 and won in 1976. Special circumstances, to be sure, but our politics are full of special circumstances, including the emergence of such remarkable men as FDR and Ike.

Eisenhower was not a strong party leader. In his memoirs he says: "One of the goals I set for myself when I agreed to run again for the Presidency [he went through some hesitation about 1956, but nothing like 1951–52], was to unify and strengthen the Republican Party. My success was slight."* He talked of leaving a "progressive" stamp on the party but was not much interested in the party as a mechanism, and could never quite conceal his impatience with patronage and the rest of the nuts and bolts.

One measure of his aloofness was the curious relationship with his Vice-President of eight years, a matter of some practical importance for the Republican future. Eisenhower didn't much like Richard Nixon, but he didn't dislike him enough to ease him off the ticket in 1956. By 1960, though Ike was incensed at the things the Democrats were saying about his Administration, he and Nixon were still not comfortable enough with each other to work out the most effective campaign stance for the President. This would have been a delicate job: it would have required Ike to express warmer admiration for Nixon than he felt privately, without in any way suggesting that Nixon in the White House would simply be Ike's man.

In managing the office of the Presidency, Eisenhower was highly effective. He left the office stronger, as an institution, than he found it. He extended and systematized the staff support that had taken shape in the Roosevelt and Truman administrations. Like a good military man, he had a strong sense of order and a readiness to delegate, and he liked clean-looking lines of authority. He had no taste for the in-house infighting that delighted FDR and sometimes overwhelmed Truman. Officials in the Eisenhower Administration generally did what their titles would imply. Dulles, for instance, had no rival on the White House

*Dwight D. Eisenhower, *Waging Peace* (New York: Doubleday, 1965), p. 652.

staff—a situation future Secretaries of State would envy—but the President himself was very much in charge of foreign policy.

As Donald Neff observes in his fascinating *Warriors at Suez,* * "A shibboleth about Eisenhower's presidency was that he allowed his Secretary of State to run the nation's foreign affairs with almost total independence. Nothing could have been further from the truth. Eisenhower kept Dulles on a short leash, though he did grant him considerable latitude in handling the department's day-to-day routine. But when it came to major issues or crises, it was Eisenhower who made the decisions." He did genuinely admire his Secretary of State. Speaking to Emmet Hughes, he said, "There's only one man who has seen *more* of the world and talked with more people and *knows* more than he [Dulles] does—and that's me."†

He used the Cabinet as a Cabinet more than any President has since, presiding over nearly three hundred meetings in eight years. But he did not overcome the difficulty that the Secretary of Agriculture and the Secretary of Defense really have little to say to each other. The interplay will only occasionally enlighten a President, though the sensation of being an insider in all policy areas may be good for Cabinet members' morale. By enlarging Cabinet meeting attendance to about twenty-five people (it was ten to twelve, plus a secretary, under FDR and got up to about fifty under Carter), he diluted the importance of the sessions, though for some reason he was proud of this move. "Cabinet government" is highly desirable in the sense of a President trusting Cabinet officers to run their departments, subject to his ultimate authority, rather than his trying to control all these policy areas out of White House staff offices. But Cabinet government has become quite meaningless as a vehicle of collegial advice to a President. The separate policy areas have grown too complex, and Presidents-elect have grown more reluctant to appoint Cabinet officers with significant political constituencies of their own.‡

For the coordination of domestic policy, analyzing and reconciling the legislative proposals originating chiefly in the Cabinet departments, Eisenhower relied heavily on the Bureau of the Budget. His Budget

---

*New York: The Linden Press/Simon & Schuster, 1981, p. 39.

†Emmet John Hughes, *The Ordeal of Power* (New York: Atheneum, 1981), p. 251.

‡This is partly because the nomination is now won or lost in the primaries, and the winner has had little need to drop hints about Cabinet jobs along the way or at the convention. His major opponents for the nomination will almost invariably decline a Cabinet post; they keep more power and independence by staying in the Senate or the state house. Utterly different, of course, from the British system, where members of the Cabinet, except for the stray hereditary peer, are all working politicians who have won seats in the House of Commons and are a kind of governing council of their party.

Directors, among them Joseph Dodge and Maurice Stans, had the heft of senior Cabinet officers, and most of their successors, under Presidents of both parties, have enjoyed comparable influence.

Eisenhower also institutionalized the White House relationship with Congress. He appointed full-time congressional liaison officers who had a feel for Congress and its mores, and he gave them high status in the White House. One of the most skillful of Ike's operatives, Bryce Harlow, recalls: "For real effectiveness a White House congressional man must be known on Capitol Hill as a confidant of the President . . . It is not enough simply to have that access to the President; the members of Congress must know he has it and, further, that he is willing to draw down on this asset for proper congressional purposes."* Harlow himself could wake up Ike with impunity when some late-night congressional situation required the President's immediate response.

Eisenhower was up against Democratic congressional majorities for six of his eight years. He had generally harmonious relationships with the Democratic leaders on the Hill, Speaker Sam Rayburn and Senate Majority Leader Lyndon Johnson. He got along better with them, he often said, than with some of the leaders of his own party.

This was in part the achievement of Bryce Harlow and his colleagues. One measure of their work—and that of the Budget Office—is that Eisenhower had only two out of his 181 vetoes overridden. Some expert nose-counting went into this record.

President Kennedy continued this legislative liaison setup almost unchanged, though his agents were more aggressive than Ike's. The liaison men were less important under LBJ, who felt with some justice that he knew the congressional levers quite intimately. Harlow came back to the White House to try to help Nixon on the Hill, but he had a more difficult client this time. Under Carter, the White House–Congress relationship was the worst since Truman. The reasons went deeper than staff structure.

Eisenhower made the National Security Council his most significant vehicle of presidential management. The NSC was dealing with the issues closest to his own training and interests. Over eight years he presided almost once a week, on average, over NSC meetings which were true deliberative sessions among the six, eight, ten most senior officers in defense and foreign policy.

The importance of the NSC declined under Kennedy and Johnson, then grew again in subsequent administrations, dramatized or overdramatized by the tendency of the President's Assistant for National

*Bryce Harlow, Center House Bulletin, Vol. IV, No. 1, Winter 1974.

Security, originally conceived as the low-key chief of a kind of secretariat, almost a civil servant, to become a second Secretary of State. Even Reagan's Judge Bill Clark became an aw-shucks version of Drs. Brzezinski and Kissinger. Secretaries Shultz, Vance, and Rogers all know the feeling.

The Mixed Domestic Record

With all this impressive management apparatus, and with his own great gifts, how well did Eisenhower handle the substance of policy?

He did not distinguish himself in the matter of McCarthyism. Ike's instinct was that Joseph McCarthy, given enough rope, would hang himself. Meanwhile he would not risk the dignity of the Presidency, and his own, by open combat with the senator. He thought denunciation by the President would simply be a publicity bonanza for McCarthy. "I will not get into a pissing contest with that skunk," Ike told his brother Milton.* It is true that McCarthy had thrived on the attacks of critics who inflated his importance—Joe could easily "run against" the press and the professors. It does not follow that he could have exploited a rebuke from an immensely popular President. Sixteen months into his Presidency, still without naming McCarthy, Eisenhower finally drew the line, invoking "executive privilege" against McCarthy's invitation to federal employees to testify to him on "graft, corruption, communism, and treason" in the government. In this demand, McCarthy did indeed prepare his own noose, and by December 1954, when the Senate voted to condemn his conduct, McCarthyism was dead.

I thought at the time, and still do, that Eisenhower should have risked some of his own political capital to destroy McCarthyism sooner. It was allowed to flourish for almost half of Eisenhower's first term, an unnecessary distraction for government and public opinion from issues fundamentally more important.

Some of the same coolness and caution marked Eisenhower's approach to civil rights. He was a gradualist, sensitive to the attitudes of the powerful southerners on the Hill and their constituencies back home. In this he resembled Roosevelt, though it should be noted that he was elected twenty years later, and the world does move. Eisenhower didn't identify himself audibly and emotionally with the aspirations of the blacks, as Truman had eventually done, and as Johnson and Carter later did (interestingly, a Border State man, a Texan, and a Deep

*Quoted in Stephen Ambrose, "The Ike Age," *The New Republic,* May 9, 1981.

Southerner). There is no evidence that Eisenhower did much private seething about discrimination, as he did about Joe McCarthy.

When the Supreme Court handed down *Brown* v. *Board of Education* in 1954, Eisenhower gave reporters a reaction that was constitutionally impeccable but not exactly a clarion call to the nation: "The Supreme Court has spoken, and I am sworn to uphold the constitutional processes in this country; and I will obey."

He did obey, dramatically, in 1957, sending elements of the 101st Airborne into Little Rock, to enforce federal court integration orders against the defiance of Arkansas Governor Orval Faubus. Just before Little Rock, Eisenhower had signed the first major civil rights bill since Reconstructionist days. It was less of a bill than his enlightened Attorney General Herbert Brownell wanted. Ike had helped water it down, partly because he needed the support of southern congressmen on other legislation, partly because he himself didn't want to go as fast as Brownell did. On civil rights, in sum, Eisenhower was correct and uninspiring, a stout conservator of process, not a groundbreaker.

Eisenhower was an excellent President of the U.S. economy. He had the wisdom to let a lot of things alone. This was anathema to the "strong President" scholars, who could not forgive Ike for not being a Roosevelt, even Theodore, Republican but hyperactivist. The business cycle was in fact poised for growth and prosperity in the early fifties, if the government did not mess it up and if no external crisis intervened.

With his preference for orderly flows of advice and information, Eisenhower entrusted his first chairman of the Council of Economic Advisers, Arthur Burns, with much more responsibility than most CEA heads have enjoyed since. The redoubtable Dr. Burns, later chairman of the Federal Reserve and under Reagan ambassador to Germany, found Ike "highly educable" in economics. At their first meeting, Burns proposed to send him a memo indicating how economic advice to the President could best be organized. "Keep it short," said Ike. "I can't read." Burns said, "We'll get along fine. I can't write." Ike was delighted, and Burns thereafter had a standing appointment, an hour every week, on the President's calendar.

I was managing editor of *Fortune* during the Eisenhower years. I argued that the economy was the biggest story in America in the 1950s; it was in any case, a great story for *Fortune*. It is hard to remember now, but in the early 1950s there were many Americans who had never known in their adult lives a long period of good times in a country at peace. The country had experienced the ten-year depression of the 1930s, five years of a war economy, the dislocations of the early postwar, a few years of prosperity in the late 1940s—though many businessmen and economists feared an early bust—then the semicontrolled economy of the Korean War.

So as the great boom of the 1950s took hold, *Fortune* analyzed and celebrated the phenomenon in almost every issue. We gave the Eisenhower Administration some of the credit.

The Eisenhower Administration pursued orthodox conservative economic policies, but there was no effort to repeal the New Deal. Indeed, old-age and unemployment security benefits were substantially enlarged, and the Department of Health, Education and Welfare was established. The biggest public works program in our history was put in motion—the building of the Interstate Highway System (roads were a special enthusiasm of Ike's), with invigorating effect on the economy and great impact on the whole American life-style. U.S. participation in building the St. Lawrence Seaway, after decades of talk, was finally authorized. Eisenhower put through a large tax reduction in 1954, but also came up with a budget surplus in three years out of eight. (Truman ran a surplus four years out of eight.) It has happened in only one year since.

In 1956, I thought neither Eisenhower nor Stevenson quite so attractive (in their very different ways) as they had looked in 1952. But Eisenhower again seemed much the better choice. In an endorsement editorial I wrote for *Fortune* (October 1956) I particularly admired four stands he had taken contrary to the "rules" of election year politics: he did not recommend a further tax cut, he vetoed a farm bill laden with goodies, he supported the Fed's very tight money policies, and he vetoed a big pork barrel bill. The Democrats denounced him as "arbitrary" and "heartless," I wrote, and "Mr. Stevenson (who long ago said something about 'talking sense' to the American people) chimed in soon afterward."

When Eisenhower left office, despite three recessions—two very mild, one rather sharp—the gross national product (real) was 20 percent higher than when he came in. Over the eight years, inflation averaged only 1.4 percent a year. A remarkable record. In a nice bipartisan way, the economy did equally well for Kennedy, who had the good sense not to tinker much with a going concern.

Five-Star Prudence

In foreign policy, Eisenhower was also a remarkably successful President through a period that presented endless opportunities for America to get into trouble. Not much gets permanently "solved" in foreign policy, but it is no small achievement to keep the country at peace for eight years and leave no time bombs for the next President.

Eisenhower in six months converted the shaky cease-fire in Korea to a permanent settlement, on about the best terms we could get, short of renewing the war on a large scale. All his diplomatic skills came into play, as well as a touch of soldier's steel. To prod the Chinese and North Koreans toward a settlement, Ike conveyed a strong hint that if the war had to be renewed, the use of atomic weapons could not be excluded. At the same time, he had to rein in our maddening client Syngman Rhee, the President of South Korea, who still wanted to invade North Korea. Ike had to concert our policy with the twenty-one other countries that, under UN auspices, had taken some part in the war. Those countries were even more eager to see the war ended than the U.S.; though they hadn't done much in Korea, they were friends and allies who mattered to us.

In 1954, Eisenhower made a painful and profoundly farsighted decision about Indochina. In the agony of Dien Bien Phu, the French were losing their last battle against the Vietminh guerrilla forces. A strong case could be made for a major U.S. military intervention. France was an ally, the Vietminh were a Communist-dominated movement backed by China and the Soviets, and Indochina was a highly strategic piece of geography. But Eisenhower decided to stay out. The British wanted no part of any intervention in Indochina, and Eisenhower did not want the U.S. standing alone with the French in trying to defend a colonial regime that had no popular support. In 1963, he wrote a prophetic memo about his decision, published nineteen years later, in William Ewald's *Eisenhower the President*:

> It is exasperating and depressing to stand by and watch a free world nation losing a battle to slavery without being able to commit all your resources, including combat troops, to its aid . . . The jungles of Indochina, however, would have swallowed up division after division of United States troops . . . The presence of ever more numbers of white men in uniform probably would have aggravated rather than assuaged Asiatic resentments.

Thus, even had all of Indochina been physically occupied by United States troops, their eventual removal would have resulted only in a reversion to the situation which had existed before . . .

The standing of the United States as the most powerful of the anti-colonial powers is an asset of incalculable value to the Free World . . . It is essential to our position of leadership in a world wherein the majority of the nations have at some time or another felt the yoke of colonialism. Thus it is that the moral position of the United States was more to be guarded than the Tonkin Delta, indeed than all of Indochina.*

Indochina was split up, after the French defeat, into four more or less sovereign states; North Viet Nam, South Viet Nam, Cambodia, and Laos. Freed of the onus of defending a colonial power, Eisenhower gave limited aid, economic and military, to the anti-Communist regime of South Viet Nam. Along with weapons, military advisers were sent to the Diem government—their number had reached 800 when Eisenhower left the White House. Kennedy, in less than three years, increased this to 16,500, and under Lyndon Johnson, of course, we eventually had more than half a million men in Viet Nam.

The last time I saw Eisenhower was in October 1965, after the Johnson buildup had begun. I was about to make a trip to Viet Nam and Eisenhower wanted to be remembered to General William Westmore-land. "Westy's as good as we've got," said Ike. "It's going to be tough out there."

The strong anticolonial strain in Eisenhower's thinking contributed to the only major foreign policy failure of his Administration. Eisenhower and Dulles may have helped bring on the tragic folly of the Anglo-French attack on Suez in November 1956. They then had to side with the Soviet Union, its hands freshly bloodied in Budapest, in denouncing our principal European allies.

After Gamal Abdel Nasser came to power in Egypt, the Eisenhower Administration vacillated between friendliness and hostility toward his regime. The overthrow of the corrupt King Farouk, propped up by the British for years, was a certifiable victory over colonialism. And the dynamic young Nasser was a leader whose friendship might be useful to the United States throughout the Arab world. Rebuffed by us, he might "let the Soviets into the Middle East." But our most intimate ally, Britain, still had considerable military force in Egypt and elsewhere in the Middle East and, with the French, still owned and ran the Suez

*Englewood Cliffs, New Jersey: Prentice-Hall, 1981, pp. 118–120.

Canal. And the British were convinced Nasser was a very dangerous man.

The dilemma was more difficult for Eisenhower than for his Secretary of State. Eisenhower knew the strategic value of the British presence in the Middle East and was not so rigidly virtuous as Dulles in his views on colonialism. Eisenhower was deeply Anglophile and, unlike Dulles, had warm friendships with Churchill, Eden, and Macmillan.

U.S. policy zigged and zagged. The big anti-Nasser zag came in July 1956 when the U.S. withdrew from negotiations for funding the Aswan high dam above the Cataracts of the Nile. To realize his dream of the great dam, Nasser did indeed turn to the Russians (he was already getting Soviet arms), and he promptly nationalized the Suez Canal Company.

The British, French, and Israelis began coordinating their plans for the attack on Egypt. U.S. policy began zigging back toward support of Nasser. Through maneuvers in the United Nations, Eisenhower and Dulles skillfully delayed the invasion for some weeks, but in the end they could not prevent it. The Israelis attacked in late October, the British and French on November 1. On November 7, they were compelled by the UN, in effect by the U.S., to accept a cease-fire.

The result was a major victory for the Soviets, who could piously vote on the "moral" side of the UN resolutions and see the world's attention diverted from their brutal suppression of the Hungarian freedom fighters. Suez completed the descent of Britain and France to second-rank powers, and indeed some bitter Europeans thought this was the precise purpose of the seeming vacillations in U.S. policy. Nothing could have been further from Eisenhower's intent, but Suez left strains within the Western alliance that persisted for years. It is possible, though by no means certain, that a more coherent U.S. policy, developed earlier and pursued consistently, could have prevented the tragedy.

Eisenhower conducted our end of the Cold War with firmness and a controlled calm. He allowed Dulles and Vice-President Nixon a certain stridency in anti-Soviet rhetoric; he seldom indulged himself.

In a speech after he left office, he boasted that in his eight years communism had not gained "an inch" anywhere in the world. This was almost true. The Communists took over North Viet Nam during his first term, and late in his second term, Fidel Castro, soon revealed as a Marxist, came to power in Cuba. Otherwise the lines held.

When the Soviets put down the Hungarian revolution in 1956, and lesser disturbances in Poland and East Germany, they were not enslaving new territories, but confirming previous conquests. Our tacit acceptance of the Iron Curtain led to a kind of stabilization of the Cold War, following the death of Stalin and the end of the Korean War. Dulles no longer talked of "liberation" of the satellites. My friend C. D. Jackson, a psychological warfare expert in World War II, found little relish in the White House for "rollback" scenarios. Ike did not agonize very long when the moment of truth came in Hungary; he was simply not ready to risk World War III to liberate a Soviet satellite. He made it amply clear that he would risk the big war if the Soviets thought of moving against the West. These were sound positions (we said so in *Fortune*). For the rest of Eisenhower's Presidency, they introduced a measure of predictability, "rules" of a sort, into the Soviet-American relationship.

In his first term, Eisenhower had already made two moves toward détente (though the word was not yet used). Neither was acceptable to the Soviets, but each signaled in a dramatic way a U.S. desire to negotiate about the atom. One was the proposal, in his "Atoms for Peace" speech before the UN in December 1953, that the United States would contribute nuclear materials to the UN for the "peaceful pursuits of mankind." The other was his "Open Skies" proposal at the Geneva summit conference in 1955, which would have allowed Soviet and American planes to conduct reconnaissance of each other's homeland.

The Open Skies overture having failed, Eisenhower prudently authorized the U-2 overflights of the Soviet Union, starting in 1956. The Soviets were well aware of the flights but kept quiet about them, not wanting to admit they couldn't prevent them and that they had no comparable capability over the U.S. (Open Skies would not have been a bad deal for them.) When the Soviets in 1960 finally brought down a U-2 and captured the pilot, Khrushchev went into a calculated public rage over the U.S. violation of Soviet air space. He broke up the Paris summit meeting. Eisenhower's invitation to visit the Soviet Union was withdrawn.

The rich comedy of Khrushchev's visit to the U.S. had been played out the previous year. His unruffled chaperone was Henry Cabot Lodge, our Ambassador to the U.N.; the juxtaposition of the stubby commissar and the tall and elegant Brahmin made for some memorable photos. Ike in Moscow was supposed to be the quid pro quo. It takes an effort to remember that an American President was considered so popular in the Soviet Union that we really wondered whether they would dare let him come. The "Spirit of Camp David"—Ike entertained Khrushchev there in the Maryland hills one weekend—didn't impress Eisenhower as much as it did European diplomats and some of us in the press. "It was a term," Ike coldly observes in his memoirs, "that I never used or deemed valid."*

In his last year in office, Eisenhower made triumphal tours of most of the world, minus Russia, Japan (his visit was canceled because demonstrations threatened to get out of hand), and Mainland China (which Presidents didn't visit in those days). Crowds totaling into the millions cheered the President of the West. This very reserved man confessed himself more than once "deeply touched."

One evening in January 1961, shortly before he left the White House, Eisenhower gave a dinner for some thirty of the White House press corps. The host was "glowing," John Steele of *Time* reported in a memo to his editors, through "an incredible three and a half hours" of anecdote, singing—the journalistic and presidential voices were beefed up by a Navy quartet—and warm little sermons about the country, the American political system, even the press. The President appealed for understanding "in the interests of our country" for that "fine young man" who was to take the oath a few days later.

In private conversations not too long before, he had been calling Kennedy "Little Boy Blue." And soon after, though circumspect in his public statements, he was harshly critical in private comments on his successor. He took some wry satisfaction in Kennedy's discovery early in his term that there was no "missile gap" after all, the gap having been a favorite Kennedy campaign theme. He was appalled by Kennedy's handling of the Bay of Pigs operation, but loyally issued a close-the-ranks statement, and perhaps relished the young President's need to be photographed "conferring with" the old soldier at Camp David.

*Eisenhower, *Waging Peace* (Garden City: Doubleday & Co., 1965) p. 448.

7

John Kennedy

Across twenty years, the dry laconic wit still comes through pitch-perfect. The style and grace and quickness still dazzle. There was more than that, of course, to John Kennedy and his Presidency. How much more?

Of the Presidents I am trying to appraise in these essays, I find Kennedy the most difficult case. I didn't think he had much claim to the Presidency in 1960. Watching him as President, I was increasingly impressed. Thinking about him since—and learning more about him—I find almost as much to deplore as to admire. In this sketch of Kennedy, I try (as elsewhere in this book) to label hindsight as hindsight.

Candidate Kennedy bothered me, to begin with, because of his father and all his father's money (later estimated by *Fortune* at $300 million-plus). Old Joe and the money still bother me. The American right to try to get rich does of course include the right to give your children, after taxes, "every advantage." When is every advantage, as applied to a political career, too many?

Jack Kennedy could kid himself about this, too. In 1958, running for reelection as senator, he told the Gridiron Club he'd just had a wire from his father: "Don't buy a single vote more than is necessary—I'll be damned if I'm going to pay for a landslide."* It was a landslide, however, the biggest margin any candidate for any office had ever rolled up in Massachusetts, and it gave powerful momentum to Kennedy's pur-

*Herbert Parmet, *Jack: The Struggles of John F. Kennedy* (New York: The Dial Press, 1980), p. 439.

suit of the Presidency. Kennedy's victory over Nixon in 1960 was, of course, very narrow and indeed was slightly tainted—not by old Joe's money but by the vote-counting virtuosity of the Democratic machine of Cook County, Illinois, and selected precincts in Texas. But Jack Kennedy never would have been a presidential candidate at all, or a senator, without the support of his father's money and the connections that came from the money.

If Jack Kennedy had been, let us say, Jack Kennelly, same sort of mind and humor, same good looks and charm, solid parents ambitious for their children, Boston College perhaps, good war record (not nationally publicized), he might have been a successful lawyer, professor, journalist, maybe even a congressman. He probably would not have gone into business, and definitely not into the priesthood.

A fascinating presidential election that didn't happen would have been John Kennedy vs. Nelson Rockefeller. Kennedy used to express some nervousness about the outcome; he once told John Steele of *Time* he would have lost. Nelson, of course, was the grandson of the tycoon, not the son, and the Rockefeller money had been civilized by decades of good works. But Nelson Rockefeller never would have been governor and a perennial presidential possibility except for his ability to bankroll the New York Republican organization.

I would make a distinction here between the lavish use of a family fortune (whether brand-new or several generations old) to finance political campaigns, and the freedom of career that an "independent income" can confer. Both Roosevelts, Franklin and Theodore, benefited from inheritances that allowed them to concentrate on politics as relatively young men, without worrying too much about making a living. But they didn't bankroll their own campaigns. And our first six or eight Presidents were all men of property. Indeed George Washington was probably the richest man in America, though he didn't spend anything on his landslides (it was unanimous in the Electoral College, twice).

But if the politician with independent income has more than enough to live on, should he be able to spend some of the surplus on his own campaign? Is $500,000 all right? But not $10 million? I doubt if legislation can ever draw such a line. But there should be one, somewhere. The moneyless candidates, the Nixons and Humphreys, are much more troubled by the situation, it must be noted, than the general public. Many voters found John Kennedy's wealth simply one more facet of his glamour. As Kennedy himself said, in another connection, "Life is unfair."

In Washington in the time just before and after Pearl Harbor I had a few stray encounters with Ensign John Kennedy. We had some mutual friends (including Captain Alan G. Kirk, USN, who helped both of us get into Naval Intelligence). At parties and touch football games there was general agreement that Jack Kennedy was a very nice fellow. Surprisingly so, considering what a handicap he had in his father, Ambassador Kennedy, who had left his London post in bitterness, was known to be anti-Semitic, defeatist about the war, and was regarded by me and my friends as a generally unattractive specimen of buccaneer businessman.

It was a type that fascinated Henry Luce (not yet my employer in 1941 and mercifully unaware of my views). Joseph Kennedy was hardly the model of the "modern" or enlightened U.S. businessman Luce liked to think *Fortune* was addressing, but he was rich and powerful, and so was Luce. Kennedy was shrewd and salty, good company, and, to an editor, a good source and good copy. Kennedy in turn found Luce a useful man to know. In 1940, when John Kennedy, age twenty-three, was getting his Harvard honors thesis published as a book, *Why England Slept,* Luce as a favor to Joe agreed to write a foreword.

In 1960, when the Democratic convention was held in Los Angeles, Joe Kennedy, having discreetly returned to New York after the nomination, invited himself to dinner with Harry Luce so they could watch the acceptance speech together. "It's quite a thing," Luce told me afterward, "to sit with an old friend in front of the television and watch his son accept the nomination for President of the United States." Luce assured Joe he understood why Jack might have to campaign a bit "left of center" in domestic policy, and Joe assured Luce that in foreign policy "no son of mine" would ever be soft on communism.

No less an authority than Joe McCarthy would have vouched for Jack as an anti-Communist. Kennedy's record on McCarthyism bothered me in the 1950s and still does. Jack's father had been a friend and admirer of Senator McCarthy's, and a financial supporter, and brother Bobby had worked for a time on his subcommittee staff. But Jack was contaminated in his own right. He conspicuously and repeatedly refrained from criticizing McCarthy. He had a lively respect for McCarthy's Irish Catholic support in Massachusetts and he had a visceral distaste for some of the people most likely to be frightened by a McCarthy. He also had a personal liking for the man and a belief that McCarthyism itself was not all bad.

If Dwight Eisenhower was guilty of a disgraceful expediency about McCarthyism at a moment in his 1952 campaign, Kennedy as congressman and senator was consistently expedient over several years and was also guilty of genuinely bad judgment about a nasty demagogue. After McCarthy was broken, no thanks to Kennedy, Jack's record on the subject embarrassed him all the way to 1960, as he sought to rally liberal Democrats, and their great icon Eleanor Roosevelt, to his ambitions for national office.

Perhaps it was discomfort over the McCarthy business that led Kennedy to launch the *Profiles in Courage* project, to associate himself, between hard covers, with politicians who put principle above expediency. *Profiles*, a study of eight great senators who took unpopular positions, was a perceptive historical essay, not unworthy of the Pulitzer Prize it received. The difficulty is that John Kennedy didn't really write it.

Journalists at the time heard about some of the ghostwriting assistance, but tended to accept the official Kennedy line that the senator himself, naturally drawing upon scholarly papers and suggestions, was indeed the author. The Kennedys threatened lawsuits against journalists who didn't accept that line.

Kennedy did think up the book, made the final choice of the senators to be included, contributed many ideas and some language. As to the completed text, he was approximately the editor (a line of work I think well of). Herbert Parmet, in his painstaking reconstruction of the whole *Profiles* process, including the drumbeating role of Joe Senior, concludes: "Neither the chronology of Jack Kennedy's life in 1954 and 1955 [when the book was written] nor the materials accumulated in the preparation of the book [which can be inspected in the Kennedy Library in Boston] even come close to supporting the contention that Jack could have been or was its major author."*

The book and all the hype surrounding it made Kennedy seem a heavyweight, and gave him a special prominence on the eve of the Democrats' 1956 convention. That in turn became a major milestone in his progress toward the White House. To have foreseen all that when he started on the book would have been political genius, worthy of its own prize. What he did put into the book was some Kennedy money and organization, his own ambition and energy, and an honest and thoughtful interest in American political history. The dishonesty arose when he accepted the Pulitzer, but by then he was in too deep—or was

*Parmet, *Jack*, p. 331.

he?—to announce that the prize should really go to his versatile assistant, Theodore Sorensen, and he was proud to be Ted's editor.

Kennedy, as congressman and senator, had been attentive to the
Time Inc. publications, and our correspondents and editors had good
access to him. (After his first European trip as President, he remarked
with some irritation that the leaders he had met knew nothing of the
U.S. except what they read in the *New York Times* and *Time.* If so, I
felt this made them tolerably well informed.) *Life,* with something of
the same national impact that TV later enjoyed, gave priceless exposure
to the stylish young senator and his beautiful bride.

The Right to Be President

My own impression at the time was that Kennedy was a playboy,
and a remarkably bright one. As a young congressman, he had sometimes appeared on the House floor in chino pants and tennis shoes.
Advancing to the Senate, he was not especially industrious or influential
as a legislator, and seemed excessively preoccupied, for such a junior
senator, with higher office. I would have been more generous about his
legislative record had I known what the whole Kennedy clan and staff
took great pains to conceal—the full extent of the agonizing disabilities
and sickness he bore with such stoic courage.

But the ambition was unmistakable, at least the equal of Richard
Nixon's, his likely opponent if he could get past all the Democrats. In
both men, as I came to know them at that stage of their lives, it was an
ambition almost totally empty of any purpose for the country. The
object of winning was to win. The Kennedy style gave his effort the air
of a high-stakes game played by a spirited aristocrat, while poor Nixon
came on as a somewhat ill-used Vice-President earnestly trying to better himself.

Kennedy himself had actually sought a VP nomination. At the
Democrats' Chicago convention of 1956, in one wildly exciting night
and day of politicking (wonderful fun to watch as a monthly magazine
editor, less fun for people filing for daily papers), he came very close to
beating out Estes Kefauver. Then he made a swift and graceful platform
appearance to thank his supporters and congratulate the victor. It is not
likely he thought Adlai Stevenson had any real chance of beating Eisenhower (his father thought he was crazy to try to get on the ticket), but
he wanted the press coverage and the personal contacts of a national

campaign, perhaps on the model of FDR's unsuccessful and useful candidacy for Vice-President in 1920, when he was only thirty-eight. (To put trivia addicts out of their misery—the Democratic presidential candidate was James B. Cox, Ohio newspaper publisher.) Kennedy, thirty-nine, was lucky to lose; he got a publicity bonanza from the convention itself, and nobody could blame Stevenson's defeat in November on a Catholic running mate. From 1956 on, every move he made in his public life was aimed at the White House.

In private life, notwithstanding the storybook marriage, he soon resumed the diversions of bachelor days. Washington journalists gossiped knowingly, but few hints of his womanizing got into print. The press, as Jack's youngest brother can testify, was far more protective then than now about the private lives of politicians. After Kennedy entered the White House, the flagrant vulgarity and political recklessness of his philandering perhaps gave it an extra fillip. I knew much less of this then, even as an editor somewhat on the inside, than all of us have been able to read since.

I aspire not to be priggish, but the thought of the President of the United States setting up assignations in the White House with a woman also enjoyed by a Mafia chieftain does, as they say, stretch the mind. The President presumably was not aware—would any thriller writer have dared cook this up?—that the Mafia character, Sam Giancanna, had been approached by the CIA to help knock off the Castro regime.

The woman had been introduced to Kennedy at Las Vegas by Frank Sinatra—the same Frank Sinatra who has often been in the company of the Ronald Reagans, not arranging dates but helping plan White House galas. What invincible bad taste is at work here? I tax the Presidents more than the entertainer.

Does Kennedy's philandering matter to our appraisal of the man as President? Perhaps a man can be dishonest and heartless in marriage and still be completely honest and compassionate in his public life. Or perhaps character is not so easily compartmented. Lyndon Johnson, another wholesale womanizer, was notoriously deceitful as a politician, where Kennedy was fairly straightforward. Johnson, however, had a much deeper strain of compassion. Johnson became intensely religious —Kennedy was not—and in the White House spent many hours in prayer with the Rev. Billy Graham. Complicated people, these Presidents.

A man as willfully self-indulgent as Kennedy in private life can carry over into public life a lordly assumption that what he wants he damned well should have. (Nelson Rockefeller showed something of the same seigneurial approach to women and politics.) In Kennedy's whole nervy drive for the Presidency, there was somehow an underlying premise that the office was rightfully his. Or, we brought the football.*

A few weeks before the 1960 convention, Kennedy came to lunch with fifteen or twenty of us in New York, the top editors of the Time Inc. magazines and our senior political correspondents. Jack took no cocktail, ate lightly, and drank one bottle of Heineken's beer. He got out one of his slender cigars, asked me for a light, and I was surprised to see his hand trembling. Maybe his father's friend Henry Luce awed him a little; I doubt the rest of us did. (Or maybe it was a bad day for his back.)

The senator politely asked me how come with a name like Donovan I wasn't a Catholic. I have always enjoyed explaining to Catholics that my great-grandfather James Donovan, a studious Irish lad intended by his parents for the priesthood, did not like that idea, and ran away from County Cork to America. A vocation did finally surface; one of James's sons, my grandfather David, became a Congregationalist minister. Kennedy began to fidget; I think I was telling him more than he needed to know. In any case, he was aware of the restiveness on his left of Luce, eager to make his editors—and the candidate—get to work.

Under "background" not-for-attribution rules, Jack was fluent on Berlin, the Formosa Straits, unemployment, depressed areas, the "missile gap," etc. In a pause during all the serious dialogue about "the issues," George Hunt, later managing editor of *Life,* put the beautifully simple question, "Senator, why do you want to be President?" Jack did much better than his brother Ted did when Roger Mudd put the same question to him on TV nineteen years later. Jack didn't fumble around. "Because that's where the real authority is," he said briskly. An individual senator could have a little influence, but "the other end of Pennsylvania Avenue" was where "the action" is. We could have gone on to ask: Action, authority, in behalf of what? But he had given us a revealing answer, and it would have been a pity to make him clutter it up with campaign-speech platitudes.

*There was some of this, too, in Robert Kennedy's feeling that Lyndon Johnson, succeeding his brother, was almost a usurper. In running for the nomination in 1968, Bob was attempting a restoration, so to speak, of the legitimate line. His assassination was perhaps a larger tragedy than Jack's; Bob Kennedy was a more serious man and was still growing, intellectually and in his heart.

I next saw him pursuing "the action" at the convention in Los Angeles. He and Lyndon Johnson, by then his only important rival for the nomination, had arranged a joint appearance before a joint caucus of the Texas and Massachusetts delegations. Kennedy at that point was well ahead, but a weak performance in this heavily billed confrontation might have derailed him. I was standing with some other press people a little behind the lectern, where we could see Kennedy's knees shaking. Texas couldn't see that, and heard a firm, confident voice. Having had my own moments of terror as an amateur public speaker, I was touched to see a big-league politician so nervous.

During the campaign, Luce was amused by occasional column items speculating that Time Inc., which had never endorsed a Democrat for President, might back his friend Joe's boy. *Time,* which had been so partisan for Ike in 1952 and 1956, covered the 1960 campaign quite evenhandedly ("too *damn* evenhandedly," one Nixon man said). The photogenic Kennedys continued to fascinate *Life.*

I was now editorial director of the company, Luce's deputy. I had something to do with the evenhanded reporting in *Time.* * I was also involved in the decision that we should support Nixon on the *Life* editorial page, the place where Time Inc. did its formal endorsing. Luce was never seriously tempted by the notion of endorsing Kennedy, though he would have enjoyed the ensuing commotion. "The College of Cardinals," as Luce sometimes called us (leaving it clear who was Pope)—the editorial director, managing editors of the magazines, and the chief editorial writer of *Life,* John K. Jessup—were all for Nixon.

Jessup's balanced editorial, published in two parts in successive weeks in mid-October, called both candidates "patriotic, full of fresh ideas and serious purpose."† Kennedy "has personal style and eloquence, great assets for a free world leader." But Nixon had the edge in experience, and the Kennedy attacks on Eisenhower policy, foreign and domestic, were generally unconvincing.

Shortly before the election there was something of a flap when the Kennedy people heard that *Life* was going to publish an article by Billy Graham endorsing his friend Nixon. Kennedy staffers were complaining to Edward Thompson, managing editor of *Life;* the candidate (and perhaps his father) phoned Luce. The published article, "We Are Elect-

---

*Thomas Griffith had more to do with it. *Time*'s managing editor, Otto Fuerbringer, was ill, and Griffith was acting M.E. He had long argued with Fuerbringer, Luce, and others for more dispassionate campaign coverage in *Time.* Luce did not try to interfere with Tom's experiment; I actively encouraged it.

†*Life,* October 24, 1960, p. 36.

ing a President of the World" (*Life,* November 7, 1960), was an innocuous appeal to everybody to get out and vote. If there was any Nixon tilt, it was only in the passing thought that "we should not decide on the basis of which candidate is more handsome or more charming."

A Classic Pragmatist

After Kennedy won, Jessup wrote an editorial expressing "hopeful curiosity." I sent Luce a memo speculating that Time Inc. might have more influence on Kennedy than we had had on Ike:

> Partly the difference between the two men, partly the difference between a 300,000 plurality* and a 9,000,000 plurality, partly because Time Inc. is in no way committed to, or to be taken for granted by, the new Administration.
>
> But Kennedy, because he is a reader, a student, a believer in "a constant flow of ideas," etc., is going to bring down upon himself a stupendous flow of advice from the faculties, the press, and all over the place. Among all these self-appointed advisers, a good many will soon talk themselves out of any influence by trying to know too much about everything. As editorial writers, we should "concentrate on a relatively small number of key issues."

As editorial writers, I doubt we had much influence on Kennedy. But as editors, photographers, reporters covering him, we did have influence, and he was very sensitive to it. Hugh Sidey, *Time*'s White House correspondent, recalls phone calls to his home on Sunday evenings (the White House got a special early delivery of *Time,* a day ahead of other Washington offices) in which the President of the United States would complain, in cheerfully profane style, about some choice of phrase or photo in one of our magazines, usually *Time.* We loved being read so closely. He loved the internal gossip of the press—what publications were making money, who was up, who was down at the major papers, the networks, the newsmagazines. He was a journalist's President.

In February 1961, I wrote in a memo to my colleagues: "I am evolving a theory that it is rather pointless to analyze whether Kennedy is at heart 'conservative' or 'liberal.' Kennedy is Kennedy. Either the least ideological of our 20th Century Presidents, or the inventor-to-be of a new ideology cutting across the traditional right-left patterns of U.S. politics."

*When the official tabulation was in, Kennedy's margin was only 118,000.

He grew only a bit more liberal as he settled into his Presidency. Arthur Schlesinger, Jr., recalls pressing on Kennedy a case for a bolder liberalism. "He felt that there were greater limits on what he could do than I felt there were. Yet one has to admit the possibility that Presidents may know more about politics than their special assistants. Perhaps that is one reason why Presidents are Presidents and their special assistants are only special assistants."

Kennedy owed little to the liberal wing of his party, and there was a touch of the Irish grudge-bearer in him. Early in his term, however, he did please the liberals, and defy the southern conservatives, by tackling the formidable "Judge" Howard Smith of Virginia, chairman of the House Rules Committee. The Administration succeeded, in effect, in packing the Rules Committee, theoretically opening the way for civil rights legislation and other liberal social and economic measures. But it had been a bitter fight, leaving Kennedy with little stomach for further battle any time soon with the southern Tories.

In economic policy the atmospherics were different from the Eisenhower era—as in Kennedy's populist outburst over the U.S. Steel price increases of 1962—but the Administration did not press for any changes remotely comparable to Truman's Fair Deal shopping list. Kennedy was a fiscal conservative. He was basically friendlier to business than Truman or FDR, and in 1962–63 proposed tax reductions (finally enacted in the Johnson Administration) that even anticipated one aspect of Reaganomics—the heretical notion that tax rates could be reduced in the face of a federal budget deficit.

In civil rights, though the Justice Department under Bobby Kennedy was a zealous enforcer of existing law, his brother did not propose major new legislation until he had been in office more than two years. He was finally galvanized by the violence at Montgomery, Ole Miss, and Birmingham. (This legislation also was enacted under LBJ.)

Kennedy was a classic pragmatist. Once in his Senate days, talking with a liberal-wing Democrat about the touchy matter of birth control, he said: "I intend to be as brave as I dare." He focused fast on the immediate and practical. My colleague Louis Banks, later managing editor of *Fortune,* reported after a session in the Oval Office: "Kennedy is a man completely and vigorously engaged in events *of the moment.* Thus he regards his past acts as more or less irrelevant prologue; his future acts as something to be determined under future circumstances. One could talk to him all day and be unable to say what his attitude toward business will be, because what he says or thinks on that day has a bearing only on the effect he is trying to achieve that day."

Kennedy's keen mind was sharpened and disciplined by the alarums and demands that beat in upon the White House. He had a far-ranging curiosity, but it could be quite swiftly satisfied. He had never been much given to philosophical ruminations, and the pressures of the Presidency made him even more impatient with abstractions. He did like "history," but on his own terms—preferably making it, also reading it at high speed, skipping and skimming, not listening to someone else hold forth about it. He was perfectly comfortable with intellectuals if they did not run on too long. He used them extensively in his Administration and, for all his pride in his own practicality, he perhaps overrated the adaptability of intellectuals to high government posts. The vanity, of course, was to think he would always know when to ignore them.

His administrative style was far less formal than Eisenhower's. He thought Cabinet meetings a boring waste of time. He promptly junked most of Ike's NSC apparatus. He liked to bypass the bureaucracy (especially State), thought nothing of phoning an official three tiers below the man's ostensible boss, and relied heavily on his senior staff people, without putting them into the tidy structure of meetings and mechanisms that Ike found comfortable. He could be a superb motivator of sophisticated people, inspiring as much devotion in Harvard professors as in the teenage "squealers" who lined his motorcade routes in 1960. He was a generally thoughtful boss, but made a few exceptions. One was his ambassador to the United Nations. He once casually confided to a reporter that he and brother Bobby had been having some fun "seeing how much old Adlai would stand for." (He would stand for quite a lot.)

Along with Kennedy's inbred pragmatism, he developed a strain of idealism. Having won the prize, he naturally wanted to give his Presidency some content (and of course be reelected). Even Chester Bowles, the kind of liberal especially uncongenial to him, thought Kennedy during his Presidency moved steadily toward a "broader concept of using power constructively."

On-the-Job Training

The use of presidential power in foreign affairs held stronger attractions for Kennedy than the domestic arena. All the modern Presidents, except for Reagan in his first two years, have felt this pull, in good part because the President, relative to Congress, the courts, press, public opinion, has so much more authority in foreign policy than domestic.

Kennedy ever since prewar days at Harvard and in his father's London embassy had been intellectually engaged by world affairs. He dared flout the Anglophobia of his father and their Boston Irish antecedents. He developed a powerful admiration for the historical role of Britain and the British, especially the aristocrats managing the empire and the European balance of power. In the new post-Britain world, the United States, bigger, stronger, unflawed by colonies, could take up the task of operating a global balance. This indeed was what a couple of plain Middle Westerners, Harry Truman and Dwight Eisenhower, had already been doing for fifteen years.

Kennedy was driven to escalate the rhetoric of the Cold War. The swollen language of his inaugural—"let the word go forth," etc.—is now embarrassing. I must confess I admired it at the time, and thought it augured well for his foreign policy.

His first major foreign policy decision was a disaster. He had inherited the broad outlines of the Bay of Pigs plan from the Eisenhower Administration. There was plenty of time to call off the operation if he chose, but it appealed to his urge to be bold and activist; indeed in his final campaign debate with Nixon he had belabored his opponent for the Eisenhower Administration's passivity in allowing communism to take over a country ninety miles from our shores. He was also sensitive, however, to anxieties of the State Department and some of his White House advisers that the hand of the U.S. was too heavy and visible in the whole Bay of Pigs scheme. He approved various changes intended to make the operation look more Cuban and less Yankee; most crucially, he cut down on air support for the landings. (Eisenhower's private comment: "Any commander who knows anything knows you must have control of the air before you launch any invasion.")

"Bit by bit, an operation that was marginal to begin with was so truncated as to guarantee its failure." This was the judgment in a *Fortune* article* that infuriated Kennedy. The author was Charles J. V. Murphy, a respected journalist with excellent sources in the Pentagon and CIA. Murphy talked out his story on the porch of my Sands Point house one evening a month or two after the Bay of Pigs. Murphy was well aware, of course, that his military and intelligence sources were trying to exonerate themselves from any blame for the fiasco. Kennedy, I said, was getting preposterous praises—and amazingly high ratings in the polls—for simply stating the inescapable constitutional fact that he was "responsible." Which did not stop him from telling scores of friends, senators, journalists, only slightly privately, that his mistake was to pay

*"Cuba: 'The Record Set Straight," September 1961.

any attention to the CIA and the military brass. I encouraged Murphy to pursue his story.

After the article was published in *Fortune* and then condensed in *Time*, it was promptly denounced by Kennedy at a press conference as "the most inaccurate thing I have ever read." Luce asked the President to elaborate. The White House drew up a seventeen-point bill of complaint and assigned General Maxwell Taylor, the brilliant Normandy paratrooper who was then the White House military adviser, later chairman of the Joint Chiefs, to come up to New York and straighten us out. Murphy and Duncan Norton-Taylor, my successor as managing editor of *Fortune*, prepared a point-by-point rebuttal. In a rather strained meeting in Luce's office, General Taylor read to us a vague and angry letter from Kennedy, then put it back in his briefcase. The general and *Fortune* finally agreed that some of the disputed points were perhaps questions of "interpretation." Taylor tactfully suggested the matter could be considered closed. I made bold to disagree, noting that we had often said in our magazines that the President was a prodigious reader, so if something was the "most inaccurate" thing he had *ever* read—wow! Shouldn't the President issue a correction? Taylor, none too comfortable during the whole meeting, smiled a very small smile. Needless to say, no presidential confession of error ensued.*

It took guts for Kennedy, only weeks after the debacle in Cuba, to go through with his earlier plans for a meeting with Nikita Khrushchev. It was to be a low-key non-summit summit, announced at the last moment, so no great public hopes would be aroused. Vienna turned out to be one of the toughest confrontations of the Cold War. Khrushchev declined to budge an inch from the bristling positions he had taken on Berlin and East Germany. Kennedy told him it looked like "a cold winter" coming up.

The summer was tense enough. In a grim TV speech on July 25, Kennedy urged the building of air raid shelters (they made slightly more sense then than they would now). He doubled the monthly draft call-ups, activated reserve units, and called for a big supplemental increase in the defense budget. In mid-August, to cut off the exodus of the East Germans to the West, the Soviets threw up the infamous Wall. Kennedy, to assert our right of access across East Germany, ordered 1,500 U.S. troops to move via the Autobahn to West Berlin. In late August, Khrushchev announced an end to the moratorium on atmospheric testing of nuclear weapons, and over the next two months

---

*Murphy was wrong on one factual point (oddly enough, not mentioned in the White House complaint), and the error was acknowledged in *Fortune*'s next issue.

exploded a series of the biggest and dirtiest devices yet built. Kennedy in September announced a resumption of underground testing in Nevada, and in April 1962 the resumption of atmospheric testing. Meanwhile the Soviets had quietly set aside their demand for a separate peace with East Germany.

It is in no way condescending to say that 1961 was an educational year for John Kennedy. His East-West policy was settling into the general matrix established by his two predecessors, and particularly by Eisenhower, who in a sense "administered" a confrontation that took form in the days of Stalin and Truman. After a year in the White House, Kennedy was muting the Cold War trumpet calls; but the language was adequately firm, and the firmness was becoming credible. Along with the firmness was the equally essential sense of restraint. The U.S. would have had an excellent case in international law if we had rushed in tanks and bulldozers to knock down the Berlin Wall in 1961. The U.S. would have had a moving case in "the court of world opinion" if we had gone in to help the Hungarian freedom fighters in 1956. I think Presidents Kennedy and Eisenhower (neither would have relished the pairing) were each right to hold back. Nobody knows for sure, which is perhaps the salient feature of Cold War decision making.

Staring down the Soviets

Kennedy's rugged indoctrination in 1961 prepared him well for the great East-West transactions of 1962–63. The first, of course, was the missile crisis. Kennedy has been variously quoted on the odds of war. One friend recalls his saying the chances looked like three out of five. The guess more commonly attributed to him was one chance in three. That is frightening enough.*

Perhaps it was not quite the *High Noon* face-off it seemed to Kennedy and his anxious countrymen. Later evidence suggests the Soviets knew they simply didn't have the nuclear strength to fight an all-out war with the U.S.—and they came out of the crisis resolved never to be at such a disadvantage again.

*If the U.S. and Soviet Union had fought World War III over the Cuba missiles, it is hard to imagine a protracted struggle confined to conventional weaponry. The U.S. apparently would have allowed the Soviets the first nuclear strike. Robert McNamara, Defense Secretary under Kennedy and Johnson, relates that in long private conversations with both Presidents, "I recommended, without qualification, that they never initiate, under any circumstances, the use of nuclear weapons. I believe they accepted my recommendation." (Robert S. McNamara, "The Military Role of Nuclear Weapons," *Foreign Affairs*, October 1983.)

I remember standing on a subway platform on one of those eyeball-to-eyeball days, on my way to work with two colleagues, Robert Lubar and James Shepley.* We were speculating on the chances of waking up the next morning. I told them as a gesture of confidence I had just bought ten subway tokens (then only $1.50).

I thought Kennedy's handling of the missile crisis was masterly—not least in his wise instruction to his people not to gloat after we had "won." I said so at the time, in memos to colleagues, speeches, lunch table arguments. I still think so today, even though we now know the risks in a firm stand were not so grave as Kennedy then thought.

Or do we know? We still don't really know why Khrushchev was fired two years after the missile crisis, or just how Leonid Brezhnev and Alexei Kosygin were chosen to succeed him, or exactly how Brezhnev became the indisputable boss. Or whether, if Brezhnev and his doctors could have defied the odds for a few years more, the Politburo would have let him stay. Or exactly why and how Yuri Andropov was chosen his successor. Nor in 1984, in the continuity of our ignorance, did we know exactly how and why the elevation of Konstantin Chernenko was arranged.

Have some sympathy for the President of the United States, Republican or Democrat, any time in the last thirty years, trying to size up our principal opposition.

Seventeen years after the Cuba missile crisis, I was working in the Jimmy Carter White House during the flap over the "Soviet Combat Brigade" in Cuba. This rather synthetic 1979 crisis, described in Chapter 12, was to some extent manufactured out of memories of the 1962 missile crisis, with "lessons" of that crisis sometimes cited by White House staffers who were in junior high school at the time.

How that island has come to haunt the White House! When Lyndon Johnson in 1965 sent the Marines into the neighboring Dominican Republic he was determined to scotch "another Cuba." Richard Nixon and Henry Kissinger, certainly unwilling to seem less resolute than Johnson or Kennedy, spent many arduous hours in 1970–71 negotiating the Soviets out of their furtive attempt to establish a submarine base at the Cuban port of Cienfuegos. For Ronald Reagan, behind his concerns about El Salvador and Nicaragua, there is always the specter of Communist Cuba. Watching Castro nowadays on TV, the gray showing in his beard, I am jolted to realize he has outlasted

*Later respectively, managing editor of *Fortune,* and president of Time Inc.

six U.S. Presidents, and is now much the most senior political leader in the Western Hemisphere.

John Kennedy came out of the missile crisis with the credentials, or as Kennedys might say, the balls, to dare talk peace with the Soviets. Just as the five-star General Eisenhower could make some conciliatory gestures without being accused of "softness" (except by crazies), and just as the hard-line Nixon could go to China, Kennedy was now free to explore détente.

In his American University speech of June 1963, he was an eloquent man of peace, and he announced the opening of atmospheric test ban negotiations with the Soviets. Only a few weeks later he committed a major zigzag. In the famous *Ich bin ein Berliner* speech, perhaps carried away just by being in the beleaguered city, he reverted to some of the most provocative Cold War rhetoric of his Administration. But the test ban negotiations were completed with remarkable speed; the treaty was signed in the Kremlin in August and ratified by the Senate in September, by the overwhelming margin of 80–19.

Taken together, the treaty and the response to the missile crisis were Kennedy's chief accomplishment in foreign policy. They constituted an effective continuation, in new and difficult circumstances, of the firm-but-reasonable line two previous Presidents had sought to lay down in our relations with the Soviets. No succeeding President has been able for very long to operate very far from that line. The Russians, or rival American politicians, or their own native good sense will haul Presidents back—Carter after sallies to the gentle side; Reagan grudgingly coming in from the hard side—to the central logic. Kennedy, after the early fumblings, caught on fast.

Less important, but a genuine innovation, was the Peace Corps. It is often the first thing mentioned—sometimes the only thing—when people are asked, "But what did Kennedy *do?*" The Peace Corps (initially a Hubert Humphrey idea) was indeed a good thing for the U.S. to do, certainly enlightening for the 100,000 Americans who have gone out, and probably beneficial, net, to the places they have worked. Symbolically it has been valuable, abroad and probably more so at home, especially among the young. The Peace Corps became the idealistic, unarmed answer to the "Ask not" challenge of the inaugural.

Legacies and Legend

In a more fateful region of foreign policy, Kennedy left a legacy still bitterly disputed. In Viet Nam he increased the U.S. military adviser group by twenty-fold. They were not a combat command but Kennedy sent them out—16,500—almost in division strength. Three of the advisers were killed in Viet Nam during the Eisenhower years; 109 were killed in the Kennedy years. Our investment, of prestige and emotion, had been greatly enlarged. And when the Kennedy Administration encouraged the overthrow of Diem in 1963, the U.S. assumed a kind of obligation to his successors it had not had to Diem himself.

Kenneth O'Donnell, in a *Life* article seven years after Kennedy's death, argued that had he lived and been reelected in 1964, Kennedy would have pulled out of Viet Nam. If he tried to do it before the election, O'Donnell quotes Kennedy, "We would have another Joe McCarthy Red scare on our hands."* This speculation was recently revived in Ralph Martin's biography of Kennedy, *A Hero for Our Time.*† But the weight of opinion among the former members of the Kennedy Administration is strongly to the contrary. Kennedy's Secretary of State, Dean Rusk, in an interview with Herbert Parmet, notes that for Kennedy to decide in 1963 to take the advisers out in 1965, subjecting them to many more months of casualties until an election was out of the way, is a kind of cold-bloodedness that no President "could live with."‡ In offering his theory, even at a time when the Viet Nam war had become such a national trauma, it is odd that O'Donnell thought he was burnishing Kennedy's memory.

I thought Kennedy was doing the right thing in Viet Nam, and the Time Inc. publications supported him, urging still more vigorous measures. With hindsight, it is clear the U.S. should not have gone in at all unless we were prepared to win. This does not imply the use of nuclear weapons, but it would have meant putting the U.S. on a war footing, and in Viet Nam carrying the war to the North. It is a fair question whether "victory" in that war would have been worth the price, but it surely would have been preferable to our defeat in the very costly war we did fight.

In his own decisions, and in the influence of his appointees who

*"LBJ and the Kennedys," August 7, 1970.
†Macmillan, 1983.
‡Dean Rusk in Herbert Parmet, *JFK: The Presidency of John F. Kennedy* (New York: The Dial Press, 1983), p. 336.

stayed on in the Johnson Administration, John Kennedy must be charged with a heavy responsibility for the ultimate outcome in Viet Nam. He was intelligent enough to be very unhappy about his choices in Viet Nam.

I am constitutionally optimistic about a new President, whether or not I voted for him. There is something exciting about a new Administration—some journalistic bias is at work here—a new Cabinet to write about, new White House staff, the habits, hobbies, and working style of the new personality in the Oval Office. The new "First Family" is interesting, for a while.

At the end of Kennedy's first year, despite the early blunders—the Bay of Pigs and some unsuccessful bluffing about Laos—I thought he was growing fast. My colleagues on *Time* were preparing to make him "Man of the Year" for 1961, and I urged in a memo: "He has been a generally good President so far, and might become a great one." The *Time* story (January 5, 1962) concluded: "In his first year as President, John Fitzgerald Kennedy showed qualities that have made him a promising leader in that battle [against communism]. Those same qualities, if developed further, may yet make him a great President."

In the summer of 1962, Kennedy made a petulant complaint to Harry Luce that *Time* switched around its own positions to "come out against me whatever I do." This astonished Luce and me. Albert Furth, Luce's executive assistant, reviewed the eighty or ninety substantial stories *Time* had run on the Kennedy Administration thus far that year. Our stories had been sympathetic to the Administration much more often than not, but we did find one story where *Time* had criticized Kennedy for a position (having to do with taxes) *Time* itself had previously advocated. I suggested to Luce he acknowledge to the President this lapse, and defend the rest of our record. He did so in a courteous letter; if there was a reply, it is lost to history.

A few days before Kennedy was assassinated, I was at a heavily Democratic dinner party in Westchester County (some of the Democrats had to be shipped in from Manhattan). Out of a dozen or more people around the table, I was the only one who had voted for Nixon in 1960 and the only one who had a good word to say for Kennedy that evening in November 1963. I admired his firmness in foreign policy—most of the Democrats felt he ran excessive risks—and they were far more disturbed than I by his caution and conservatism in domestic policy.

That John Kennedy might have become a great President, as *Time* and I once thought, I now strongly doubt. He had fewer accomplishments to show for his Presidency than Lyndon Johnson, who left the office broken, or Richard Nixon, who left in disgrace. He had somewhat less time to work than Nixon, who had four full years before being crippled by Watergate, and almost the same length of time as Johnson, whose Presidency was effectively paralyzed by Viet Nam toward the beginning of his fourth year.

I am not at all certain that Kennedy, had he lived, would have come out of Viet Nam looking any better than Johnson did. The two Presidents relied on the same advisers on Viet Nam—Kennedy appointed them and Johnson kept them on—and they shared the same general view of the strategic importance of Southeast Asia, heavily influenced by the "Munich" and "domino" metaphors (I shared it, too). If John Kennedy had still been President in 1968, he would at least have been spared the experience of brother Bobby campaigning against his Administration's war. Perhaps Vice-President Johnson would have slipped over to the dovish side to contest the 1968 nomination with a gung-ho Bobby. Jack Kennedy himself foresaw a Bobby-Johnson battle some day, and didn't relish the bind he would be in.

In my present appraisal of Kennedy, I am also influenced (for the old-fashioned reasons already admitted) by the disclosures about his private life. I am further influenced by the full story of *Profiles in Courage,* also by the revelation that Kennedy ran a secret taping system in the White House. Without the knowledge of the people being recorded, he taped about six hundred of his telephone conversations and meetings in the Oval Office and Cabinet Room. Richard Nixon was brought down by the evidence on his tapes, not for having a taping system, but in the press and the academy there were many denunciations of the practice itself as typical Nixonian sneakiness. Arthur Schlesinger said at the time it was "inconceivable" Kennedy could have done such a thing.

When the full extent of the Kennedy taping system was disclosed in 1982, some of the old New Frontiersmen loyally shrugged it off. The most heartrending comment, however, came from Mike Feldman, deputy special counsel to Kennedy. He was asked by the Washington *Post* if people should have been told they were being recorded. He said, "I can never say anything bad about Kennedy—he's my idol. I'm struggling to say 'No,' but the answer is yes. Yes, he should have told us."*

*Mike Feldman, Washington *Post,* February 5, 1982.

The flaws in the Kennedy character, and the rather meager accomplishments of his Presidency, do not seem to have shaken his powerful hold on the American imagination. Public opinion polls over the twenty years since his death have consistently placed him among our greatest Presidents. As recently as August 1983, a Lou Harris study of public attitudes toward the nine modern Presidents found that 40 percent of those surveyed ranked Kennedy as the President who "most inspired confidence in the White House," followed by FDR at 23 percent, Truman and Eisenhower at 8 percent. An astounding judgment. As the President "best in domestic affairs," Kennedy led FDR by 27 percent to 22 percent. Nixon, interestingly, led in foreign policy, 25 percent to 21 percent for Kennedy and 14 percent for FDR. As to "the most appealing personality," it was 60 percent for Kennedy, 11 percent for FDR, and 8 percent (his highest vote in any of the categories) for Ronald Reagan.

For millions, not just in America, John Kennedy is the romantic hero, martyred and forever young. More than any concrete deed or policy, his greatest achievement is precisely his legend.

PART IV

---

*The Broken
Presidencies*

8

———◆———

Lyndon Johnson

America and the Presidency changed profoundly in the mid-sixties. The postwar bipartisan consensus on foreign policy had prevailed for more than two decades, under the "Presidents of the West" and on into the first two to three years of the Johnson Administration. The consensus was shattered in Viet Nam, and none has been put together since. No President since Viet Nam has enjoyed the worldwide power that Truman commanded, the power and personal respect that Eisenhower commanded, the power that was still there in Kennedy's day. And certainly no President since Viet Nam has inspired the love that is still felt, not just in Irish pubs but in so many parts of the world, for Kennedy. Viet Nam damaged our repute with our allies and in the Third World, in part for the same reasons the war became offensive to many Americans, but at least equally important, because we lost.

As America's wounds deepened and festered in Viet Nam, the social contract seemed to be coming apart at home. The violence in Watts, Newark, and Detroit ended the illusion, if any still held it, that "the race problem" was some special sin and burden of the South. When Martin Luther King was assassinated in Memphis in 1968, there was burning and looting and gunfire in Chicago, Cleveland, Baltimore, and Washington, where empty blocks of the "riot belt" can still be seen less than a mile from the White House.

The crisis in race relations, coinciding with Viet Nam and the military draft, created within the U.S. something approximating a revolutionary age: domestic order in doubt; polarizing tendencies in our politics; some of the best of our youth embittered; most of our major institutions, much of the familiar morality, and many of our most cherished ideas about America under skillful and determined attack. It seemed in some ways a more formidable challenge to the American system than the Great Depression was.

It was an age in which two Presidents, in succession, found themselves unable to govern.

In his first hours and weeks as President, Lyndon Johnson, the ferociously ambitious politician, the vulgar, ruthless wheeler-dealer, was a magnificent national leader. He radiated strength and dignity. He never struck a false note in his dealings with the grieving Kennedy people (who did not always make it easy for him) or in his messages to a stunned and sickened country.

I thought of the extraordinary depths of the man as he talked with eight or ten of us from *Time-Life-Fortune* a few weeks after the assassination. It was a dazzling day, fresh snow on the ground, the sun flooding into the living room of the family quarters of the White House. Over drinks (I think he had Dr. Pepper) and lunch, he touched on fifteen or twenty of the principal problems before him. He was guarded in some areas of foreign policy and domestic politics, more expansive on domestic issues. There were appealing touches of humility, but if his purpose was to show us how fast and firmly he had taken hold of the President's business, he was entirely successful.

I had first met Johnson some twenty-five years before—glib, glad-handing, and unmistakably bright, tirelessly building connections all over Capitol Hill, and remarkably well plugged in, for a junior congressman, at the New Deal agencies and the White House. The press understood he was FDR's favorite young congressman, or at least his favorite young Texas congressman. Lyndon did nothing to discourage these impressions, and reporters working on the Hill (as I was in 1939–41) paid him a fair bit of attention.

Lyndon Johnson as a boy often announced that he was going to be President some day. More remarkable, he went right on saying it as a grown man in his twenties and thirties. Only when it began to be somewhat believable did he become more circumspect—somewhat.

The mature Lyndon Johnson of the 1950s was a formidable figure, and he fascinated the press, including the Time Inc. publications. I saw him occasionally in those years but learned more from the brilliant reporting of *Time*'s Washington bureau, who necessarily filed far more than the magazine could print, including some items strictly for the entertainment of the editors.

Johnson had arrived in the Senate in 1949 as "Landslide Lyndon," winner by 87 votes (thousands were bought, by both candidates) in a primary that was contested in the courts for months afterward. Yet despite his well-deserved reputation for electoral chicanery, the snickers at his war record (perfectly respectable except for Lyndon's exaggerations), and the widespread talk of his gargantuan appetites, including for money, he so impressed his colleagues as a working senator that he was elected Minority Whip within two years, Minority Leader after another two years, and then only two years later, when the Democrats took over the Senate, Majority Leader. He was perhaps the most effective Majority Leader ever to operate in—and on—the Senate.

As Minority Leader, Johnson played a skillful role in the maneuvering that led to the censure of Joe McCarthy. But he carried at least as great a burden of McCarthyism on his own record as John Kennedy did —except it was his own made-in-Texas creation. In his successful campaign for the Senate he had gone through incredibly brazen contortions to label his opponent, a man with a far more conservative record than his own, as a dupe of the Kremlin. It was an even less edifying campaign than Richard Nixon's against Helen Gahagan Douglas; she was at least more liberal, unmistakably, than Nixon.

Johnson in those days was rapidly distancing himself from his New Deal antecedents. He could not win and consolidate statewide support in the increasingly conservative Texas of the late 1940s and early 1950s by invoking the memory of FDR. Nor could he commend himself to the powerful southerners who were the key to control of the Senate. But once he had power—no matter how acquired—he was capable of using it for lofty purposes. Lyndon Johnson was the ends-and-means question writ very large. His masterwork as Majority Leader was the passage of the Civil Rights Act of 1957. The legislation emerged from the close and subtle relationship Johnson and Speaker Sam Rayburn had with the Republican President (Ike also knew what he was doing). It was guided, above all, by Johnson's superb sense of timing and his astute reading of what could move, or not move, dozens of individual senators.

His reign as Majority Leader brought to perfection the famous Johnson "treatment," the overwhelming face-to-face plea, the calling-in of debts, the soft, sorrowful aside that could be taken as a threat. All this included an almost infallible sense of when to stop.

*

I think few of us in the press could have visualized this great cloak-room tactician as President. Senator Jack Kennedy could. He thought Johnson the best qualified of all the Democrats for 1960—but unelecta-ble because he was from the South. When Kennedy brought him onto his ticket, however, he wasn't choosing Johnson as a high-quality standby President, but to carry Texas, which Johnson did.

Lyndon Johnson, who knew a good exaggeration when he saw one, would have agreed with John Adams' famous definition of the Vice-Presidency as "the most insignificant office that ever the invention of man contrived." Lyndon was stepping down, as he saw it, from the No. 3 position in Washington, as the system had worked under Eisenhower. He hated it. President Kennedy was considerate to his VP, but Johnson felt the rest of the Kennedy people condescended to him and told jokes about him behind his back (he was right).

I saw him once enduring the reading of a telegram from Kennedy at a dinner the President didn't quite want to grace himself—a Waldorf-Astoria banquet for the fortieth anniversary of *Time*. The guests of honor were hundreds of men and women who had been on the cover of *Time*. Before Kennedy's witty wire was read, the Vice-President, as ranking guest, had dutifully risen to toast the magazine and the country, first offering a sally of his own: "Many of us owe Harry Luce a very great debt for being the first publisher to select magazine cover models on a basis other than beauty." Johnson might have had some fun, but didn't, by noting that the President had been on *Time*'s cover more often than he had, as was fitting, eight times to his mere seven. It was the kind of statistic he would have been aware of. (Eventually Johnson was on twenty-three times, more often than anybody except his succes-sor, but almost half of Nixon's fifty-one appearances revolved around Watergate.)

How's Abigail?

In July of 1964, shortly before the Democratic convention, Harry Luce and I were invited to dinner in the White House family dining room. Johnson was in the process of massaging more or less influential politicians, editors, opinion makers, by asking their views on the per-formance of his Administration thus far, and their suggestions as to who his running mate should be. I had recently been appointed Editor in Chief of Time Inc., and when Johnson addressed his questions to Luce,

Harry would buck them along to me, repeatedly telling the President I was now responsible for such judgments. Johnson was eventually persuaded. I suggested Hubert Humphrey for Vice-President, as did most of the people Johnson was seeing during those weeks, and as Johnson himself had doubtless decided long before.

He kept poor Hubert dangling up to a few hours before announcing his choice, in part so he could go through a charade of considering certain Catholics. This necessity ensued from a previous charade in which he had announced that none of his Cabinet officers was eligible for the VP nomination—he didn't want any of them distracted from their present work. The point of this, of course, was to eliminate the Attorney General, but lest any Catholic voters be offended by the dumping of Bob Kennedy, Johnson now pretended to give serious thought to two Catholic Senators, Thomas Dodd of Connecticut and Eugene McCarthy of Minnesota. Dodd and Humphrey were brought by presidential plane from Atlantic City, where the convention was in progress, to audition at the White House. The sardonic McCarthy had asked to be withdrawn after a conversation of which he recalled: "I guess I was in there about twenty minutes. Lyndon says, 'How's Abigail?' I say, 'Fine. How's Lady Bird?' He says, 'Fine.' We had some coffee. Then he says, 'Well, Bird and I sure think the world of you and Abigail.' I couldn't think of anything to say except 'Abigail and I think the world of you and Bird.' "

In the coronation ceremonies at Atlantic City, where the P.A. was pounding out "Hello, Lyndon [Dolly]" night and day, the only business of substance was which Mississippi delegation would be seated—the "Freedom" delegates or the lily-white regulars. (The eventual compromise was to seat two Freedom delegates in 1964 and open the way for more blacks in the future.) The chief emotional tension built around the "Kennedy night," deferred by Johnson until the VP roll call was out of the way. Lady Bird sat in a box with Robert and Ethel, as the JFK film *A Thousand Days* was shown. Robert Kennedy had his turn at the podium, and Johnson was finally free of him—until Viet Nam overtook his Presidency. Carrying himself with somber dignity, the President appeared in the box when the film was finished.

My next encounter with Johnson came a few weeks after Atlantic City, when one of his "Great Society" task forces was gathered in the Cabinet Room. I had agreed to serve on the task force on education (there were thirteen panels in all), and our chairman was John Gardner,

then head of the Carnegie Corporation, later Johnson's Secretary of
HEW.

Johnson's charge to the task force was as shrewd—and moving—as
any pitch I have ever heard addressed to a small group of sophisticated
people taking on some *pro bono* chore. He said there had been some
surprises and disappointments for him in the workings of the Presidency, but one wonderful thing he had always heard was certainly true,
and our presence in the White House that morning proved it. The
President of the United States could call on busy, important people, of
either party, or no party, to donate time to their country, and no matter
what they thought of the fellow in the Oval Office, they would gladly
serve. As a public official, he would rather be remembered for widening
opportunities for a good education for all American children than for
anything else he could think of. (This was deeply true—and infinitely
sad, as one looks back on his Presidency today.) "Now I just ask you good
people to consider what we *ought* to do about education. Tell me that
in your report. Don't get yourselves all messed up with what you think
Congressman So-and-so will let us do. Let me handle the politics."

We walked across the street to our quarters in the Executive Office
Building and went to work well motivated. Apart from one low-key
White House announcement that the task forces were being formed,
there was no further publicity about them, their membership was never
announced, and their reports, not due until after the election, were
never made public. Some of these precautions made it possible for
Republicans and independents to serve on the task forces in the autumn
of a campaign year without fear that they were being exploited by a
Democratic President. With characteristic canniness, Johnson was also
protecting himself. He wanted to pick and choose what he liked from
the task force reports, when he worked up his legislative agenda for
1965–66, without any press stories that he had turned down this or that
recommendation of "his own" advisers.

The education task force turned out to be one of the more influential. The recommendation that parochial schools could share indirectly
in federal aid to secondary and primary schools, largely the work of John
Gardner, became a key provision in Johnson's education bill of 1965.

I was enmeshed with Johnson on several levels in the autumn
of 1964, a circumstance doubtless more fascinating to me than to
him. But I marveled at whatever central switchboard must be hum-
ming away in the Johnson head, sorting out all his multichannel relationships with thousands of individual politicians, officials, business-

men, journalists in Washington, New York, Texas, all over the U.S.

Even as I accepted Johnson's high-minded summons to his task force on education, I was engaged as an editor with a distinctly seamy side of the man. *Life* had put months of painstaking research into a study of Johnson's personal fortune. *Life* figured he was worth $14 million—after thirty-two years in which his salary as a public official totaled about $550,000 before taxes. Lady Bird had a modest inheritance which was useful seed money once or twice in their earlier years. But it was hard to escape the conclusion that Lyndon's magic touch at business and investment, including properties subject to federal regulation, had something to do with who he was in politics, and everybody's awareness of that.

When he heard how deeply the *Life* team was digging, Johnson granted the interview they had been seeking, asked that their editors should be with them, and was himself attended by his lawyer friend Abe Fortas, whom he later appointed to the Supreme Court. The session in the family quarters of the White House went on more than five hours, ending after Lady Bird offered roast beef and tapioca pudding at midnight. He ranged all over the issues of the day, told a lot of stories, dirty and otherwise, and from time to time noted that he was "the only President you fellows have got." But he came back always to the *Life* story, and it was clear that he knew, in considerable detail, whom *Life* had seen and what had been said.

In the published article,* *Life* included a tabulation of the Johnson holdings by his trustees and lawyers (based essentially on cost rather than 1964 market) that added up to about $4 million, and quoted one White House man as saying *Life*'s $14 million estimate was "crazy." *Life* was probably too conservative; later researches suggest that $25 million might have been more realistic.

While Time Inc. was enraging Johnson with this report on his money, we were also preparing to endorse him for election in his own right as President. I wrote an article for *Life*, "The Difficulty of 'Being Fair' to Goldwater."† This was a lengthy analysis of the Republican candidate's views over the years and the complaints of his supporters that the press and the Democrats kept misrepresenting his views. I argued that the candidate himself was chiefly responsible for the confusion over his views. An angry Goldwater aide had snapped at a reporter, "Don't print what he says, print what he means." This, I concluded, "is

*August 21, 1964.
†September 18, 1964.

easier said than done." Since the article was published under my by-line as Editor in Chief of Time Inc., it left little suspense about our endorsement. This came three weeks later in a *Life* editorial* that called Johnson "a very effective President" with an "immense hunger for approval and votes" which would "probably be directed at the approval of future historians, by whom he would like to be voted a great President." Once more that optimistic theme. "That is the best ambition a master politician can have. We hope he makes it."

It was the first time Time Inc. had ever endorsed a Democrat for President. Johnson phoned me to say the editorial was "simply wonderful," and "I'm going to do my dead-level best to be worthy of it."

The Need to Be Loved

Within a couple of months we were in the doghouse again. *Time* was working on a story on Johnson as "Man of the Year" for 1964. He summoned John Steele, our Washington Bureau chief, to the Oval Office one evening and chewed him out unmercifully. He said the Time Inc. editors and reporters were liars and cheats, men determined to tear his Administration apart. "They warp everything I do, they lie about me, they don't know the meaning of truth." When *Life* did its story on his finances, "they took the word of some drunks in Texas against the word of the President of the United States." If Steele had any influence with the home office, would he please get the *Time* project canceled because the story "can only make my job more difficult." The tirade went on for an hour and ten minutes, at which point Steele simply excused himself.

Early the next morning Steele had a phone call from Press Secretary George Reedy offering full White House cooperation in the *Time* story and as much of the President's time that day as Steele, Hugh Sidey, and Peter Hurd, the artist who was to do the cover, would need. Late in the interview Johnson edged his way to an apology: "It's my job to try to understand people and to realize that save in rare instances they don't get up in the morning deciding to do something wrong. Now with John last night, I forgot that. . . . I was sorry."

What was it all about? Steele and Sidey guessed that a few nonworshipful points in recent *Time* stories—generally favorable—had triggered the outburst. Johnson's staff fed his immense vanity and sensitivity to any criticism. A need to be completely loved and appreciated "dominates this difficult, complex, and totally interesting though some-

*October 9, 1964.

times reprehensible man." That judgment by Steele, in a rapidly written memo nineteen years ago, stands up very well today.

The Man of the Year story mentioned some of the Johnsonian foibles, but was an essentially enthusiastic account of his first year in the Presidency. He let it be known that he liked it. (One of his aides thought —far off the record—it was too laudatory.) The Peter Hurd cover painting showed a strong, weathered face, eyes squinting into the Texas sun, in the background a replica of the "boyhood home." In his mid-fifties Johnson from some angles could be a ruggedly handsome man. Hurd used the best of all possible angles. Johnson professed not to like the picture, and pointed out, quite accurately, that his right shoulder seemed to go on and on. I later saw that the original was hanging in his office at the LBJ ranch.

The period 1964–66, the year he inherited from Kennedy and the first two years of his own term, was the peak of the Johnson Presidency. In Washington, Isaiah became the best known of the Old Testament prophets. "Let us reason together." Johnson thought of the Congress as a truly coequal branch, especially when it was doing what he asked, but even when it wasn't, he never descended into the kind of trench warfare that Roosevelt, Truman, and Kennedy all sooner or later fought against the Hill.

Johnson was the first President in more than a century with top leadership experience in Congress (James Polk had been Speaker of the House), and the richness of his legislative record in 1964–66 suggests this is a solid credential for the Oval Office. In the congressional leadership of 1984, Speaker Tip O'Neill had said he would serve just one more term, then would love to be U.S. Ambassador to Ireland. Could his fellow Irishman Ronald Reagan, Republican though he is, be so flinthearted as to deny him? Howard Baker of Tennessee gave up his Senate seat and role as Majority Leader to position himself for a full-time run for the Republican nomination in 1988.

Johnson in his first three years as President got almost two-thirds of his legislative proposals enacted. This included the tax and civil rights bills* initiated by Kennedy, but from there on, it was essentially Johnson's own tremendous agenda. He struck the Great Society theme at the University of Michigan, May 22, 1964, in an eloquent speech

---

*In the Senate, Hubert Humphrey was chief strategist for the civil rights bill, which was fitting enough, since it was as a fiery civil rights advocate at the Democratic convention of 1948 that Humphrey, then merely Mayor of Minneapolis, first became a national figure.

drafted by Richard Goodwin. The phrase was not newly coined (it had been used by Walter Lippmann and Henry Luce among others), but Johnson found it a satisfying successor-slogan to the New and Fair Deals and the New Frontier.

"We have the opportunity to move not only toward the rich society and the powerful society, but upward to the Great Society. The Great Society rests on abundance and liberty for all. It demands an end to poverty and racial injustice, to which we are totally committed in our time. But that is just the beginning."

The Great Society "serves not only the needs of the body and the demands of commerce, but the desire for beauty and the hunger for community...." It "is not a safe harbor, a resting place, a final objective, a finished work. It is a challenge constantly renewed, beckoning us toward a destiny where the meaning of our lives matches the marvelous products of our labor."

The bills poured forth: voting rights, mass transit, federal aid to education, help for Appalachia, medicare, help with the rent for low-income families, food stamps, the war on poverty.

This legislation evoked no widespread alarm among conservatives who were basking, along with liberals, in the country's unprecedented prosperity. (One occasional dissident was *Fortune*, which was bothered by the inflationary potential in all these programs at a time when prices were already edging up 1 to 1.5 percent a year. The good old days!) In a speech at Yale in April 1965, I noted that the U.S. economy was in its *fiftieth* month of expansion, the longest such cycle we had ever experienced in peacetime, and I speculated that one reason was "the extraordinary man in the White House." He "exudes positive affection for businessmen and bankers. Uniquely among modern Democratic Presidents, he is not mad at anybody, except occasionally the press. And it may be that this combination of neo-Republican warmth toward business and post-Keynesian Democratic economics is exactly what so stimulates the economy."

I watched him exuding affection for businessmen and bankers (and even editors and publishers) over dinner in the White House one August evening, and he was very convincing at it. He urged us all to write him whenever we felt like it. When I sent my thank-you note for the evening, I said I would spare him any personal views "since my colleagues and I have already been offering you a fair amount of free advice via the pages of *Time, Life* and *Fortune.*"

On another occasion, walking through the Rose Garden to a lunch in the residence, he dropped the thought that if "you ever get tired of what you're doing, I'd love to have you helping out around here." I was not tired of what I was doing, and I assumed he issued a fair number of these vague invitations that were in small danger of being accepted.

But did this kind of flattery affect my judgment of Johnson? I suspect it did, at least around the edges. I also learned more about the man, in these personal contacts, than I would have by observing him from an antiseptic distance.

It would have been ridiculous, in any event, to decline an invitation to the LBJ ranch. So my wife and I found ourselves guests there, along with three other Time Inc. couples, one December weekend in 1966. Lady Bird had obligingly written the captions for a *Life* article on the Johnsons at home in the White House and back in Texas. *Life* in appreciation had made a donation to the building of a little park in Johnson City, and Lady Bird that weekend was lighting the Christmas tree there.

Johnson was a tireless host, showing off his three ranches in the lovely Hill Country, driving us around Johnson City and Fredericksburg, delighting in eluding any press cars, relishing for the nth time a movie of his triumphal visit to Australia, eating and drinking robustly (no visible effects), clutching, pawing, and talking, talking, talking. Some of the talk was local and family lore, most of it was politics and policy.

He had also been to Korea on his Far Eastern tour. There was a huge rally at a park outside Seoul, the most people Johnson had ever seen in one place. "So I asked President Park how many people were there, and President Park said he didn't know, but he'd ask the mayor of Seoul. Well, the mayor of Seoul didn't know, but he asked the chief of police to check on it. Well, the word came back through the interpreter: Chief of Police says to tell Mister Mayor to tell President Park to tell President Johnson there are two and a half million people here, and he's sorry there aren't any more people here, but that's all the people he's got." So the President said to us, "*I'm* sorry I can't show you any more ranch, but that's all the ranch I've got."

He hadn't forgotten *Life*'s hateful $14 million. Driving along one of the ranch roads, he said, "You know, I paid fifty dollars an acre for this place. And you folks in your *Life* story said this place is worth three hundred dollars an acre. Maybe nowadays it's worth eighty or ninety dollars. Look, look at this stuff, that isn't worth three hundred dollars an acre, is it?"

If Johnson had some message to deliver—having given up the weekend before Christmas to eight not very intimate friends—it was that we should understand what a tough job he had. This subject was introduced through the parable of Hardhead. There's been this very close football game, and one team has this star fullback Hardhead, and he's been doing all the work that afternoon. His face is all chewed up, one eye has been gouged and he's really beat up. I think he is meant to be black, though the President didn't specify that. Hardhead's team is behind 7–6, three minutes to play, on their own 30. "The coach sends in word, 'Keep feeding the ball to Hardhead.' Well, on the first down the little quarterback takes the ball himself and he loses eleven yards. The coach jumps up and down and says: 'Goddammit, I said give the ball to Hardhead.' Second down, the quarterback takes it again and loses seven yards. The coach is beside himself. He rushes onto the field and breaks into the huddle and grabs the poor quarterback and says, 'Goddammit, I said give that ball to Hardhead,' and the quarterback says, 'Hardhead, him don't want the ball any more.'"

That was the thought the President wanted to leave with us—it's hard work being Hardhead. "Okay, *you* be Hardhead," he said to me several times, posing some question about taxes, the defense budget, the Middle East. I adopted a policy for the weekend of responding to all such questions more or less instantly, rather than saying, Gosh, you sure have it tough, Mr. President. And he could listen, for all his love of talking, very patiently, though he had a disconcerting ability to make no reply whatever, unless he chose to. Once or twice, like the high school teacher he once was, he would indicate I showed some promise as an amateur Hardhead.

Decline and Fall

That weekend, though I saw it only tentatively, Johnson was just past the zenith of his Presidency. In the congressional elections of November 1966, after strenuous campaigning by LBJ, the Democrats had taken a beating. Over cocktails at the ranch, Johnson brought up the subject himself, volunteering how really the election results were no defeat for him or the Democrats: it was a perfectly normal off-year result. In fact, better than usual, he claimed, and then he ticked off the statistics of Roosevelt's mid-term defeat in 1938, and Eisenhower's in 1954 and 1958. He was jabbing me in the chest throughout this recital, and this perhaps made me a little argumentative.

So I said I didn't think those comparisons were quite the whole story. After all, Eisenhower and his administration hadn't accomplished anything in particular between '56 and '58, and there had been quite a serious recession in '58. So it wasn't too surprising that the Republicans lost seats. In '54 there had also been quite a noticeable recession, and it was still on at the time of the election. So again it wasn't surprising the Republicans lost some seats. And then in '38—Roosevelt had no important new legislation he could point to, except for the minimum wage and hour law; there had been the Supreme Court fight; and there was a bad recession-within-the-depression in '37 and '38.

By contrast, Johnson's Administration really had accomplished a lot legislatively in 1965–66 and there certainly was no recession, quite the opposite. There was a somewhat unpopular war on, but nobody in either party thought it entered into the election very much. So in the circumstances, I thought it was quite a defeat for the Democrats—there must have been something more at work than just the normal off-year effect. Johnson didn't like that suggestion at all. He must have thought it implied some decline in his own appeal. (It did.) He didn't respond except with a kind of footnote—"You're right about the New Deal ending in 1937. I remember that very well because it was just when I came there in the Congress."

Johnson was not a compelling national campaigner. His supreme skill as a politician was in parliamentary management and the analogous arts of dealing with influential private citizens in small numbers. He understood individual senators better than he understood the people of their states. He had none of the mass appeal of a Roosevelt, Eisenhower, Kennedy, Reagan.

In his best form, with prepared text, he could be a dignified speaker, though generally dull, but out on the trail he could also be strident and flailing. On TV, his facial expression was often out of sync with his words, and he seemed to project insincerity.

His one successful national campaign was his landslide victory over Goldwater in 1964. He won the biggest percentage ever of the popular vote, and though he used to say Roosevelt was "like a daddy to me," he got a particular kick out of beating daddy in this department—61.1 percent to 60.8 (FDR in 1936). His vote was not a response to his platform personality, but to the many solid achievements of his first year in the White House—and to the singular weakness of his opponent.

Through most of 1964, Johnson's approval ratings in the Gallup Poll were running well above 70 percent. By the autumn of 1966, they had dropped to 48 percent. Many of his deceits, some in ridiculously small things, had been exposed. "Credibility gap" had passed into the language. (On our ranch weekend, my wife asked him how old Johnson City was, and he said he used to tell people it was founded in 1853, but now he had some University of Texas people studying the question, and he just wasn't saying anything more until he heard from them, because, "You know, Ma'am, all this talk about Credibility Gap.")

After Johnson's setback in the mid-term elections, he took a number of defeats in the new Congress. Most of his major legislative proposals were turned down, and funding for some of the Great Society programs was cut below his requests.

Though the great economic boom continued all through the Johnson Presidency, he was no longer getting much credit for it. The temper of the country had turned very sour. Spreading crime, urban blight, racial disorders mocked the aspirations toward a Great Society.

But it was half a world away, in a very different society, that Lyndon Johnson was being undone.

James Hester, the president of New York University, had invited Johnson to give the 1967 commencement address. But the White House couldn't commit him much in advance, and these were the days when it was getting more and more unpleasant, and possibly dangerous, for LBJ ("How many kids did you kill today?") to appear on campuses.

Hester asked me to be the backup speaker in case Johnson declined at the last minute. I was an NYU trustee, "in the family," and would not be offended at speaking or not speaking on short notice. As it turned out, I did speak, "On the Possibility of Being Wrong."

I said that within a year or two it would be clear that a large body of Americans had been wrong about Viet Nam—it would be seen either that the Johnson policies had worked or that they had failed. But articulate Americans, the politicians, professors, clergymen, journalists, were not very good at admitting they had been wrong. (I couldn't refrain from noting that only two years before much of the U.S. intellectual community was in a furor of indignation over Johnson's intervention in the Dominican Republic. In fact it had worked pretty well, but I hadn't heard any professor say, "Well, Johnson was right, and I was wrong.")

Presidents, I told the graduates, were especially prone to infallibility. FDR never acknowledged error. Harry Truman once told a seminar at Columbia: "On the big things, I was right. And on the little things

. . . well, if there's anyone listening here who hasn't ever made a mistake, let him put on his wings and fly the hell out of here." Even this confession of the occasional little mistake did not come until 1959, six years after Truman had left the White House.

Lyndon Johnson had said at a press conference in February 1967, "From time to time we will make mistakes," and then in May he had said, "We try not to think ourselves in possession of all truths." At first glance, I said, "these are appealingly humble statements, but then you begin to wonder a little about that 'We.' It's perhaps a trifle imperial."

I hoped that those of us who turned out to have been wrong about the war would have the grace to say so, and that the country could then turn to a fresh agenda in an atmosphere of mutual trust and confidence. I was beginning to have doubts about Viet Nam, but there was a slight tilt in the speech, I must admit, toward a presumption that I was not among those who would be wrong.

Over the summer of 1967, my doubts increased. By October, we were preparing a *Life* editorial that would end Time Inc.'s unswerving support of Johnson's Viet Nam policies. Johnson got wind of it and wanted to send Dean Rusk to New York to argue with us. I declined the offer; we were thoroughly familiar with the Administration's case, and I felt the errand was an imposition on Rusk and an embarrassment for us. The *Life* editorial (October 20) advocated a pause in the bombing of North Viet Nam and "energetic diplomatic probing" of the possibility of talks with Hanoi. If it failed, this good-faith effort at negotiating might at least recapture some home-front support for the war. Read alongside the anti-Johnson polemics of the time, the editorial was quite sympathetic to the President, but he was hurt and angry. He became increasingly so as *Life* and *Time* in subsequent months diverged still further from the Administration line. I heard he was telling people I had "betrayed" him. After Walter Cronkite turned against the Administration policy, in a broadcast in February 1968, Johnson would tell people that Cronkite and Hedley Donovan had cost him the war. He was never given to understatement.

He received me very courteously, however, along with several *Time* editors, one evening in March. He drew me aside for just one brief, bitter comment: "I've only been doing what you fellows always said I should be doing out there." I could only say: "I think we were wrong, Mr. President. It doesn't seem to be working." Much of our conversation turned on the Middle East, and he let us riffle through a green loose-leaf binder containing some of his hot-line exchanges with Kosygin during the Six-Day War of the previous June.

As we were leaving, I said, "Mr. President, I've understood that when you retire you'd like to be a lecturer in government and politics at the University of Texas." When I spoke the word "retire," he looked at me narrowly. I said I'd like to come and hear some of his lectures, especially the one on the problems of running a war in a democracy without declaring war, so therefore the war is up for discussion every day in the fullest and freest way, with a very large minority actively, articulately opposed to the war. This was a problem in presidential leadership no other man had faced. Apart from the merits or otherwise of the Viet Nam war, this would be an important chapter in the history of the Presidency. He continued to regard me with some suspicion but finally said, "Yes, that would be a good subject."

Then he turned slightly cheerful and said, "Well, it's true like your magazines say, I feel sorry for myself, yes. I enjoy being a martyr, yes. But every so often I count my blessings." Then he gave us a flash of the history professor. "I count my blessings that I don't have a Speaker of the House like Champ Clark [1911–19] who's fighting me. I don't have a Secretary of State like William Jennings Bryan [1913–15] who's fighting me. And I don't have a general out there like Douglas MacArthur." He slapped me on the back a couple of times and I departed.

A week later, Johnson announced he would not be a candidate for reelection. Not long afterward, at a White House Correspondents' dinner, he got off a very good line: "There has always been some friction between the press and us in the academic community."

But he was not in a generally mellow mood. Gene McCarthy, the twenty-minute VP "possibility" of 1964, had put in long and arduous months campaigning in 1967 and early 1968 against Johnson and the war. He severely wounded the incumbent President in the New Hampshire primary on March 12, losing only 42 to 49 percent.

McCarthy and Johnson viewed with almost equal bitterness the neatly timed decision of Senator Robert Kennedy, legend-bearer and formidable politician in his own right, to come in now as another anti-war candidate for the Democratic nomination. For Johnson the bitterness was compounded by the years of hostilities with Bobby, and his aggrieved view that in Viet Nam he was simply trying to honor a commitment John Kennedy had made. He was incensed by the assumption of many McCarthy and Kennedy supporters that he had secretly planned all along to put half a million men in Viet Nam. The truth was that he was as disagreeably surprised as the American people by the growing scope and cost of the war, and was essentially improvising his responses to the disappointments in the field. A further poignance was that Johnson—unlike Kennedy—had no intellectual interest in military matters. He didn't enjoy the company of generals and admirals.

As the important Wisconsin primary approached, the question was which of the two antiwar Democrats would do better in that activist state. There were newspaper dope stories guessing that the incumbent President would get as little as 10–15 percent of his own party's vote.

These portents surely figured in Johnson's decision to withdraw. For this proud man to run and fail of reelection, or even, conceivably, be denied renomination by his party, would have broken his heart. It was not much less wounding that he administered the heartbreak by his own hand. He was not cut out to be Cincinnatus. After the White House, he lived just four restless years, prowling the ranch and Austin, not greatly esteemed or consulted as any sort of elder statesman, never settling into a reflective, semischolarly mode.

In the motivation for Johnson's 1968 withdrawal, inseparable from the man's vanity, I would argue there was also something noble. He was concerned that he personally might have become an obstacle to negotiations in Viet Nam and reconciliation within the U.S. He also felt a sense of stewardship for the office of the Presidency.

In June 1968, in the same University of Rochester speech cited in the Foreword, I argued that Johnson in retiring might have regained a measure of "moral authority." I reminded the graduates of the historians' distinction between activist and passive Presidents, and that "just about everybody, historians and all the rest of us, had decided activist Presidents were the best kind." But now in 1967–68 "we have seen a strong and activist President get into a tremendous amount of trouble." We see

a dimension of the Presidency which goes much beyond the familiar contrast between strong and weak Presidents. It is the element of moral authority in the Presidency. When it's not there, the United States, no less than the President, is in trouble.

Moral authority includes not just the factual accuracy of what the President says, which surely we are entitled to take for granted; it includes the idea that what the President says, subject only to security or diplomatic limitations, is a full disclosure of his motives, that you're not being presented something on one set of grounds which actually was thought up for different reasons, that you can be sure anything he urges represents his best judgment of the best interests of the country.

Moral authority is not the same as popularity, indeed the two may sometimes be in conflict. Moral authority is something quite different from that rather overworked word charisma. I heard Vice-President Humphrey the other day pronounce charisma as though it were some kind of foreign disease; I think he had read in some columnist that a couple of the other candidates are supposed to have more of it than he has.

Moral authority implies successful experience with difficult moral decisions; a politician accumulates moral authority by acts of visible integrity amid conflicting temptations and pressures, and by forthright words in situations where lesser men would tell less. I do not mean that a President can afford no enemies, detractors, or doubters. A certain number of these, in the right places, can be very helpful to a President. But he cannot afford as many doubters as President Johnson had gathered in 1966 and 1967.

Hugh Sidey once quoted a man who knew Lyndon Johnson well: "Johnson is bigger than anybody else. He hates more, he loves more, he eats more, he sleeps more, he drinks more, he has more kindness, he has more contempt, he saves more, he spends more, he does everything more. He's just more."

Robert McNamara, Secretary of Defense, told his aide Joseph Califano, departing the Pentagon to join the White House staff: "You will never work for or with a more complicated man than Lyndon Johnson so long as you live. I guarantee it."

George Reedy, who worked for the man for fifteen years, says "He could be an 'insufferable bastard' to his staff, a bully and a sadist." He was a "tormented" man; why, Reedy does not pretend to know. "He may have been a son of a bitch but he was a colossal son of a bitch . . . No one could avoid the feeling of an elemental force at work when in his presence. . . . His feelings for Blacks, Chicanos, dirt farmers were not feigned. He felt their plight and suffered with them—as long as they did not get too close."*

The most ambitious biography of Johnson is an unrelenting assault by Robert A. Caro. *The Years of Lyndon Johnson: The Path to Power,† the first volume in a proposed three-volume work, tells in massive detail of his maneuverings in Texas and in his early years in Washington. Some former Johnson aides and assistants rushed into print to denounce Caro. One of the wisest of LBJ's men took a different line. Horace

*George Reedy, *Lyndon B. Johnson: A Memoir* (Fairway, Kansas: Andrews and McMeel, Inc., 1982), pp. 157–58.
†New York: Alfred A. Knopf, 1982.

Busby, who had worked on the Johnson staff but also in private life served as a confidant and counselor, wrote: "The Lyndon Johnson appearing in Caro's prose is not a fiction. There was such a man. There were many other Lyndon Johnsons as well, but the man's stature requires no protective purging of his past." Some of the Lyndon Johnsons were "detestable, small, abusive." Some were "admirable, brilliant, even . . . awesome."*

I did not have to be so close as a Busby, Reedy, or McNamara to be challenged, as part of my job, by the job of understanding Lyndon Johnson. This mercurial, secretive, conniving, in some ways monstrous man was also capable of deeply generous impulses and great visisons for America. If Shakespeare were working with our nine modern Presidents I think he might have found in Lyndon Johnson the richest theater. Or perhaps he would have been as powerfully attracted to the Presidency of Richard Nixon.

*Horace Busby, "Remembering LBJ, Warts and All," Washington *Post,* May 29, 1983.

9

---◆---

Richard Nixon

One of Nixon's favorite historical figures was Benjamin Disraeli. He had admired the brilliant biography by the English historian Robert Blake,* and at least one well-read member of his staff, Pat Moynihan, the in-house Democrat, encouraged Nixon's desire to see parallels between his own leadership and Disraeli's enlightened Toryism. In domestic economic and social policy, Nixon's Republicanism was indeed of a moderate centrist character, and in foreign policy, with at least as much adroitness as Disraeli, he was managing the interests of a world power in an age when its relative strength was declining.

A senior Nixon official goes on from this to attribute Nixon's resignation to Blake's book. Elliot Richardson, the "Secretary of Everything" who held three Cabinet posts under Nixon, came away from the Disraeli biography with a sense that this "exotic, even bizarre, creature remains elusive.

"How the dandy, the satirist, the Jew, the alien even, could ever have become leader of the Conservative party, Chancellor of the Exchequer, Prime Minister and favorite of Queen Victoria still remains to a significant extent a mystery. Now, it seems reasonable to assume that Nixon put down the Disraeli volume with the same thought. When the time came, therefore, when it was the obvious move in self-preservation to destroy the [Oval Office] tapes, he couldn't do it. The tapes were going to be the indispensable tool whereby *his* biographers would gain the insights denied to Blake in accounting for the career of Disraeli." (Richardson offered this ingenious theory in a speech at the White

Disraeli (New York: St. Martin's, 1967).

108

Burkett Miller Center of Public Affairs, University of Virginia, March 21, 1983.)

Maybe so. Nixon did in fact urge various of his people to read the Blake book. In this he may have been competing, as he always was, with John Kennedy. During the JFK Administration it was prudent for White House staffers to have read David Cecil's biography of Lord Melbourne, a Whig whose politics and personal style were much admired by Kennedy. Nixon had much the more substantial Prime Minister.

I never heard Jimmy Carter mention any of the nineteenth-century prime ministers, and I doubt if Ronald Reagan thinks about them much. (I believe he would admire the Duke of Wellington, and Elizabeth Longford's great biography of that classic Tory and patriot hero, even if he found the Duke's crusty style a touch intimidating.)

In my first brief encounters with Richard Nixon, when he was a congressman and then Senator, I was struck by his swift and coldly analytical intelligence. I thought he was on the right side in the Alger Hiss affair, and I had not been distressed that he had retired the ultra-liberal Congressman Jerry Voorhis, then beat Helen Gahagan Douglas for the Senate. Some of his campaign tactics had been unattractive though, as he would note, scarcely unprecedented. Here in 1946–50 was a prefiguring of the "Everybody Does It" theme central to events of 1970–74. I did not see Congressman or Senator Nixon as any sort of Fascist, and I thought he was many cuts above Joe McCarthy (with whom he was lumped in some feverish anti-anti-Communist polemics) in diligence and brains.

I was not captivated aesthetically. His personal style—as in the exploitation of his family in the Checkers speech—was an embarrassing blend of the slick and the corny. And in seeing him from time to time while he was Ike's Vice-President, it was sometimes hard to give him due credit for his discretion in a difficult role, and for his impressive grasp of the issues of the day, because of his excessive desire to please and his sudden off-key efforts to be one of the boys.

I remember an awkward dinner at Luce's apartment, when Nixon seemed not to realize there might be several different points of view among a dozen senior Time Inc. editors. He reacted sympathetically to the rigidly laissez-faire line of his first questioner, the most conservative man at the table, then tried to adjust to the more pragmatic conservatism of his second questioner, then realized with increasing discomfort that Luce was to the left, so to speak, of the editors who had spoken thus far. In due course others emerged to the left of Luce, but Nixon, instead of letting Time Inc. debate with itself (one of our chief hobbies), kept on trying to agree with everybody. Luce was always vexed when I cited this kind of expediency as a question mark about Nixon's character; he thought Nixon's "flexibility" was well within acceptable political practice.

Notwithstanding my question mark, I voted for Nixon with conviction in 1960, on the grounds given in the *Life* editorial already quoted in Chapter 7. After he lost, I wrote him a personal letter urging (unnecessarily) that he try again some other time. We corresponded and met a few times while he was out of office. I watched some of his moves back toward the center ring, starting with his powerful speech at the Republican convention of 1964, a plea for party unity after the Goldwater nomination. In 1965, I saw him put on an entertaining performance at one of those white-tie insider evenings Washington used to take quite seriously, the Alfalfa Club dinner. Ghostwritten stuff no doubt, but beautifully delivered, with himself the principal butt. He seemed fully recovered from the snarling self-pity ("You won't have Richard Nixon to kick around any more") that had engulfed him after his defeat for governor of California in 1962. And through the mid-sixties there was a cool purposefulness in the way he used his international law practice not only to make money but to finance fact-finding and contact-cultivating trips all over the world.

Against my friend and fellow Minnesotan Hubert Humphrey, I supported Nixon again in 1968. I had written to the Managing Editors that the "charge of a grave flaw in character" lay against both men. Humphrey's compulsive garrulousness raised the question "whether this man is in full control of himself"; against Nixon, "it is the old question of whether or not he is a principled man." I would have preferred to see Nelson Rockefeller the Republican candidate. His foreign policy credentials were as impressive as Nixon's, his personality was decidedly more appealing, and he had shown enlightenment and executive talent in his ten years as governor of New York. But as the 1968 election approached, Rockefeller conducted some Byzantine out-again, in-again maneuvers that ruined whatever chance he might have had.

In our *Life* editorial endorsing Nixon, we said he and his opponent were both "well equipped to be President."* We guessed that a Nixon Administration would be "cool, guarded and efficient," a Humphrey Administration, "warm, open and sloppy." We thought the Democrats had simply held the Presidency too long—twenty-eight of the previous thirty-six years—and even the Eisenhower interruption was "almost too nonpartisan" to reinvigorate the two-party system. Nixon offered us "political competence, a coherent national party and a change in the cast of characters," a good start toward a recovery of national morale.

Nixon phoned me at my house to thank me for the editorial before he had seen the text, so I thought I should tell him the endorsement was quite "measured." That didn't bother him—he said he also was very fond of Hubert Humphrey. If he was elected, he hoped he could call on me for advice from time to time.† I said I was complimented, but of course we would be giving him advice every week, at forty cents a copy, in *Time* and *Life.* My wife, though scarcely a Nixon admirer, told me I had not been very gracious.

As the campaign wore on, I was offended (as I wrote in a memo to my colleagues) at the double standard that "fastidious" liberal columnists were applying. Humphrey was "talking a stream of really fantastic nonsense about the dark ages Nixon would plunge the country into. Somehow this kind of demagoguery is OK from warm-and-generous Humphrey; he doesn't really mean it; whereas the fact that Nixon [being ahead] is doing very little outrageously partisan talk becomes one more example of what a tricky fellow he still is."

Nixon was making some remarkably thoughtful radio speeches that fall. The best of them, "The Nature of the Presidency" (September 19, 1968), makes poignant reading today. Some of his points:

> The President cannot isolate himself from the great intellectual ferments of his time. On the contrary, he must consciously and deliberately place himself at their center. The lamps of enlightenment are lit by the spark of controversy; their flame can be snuffed out by the blanket of consensus. . . .
>
> The President's chief function is to lead, not to administer; it is not to

*October 25, 1968.

†He did invite me twice to serve on nonpartisan panels—one to review the work of the U.S. Information Agency, the other to come up with recommendations on U.S. foreign trade policy. Though I had served on the Lyndon Johnson task force on education, and found it a fascinating experience, I decided not to take up presidential commissions as a habit.

oversee every detail, but to put the right people in charge, to provide them with basic guidance and direction and to let them do the job. . . .

The tasks confronting the next President abroad are among the most complex and difficult ever faced. And, as Professor Clinton Rossiter has observed, "Leadership in foreign affairs flows today from the President—or it does not flow at all."

The Professor and the Pol

Foreign policy became the chief preoccupation—and ornament—of the Nixon Administration, and the leadership did indeed flow from the President. Yet his role was inseparable from that of his extraordinary agent Henry Kissinger. These two men, to understate the matter, were well met. The politician had an excellent mind, and in the professor there was latent a profound aptitude for political maneuver.

In the kind of "disclosure of interest" required by the Securities and Exchange Commission, I should state that I was and am a friend of Henry Kissinger's.* I have known Nixon longer but Kissinger better. It is of course easier to know a presidential assistant than a President.

John Rhodes of Arizona, who came to the House in 1953, and in 1973 succeeded Gerald Ford as Minority Leader, says that, as well as he knew Nixon, "I'm not sure whether he created Kissinger, or Kissinger created him." Each surely used the other and understood very clearly the other was using him. They were at once admiring and fearful of each other, rivals at times, sometimes suspecting plots and manipulations the other man hadn't even thought of (or hadn't thought of yet).

It was a collaboration unique in the modern Presidency. A Kissinger would have been an absurd impossibility under FDR. Ike and Dulles were a team, up to a point, but Dulles never became as powerful as Kissinger. Truman-Acheson were a team, but the Truman role was not as large as Nixon's. Most of those who saw the Nixon-Kissinger policy process up close concluded that the large designs and concepts came chiefly from Nixon. Kissinger could brilliantly elaborate—and negotiate.

Nixon brought to foreign policy his first-rate legal mind, two decades of exposure to the principal issues—as a member of Congress, Vice-President, and world traveler—and a broad imagination not de-

*Seymour Hersh, in *The Price of Power* (New York: Summit Books, 1983) stresses Kissinger's assiduous cultivating of the press, especially columnists James Reston and Joseph Kraft. More or less in passing, he accuses *Time* of "fawning" on Kissinger. I escape mention by name.

void of idealism. He also had a remarkable ability to apply his precinct-level foxiness (a quality that does not always travel well) to international politics.

Kissinger, along with his past scholarship in diplomatic history and his elegant expositions of balance-of-power theory, had dazzling gifts at seeing into political leaders of other countries and cultures.* As sometimes happens with the most talented negotiators, Kissinger could get too caught up in what he was so good at, the game almost for its own sake, savoring all the intricacies and subtleties of (one of his favorite phrases) "the state of play." Nixon from time to time asserted a certain common-sense instinct to haul the proceedings back to basic objectives, to keep the Nixon-Kissinger initiatives from getting too intricate for congressional or public taste.

The great labor of the Nixon-Kissinger foreign policy was to adjust the United States to somewhat reduced circumstances. This does not sound like a heroic undertaking—but it was. We could no longer dominate world politics to the degree we had in the fleeting years of the "Presidents of the West." But to accept this without demeaning or dissipating any of our still formidable power and will was not an easy transaction. It was done with success everywhere except Viet Nam.

"The Nixon Doctrine," put forward only a few months after he became President, represented a certain retrenchment of our role in Asia. We would stand by our treaty commitments, we would "provide a shield" if a nuclear power threatened a nation vital to our security, but nations resisting "other types of aggression" (civil wars, wars across borders the U.S. had not guaranteed, mixtures of both), should not look for American troops. In other words, no new Viet Nams. But the Nixon Doctrine could not extricate us from the Viet Nam we were already in.

Meanwhile Nixon made his visit to Romania, the first by an Ameri-

---

*In his massive memoirs, Vol. I, *White House Years* (Boston: Little, Brown, 1979), and Vol. II, *Years of Upheaval* (Little, Brown, 1982), Kissinger has sketched superb vignettes of Mao, Chou, Brezhnev, Sadat, Golda Meir, Pompidou, and several dozen more foreign leaders and diplomats he dealt with. Nor does he neglect Secretary of State William Rogers, Secretary of Defense Melvin Laird, or principals in the Watergate cast, John Mitchell, H. R. Haldeman, John Ehrlichman. But the most valuable portrait of all, accumulating through the two volumes, adding up to perhaps 50 pages out of his demanding 2,700, is of his boss and patron. Kissinger's version of Nixon is of course self-interested (and also revealing of Kissinger), but it is the wisest and fairest appraisal we have yet had from anybody who was up close.

In commending Kissinger's memoirs, I must again make a declaration of interest. Toward the end of his time as Secretary of State, he and I had a two-minute conversation, and hand-shake understanding, that Time Inc., which owns Little, Brown, would have first refusal if he decided to write. How he did write! And he is still at it; a third volume will deal with his diplomacy during the Ford Administration.

can President to one of the Communist states of Eastern Europe. The principal attraction in this imaginative journey was that Romania, unique among the Soviet satellites, had close relations with China. In 1969, Nixon already had his heart set on the boldest diplomatic move an old Cold Warrior could make.

Nixon and Kissinger loved back channels and back-back channels to bypass the State Department bureaucracy and Bill Rogers, the nominal Secretary of State. Along several of these private circuits, they patiently probed for two years, and finally landed the invitation for Kissinger to make his secret visit to Beijing in 1971. This paved the way for Nixon's historic visit of February 1972, and the signing of the Shanghai Communiqué.

There was a cost in all the secrecy. The news of the Kissinger trip, after the event, hit our ally the Japanese as the "Nixon Shokku." (They were to receive a second *shokku* only a month later when Nixon devalued the dollar.) A more lasting cost was exacerbation of our relations with India, always difficult, because of the Nixon-Kissinger "tilt" toward Pakistan, in part to protect our Pakistani back-channel to Beijing. (When I saw Kissinger at a small dinner party in New York shortly after his triumphal return from Beijing, I asked why, in view of Nixon's public hints that he wanted to go to China, and Mao's public statement that he would be welcome, was all the secrecy necessary? I think Kissinger thought I was very dense; I didn't think he was very convincing.)

If he and Nixon relished the melodramatic flourishes, if he gloried in the upstaging of Rogers, if Nixon was keenly aware of the uses of China in election year 1972, the China opening still remains an act of high statesmanship. Most of the credit should go to Nixon; the key was the presidential decision to *do it;* there was not all that much for Kissinger to negotiate about. In effectively recognizing the People's Republic, the U.S. had recognized the real world, in which many countries, even the most populous of all, may pursue political and economic policies very uncongenial to Americans. We had recognized the staggering potential of China, including a potential for ideological change.*

In the China opening, the U.S. also was acquiring a new flexibility in its dealings with the Soviet Union. Nixon and Kissinger were circum-

---

*On October 25, 1983, Jude Wanniski could report in the *New York Times* that "China is running, not walking, down the capitalist road . . . all known Communists are being purged from the [Communist] party." Wanniski's book on supply-side economics was being translated into Chinese at Beijing University. In late 1984, the Central Committee of China's [sic] Communist Party announced bold reforms that would limit central planning for state enterprises and open up pricing to free-market forces. The party newspaper said it would be "naive and stupid" to try to apply Marxism to all contemporary problems. (The *New York Times,* December 9, 1984.)

spect in their public statements on this point, and were much too adroit to be caught in any blatant playing upon the Soviet-Chinese tensions. As Kissinger virtuously puts it: "To have the two Communist powers competing for good relations with us could only benefit the cause of peace; it was the essence of triangular strategy."*

We went Kissinger one better, or actually two better, in a *Life* editorial (August 6, 1971) on pentagonal diplomacy. We thought a new "Five-Cornered World" was emerging (Japan and Western Europe being the other corners), and that the Nixon Administration was approaching it with "prudence," a sensible lowering of the U.S. profile, and generally "conciliatory diplomacy."

Triangular diplomacy may well have stimulated Soviet interest in détente and in a meaningful outcome for the Strategic Arms Limitation Talks that had begun in 1969. Détente, for the Nixon Administration, was another major act of realism about a world that had changed. The Soviets were approaching parity in nuclear power. In 1970–71, in complex negotiations over Berlin, Nixon and Kissinger were tacitly accepting West German Chancellor Willy Brandt's *Ostpolitik,* the dealings with East Germany and the Soviet Union that in effect recognized the existing boundaries in central Europe. Our allies in Europe and Japan in their combined economic capacities were about to overtake the U.S., and they were increasingly and understandably independent in foreign policy. They wanted, among other things, serious and audible U.S. dialogue with the Soviet Union—but not a U.S.-Soviet condominium.

Nixon and Kissinger were sensitive to these changes and currents and saw value for the U.S. in careful arms negotiations, always recognizing there had to be something in it for the Russians, too. Out of this came Nixon's Moscow visit in 1972, SALT I, and a variety of U.S.-Soviet agreements on joint space ventures, environmental protection, exchanges of science and technology.

The Moscow summit was of course superb theater, as China was, for Nixon's reelection campaign. SALT I had its flaws, and Nixon tended to oversell détente in general. But in his dealings with the Soviets, as with China, the old Cold Warrior was a farsighted statesman. Equal credit belongs to Kissinger. Détente brought all his diplomatic skills into play.

The other major breakthrough came in the Middle East. Responding to the vision and courage of Sadat, the U.S. restored relations with Egypt, and undertook in the aftermath of the Yom Kippur war to lay the groundwork for an eventual settlement between Israel and its neighbors. Kissinger's virtuosity (and stamina) were spectacular in his

The White House Years (Boston: Little Brown, 1979), p. 836.

shuttle diplomacy between Cairo, Jerusalem, and Damascus. Here the negotiating, detail by excruciating detail, the brokering between deeply suspicious principals, was the essence of the achievement, which can properly be called a Kissinger-Nixon breakthrough. The disengagement agreements Kissinger extracted in 1974 from Egypt and Israel and from Syria and Israel made possible another brilliant piece of negotiating, by a very different sort of diplomat, Jimmy Carter, at Camp David in 1978. It is no denigration of the gallant efforts of Carter, Kissinger, and Nixon, which all seemed immensely hopeful in their time, to note that the Middle East looks just about as intractable today as it did ten years ago. The only solid achievements are that Israel has given the Sinai back to Egypt, and the U.S. retains some limited credibility as a mediator with some of the Arab states as well as with Israel.

In admiration for his first-term foreign policy initiatives, *Time*'s editors decided to make Nixon their Man of the Year for 1971. (We had not picked him for 1968, the year of his narrow win over Humphrey.) Four of us went to interview him one December evening. He came into the Oval Office from a staff Christmas party; he was in a sports blazer and slacks, more relaxed and sure of himself than I had ever seen him. We had asked if we might bring a recorder, but the press office said that wouldn't be necessary; Army Signal Corps technicians could tape the session. After the interview, an embarrassed aide told us there had been some snafu about the taping. We went straight back to the *Time* Washington office and reconstructed the two-hour interview from memory. Nixon accepted our version with no argument. He might have wished for other taping snafus a few months hence.

Time Inc.'s relations with the Nixon White House were generally friendly through his first term. Once when he was meeting a delegation of *Fortune* editors, I sought to loosen things up by saying, "The last time I saw you, Mr. President, was from under water." I had just been vacationing at Caneel Bay Plantation in the Virgin Islands at the same time he had been there, and one morning I had snorkeled over to his beach —evoking no interest on the part of the Secret Service—and spotted the President and his friend Bebe Rebozo conversing waist-deep in the water. I surfaced briefly, decided I shouldn't eavesdrop, and withdrew. The President seemed uncomfortable with my laborious pleasantry; he launched into a somewhat overemphatic discussion of his tastes in swimming and exercise. He also volunteered that sportswriters had the best job in the world; they should really pay to do it. I said I would pass along this thought to the managing editor of *Sports Illustrated*.

Nixon the sports fan had a touching kind of Walter Mitty side. At a White House dinner in April 1970, he was awarding eight journalists the Medal of Freedom. His remarks about seven of them were witty and graceful, no more than two minutes per medal, but for the eighth, Bill Henry of the Los Angeles *Times*, he really took off. Henry, a sports reporter and columnist who had died a few days before the White House dinner, was manning the public address system during a running of the 5,000 meter event at the Los Angeles Olympics of 1932. Nixon, who had been in the stands, seemed in 1970 to have total recall of the race, lap by lap, and played the sports announcer for what seemed like a good ten minutes. Near the finish, the crowd thought the front-running Finn had crowded the American just behind him, forcing him to break stride. When the Finn later came up to receive his gold medal, "a ripple of boos swept through the Coliseum." Then Bill Henry–Richard Nixon cries into the mike: " 'Ladies and gentlemen, remember, these men are our guests!' The boos stopped."

Most of the Freedom medalists were in their seventies and eighties. In a conversation after the ceremonies Nixon asked me how old I was. Fifty-six. "Oh," said the President, "you've got lots of time!"

On the economy and the welfare state, Nixon was much more liberal than the Barry Goldwater wing of his party in the sixties and early seventies. He thought the pure-right doctrine was a loser in national politics, but I believe there was also some conviction on his part that it deserved to lose. (Again, Benjamin Disraeli.) Under Nixon, appropriations for Lyndon Johnson's Great Society programs grew more in percentage terms than they did under Carter. Ronald Reagan did not try to "repeal" the Great Society (let alone the New Deal) but was attempting to arrest the rate of growth of these programs—i.e., reduce velocities that first built up under Nixon. Philosophically, President Nixon stood well to the left of President Reagan, though Nixon, the thoroughly professional pol, of course saw in the late seventies that the country had moved, and by 1980 that Reagan was on to a good thing.

In 1972, to the distress of most of the *Life* editorial staff, the magazine endorsed Nixon for reelection. We were for him "on the whole." Our editorial (October 27) said, "He makes it hard for independent voters to give him unqualified support." (I was not angling for the Medal of Freedom.) His performance in race relations had been "uninspiring," on other domestic issues "respectable." In most respects the record in foreign policy was "excellent." And again the dream: "If he wins the second term that now seems so likely, we hope at the end to be able to salute him as a great President."

The Quagmire

Four years earlier, I had supported Nixon in good part because he was home free on Viet Nam. Not that he would or should have pulled out abruptly. But he certainly had more freedom of maneuver—vis-à-vis South Viet Nam as well as North, and vis-à-vis U.S. opinion—than did Humphrey, who as Vice-President had been faithfully defending Johnson's war policies up and down the land.

A few weeks after the 1969 inaugural, a group of business executives and Time Inc. editors who had just returned from a "news tour" of the Far East, including a short stop in Viet Nam, met with the President in the Cabinet Room. He listened patiently to our impressions. We recommended an early first installment in a schedule of gradual U.S. troop withdrawals—up to fifty thousand of the half-million plus in Viet Nam. Nixon of course had such an obvious policy already in mind (and probably welcomed all evidences of support for it). He had claimed during the 1968 campaign he had a "plan," never specified, for ending the war. What it amounted to, in practice, was U.S. troop withdrawals keyed to South Vietnamese progress in fighting and in governing, i.e., "Vietnamization" of the war, and intensified negotiation with the North. He was also prepared to intensify the air war as the U.S. ground force was drawn down, in part to support the South militarily, in part to pressure the North into serious negotiating. He never complained, at least in public, of inheriting a Democratic war, and indeed he and Kissinger pursued their two-track policy with a principled stubbornness.

Nixon consistently underestimated the damage the war was doing inside the U.S., and tended, as Johnson had done, to equate dissent with aid and comfort to the enemy. Even as he was moving us slowly out of the war, he kept inflaming the home front with divisive and belligerent language. Toward the end of his first year of grappling with Viet Nam, I wrote in a *Life* editorial:

Richard Nixon has said he does not propose to be the first American President to lose a war. He might, however, if he and we are lucky, become the third President to settle for a tie. The others were James Madison (War of 1812) and Dwight Eisenhower (Korea), perfectly respectable company for any President to keep.

It is a profound question how—and whether—a democracy should conduct a war with only, say, 60 percent of public opinion in support. Our Constitution specifies no fewer than nine matters, none as serious as a war, which require a two-thirds vote for congressional approval. When we are in a war which has never had explicit congressional sanction, and never even been legally "declared," being fought in good part by draftees (chosen by a fantastically capricious system), a war which many (*Life* included) have thought important to win but almost nobody has ever claimed was imperative, and when this war has dragged on inconclusively for years, the wonder is not that there is protest but that there is so much willingness to serve and sacrifice. Mr. Nixon and Mr. Agnew too would do better to marvel at the stability and patience of the nation they are privileged to lead, rather than purse lips and wonder how Hanoi is reading our students today.

What an irony that we should be on fairly good terms with Communist Russia, talking cautiously about a possible thaw in relations with Communist China, and still so bitterly embroiled with one of the smallest Communist states.*

Troop withdrawals began to establish their own momentum, regardless of the meager progress in Vietnamization. Reescalation became unthinkable by 1970–71; more and more, it was up to the bombers to make up for the departing infantrymen. At the same time, Nixon and Kissinger were moving away from the LBJ concept of victory ("nail that coonskin to the wall") to the much more modest goal of "a fair chance" for a non-Communist South Viet Nam to survive.

But as the war ground on, and the frightful costs kept piling up, in Viet Nam and the U.S., Nixon seemed to be losing control of his own policy. It seemed as though either Viet Nam—North or South—could force us to stay out there, in much reduced numbers, indefinitely.

Thomas Griffith, then the editor of *Life,* wrote an editorial (April 2, 1971) saying, "The U.S. has done a great deal in, for and to Viet Nam —probably too much. According to President Nixon, one of his major difficulties in Viet Nam is that 'Americans are very impatient people; they feel that if a good thing is going to happen, it should happen instantly.' This is an almost unbelievable complaint for a U.S. President to make in 1971. Americans have been extraordinarily patient in waiting for a resolution of the Viet Nam war—the longest and most inconclusive in U.S. history and the most marginal to our vital interests.

*October 24, 1969.

"Though we do not ask the President to say this, his statements should permit Americans to conclude that if worse came to worst, Communist victory in the South could be borne more easily than an indefinite U.S. role in an endless war: this indeed would be to become the 'pitiful, helpless giant' of Nixon's midnight fears."

In 1972, in endorsing Nixon's reelection, *Life* called Viet Nam his one serious foreign policy failure. It was becoming "the long stay for less and less."

A few weeks later, however, we were sufficiently hopeful about Kissinger's burst of negotiations with North Viet Nam to think we should make Nixon and Kissinger *Time*'s co-Men of the Year for 1972. Peace was "at hand," then not quite at hand, but things clearly were in motion. *Time*'s choice was based chiefly on the opening to China, détente with the Soviets, and Nixon's reelection landslide, but the story would not have read well if the Men seemed still hopelessly mired in Viet Nam. The story did not read too well as it was, because it appeared during the savage "Christmas bombing" launched by Nixon and Kissinger on December 26, 1972, to impress North *and* South Viet Nam with our resolve.

It seems plausible that Nixon-Kissinger did bomb the North back to a negotiating mode, for the moment, and did convince the South, for the moment, that we were dependable allies. That the latter proof should have seemed necessary, after all the dollars, years, and lives spent in behalf of a remote place of no overwhelming strategic concern to the United States, is a terrible judgment on policies of the Kennedy, Johnson, and Nixon presidencies. But the Paris Agreement was finally initialed by Kissinger and Le Duc Tho, of the Hanoi Politburo, on January 23, 1973. The war was ostensibly over.

Saigon and the countryside were deceptively agreeable when I made my first "peacetime" visit to Viet Nam in April. From travels into the provinces and talks with U.S. and Vietnamese officials, I thought I saw progress in the economy and political structure of the South, and presumably in its capacity to stand on its own. There was in fact some progress, but nowhere near enough. The South had only two more years to live as an independent country.

Nixon and Kissinger are right to argue in their memoirs that the Paris Agreement was not simply the same deal we could have had four years earlier without the intervening bloodshed. At Paris, Hanoi finally gave up on its previous insistence that there could be no peace as long as the regime of Nguyen Van Thieu was in power in Saigon. The Paris

Agreement would have been a tolerable outcome for the South and the U.S.—if it could have been enforced.

But our diplomatic victory was empty, since the North never had any intention of abiding by the agreement, the South was not yet strong enough to go it alone, and the only real sanction was U.S. air power. Many Americans would have been outraged by more "Christmas bombings," and from mid-1973 on, Nixon was so weakened by Watergate that he could not risk public and congressional wrath by any measures that seemed to reescalate the war. Indeed he would have been accused of trying to divert public attention from Watergate.

In the end it was not Watergate that wrecked the Nixon-Kissinger settlement of the war. Even for the well-liked Gerald Ford, Congress would not approve a mere $300 million of emergency military supplies to the South after Hanoi began its massive offensive in December 1974. The Nixon-Kissinger policy foundered on two facts: the North had a superb fighting machine, and the U.S. was sick of the war.

Covering Up the Cover-Up

Viet Nam was one of the fathers of Watergate. When the Pentagon Papers were stolen and published in the *New York Times,* Nixon might have chosen to sit back and enjoy the embarrassment of various Democrats who fashioned Viet Nam policy in the Johnson and Kennedy administrations, for the documents all pertained to those years. Instead, the Nixon Administration treated Daniel Ellsberg's theft of the papers as a major breach of national security and attempted to enjoin publication. In an Administration already obsessed with leaks and lavish in its use of wiretapping, the infamous "Plumbers Unit" broke into the office of Ellsberg's psychiatrist, and there was even half-serious talk in the White House of trying to "firebomb" the Brookings Institution to get Ellsberg papers out of a safe. Anti–Viet Nam demonstrations within sight and hearing of the White House contributed to a siege mentality.

The Watergate break-in itself derived from a different culture— old-fashioned dirty-trick politics—but it was not the break-in that brought Nixon down. It was the cover-up that destroyed his Presidency, and the cover-up of the cover-up ad infinitum—in short, obstruction of justice and lying.

In this "Watergate," the serious one, the poisons that Viet Nam released into American political life worked on the old insecurities of Richard Nixon. The break-in could have been handled in other ways, including firing a Nixon friend or two, and telling the truth. But within days of the break-in, the cover-up began. The first lies were told.

Many successful and self-confident politicians will say they believe in always running scared, but Nixon *was* scared. In 1960, as he saw it, the great prize had been snatched away from him by the undeserving Jack Kennedy, rich and glamorous, and in 1962 even Pat Brown, neither rich nor glamorous, had beaten him badly for governor of California. In 1968 he himself had barely beaten Hubert Humphrey. Even as the incumbent President in June of 1972, it was not at all obvious that he was going to crush George McGovern in November. So in the first stages of the Watergate cover-up, he was suppressing a possible threat to his always precarious political fortunes. But if the obstruction of justice caused any twinge of conscience, he could cite a higher good. In his reelection campaign, he saw himself doing just battle on a broad front: against all the forces in the Democratic Party, in the media, on the campuses, that were insufficiently loyal to the United States.

Watergate in fact was not a noticeable issue in the 1972 presidential election. It would have been difficult to find a voter who had shifted from Nixon to George McGovern because of it. I can remember, much as I would prefer not to, telling my friend Clark MacGregor, the former Minnesota congressman who had become chairman of CREEP (the Committee to Reelect the President), that White House Press Secretary Ron Ziegler was wrong to call Watergate a third-rate burglary. It was second-rate, I said, but too complicated ever to catch on as a "popular" scandal. Nobody seemed to be on the take. Clark, I hope in full innocence, agreed.

In early 1973, the case against the Nixon White House began to build up, and *Time* reporting made some worthwhile contributions. A project I had thought up as a celebration of *Time*'s fiftieth anniversary, a series of symposia and dinners around the country on the role of Congress, became a kind of critique of the "Imperial Presidency," with Watergate always the backdrop. Ford, Humphrey, and Speaker Carl Albert were among our speakers at the windup dinner in Washington. I spoke too, and said we were not attacking any President, past or present, but were concerned with whether "the legislative role is eroding, and our system of government is moving out of balance."

At another big Time Inc. dinner in Washington, April 30, 1973, TV was brought in so we could watch Nixon's TV speech on the firing of Haldeman and Ehrlichman. A Washington *Post* reporter asked me what I thought of the speech. I said, "Not very good." She asked if she could use that and seemed startled when I said, "Sure." So in the paper the next morning I came out "forthright." The main trouble with the speech, and indeed Nixon's irreducible Watergate dilemma, was why, if these men were two of the "finest public servants it has been my privilege to know," was he firing them.

I wrote an essay for *Time* on the "Good Uses of the Watergate Affair":

> Watergate could be a historic check upon the long and dangerous aggrandizement of the presidency . . . under Kennedy, Johnson and Nixon, for all their differences, there has been a driving personal urge to power, a philosophical view of the presidency as the central institution in American life, and a whole series of external events and circumstances that gave vast scope for presidential activity.
>
> In the past fortnight, some of the most anguished comments about "preserving the presidency" have come from liberal Democrats profoundly unsympathetic to Richard Nixon the man but devout believers in the near mystical view of the presidency. They lament "the crippling of the presidency," a "collapse" of the American form of government, etc., etc. Nonsense. . . .
>
> There is obviously more to come about the Watergate affair and more the President himself will have to do, including eventually a fuller and franker account of his own discussions and decisions from the beginning. Meanwhile, Congress, courts, and press show us the American democratic "system," an even grander and more important thing than the presidency, is still running.*

By late July, after the Ervin committee hearings, I was among those now convinced that Nixon must have committed impeachable offenses. Morally and constitutionally, his Presidency had lost legitimacy. But the apparent alternative was Spiro Agnew.

I had found Agnew's bluff style rather appealing when I first met him during the 1968 campaign. In 1969, I enjoyed putting a little editorial in *Life* on "The First Hundred Days of Spiro Agnew."† I wrote that he had been diligent and discreet, maintaining "that low political silhouette which his employer is said to have recommended." And in 1970, I had offended some colleagues, in Time Inc. and elsewhere in journalism, by arguing that Agnew was halfway right in some of his attacks on the "Eastern Media Establishment" for negativism and elitism. In one speech I offered the bold thesis that "a statement does not become untrue just by being spoken by the Vice-President."

*May 14, 1973.
†May 2, 1969.

But the Vice-President did not wear well, and there were other Republicans clearly better qualified for the office. While Nixon still seemed to be weighing his choice of running mate for his second term, we said in a *Life* editorial: "It is hard to imagine that Nixon, with four years' knowledge of the presidency and eight years' experience as Vice-President, really thinks Spiro Agnew is the best the Republicans can offer as Vice-President."* We helpfully suggested a number of better candidates from both the conservative and liberal wings of the party. Among them: Rockefeller, Elliot Richardson, John Connally, Senator Charles Percy of Illinois, Mayor Richard Lugar of Indianapolis.

Nixon would not have disagreed with our general thesis. "He never considered Agnew up to succeeding him," according to Kissinger.† "He once said, only partly facetiously, that Agnew was his insurance policy against assassination." But Presidents tend not to believe they could die in the next four years; Agnew was popular with hard-shell regulars and Nixon decided not to stir up any trouble.

After Agnew was duly renominated, we invited him to an editorial lunch. He insisted we meet instead in his suite in the Executive Office Building. He took one or two questions from me about the campaign, then when one of our correspondents tried to follow up, Agnew abruptly said this was not "one of your usual *Time-Life* lunches." This was *his* lunch, he wasn't there to answer questions, he wanted to ask us how we possibly justified the tone of the *Time* coverage of him and the insult of the *Life* editorial. I was offended that he had wheeled on one of my younger colleagues instead of attacking me directly. I told the Vice-President he was a servant of the public, and for that part of the public that read our magazines, we had a duty to report on his performance as we saw it. As to the *Life* editorial, I said no insult was intended, and I came up with the somewhat Jesuitical point that there were a number of my best friends, close colleagues, and even relatives that I did not consider qualified to be next in line as President. It was an awkward meal.

But when Agnew's violations of the law became known the next summer and when he was forced to plead *nolo contendere* to bribery charges and resign in October 1973, the way opened up for the final resolution of Watergate. (Elliot Richardson, who as Attorney General negotiated Agnew's *nolo* plea, surely had more to do with Nixon's eventual resignation than Disraeli's biographer did, despite Richardson's engaging theory to the contrary.)

July 28, 1972.
†*Years of Upheaval*, p. 92.

On October 22, 1973, in a speech to the *Time* staff at a fiftieth anniversary banquet, I said: "Long before the last Watergate trial ends, we surely must demand a solemn and unmistakable national verdict that Watergate was a gross abuse of executive power and a subversion of the American political system. There are several ways such a verdict might be rendered. Impeachment becomes more thinkable by the day. But in one way or another I believe it will be lodged irrevocably in our history that the American people did not consider Watergate just a case of Everybody's Doing It.

"And we in journalism, for all our worldliness, must be willing to speak quite directly and quite simply of the moral qualities we require of our public men: truthfulness, courage, compassion, the willingness to give trust, and a sense of restraint, the sense of where to stop."

My stout colleagues at the top of "the business side" of Time Inc., Chairman Andrew Heiskell and President James Shepley, said OK, we hear you, when are we going to do it? They knew full well some of the perils for a communications company—postal rates, TV franchises, etc. —in challenging an alley-fighting Administration, but they were eager for me to get on with it.

The brilliant managing editor of Time, Henry Grunwald (now Editor in Chief of Time Inc.), had drafted an eloquent article calling on Nixon to resign. I am of somewhat more cautious temperament than Heiskell, Shepley, or Grunwald (they have told me so), and there was one detail I wanted cleared up. A large detail.

Agnew gone, the next in line, by statute, was House Speaker Carl Albert, a Democrat. To advocate a Nixon resignation before there was a Republican Vice-President on hand would have been a proposal to rewrite the 1972 election results.

Nixon had nominated Gerald Ford as Vice-President on October 12, two days after the Agnew departure, but it was not clear how soon he would be confirmed (there were complicated Democratic vs. Republican calculations involved, jockeying within both parties, and maneuverings toward 1976). Grunwald freshened up his unprinted article week by week.

By late October it seemed certain Ford would be confirmed (though it didn't finally happen until December 6). We decided to go ahead, and to run Grunwald's article as an unsigned "Editorial," leading off the issue of November 12, the first overt editorial in *Time*'s fifty years. (Ten years later, it was still the only *Time* editorial.) Grunwald's eloquent argument:

Richard Nixon "has irredeemably lost his moral authority, the confidence of most of the country, and therefore his ability to govern effectively. The most important decision of Richard Nixon's remarkable career is before him: whether he will give up the presidency rather than do further damage to his country. . . .

"The nightmare of uncertainty must be ended. A fresh start must be made. Some at home and abroad might see in the President's resignation a sign of American weakness and failure. It would be a sign of the very opposite. It would show strength and health. It would show the ability of a badly infected political system to cleanse itself. It would show the true power of popular government under law in America."

I inserted in the editorial an unapologetic statement that Time Inc. had endorsed Nixon for President, on the *Life* editorial page, every time he ran. The editorials were not rave notices, but we had been generally impressed, three times, with his qualifications for the office. This acknowledgment caused wincing among some colleagues, but I thought our *Time* editorial would be more effective if we reminded readers (and Nixon) we were not speaking as old Nixon-haters.*

I had no swollen notion that Time Inc. or Grunwald or Donovan was decreeing the fall of the Nixon Presidency. I thought then, and think now, that our editorial did contribute to public awareness that resignation was a thinkable outcome, that the country and the Presidency need not be dragged through the whole impeachment process.

*A few days earlier I had received a letter from William Owens, of Cambridge, Maryland, advising me that "the transfer of *Time* magazine from an independent well-run magazine under Henry R. Luce to an oracle of the Democratic Party is one of the most disgusting things in modern-day journalism. You have consistently . . . shown your hate-Nixon Get Him at Any Price attitude."

The writer was not known to me personally, and ordinarily the letter would have been answered by *Time*'s corps of full-time letter-answerers. But I couldn't resist a personal reply because of Mr. Owens' arresting final sentence: "Unless you change your attitude and become a little more non-biased I shall be forced [into] buying substantial portions of the stock and throwing you, unqualified as you are, out of office."

"Dear Mr. Owens," I wrote:
"Far from having a 'Hate-Nixon Get Him At Any Price attitude,' the Time Inc. publications supported him three times for President. We also deplore many of the activities now shown to have been carried out by some of his most intimate advisers and appointees. These inevitably reflect on his own capacity as an executive and his own sense of propriety.

"On the basis of new information, in other words, we are revising our previous opinion. The willingness to go through that painful business is known as open-mindedness.

"Please feel free to buy as much Time Inc. stock as you wish."

If he did buy, Mr. Owens would have done quite well. Allowing for splits and a spinoff, the stock was selling in late 1984 at about five and a half times the level of late 1973.

The day the *Time* editorial appeared, I saw Alexander Haig, then Nixon's Chief of Staff. What did he think of it? It was like "being hit in the face with a cold fish." Had the President read it? "You may assume he has."

Forbes ran an editorial condemning *Time* and others who were calling on the President to resign, saying we were asking Nixon to violate his Constitutional duty. Nixon wrote *Forbes* a grateful letter reiterating that he had "no intention of walking away from the job I was elected to do." In the same issue the magazine published a letter from me saying "I can't forbear reminding you that the Constitution does contemplate that a President might some day resign . . . So it hardly would seem the 'ultimate betrayal of trust' [*Forbes'* words] for him to consider this course or for others to urge it upon him."*

Clare Luce, a Nixon loyalist to the end, sent me an impassioned letter for publication in *Time,* also arguing that it would be unconstitutional for a President to resign. I sent word back that we would be glad to print her letter but would follow it with an Editor's Note (in old-fashioned *Time*-speak): "Let Reader Luce reread her U.S. Constitution, Article II, Section 1, Paragraph 6, and the twenty-fifth Amendment." She withdrew that letter, though we later printed one in which she denounced *Time* for "its editorial overinvestment in the destruction of the President."†

A Time Inc. director, catching up with our editorial in Hong Kong, fired off a blistering cable to Board Chairman Heiskell, saying that he refused to take any responsibility for the editorial. Heiskell replied pleasantly that that was just right; the editors were responsible for the magazine's views.

Mail from subscribers (some announcing they were now ex-subscribers) was heavy and heated. One reader wrote *Time* after John Mitchell and Maurice Stans were acquitted on conspiracy and perjury charges: "Well how do you rotten bastards like that verdict? Didn't end up according to your prepared script, did it? You've got egg all over your face." Another reader was incensed at the jury: "I

*January 1, 1974.
†Clare Boothe Luce, *Time,* April 5, 1974, 9.5.
As late as May 1974, with bad news crashing in on Nixon every day, he received a touching note from Clare: "From 'The Ballad of Sir Andrew Barton': "Sir Andrew Barton said, 'I am hurt but I am not slain! I'll lay me down and bleed awhile, and I'll rise and fight again!' " (*The Memoirs of Richard Nixon,* vol. I [New York: Grosset & Dunlap, 1978], p. 858).

just heard the verdict in the Mitchell-Stans trial and went into the bathroom and threw up." Some of our letters showed a defter touch: "The Nixon tape transcripts make one thing perfectly clear. When the President says that he has never known two finer men than Messrs. Haldeman and Ehrlichman, he is—more's the pity—probably telling the truth."

I was given an exotic perspective on Watergate during a visit to the Soviet Union in May 1974, just three months before the end. In meetings with Soviet think-tankers and second-tier officials, I was pumped daily about Watergate. The offenses or alleged offenses—bugging, breaking and entering, perjury, conspiracy to obstruct justice, personal enrichment at the public expense, etc.—could scarcely impress my Soviet friends. Their question was, Why are these things being brought up, and by what forces? Was it a plot by the "military-industrial complex" against the author of détente? Can it really be that the American ruling class is at war within itself? The thought that an open and genuine process of inquiry and judgment was about to begin—that by these procedures the President of the United States might really be removed from office, *but nobody could be certain*—all this left them profoundly, one can say sincerely, mystified. Imagine the fate of Soviet politicians who challenged the leader and failed to bring him down!

I am not proud of this, but I enjoyed Watergate. To a journalist, it was a stupendously exciting story, fascinating in its complexity and fecundity, new sensations constantly leading on to more sensations. Beyond the sensations, however, I thought in the spring and summer of 1974 I was also seeing a majestic republican drama: Congress, the courts, press, and public opinion combining to establish that the holder of the most powerful political office in the world, elected in a landslide, could be forced to abdicate for breaking the law. To witness all this, and even take a small part in it, was like being at the Constitutional Convention in Philadelphia (with a delegate's badge; the press was not admitted).

Overlaying its legal and constitutional dimensions, Watergate was of course a political struggle on a grand scale, and a kind of war of cultures. Senator Sam Ervin's committee and the House Judiciary Committee were not totally free of partisan calculation; Judge "Maximum John" Sirica and Special Prosecutor Archibald Cox had their biases; the press (as a Washington *Post* editor later said) smelled "blood in the water." Nixon to this day can only concede that he made "misjudgments" that cost him his "base" on Capitol Hill. Many unfairnesses of detail can be found in the overthrow of Nixon.* I think the result was broadly, roughly fair.

I could not think of Watergate as a "national tragedy." It was a shattering personal tragedy (of the Greek variety, as so many moralists instructed us) for Richard Nixon, and a cruel ordeal for his family. Many of his men paid a harsh price for their eagerness to fulfill what they thought, not unreasonably, to be his wishes.

Watergate was an embarrassment, in a way, for all of us who had voted for Nixon, and especially those of us who had urged others to vote for him. To this day, however, I cannot wish that George McGovern had won in 1972; Nixon—disgrace—resignation—Ford was a better outcome. Humphrey vs. Nixon in 1968 is a tougher call, looking back. I am not sure a liberal Democrat could have made the China and Russia moves that Nixon did. Humphrey would not have done worse in Viet Nam, but I doubt he would have done better.

I had thought Nixon would be enlarged and mellowed when he finally won the job he had so strenuously sought, but it didn't work that way. And after his huge victory over McGovern in 1972, he went within hours into a strange and nasty funk, asking for the resignation of everybody, brooding for days up at Camp David.

This lonely, strangely tortured man, who liked to think of himself as a fearless fighter, dreaded face-to-face confrontations. He asked the long-suffering Bill Rogers to fire Haldeman and Ehrlichman, but that was one thing too many for Bill; Nixon had to do it himself, and it left him, according to Kissinger, "nearly incoherent with grief."† When it came Rogers' time to go, Rogers being Nixon's oldest friend in his Administration, Nixon sent Al Haig to do the job. Rogers refused to be fired by proxy, though when Nixon finally got up nerve to summon him, Rogers thoughtfully arrived with a prepared letter of resignation.

But in his musings in the Oval Office, confided to a few intimates (and the tape), Nixon could be casually brutal. "The coarse side of his nature," writes Kissinger, "was a kind of fantasy in which he acted out his daydreams of how ruthless politicians behaved under stress."‡ Bryce

---

*The principal historical unfairness, arising from the sheer bulk of the Watergate literature and documentation, is the impression that Watergate totally dominated the Nixon Presidency from the moment it happened, June 17, 1972. It probably occupied no more than 1 or 2 percent of Nixon's attention (if we can devise such a statistic) until March or April 1973, when John Dean began to sing. Whether Nixon would have handled it better if he had spent more time on it is not clear. But it does an injustice to the work of his Administration, foreign and domestic, to chop off nine or ten months of his effective Presidency before Watergate did indeed start consuming it.

†Kissinger, *Years of Upheaval* (Boston: Little Brown, 1982), p. 102.
‡*Ibid.*, p. 105.

Harlow, who greatly admires Nixon, worked for him for a while in the White House, and believes he got a raw deal in Watergate, thinks somebody must have wounded Nixon very deeply when he was young, "somebody in his family, or maybe a girl." Elliot Richardson tells of a moment when he tried to break through the tough-guy shell. At Camp David, on April 1, 1973, after he had accepted the appointment as Attorney General, he said: "Mr. President, there's one thing I've been wanting to say to you for a long time. I wish somehow down inside yourself you could come to believe that you have really won . . . If you could only bring yourself to reach out with magnanimity toward your former opponents . . ." Richardson says, "I don't think he really got it."

The political consequences of Watergate are still working their way through American government. The reminder that Presidents are not above the law should not have been necessary, but it was, and it is good to have the lesson there in the history books. Watergate was checks and balances on a heroic scale. The system did work, and after many years of domestic disorder, the trauma of Viet Nam, and the struggle of Watergate itself, that was welcome news for a nation that had not had recent cause to congratulate itself.

There were costs: some decline in respect for the Presidency, especially a decline in public willingness to assume the President and his Administration are telling the truth. Skepticism lingers. But the office of President is substantially recovered—partly the passage of time, and equally important, Ronald Reagan's superb enactment of Being President, including the ability to get reelected and break the string of one-term Presidencies.

Perhaps the most enduring political consequence of Watergate was the line of succession it set up, extending into three Presidencies. Watergate put Gerald Ford into the White House in 1974, it certainly helped the under-experienced Jimmy Carter get nominated and elected in 1976, and Carter's vulnerabilities helped Ronald Reagan win in 1980. In the fall of 1984, Reagan was still running against Jimmy Carter—in the shape of the "Carter-Mondale Administration." By then, to be sure, Reagan's phenomenal personal appeal had transcended the Watergate antecedents of his Presidency. He never mentioned Ford or Nixon, his two immediate Republican predecessors, during the 1984 campaign. Richard Nixon, for his part, in conversations before the 1984 election could offer a very detailed and accurate prediction of the voting results without ever mentioning Ronald Reagan by name. These two Californians have intensely mixed feelings about each other.

PART V

"Disgustingly Sane"

10

—◆—

Gerald Ford

I was first introduced to Gerald Ford by Neil MacNeill of *Time*, one of the rare Washington journalists who think Congress—and particularly the House—is the best beat in the world. Neil told me this Michigan congressman, then of only middling seniority, had a bold ambition—to be Speaker of the House. He would make it, too, if the Republicans could ever recapture the House. They still haven't.

In a complexity contest among the nine modern Presidents, one is tempted to say right away that Jerry Ford would come in last. But that isn't quite right. Perhaps it would be a three-way tie between Ford, Kennedy, and Reagan—each being mainly what they seem to be but not entirely. In Ford's case, along with the hearty, gregarious Big Ten pol, the quintessential good guy, there is also a very contained, stolid man who can keep his own counsel.

"I am disgustingly sane," Ford once admitted. It is possible, of course, to be totally sane and quite complicated—witness Dwight Eisenhower. Ford is more open and less complicated than Ike was, and his mind doesn't move as swiftly as Ike's did. Not that speed—or complexity—necessarily equates with intelligence.

The performance of Presidents compels us to think what we mean by "intelligence" as applied to the highest level of political leadership. I have more to say about this in Chapter 19 in appraising the indisputably bright Jimmy Carter. But Ford conveyed none of the pent-up nervous energy of Ike or JFK, the hooded cunning of LBJ, or the darting, calculating agility of Nixon. Ford's calm and often plodding public style could fool people. Hence the discovery, periodically announced by someone coming away from a first private meeting with Ford, "You know, that man is *smart!*" (Ford graduated in the top third of his Yale

Law School class.) Lyndon Johnson loved telling his Ford stories—Jerry had played too much football without a helmet, and so on—but Lyndon was himself smart enough to know better.

The Honeymoon

I thought Gerald Ford was somewhat overpraised, and still is, for his "healing" role after Watergate, and was and still is underesteemed for the rest of his Presidency. The title of his autobiography, *A Time to Heal,** perpetuates this approach to his Presidency. And Jimmy Carter, in the gracious opening sentence of his Inaugural, January 20, 1977, said, "For myself and for our nation, I want to thank my predecessor for all he has done to heal our land."

But unless Nixon had been succeeded by, say, Bob Haldeman or John Mitchell, no successor could have failed to "heal." I sat in the House Press Gallery on the night of August 12, when Ford made his acceptance–inaugural–State of the Union speech to Congress. This was perhaps the most moving presidential speech I have ever heard. The language was mainly that of the gifted and cantankerous Robert Hartmann, but the ideas and mood were pure Jerry Ford. You could sense how deeply the Congress, the Democrats no less than the Republicans, wanted him to do well. And the almost athletic delivery, as this very confident and well-coordinated man rocked back and forth behind the rostrum, reinforced the rapport with the very masculine body that was his immediate audience.

"Part of my heart will always be here on Capitol Hill," Ford said. In recent months he had often "protested that I was my own man." But this was wrong. "I am your man, for it was your carefully weighed confirmation that changed my occupation. The truth is I am the people's man, for you acted in their name . . ."

It was exactly the right note. But I think any reasonably presentable Republican untainted by Watergate could have carried off the transition. The country was all ready to be vastly "relieved." The press, *Time* and *People* included, delighted in reporting how the new President in his modest suburban Alexandria, Virginia, house went to the door stoop to pick up the morning paper, swam some laps out in back, and even toasted his own English muffins!

Ford, in short, was not Nixon. And the country, whatever trauma it had been undergoing, seemed to adjust within days to not having a trauma. TV may have played an oddly therapeutic role, by familiarizing

*Harper and Row, 1979.

people with fantastic situations. Thus Gladys and Kurt Lang, in their Watergate study *The Battle for Public Opinion* cite Frederick Davis, sociologist at the University of California, San Diego: "The depiction of the most extraordinary events through the everyday routines and practices of news coverage familiar to audiences everywhere helped make the extraordinary ordinary, thus contributing to the tranquil, unemotional response to the end of Watergate."*

In any event, there were no riots in the streets, nor recorded fistfights in bars, when Nixon fell. There were substantial numbers of Americans, up to 24 percent in the Gallup Poll just before the resignation, who still generally "approved" his Presidency. But even in his best days Nixon had not attracted truly fervent followers, comparable to those who worshiped JFK, Ike, and FDR. Nixon supporters admired his ability without particularly warming to the man. Jerry Ford came in on a wave of goodwill and welcome.

I think Lyndon Johnson's performance in November–December 1963 was much more remarkable. He was the crude and graceless fellow succeeding the martyred prince, murdered in Johnson's own state. Ford was the friendly and likable fellow succeeding the odd and awkward President who had been forced to resign. In that role, Ford did very well at an easy job.

The honeymoon lasted exactly one month. When Ford announced his pardon of Nixon, I was among the many who were outraged. (Ford's approval rating in the polls fell from 71 percent to 50 percent.) I thought the legal process should have been allowed to run: Nixon should be indicted, tried, and then if convicted, given a pardon. I didn't want to see him in jail, but I did want to see him in court. It was not just a matter of justice; I'm afraid also I may have become something of a Watergate junkie. This was probably true of a good many journalists and at least a part of our audience. We were glad to have a clean new President, but we wanted to keep on learning scandalous things about the old President.

Today I think that Ford made a wise decision, essentially for the reasons he stated at the time. He believed the pardon would help "put Watergate behind us," and free him, the Congress, the press, and the country to turn to other concerns. Word reached him that the Special Prosecutor, Leon Jaworski, thought it would take at least a year to bring Nixon to trial. Ford was right to question whether a fair trial of Richard

*Gladys and Kurt Lang, *The Battle for Public Opinion* (New York: Columbia University Press, 1983), p. 8.

Nixon would by then be possible. Appeals, if there had been a conviction, would drag on, and Watergate would endlessly preoccupy the public—and upstage Ford's Presidency. He was also influenced, more than he wanted to say at the time, by what he was told of Nixon's health, physical and mental. Ford's sensitivity to this and his restraint in discussing it, for the sake of a friend of twenty-five years and for the honor of the Presidency, do him credit.

But was there a deal, the pardon in payment for the resignation? No, though Ford on August 1, 1974, foolishly permitted Al Haig, Nixon's Chief of Staff, to discuss the possibility of a pardon in front of him. Even if Ford had been so unscrupulous as to want to deal, there was no need of it. By that time everybody in Washington knew Ford was soon to become President, either through Nixon's resignation or his impeachment and conviction. And Ford didn't need Haig to tell him that Presidents have the power to pardon. Still, the mention of a pardon to the President-to-be was an impropriety on Haig's part, and Ford was careless not to cut him off at once. He recognized as much by phoning Haig on August 2 and in the presence of witnesses reading off a stiff little statement: "I want you to understand that I have no intention of recommending what the President should do about resigning or not resigning and that nothing we talked about yesterday afternoon should be given any consideration in whatever decision the President may wish to make."*

Controversy over the pardon boiled on for weeks, and so on October 17, Ford voluntarily appeared before a subcommittee of the House Judiciary Committee to reaffirm: "There was no deal, period, under no circumstances." He was the first President to testify before a congressional committee since George Washington. Three liberal Democrats, led by the implacable Elizabeth Holtzman of Brooklyn, remained skeptical; the rest of the subcommittee, the Democrats as well as Republicans, were satisfied.†

---

*A Time to Heal, p. 13.

†Seymour Hersh revived the charge of a deal in an article in the *Atlantic Monthly,* August 1983. A powerful rebuttal appeared in the *National Review* of October 14, 1983, written by Robert McClory, a Republican congressman from Illinois for twenty years, author of one of the articles of impeachment brought against Nixon and coauthor of another. McClory calls the Hersh article a mishmash of "unidentified sources, clandestine conversations and unsupported allegations by some of Ford's bitterest political enemies." McClory points out that even after the Haig-Ford conversations of August 1–2, 1974, Nixon for several days still talked of fighting it out in the impeachment proceedings. In his article McClory discloses for the first time that he conveyed to the White House on August 6 assurances from several key Democrats, including Speaker Albert and Chairman Peter Rodino of the Judiciary Committee, that if Nixon resigned, they hoped there would be no criminal proceedings against him. It was after hearing this news, McClory believes, that Nixon finally made up his mind.

A Bad Case of Stagflation

If he could get Watergate to go away, Gerald Ford could take a good look at the most difficult economic situation inherited by any of the postwar Presidents. Inflation was running over 12 percent, the highest rate (until Carter) in our peacetime history. Interest rates were the highest in a century, and the housing industry was flat. The securities markets were sickly.

Some of the troubles had been stored up for Ford by the Johnson Administration with its guns-plus-butter policy during the Viet Nam buildup, and by the Nixon Administration, with its expansion of social programs and its misguided wage and price freeze of 1971–72, followed, of course, by a wage and price surge. Then in 1973–74, triggered by the Yom Kippur war and Arab oil embargo, prices of crude increased fourfold. The malady known as stagflation was appearing all over the Western industrial world.

Ford tried to rally the country in September and October to Whip Inflation Now—WIN. The pep-talk assault on inflation was predictably getting nowhere even as unemployment was becoming a bigger worry to the White House. The country was heading into the worst recession since 1937–38.

The gathering recession and Watergate and the pardon all figured in the congressional elections in November. When the Republicans lost forty-three House seats and four in the Senate, it could not be dismissed as a normal off-year result: there had been no "abnormal" Republican gains in the previous election; the Nixon sweep against McGovern in 1972 had scarcely dented the substantial Democratic majorities in both houses.

While Ford was a congressman his voting record had been a touch to the right of President Eisenhower and noticeably right of Nixon. In national office, he moved to the center. In one blunt conversation about civil rights, after he had become Vice-President, he said: "Forget the voting record. The voting record reflects Grand Rapids."

There was an amalgam of Grand Rapids and presidential perspectives in an interview Ford gave half a dozen of us from *Fortune.** Wariness about "expectations" was a major theme:

"When you set a timetable or a goal you do raise expectations. In our energy program we say by 1985 we have to be invulnerable to foreign challenges as far as energy is concerned. I don't think that

*April 1975.

is bad. But setting a goal for the total ending of segregation by a certain date is raising an expectation which you cannot necessarily achieve.

"An energy goal is something material. Desegregation involves such a human element, as well as what the law says, that raising that expectation can bring about some disillusionment and loss of faith in government and loss of faith in the system."

And another favorite theme, the menace of ever-rising transfer payments (Social Security, medicare, food stamps, etc.):

"If you take the transfer-payment growth for the last two decades —it is about 9 percent per year—and continue [to] the year 2000, 50 percent of the people will be living off the other 50 percent.

"I don't think that we are over the cliff, but it is something we have to stop now. As more people get on those transfer payments, they become a political force and the programs are . . . self-perpetuating."

In 1975–76, considering the Republican weakness in Congress, Ford did fairly well with his legislative program. He initiated an ambitious energy program and got some of it through Congress, he chipped away at excesses of the regulatory agencies, and put through a $23-billion tax cut for individuals and corporations, the first cut since the Kennedy-Johnson measure of 1964. Ford was sustained in forty-nine out of sixty-one vetoes, mainly of spending bills, including Democratic programs for higher farm-price supports, bigger housing subsidies, and more public service jobs. The unemployment figures began leveling out in late 1975. With a large assist from the recession, the rate of inflation had been reduced to 4.8 percent when Ford left office.

Ford "hung tough" on monetary policy, as Richard Cheney puts it. Cheney, senior White House administrative aide for the last half of Ford's tenure, now a Wyoming congressman, means by this that Ford made it clear to his own staff and Cabinet and to congressional leaders that he supported the Federal Reserve's rigorous measures to wring inflation out of the economy. Chairman Arthur Burns met once a month with Ford and recalls a President of "immense integrity," who never by any remark or question trespassed on the independence of the Fed. Once Ford told Burns he had a question that might be inappropriate, and if so, the chairman should of course ignore it and the President would understand. The Washington *Post* and *New York Times* were publishing alarming stories about a federal list of "problem banks," including some of the biggest in the country—how serious was the situation? Burns assured Ford the question was entirely proper and analyzed the problems of the problem banks as being manageable.*

Presidents tend to get too much credit, and too much blame, for the ups and downs of the business cycle. But they do have important influence on the economy. Ford's basic free-market orientation led him, as a *Fortune* editorial said in October 1976, "to insist that the economy would pull out of the recession without massive stimulus and that the recovery would be healthier without it." He was right on both counts.

Ford was an excessively amiable administrator—with clear and sensible views of the job of President. "Almost by definition," he writes, "the decisions that must be made in the Oval Office are difficult. If they're easy, they're made elsewhere in the federal bureaucracy." He freely admitted that he liked the work. "I couldn't wait to start the day."†

But he worried about the future of the office. Four years after he left the White House, he wrote in *Time* (November 10, 1980): "We have not an imperial Presidency but an imperiled Presidency," imperiled mainly by Congress. Some of Ford's staff had thought his relationships with his old buddies on the Hill were "all too good"—the congressmen kept invading "the time of the President, the most valuable natural resource in this city." But for all his love of the Congress, Ford thought it was gaining too much power even as it was losing the ability to act responsibly. The "reforms" of the late 1960s had "messed up" the real workings of Congress; the leadership could no longer lead; party loyalty had eroded.

As a boss, Ford presided over an unholy amount of White House infighting. He was not deliberately pitting people against each other, as FDR did, but seemed unable to control his staff. Ford people fought with leftover Nixon people. Vice-President Nelson Rockefeller and his staff contended with the able and fiercely ambitious Donald Rumsfeld, chief administrative assistant to the President, then Secretary of De-

---

*Burns found Ford a refreshing change after Nixon. Early in 1971, Burns recalls, Nixon "released" Charles Colson, one of his nastier operatives, to work on the Fed. First Colson floated a Nixon "plan" to put the Fed under Treasury control, then a plan to enlarge the Fed's Board of Governors from seven members to perhaps fifteen. Then he spread a report that even as Arthur Burns was making speeches urging wage restraint, he was privately lobbying to get his own salary raised. "That hurt," Burns says. The fact was he had written the Office of Management and Budget supporting previous presidential recommendations that the Fed chairman's pay be restored to parity with Cabinet officers; but Burns urged this not be done until inflation was brought under control and in any event should not apply to him but to his successors.

Years later Colson, having been born again, came to Burns and begged forgiveness, which the good doctor issued. Colson also proposed that Burns pray with him, and Burns saw no harm in that.

†*A Time to Heal,* p. 259.

fense (later President Reagan's Middle East negotiator for a brief period). Rumsfeld's protégé and successor, Dick Cheney, fought with the same people Rumsfeld had.

Ford simply hated to lay down the law. He could never bring himself to rein in Robert Hartmann, his senior aide for years on Capitol Hill, who could craft superb speeches that sounded exactly like what Jerry Ford would say if he were more eloquent. (Unlike some of the rich purple passages my friend Emmet Hughes drafted for Eisenhower; I was often surprised when Ike was willing to speak them.) But Hartmann was also a terrible-tempered prima donna who expected the same primacy and access in the White House he had enjoyed when Ford was a congressman. His highly readable and colored memoir is aptly titled *Palace Politics.**

Ford's executive permissiveness also exposed him to some costly "Oh-By-the-Way" situations—Cheney's nice description of a White House staff nightmare. Thus Secretary of Labor John Dunlop, coming to see the President for half an hour about something else, says on his way out of the Oval Office, Oh, by the way, he thinks he should testify in behalf of the bill to legalize *common situs* picketing. He briefly recalls the reasons, and Ford says, Sure. Dunlop goes way out on a limb advocating the bill, Ford vetoes it, Dunlop honorably resigns, the building trades unions are incensed in an election year. The question had not been at all "staffed out"—by the White House, OMB, etc.—when Ford gave his casual OK to Dunlop.

Ho Chi Minh City and Vladivostok

In his first months in office, even as he was contending with a fractious staff and a severe recession, Gerald Ford was facing the most severe foreign policy defeat ever suffered by the United States. The Viet Nam defeat was in no way of his making, but it was his lot to sit helpless in the Oval Office during the collapse of a country and government we had sacrificed so much to defend. The Communists no longer made any pretense that indigenous Viet Cong "cadres" could conquer South Viet Nam and humble Thieu's mighty patron across the Pacific. Fourteen line divisions of North Vietnamese regulars administered the coup de grace.

The last rescue helicopters lifted from the roof of the U.S. Embassy in Saigon—within days to be renamed Ho Chi Minh City—on April 30,

*New York: McGraw-Hill, 1980.

1975. The U.S. effort in Viet Nam had gone on for twenty years, under five Presidents. It had been a major American war for eight years, the longest war in our history, under Johnson and Nixon. The total direct cost was $111 billion, 303,000 American wounded, 47,400 dead in combat. (Almost as heavy as our combat losses in World War I, heavier than our losses in Korea.)

In its last throes, the Thieu regime had appealed desperately for U.S. air support and emergency shipments of ammunition, fuel, spare parts. Ford and Kissinger with almost equal desperation pressed the case on Congress. But Congress felt the U.S. had done enough.

Some of the Ford-Kissinger language of those days was so overwrought that I thought they were making our impending defeat even more grievous than it needed to be. They had been applying to events in Cambodia and Viet Nam "a kind of twilight-of-civilization rhetoric," I said in a speech in April in Illinois, and they "even urged the world to believe that if these regimes fell, it would be because the United States had betrayed them." Much of the damage to our "credibility" was self-inflicted—"shockingly enough" by the President and his Secretary of State. These remarks ran in a *Time* Essay (May 19, 1975), and Kissinger later told me, in the English idiom: "I take your point."

Ford was large enough and secure enough to feel utterly unthreatened by Kissinger's brilliance. He thought Henry deserved his fame and the country should be proud of him. Once, toward the end of his Vice-Presidency, when Ford was talking to me about foreign policy, we were each expressing high admiration for Kissinger and I said I hoped Kissinger was aware of Ford's opinion. (I was one of I don't know how many dozen people on whom Kissinger from time to time tried out his gloomy musings as to when he should resign.) Ford seemed amazed that there could be any doubt of his esteem for Henry, but if there was, he would certainly clear it up.

Within a fortnight of the fall of Saigon, Ford and Kissinger got a chance to work off a little of the nation's frustration. On May 12 (Washington time) word arrived in the Oval Office that Cambodian gunboats had seized the U.S. merchantman *Mayaguez* in international waters off the coast of Cambodia. In his memoirs, Ford frankly describes the incident as an "opportunity" to show the world "proof of our resolve." Ford was thinking of the *Pueblo* incident in 1968 (its crew imprisoned in North Korea for nearly a year) as well as our humiliation in Viet Nam.

Diplomatic efforts to free the *Mayaguez* crew and recover the ship were pursued unsuccessfully via China and the UN. U.S. reconnaissance planes, Marines, helicopters, destroyers, and carriers were marshaled. In the fighting, the U.S. suffered forty-one dead and fifty wounded—and freed the thirty-nine crew members unharmed. Ford bounced up in the polls—a young Democratic congressman from Kentucky said, "It's good to win for a change."* Some critics took a kind of cash-register approach —the operation was wrong because more Americans were killed than freed. Another objection was that the crew might soon have been freed by the Khmer Rouge with no military intervention on our part. Possibly so. There was no way of knowing, though the subsequent record of the Khmer Rouge in dealing with their own people is not reassuring.

The modern Presidents face agonizing choices in trying to protect U.S. citizens in jeopardy from rogue governments and terrorists, and no incident is just like the last one. Carter, of course, thought of *Mayaguez* and *Pueblo* when he gambled on the Iran rescue mission, and Reagan was determined to avoid "another Iran" (among other purposes) in Grenada, where the American medical students may or may not have been in danger.

In the *Mayaguez* episode it was a relief for Ford to be able to act without seeking congressional sanction, to go in and get out—four days' elapsed time—before any congressional furor could arise. Ford was the first President to exercise his foreign policy responsibilities under the constraints of the War Powers Act. He considers it unconstitutional, and Reagan audibly chafes under its restrictions. "Every once in a while," Ford remarked recently, "the President has to have the flexibility to really stir the pot."†

Ford felt the full effects of the new congressional assertiveness in foreign policy, and aides heard this normally mild-mannered man apply "remarkably foul language" to some of his old friends up on the Hill. The bipartisan consensus of 1941–65 had been broken in Viet Nam and Watergate; Congress, including senators and representatives of the President's own party, was no longer willing to assume the President knows best. In my own view, a greater congressional involvement in foreign policy is healthy in principle, and I argued to that effect in many speeches and articles during the Nixon and Ford administrations. But the practical applications of the principle can indeed be messy.

Within his first days in office, Ford was confronted by a congressio-

*A Time to Heal, p. 284.
†The New York Times, November 8, 1983.

nal move to embargo U.S. arms shipments to Turkey, the eastern anchor of NATO's Mediterranean position. In response to a coup in Cyprus inspired by the military junta governing Greece, another (somewhat less important) NATO ally, the Turks invaded Cyprus and occupied about two-fifths of its territory, though the Turkish population on the island was only about a fifth of the total. Both parties to the old and miserable "Cyprus problem" were deeply in the wrong. But a few influential senators and representatives especially sensitive to the Greek-American vote (there is no noticeable Turkish-American vote) persuaded their colleagues that Turkey should be punished. The embargo on arms deliveries went into effect in February 1975. Jerry Ford is seldom bitter in *A Time to Heal,* but of the embargo he writes (p. 138): "Congress was determined to interfere with the President's traditional right to manage foreign policy, and if this interference had dire consequences for the country as a whole, well, that was just too bad." And again: Just before Ford left on a trip to Europe, July 1975: "Congress slapped me in the face by refusing to lift its embargo . . . I considered this the single most irresponsible, short-sighted foreign policy decision Congress had made in all the years I'd been in Washington" (pp. 301–2). (The embargo was finally lifted during the Carter Administration.)

Another reckless act in Ford's view was the Senate vote a few months later to prohibit $25 million worth of assistance to pro-West forces in the civil war in Angola, against Marxist forces propped up by Cuban troops. The large Senate majority (54–22) feared "another Viet Nam."

If "the Greek vote" was a new influence in the U.S. foreign policy, the "Jewish vote" was a much more familiar force. Its chief impact on foreign policy had been in the thoroughly understandable concern of American Jews for the safety of Israel. But in 1974, Ford felt "the Jewish vote" was being cynically interjected into a new sphere of policy, U.S.-Soviet relations, with great risk to détente. Senator Henry Jackson was sponsoring legislation denying liberalized trade treatment for the Soviets unless they agreed in writing to permit 50,000 Jews a year to emigrate. Jackson, Ford writes, "was about to launch his Presidency campaign, and he was playing politics to the hilt" (p. 139).

Kissinger has written that his protracted negotiations with Jackson made him "long for the relative tranquillity of the Middle East."[*] Kissinger and Nixon in quiet diplomacy had worked the rate of exit permits

Years of Upheaval, p. 991.

up from 400 a year to 35,000, and Soviet Ambassador Anatoly Dobrinin had told Ford the flow could go to 50,000—not, however, as a publicly acknowledged quid pro quo for the easing of trade restrictions. For broad economic policy reasons, Ford reluctantly signed a trade bill burdened by the Jackson-Vanik amendment, and the Soviets in 1975 allowed only 13,000 Jews to leave. But the Soviets seemed to get used to Jackson-Vanik. During the Carter Administration, even though the amendment remained in effect, the outflow reached a record 51,000 in 1979.

Scoop Jackson notwithstanding, Ford and Kissinger in November 1974 had a productive meeting with Brezhnev at Vladivostok. They made considerable progress toward SALT II. In a touching passage in his book, Ford tells of a limousine ride around the Siberian port, with the Soviet dictator tightly gripping the President's hand while they talked through an interpreter of their responsibility to "all mankind."* Years later I asked Ford how much weight he put on such a moment. "I've thought about that a lot . . . He was genuine. I don't think it was any trick." I asked if we should try to get Reagan and Brezhnev's successor Andropov into a limo together. Ford's somewhat delphic answer: "It is a little different because Andropov speaks English." But yes, it's good for world leaders to get to know each other.

In an interview in 1975 Ford gave me a prudent assessment of détente: "On balance, it has been a relationship that has given both sides enough benefits to justify its continuation. . . . As long as we are realistic about détente and don't expect it to be the millennium, I think we can build from that relationship and use it for not only the relaxation of tensions between ourselves and the Soviet Union, but as an instrument in calming fears, holding back rash action and keeping the world relatively quiet so we can work for the solution of the problems on a regional basis around the world." I asked, "How close do you think that would be to Brezhnev's definition of détente?" Ford: "Relatively close. Those are the words I hear, and I think the actions taken fit."†

At his second meeting with Brezhnev, in mid-summer 1975, Ford could not get SALT II totally buttoned down. Looking back now, he thinks the U.S. and the Soviets had gone "95 percent of the way" to an agreement. But "we got all involved in the political situation in 1976 and there was no practical way to push that last 5 percent without

*A Time to Heal, pp. 218–19.
†Time, July 28.

having some difficult political problems here in the United States."

Ford played no pioneering role in détente, but he managed the new relationship with the Soviets with skill and steadiness in circumstances more difficult than Nixon had faced. Ford never had the domestic political base that Nixon enjoyed through 1972; he was up against the new rambunctiousness of Congress in foreign policy, and the fall of Saigon had inflicted some damage to U.S. "credibility." The damage was not so severe, fortunately, as Ford and Kissinger were proclaiming at one time.

Ford and Kissinger were attentive to the China corner of triangular diplomacy, but achieved no progress toward a full normalization of relations. Chou was dying, Mao was increasingly feeble, and the leadership was clearly in transition. After the euphoria of the original opening to China, there was some letdown on both sides.

Ford made the now almost obligatory trip to Beijing in December 1975, and found Vice Premier Teng a tough bargainer, "cordial but firm."* After the long years in quarantine, the Chinese must be amused to have become a standard backdrop for U.S. presidential campaigns— Nixon in 1972, Ford in late 1975, Reagan in April 1984, and Carter would have loved to go in 1980 if the Iran hostage crisis hadn't intervened.

A Man of Substance

Ronald Reagan, in his almost successful effort to take the Republican nomination away from Ford, was vigorously denouncing détente and often seemed to be running against Dr. Kissinger. Ford dumped his Vice-President, Nelson Rockefeller, to try to placate the conservative wing of the party, and some years later told me it was the only act of his Presidency he was ashamed of. At the Kansas City convention of 1976, one of the more lively of recent years, there was electricity in all the appearances and movements of Kissinger, Rockefeller, Reagan, and the phlegmatic Ford himself, as well as those he pondered for VP. (I thought, not for the first time, of the appalling cruelty of politics—and the press—when Senator Howard Baker felt compelled to explain to some of us, at breakfast in the Muehlebach Hotel, all about his wife's drinking problem, instead of just saying, Go to hell.)

The vigorous assault from within his own party unquestionably hurt Ford going into the campaign against Carter—just as the Ted Kennedy

*A Time to Heal, p. 337.

attack weakened Carter in 1980 (though Kennedy came nowhere so close to unseating his own President as Reagan did). There are frosty references to Reagan in Ford's memoirs. As late as 1983 I heard him refer, in connection with a forthcoming legislative impasse, to the need for a bargain between "my good friend the President of the United States, and my very good friend the Speaker of the House [Democrat Tip O'Neill]."

Ford's best issue—détente having become controversial—might have been the economic recovery. But unfortunately for him, it was a recovery from a situation he inherited from another Republican President. And he wasn't articulate or interesting in explaining his economic policies, first against Reagan, then against Carter. To offset the Republican success in squeezing inflation out of the economy, a Democratic economist, Arthur Okun, had invented the "misery index"—inflation plus unemployment. It was running around 12 to 14 percent through most of campaign year 1976. (In campaign year 1980, Jimmy Carter would just as soon the misery index had never been discovered; it hit 24 percent.)

But the heaviest disability for Ford was probably the pardon, which linked him inescapably to Nixon and Watergate. It was the pardon that permitted Carter both in the Democratic primaries and in the general election to campaign chiefly on the plank of his own goodness. The American people were also good, he said, and deserved an administration of equal goodness.

Ford was the only appointed President in our history, he had never won a national election, and he had pardoned the disgraced President who had made him Vice-President. He didn't quite have complete legitimacy. More than for Johnson in 1964 or Truman in 1948, Ford's effort in 1976 to win a term "in his own right" had a special poignance.

To come as close as Ford did to defeating Carter, despite the pardon and despite the bruising fight within the Republican Party, was a considerable political accomplishment. Ford was a decent and generally sensible President. When I later told Carter how much trouble I had deciding how to vote in 1976, I said I thought Ford all in all was a good President. Carter said at once: "So did I." I think he genuinely admired Ford. He also preferred, understandably, to have defeated no hack but a man of real substance—and he had.

PART VI

*My Year in
the West Wing*

11

Going to Work for Jimmy Carter

From Jerry Ford all the way back to FDR is quite a span of personalities —and history. I had been lucky to be there.

From forty years of acquaintance with Presidents, a vivid miscellany of episodes and encounters and perhaps a useful insight or two came to mind as I mulled Jimmy Carter's job offer in mid-July 1979. The reporter or editor visiting in the White House carries with him some privileges and immunities, including a certain lack of responsibility. What would it be like to hurry to the Oval Office at the summons of the President as boss, who is expecting wise advice about—God knows what? And what about Carter himself? I was prepared to believe he was a pleasant man to work for, as he had touchingly assured me, but could I actually help him? Might he perhaps look better in history than he did in that summer of our discontent? Even if not, wasn't he, for at least the next eighteen months, "the only President [as LBJ used to say] you've got"?

I deliberated only a day or two. I decided that no self-respecting political reporter (and lapsed history student) could turn down a chance to know a Presidency up close.

I told the President yes. The press descended upon me; I was taciturn (but of course read my notices avidly). With my new employer's permission, I went ahead with long-laid plans for a vacation barge trip on the Marne-Saône canals.

When I reported for work on August 15, I was met by an agreeable

young man named Val Giannini, who took me through the fingerprint-
ing, pointed out the men's room, and said this must be like the first day
of school, noting, "You haven't had one of those for quite a while." Very
true.

I sat down in the Watergate Hotel that night to start a journal. I
wrote from about 10 PM to midnight. I was too tired to go on but had
only covered from 10 AM up to the last course of a lunch in the Family
Dining Room with the President, Rosalynn, and six or eight others. The
second night I wrote up the rest of the first afternoon. Meanwhile the
second day's events had piled up. I decided this was silly. A thoughtful
friend gave me a tape recorder; there had been technological developments since I kept a diary as an eight-year-old. I eventually settled into
a pattern of "evening notes" once or twice a week and "weekend
notes" on planes to and from New York.

Like any aspiring bureaucrat, I swiftly concerned myself with office
space. I got wind of a vast vacant suite in the grand old Executive Office
Building, the French Renaissance château that accommodated the
whole State, War, and Navy departments in the nineteenth century.
Now it is merely one of the overflows from the White House for the
presidential establishment. The particular chambers I lusted after had
once been the domain of Secretaries of the Navy, a point of some
additional appeal to a former lieutenant junior grade. But I was told
firmly that the President wanted me in the West Wing of the White
House, and might think it odd if I preferred an office across the street
in the EOB. "Proximity is very important around here," said the emissary.

Still more important, of course, is direct access to the President,
though it is not always spelled out who has it and who doesn't—and of
those who have it, which ones keep it only so long as they don't use it
very much. (The latter is the general lot of Cabinet officers outside the
Big Four—State, Defense, Treasury, Justice.) In the White House announcement that I would be providing the President with substantive
advice on the full range of issues coming before him, foreign and domestic, there was also a little signal to the bureaucracy: "Mr. Donovan
will report only to the President."

When the President stressed this same point in our private conversation about the job, it was just after Hamilton Jordan had accumulated
some embarrassing publicity about a questionnaire he had distributed
to the White House senior staff and all Cabinet officers. They were asked

to rate their subordinates on loyalty and various other virtues, including what time they came to work in the morning. The official filling out this report card could check one of various boxes, from 6:30 AM to 6:45, 6:45 to 7:00, and so forth. I told the President I had read about Jordan's questionnaire and said, "I think I have to warn you I tend to come to work about ten AM." The President smiled in a rather wan way and we went on from there. He got up around 5:30.

But Carter has a remarkable memory. When I reported for work a month later he began telling me some of the meetings he wanted me to attend. The first one he mentioned was his regular Friday morning "Foreign Policy Breakfast," which included only the Vice-President, the Secretaries of State and Defense, plus Zbigniew Brzezinski and Hamilton Jordan—and he wanted to include me as I came aboard. But the President said he seemed to remember "some problem about your rising habits—these breakfasts are at seven thirty." I said I thought once a week I could work it out.

I had to yield on the 10:00 AM policy (too many White House meetings were scheduled for 8:30 and 9:00), but first I did get a little publicity as the only White House staffer who dared to come in at midmorning. Early in my White House year I ran into Irving Kristol, the neoconservative high priest, who congratulated me on the wonderful thing I was doing for the country. For a brief moment I was foolish enough to think Irving was just another of my earnest friends admiring "the sacrifice" I had made in going to Washington. No, it was that I was revolutionizing government by staying in bed until a reasonable hour.

After the White House issued its spacious job description, some of my journalistic friends, clutching for historical parallels, told me there had been nothing like my position since Colonel House under Woodrow Wilson or Harry Hopkins in the days of FDR. So far as I know there literally never has been a White House position set up the way mine was. There was certainly no resemblance to the plenipotentiary roles of Colonel House or Harry Hopkins, or the political ties that bound them to their Presidents and vice versa. One newspaper said I was to be the northern Charles Kirbo. That wasn't it at all. I was secretly hoping some paper would call me the "Congregationalist Cardinal Richelieu." Nobody did, and I wasn't.

Nor was there much resemblance to two adviser experiments Lyndon Johnson had tried. In December 1963 he appointed Eric Goldman, a Princeton historian, to be a kind of emissary to the academic and intellectual world. Goldman was given an office in the EOB. He contributed to speech drafts, and sent some interesting memos to the President. Goldman was pushed around some by the senior staff, and he once enraged LBJ because a few invited guests snubbed a White House gathering Goldman had arranged to show intellectuals that Johnson, despite Viet Nam, was not a monster. Goldman chose to leave about a year after that episode. With Goldman's experience in mind, I resisted journalistic efforts to classify my job as "philosopher in residence." My line was: "No, there are a lot of philosophers around here."

Johnson brought the journalist Robert Kintner into the White House in 1966. Johnson admired Kintner, a former columnist and NBC executive, but never figured out how he wanted to use him, and Kintner left after a year.

Nixon, as Watergate was closing in on him, appointed John Connally an adviser-without-portfolio. Connally got a chance to deliver one pungent piece of advice—that Nixon should burn the tapes—but otherwise found he had nothing to do. He cleared out of the Mayflower Hotel and went back to Texas after six weeks.

I did go to those Friday morning foreign policy breakfasts. We were deployed on either side of the President at one end of the long gleaming Cabinet table, Vance on his right, Brzezinski on his left, they being the principal briefing officers. The Vice-President sat "below" Zbig, to his left, and I to Mondale's left, then to my left Counsel Lloyd Cutler, a few weeks junior to me at that table but soon to be my senior in general influence in the Carter White House. Across the table from us were Harold Brown and Hamilton Jordan.

The fate of the world might be the agenda, but people ate heartily —fruit and juice, eggs and bacon or ham or sausage, toast, Danish, doughnuts, and we were each billed, $2.55 as I recall it, by the White House Mess. I was often shocked at how frail and tired the President looked on coming into the Cabinet Room—he had had time to read and hear a good deal of bad news while most of the rest of us were still in bed. But as the white-jacketed stewards served us and the discussion flowed, Carter ate as robustly as any of us, and seemed to take on color and animation.

These were serious working sessions lasting an hour and a half, often reaching some fairly weighty decisions or at the minimum resulting in instructions, usually to State or Defense, to pursue some question further and have a memo or recommendation back by Monday, or perhaps tomorrow. I occasionally drew some assignment out of one of those breakfasts, although not often.

I had a number of private meetings with the President. Usually every other week we would have a formally scheduled thirty to forty-five minute meeting. It was understood I could get at him any time between those meetings if I had something I felt should be brought up right away. When I did want to see him, I would get to see him the same day. Those were brief five, ten, fifteen minute meetings, almost entirely on my initiative, seldom his.

He urged me to write him memos when I was so moved and I was so moved quite often. I had come from a company, Time Inc., where the memo is something of an art form, and it's a good literary exercise when the President of the United States is your audience of one. He would read my memos very promptly. I would almost always get his comment back by the end of the same day, or the following morning.

I attended Cabinet meetings, sitting not at the table, of course, but along the wall with other senior staff people. But Cabinet meetings had become a very infrequent formality. I think there were only four during the year I was in the White House.

My first morning at work the President showed me into his little private office beyond the Oval Office and spent some ninety minutes reviewing the principal problems on his mind. He talked from a handwritten list of about two dozen topics, foreign and domestic. He was in shirt sleeves, cuffs rolled halfway to the elbow, very calm and good-humored though he had just spent some painful hours wrestling with his Andrew Young problem. He talked of the black-Jewish tensions exacerbated by Young's contact with a PLO representative, and the black bitterness that could be expected if Young were fired as Ambassador to the UN. I recommended Young be fired because he was damaging national and international perceptions, never mind black or Jewish, of the President's ability to run his own Administration. I am sure Carter had already decided Young must go, though the announcement the next day of his resignation, and the explanations from the White House and Young himself, went to unusual lengths to make it seem like a voluntary departure. The White House hope, of course, was to keep Young on the reservation for 1980, and he did in fact campaign reasonably vigorously for Carter.

In retrospect the most striking thing about that conversation with the President, and a somewhat longer one, equally systematic, ten days later at Camp David, was two places that were not mentioned: Iran and Afghanistan. We talked of SALT II, NATO, Israel, Egypt, Mexico, Nicaragua, energy, the state of the dollar, the new Cabinet appointments, tensions between Cabinet and White House staff, etc., etc.—a long and sensible list, but it did not include the two countries that came to dominate the final year of the Carter Administration. I mention this not to imply that Carter (or I) should have been clairvoyant about the taking of the hostages in Iran or the Soviet invasion of Afghanistan. But holder of the modern Presidency needs to visualize contingencies, especially in foreign affairs—or at least see the need for people around him to be thinking *What If* thoughts. He and his advisers might ponder, "What if the Soviet Union moves into Afganistan?" and finally conclude it isn't likely, but at least they have had to think about possible U.S. responses.

I want to underscore the harsh fact that no matter how many tough problems a President can see on his desk, even tougher ones can materialize very suddenly—"out of nowhere." Not really out of nowhere, but feeling that way as they hit.

12

The Soviet Brigade Flap

There was no mention in my August conversations with President Carter of a Soviet "combat brigade" in Cuba, focus of a furor that was to erupt within days and preoccupy the White House for more than a month. Cuba came up only in connection with its support of revolutionary forces in Central America; the President had a farsighted view of our problems there.

The flap over the Soviet brigade gave me a memorable introduction to foreign policy management in the Carter White House. It was dismaying to see the Executive and Congress together create a superfluous crisis, in a world sufficiently dangerous with real problems.

I can't deny that it was also exciting to be in on it—to have the big black gates to the White House grounds swing open as I was arriving for an off-hours meeting, and see TV cameramen and baffled tourists peering into my car, doubtless having hoped for a glimpse of Secretary Vance or Professor Brzezinski or at least some four-star general. For at least a few days there were some gut-knotting moments. It is one thing to advise Presidents in magazine articles on everything under the sun, and something quite different to be advising *the* President *to his face* on a specific East-West showdown, and to see him listening, by all appearances with close attention. Those tremors do fade quickly, however, even for presidential advisers as for Presidents themselves. A shell begins to form: Well, somebody has to do this, and right now it happens to be me.

The White House had been justifiably concerned with the Cuban/-Soviet potential for subversion in the hemisphere. In the spring and summer of 1979 the CIA was ordered to intensify the analysis and surveillance of Soviet military activity in Cuba. This surveillance had been rather desultory for a year or two previous. Now the CIA identified a Soviet brigade of perhaps three thousand men, stationed near Havana. If this unit had "offensive capabilities," as distinct from a training role, its deployment in Cuba could have been interpreted as a violation of the Kennedy-Khrushchev agreement of 1962, which wound down the missile crisis. The distinction is a shadowy one at best since a training formation needs some combat equipment to teach with. The CIA did turn up some evidence of such equipment. But at first nobody in the Administration was very disturbed about it. There was never any indication of air- or sea-lift capability that would have allowed the brigade to operate independently outside Cuba.

Carelessly, the Administration gave assurances to the Senate Foreign Relations Committee that there were no "significant" Soviet ground forces in Cuba. Two members of the committee, facing tough reelection fights against opponents certain to label them soft-liners, were especially sensitive about Cuba. They were Richard Stone of Florida, hawkish about his neighbor island, but in trouble at home for (among other offenses) supporting the Panama Canal "giveaway," and Chairman Frank Church of Idaho, who had been indiscreet enough to visit Cuba in 1977 and get his picture in the papers with Castro. Church was for SALT II, Stone was uncommitted, and the Administration had no votes to spare. Both were indignant when in late August it began to leak all over Washington that U.S. intelligence had just spotted the brigade out of its barracks and maneuvering with "combat equipment." Church issued an ultimatum that he could not support SALT II unless the Soviets removed the brigade from Cuba.

On September 5, Secretary Vance said the presence of the Soviet brigade was a "serious matter, affecting our relations with the Soviet Union," and that the U.S. "will not be satisfied with maintenance of the status quo." On September 7, President Carter said, "The status quo is not acceptable."

I argued unsuccessfully, at two of the President's Friday morning foreign policy breakfasts and in a meeting alone with him, against such sweeping language. I suspected we were going to end up "accepting" the brigade in one way or another. We then would have to escape from the Carter-Vance formulations with, as I feared, some "hair-splitting semantic solution." Vance favored a much tougher line than Brzezinski —a reversal of their usual roles—because he feared any seeming softness on the brigade issue would be fatal to the ratification of SALT.

Carter came down on Vance's side. As late as September 25, when the artificial nature of the "crisis" seemed inescapable, the President again said publicly that the situation was "unacceptable."

Carter asked Lloyd Cutler and me to assemble some of the distinguished "alumni" of U.S. foreign policy for support and counsel.* Sixteen alumni, including all the living ex-Secretaries of State, came to the White House on September 28 and 29, a Friday and Saturday, for an evening and morning of discussions with Secretaries Vance and Brown and Admiral Stansfield Turner, director of the CIA, then a sandwich lunch with the President. (Said the *New Republic:* "The 16 men whom Lloyd Cutler and Hedley Donovan gathered to advise President Carter during the recent Cuba Panic represented just about all the accumulated modern experience of foreign policy failure.")†

The alumni, about half and half Republican and Democratic, could scarcely be considered soft on Cuba or Russia. About half of them had experienced the Cuba missile crisis firsthand, as members of Kennedy's Administration or "wise men" called in for advice. Vance and Brown had been in second-tier jobs in the Pentagon in 1962 (Carter in the Georgia legislature).

The alumni generally felt the brigade problem had been blown up out of all proportion, that very probably some such unit had been there for years. Henry Kissinger, however, was quite insistent that no such brigade had been in Cuba during his time in office. As one former naval officer at the table whispered to me: "Not on *my* watch." Some of the group felt they shouldn't have been convened at all, especially on a weekend—that it intensified the crisis atmosphere.

Yet they agreed that a crisis had indeed been allowed to arise, for the President and the country. No one refused the invitation to "advise" the President. Most of these men were in their late sixties or seventies; several came from great distances; all were senior to Carter on the national scene. To his face, however, their advice was extremely deferential. It may be that Americans are too deferential in the presence of Presidents, and that the awe for "the office," especially among men who have worked close to it, is one of the chief obstacles to a useful flow of

*Brzezinski, who thought the meeting was a bad idea, says Cutler suggested it (*Power and Principle,* p. 350). Vance, who thought it was a good idea, says Cutler and I suggested it (*Hard Choices,* p. 363). My own recollection is that it was Carter's idea. Professor Stanley Hoffman of Harvard, reviewing the Vance and Brzezinski volumes in the *New York Review of Books* (September 29, 1983), has the players all mixed up: "Lloyd Cutler supported Brzezinski, Hedley Donovan and Rosalynn Carter backed Vance."

†"Washington Diarist (M.P.)," October 20, 1979.

advice. If the alumni had any influence on the President, it was perhaps to strengthen his growing inclination to seize on any remotely helpful Soviet language as grounds for calling off the crisis.

In a national TV speech on October 1, Carter did declare himself satisfied with "significant" assurances from Brezhnev that the Soviet troops had training functions only and would stick to that. This in fact was what the Soviets had been saying all along. Diverting attention from this acceptance of the unacceptable, Carter announced increased surveillance of Cuba, creation of a new "Caribbean Joint Task Head-quarters" at Key West (still a hollow command five years later), higher priority for the previously announced Rapid Deployment Force—designed to go anywhere, but especially the Persian Gulf—and more U.S. warships for the Indian Ocean. Lest all this sound belligerent, however, he appealed again for Senate ratification of SALT II, and said the Cuba brigade uproar was "certainly no reason for a return to the Cold War."

The speech illuminated all too clearly the contradictions between the hard and soft instincts in Carter foreign policy, never really resolved. Or when they did seem briefly to be resolved, they wouldn't stay resolved.

The whole Soviet-Cuba connection, with its ramifications in Central America, Angola, and the Horn of Africa, is indeed a serious concern for U.S. security. But the old Soviet brigade in Cuba was the wrong specific to get excited about, and the whole flap did U.S. foreign policy —and Carter—considerable harm. The Soviets thought the U.S. government had manufactured this silly crisis to kill SALT II. The suspicion was understandable—and fantastically wrong. The Carter Administration and above all the President himself had seen the new arms limitation treaty as a crowning piece of statecraft as he approached the final year of his first term.

The Soviet leadership does believe some of its own propaganda— a U.S. decision to torpedo SALT, plus the U.S. rhetoric about the Rapid Deployment Force and the Indian Ocean, might have had something to do with their decision to invade Afghanistan. Or quite to the contrary, it could be that an impression of a confused and irresolute U.S. Administration contributed to the Kremlin's Afghanistan decision.

In domestic politics, certainly, the fallout was damaging to Carter. His Administration was seen to have marched up the hill, and right back down again. Not for the first time, nor the last.

In terms of my own interest in what it takes to be President, or what it should take, the brigade episode, trivial in so many ways, was richly instructive. I noted three principal points:

• In important matters, small details can become important. No chief executive of a complicated operation—especially the President of the United States—should get into details indiscriminately. (Carter seemed sometimes to have a compulsion to do this.) But there is a sort of sense of smell that warns of a certain detail that should be gotten into. Many months later, Carter told me one of the most difficult aspects of the Presidency was "how to deal with routine minutiae which could become crises." In the matter of the brigade, the fateful detail was: Are we reading a real change in Soviet military purposes in Cuba, or are we seeing a technical improvement in our reporting of what was already there? (A familiar question to police reporters asked by the City Desk to document a "crime wave.")

• Certain philosophical and practical debates about foreign policy are inevitable—and desirable—among the President's own people. But you don't want the President himself acting out both sides on prime-time TV.

• To what extent can foreign-policy-in-the-national-interest be separated from domestic politics and the personal political fears and ambitions of the principal actors? They got to be the principal actors, of course, through their prowess in our domestic democratic process or through the favor of somebody who did win an election. As elections approach, they tend to want to be reelected, or reappointed. Ex-President Carter, no less than ex-Senators Church and Stone, had perceived a personal political stake in the Cuba brigade question. To what extent are we, the voter-taxpayers, entitled to expect or hope "politics" and "policy" can be separated?

I had an understanding with Carter that I didn't want to be considered any sort of speech writer or editor of speech writers. I couldn't keep all the way out, of course. When some big foreign policy speech is coming up, the speech becomes the policy.

I sat in on a number of sessions where ten or twelve senior Administration officials were chewing, nibbling, and niggling various drafts of what became the President's October 1 speech, disposing of the brigade crisis. My magazine-editing experience was that a touch of collective editing is possible among three or four people. But the ideal number of editors in one room at one time is one.

I told the President after that speech that as a professional editor I found the whole speech-draft process appalling. He had a snappy comeback: As "a professional President" he too had found it appalling.

I stayed away from a White House staff party the night of the speech —it was the President's birthday—because I didn't want to congratulate him hypocritically on the speech, or seem churlish by saying nothing about it. I thought the President could have taken a more resolute posture toward Soviet expansionism generally, even while extricating himself from the brigade embarrassment. Admittedly that would have been a difficult literary exercise, even for a single author working alone.

I must assume (five years after Carter's crisis-dissolving speech) that a Soviet brigade is still in Cuba. Soldiers would be rotated in and out, of course, and any conscientious colonel is going to get them up off their backsides now and then and out on "maneuvers." It's just that we don't hear much about it.

13

---◆---

A Surplus of Secretaries of State

I had been in the White House six weeks or so when the President invited me to tick off some initial impressions of people and problems. I ran through various items, plus and minus, saving for last the President's peculiar preference for having his foreign policy conducted by two Secretaries of State.

I told Carter this arrangement had struck me as odd and dangerous when I was looking at his Administration from the outside, and now that I was on the inside I found the situation even more harmful than I had realized. I thought highly of both Vance and Brzezinski, but the rivalry between the two was damaging the President and confusing other governments, as well as our own.

Carter seemed startled, and for some reason a little amused. Why didn't I see if I could straighten the situation out? I said he had created the situation and was the only one who could straighten it out. Well, see what you can find out, and what you would recommend.

Most of Washington saw Zbig as the villain—a wild Polish cavalryman constantly harassing the too gentlemanly Vance. Cy is indeed a gentleman—and no slouch as a political operator himself.*

I had known both men quite well for some years and neither seemed offended by my strange mission. Brzezinski, not surprisingly, was pleased with his setup, thought "the story" was much exaggerated

---

*Some of his rivals for State noted with amusement how Vance had parked himself for a few months early in 1976 as campaign treasurer for his Yale classmate Sargent Shriver, who was never going to be nominated, while the more serious Democratic presidential candidates sorted themselves out. They also noted that Cy in his years in the foreign policy establishment had "left no tracks"—few speeches or articles, no books— in contrast with the "controversial" George Ball.

by "the media," and such trouble as there was consisted of occasional sniping by the staffs. Vance did not think the trouble was exaggerated and unburdened himself with vehemence.

After two rounds of talks with the principals and conversation with State and NSC people down the line, I told the President the situation was indeed as bad as I thought. I guessed Vance would put up with it a while longer. He had done so for three years, and he had already said publicly he would resign at the end of Carter's first term. (This was a source of some irritation to Carter, I suspected—Presidents don't like to hear Cabinet officers announce unilaterally they are leaving.)

So Carter could make a fresh start, I recommended, if he were reelected in 1980, and appoint a new Secretary of State who, I was certain, would demand a clearer charter than Vance had been allowed. Brzezinski would scarcely accept a lesser role than he had enjoyed, and Carter could appoint a more self-effacing National Security Adviser. Ideally, I thought, there should be an innovator and idea spinner as brilliant as Brzezinski, if another could be found, placed somewhere at the Under Secretary level in the State Department, or perhaps a second Deputy Secretaryship should be created for him, but he should clearly be the Secretary's man. In the White House, the model of a National Security Adviser, I thought, was General Brent Scowcroft under President Ford. Scowcroft was a man of experience, judgment, and sufficient stature to organize the flow of arguments and options that should come before the President, to order up necessary people and paper from State, Defense, CIA, without interposing his own solutions and without competing with the Secretary of State for public attention. The Secretary at that time having been Henry Kissinger, this wouldn't have been much of a contest anyway.

To all this, Carter said that a "strong President" who wants to take active direction of foreign policy is going to need a strong National Security Adviser in the White House to help him perform this large presidential role. It was hopeless to look for any creative thinking from State, whereas Zbig was constantly coming up with innovative approaches—some foolish, to be sure, but that flow of new ideas was indispensable to the President. ("Feisty" was the President's somewhat inadequate word for Zbig.) It was not new, Carter said, this competition, if you want to look at it that way, between NSC and State, and it necessarily means a somewhat reduced role for the Secretary of State. Thus Nixon, a "strong" foreign policy President (whatever else you might say about him), had Kissinger in the White House through most of his administration and a "passive" Secretary of State, William Rogers. But Ford, a "passive" foreign policy President, could be satisfied with Scowcroft in the White House since the strong Kissinger was by then at State.

Carter also thought, quite mistakenly, that Eisenhower had been a "passive" foreign policy President who therefore needed a "strong" Secretary of State, John Foster Dulles. Recent scholarship, thoroughly documented, makes it clear that Eisenhower was very much in charge of his own foreign policy. Dulles did what Ike told him to.

I suspected Carter had had some help from Zbig in evolving his pretty historical theory, so congenial to them both. It was no answer to a failure in management. Carter was extremely active in foreign policy, hardworking and minutely informed, but it was a measure of weakness, not strength, that he wanted two Secretaries of State.* To my astonishment, I heard Carter a year after he left office stand up and give his same strong-President passive-Secretary formulation at a dinner in New York for at least a hundred people—with Cy and his wife a few seats away.

Vance and Brzezinski were generally consistent in their separate approaches to foreign policy, especially on East-West issues, Cy cautious and conciliatory, Zbig more aggressive and adventurous. It was Jimmy Carter who veered back and forth. Cy Vance, as noted in the previous chapter, could take a tougher line than Zbig on the Cuba brigade question—but that was a tactic to hold Senate votes for a major act of détente, ratification of SALT II.

Defense Secretary Harold Brown, the other senior official in the national security area, did not aspire to be a third Secretary of State. Harold tended toward the hard position in most of the policy arguments of 1979–80, but seemed on good terms with Cy as well as Zbig, and quicker than either of them to adapt to a shift in the President's stance. It was my impression that this brilliant physicist, a not too beloved

---

*Brzezinski has now refined his theory, but it still amounts to two Secretaries of State. He would have the Vance role clearly understood, including by the appointee, as "chief diplomat" of the U.S. The Brzezinski title would be elevated to "Director of National Security Affairs" and he would be subject to Senate confirmation (as is the Director of OMB) and available to testify on the Hill.

I still think Kissinger-Scowcroft is a better model. So now does Kissinger, having repented of Rogers-Kissinger—at least as a management structure for foreign policy.

I believe the right President can conduct his foreign policy with and through a strong Secretary of State. This means a President with a better grasp of power than Carter had, and a better grasp of foreign policy than Reagan has.

"Whiz Kid" back in the McNamara era, liked being Secretary of Defense, and felt there was a lot to keep him busy over at the Pentagon.

The Carter Administration had gotten off to a bad start with the Russians. Instead of moving for swift completion of a modest but worthwhile Strategic Arms Limitation agreement, a SALT II along the lines already negotiated by the Ford Administration at Vladivostok, Vance went to Moscow in March 1977 with sweeping new proposals for deep cuts, which the Soviets saw as a sudden and provocative shift in U.S. policy, and a transparent attempt to deprive them of some of their most potent weapons at little cost to us.

In the U.S. move there was more than a touch of hubris, the new Administration seeking in its first weeks in office to show how arms negotiations are *really* conducted. In their memoirs, Vance and Brzezinski both say now that they considered the March 1977 proposal overambitious. Cy simply says the idea came from "others in the Administration." Zbig blames Cy. Carter still thinks the initiative made good sense and shares the credit generously; he spent "many hours," he writes, working up the proposal with Vance, Brzezinski, Harold Brown, Arms Negotiator Paul Warnke, and the Joint Chiefs of Staff.*

Over the next two years, the negotiation was slowly put back together again with due solicitude for the Soviet dislike of surprises (unless of their own devising). Carter and Vance showed admirable persistence, the "team" stayed fairly well behind the effort, and in Vienna in June 1979, Carter and Brezhnev signed a SALT II treaty that could be considered some advance over the Brezhnev-Ford understandings at Vladivostok. But precious political capital had been draining away from Carter. He was no longer a new President whom senators must reckon with for four years, maybe eight, but a third-year President in severe trouble in the polls.

Another attempt to be different from recent Republican foreign policy, less important but silly, was Carter's campaign position that U.S. ground forces should be withdrawn from South Korea. Zbig supported the idea; Cy wisely opposed it; the Japanese were almost as alarmed as the South Koreans. In the third year of the Carter Administration, U.S. intelligence conveniently discovered that North Korean troop strength had grown, and the withdrawal idea was dropped. No great harm done, but the decision process was not reassuring.

Still another of the Administration's efforts to contrast itself with

*Keeping Faith, p.218.

Nixon-Kissinger-Ford was in the field of human rights. Here Carter, Vance, and Brzezinski were in harmony; they thought the previous Republican administrations had been insufficiently sensitive to the issue. That was true. The Carter Administration was too sensitive to the issue—in a highly selective way. (I must confess the very phrase "human rights" sounds to me plaintive and somewhat squishy. I prefer the older battle cries: Freedom, Liberty. Imagine that noble moment in Beethoven's *Fidelio* with a chorale not to *Freiheit!* but to *Menschenrechte.*)

The Carter Administration's human rights displeasure tended to focus on Latin American military regimes, on South Korea, the Philippines, South Africa—and on the Soviet Union for its mistreatment of dissidents. I always thought the latter a rather quixotic concern. The Soviet Union is a prison-state. The emphasis on the plight of "dissidents" almost implies that everybody else in the country is enjoying their regular human rights. Abuses of human rights in the black African states or the Arab world were not much emphasized in the Carter Administration. At White House meetings where there was self-congratulatory discussion of our warming relations with China, I sometimes wanted to ask, "How are they coming along on human rights?"

In China policy generally, the Carter Administration did a skillful job. In some of the White House celebrating of "normalization"—the establishment of full diplomatic relations in December 1978—the original Nixon-Kissinger breakthrough of 1971 seemed to have become almost an Orwellian non-event. But that had happened seven years before, and Carter was entitled to think "normalization" was more than just an easy follow-up. The Taiwan dilemma was not "solved" in 1978 but deferred, perhaps for a decade or two. A benign ambiguity was drawn about the island, which was still prosperous and independent in 1984, still a part of the sacred "one China," still to some degree protected by the U.S.

Normalization was accomplished despite heavy infighting between Brzezinski and Vance—Zbig the winner—for the lead role in the negotiations. Zbig writes, without apparent irony, of one presidential conversation with a Chinese representative: Carter "handled it extremely well. He did exactly what I was urging him to do . . ."*

The bitterness accumulated in those bureaucratic wars merged with a serious policy dispute in the last year and a half of the Carter

*Zbigniew Brzezinski, *Power and Principle: Memoirs of the National Security Advisor, 1977–1981* (New York: Farrar Straus & Giroux, 1983), p. 198.

Administration. To what extent should the U.S. "play the China card" in dealings with the Soviet Union? Zbig was frequently tempted by gestures in that direction (some of which also appealed to me and, more significant, to Harold Brown).

Vance thought any attempt at playing upon Soviet-Chinese tensions the height of recklessness. At a foreign policy breakfast in September 1979, I saw Cy, face reddening, voice rising, issue an unmistakable threat to resign if negotiations were opened on limited categories of military assistance to China. The President papered that one over. Later he told me that was "about the fourth time" Cy had talked of leaving. One occasion had to do with Andy Young's loose-cannon (my word, not Carter's) activities. Another followed a particularly egregious Brzezinski thrust into State turf. Carter actually reproached Zbig, and told me Zbig kept a lower profile for a while. ("For a while," Vance later confirmed to me.)

I was the recipient of a further Vance distress—which I think never reached the President—when Zbig wanted to review in advance what could be said on a TV talk show by Marshall Shulman, Vance's special adviser on Soviet affairs. Shulman is a mellow and delightful scholar willing to go the very last mile in trying to understand—and explain to those less patient—why the Soviets act the way they do. Shulman and Brzezinski had been Columbia faculty colleagues (and are again); Shulman and I were old friends. Shulman came to see me about the Brzezinski demarche. Lloyd Cutler came by too, and said Carter might have to "get himself a new Secretary of State" (also a new White House Counsel) if Zbig could impose this humiliation on Cy's chosen Soviet expert. The general drift of Shulman's proposed remarks seemed to me perfectly sensible. I encouraged him to go ahead and remark them, nobody quit, and the world went on. But this kind of thing can take up a surprising amount of time and nervous energy at high levels of government.

The fractious Carter Administration achieved an important diplomatic success in the final negotiation and ratification of the Panama Canal Treaties. Three previous Presidents had supported the general outlines of such a settlement, but it was Carter, against forbidding Senate arithmetic, who pushed it through. And it may be significant that he left most of the negotiating to two prestigious special envoys beyond the reach of NSC-State feuding, both men called in from private life: elder statesman Ellsworth Bunker, former Ambassador to Viet

Nam, Italy, India, and Argentina, and the astute Sol Linowitz, former Assistant Secretary of State for Latin America and Ambassador to the OAS.

But the finest hour in Carter Administration foreign policy was pretty much the President's own show: the Camp David agreements of September 17, 1978. It is not clear today how much vitality Camp David still has in the bleak landscape of the Middle East. But at its time the agreement was a remarkable accomplishment. Camp David was Carter at his best.

Here all of Carter's intellectual and moral strengths came together in a major piece of statecraft, and some traits that I discuss elsewhere as limitations proved to be assets, vital to the outcome. After naive and clumsy beginnings in Middle East policy, Carter willed himself to become an expert. By his second summer he was. The vast Carter appetite for detail paid off—he knew the West Bank and Jerusalem problems in depth, he knew the larger implications of seemingly minute controversies, he knew the code words. He had a shrewd sense of what was negotiable and what must finally be finessed—notably, the status of Jerusalem—and he had the vision to fit the immediately attainable within a larger design for the future. He was tough when he needed to be, and he had the patience and stamina to outlast Menachem Begin and Anwar al-Sadat. For much of that time up on the mountain they were communicating only through him. He didn't do it all by himself, of course. He had strong support and advice from State and NSC, getting the best out of Vance and Brzezinski both, and this is precisely what a leader should be able to command. It was a splendid achievement.

Why were there not more like it? Well, for one thing, Carter was brokering an agreement between two other parties; he had to keep in mind U.S. political consequences, but he didn't need Senate ratification. Sadat could negotiate as a plenipotentiary, and Begin almost so—his dependence on Cabinet approval was partly real, partly a negotiating convenience. Sadat and Begin signed *for* Egypt and Israel; the document was "Witnessed by" Jimmy Carter.

The negotiation was focused in time—it couldn't drag on more than ten or twelve days at most—and in place, a setting completely controlled by the President. Sadat and Begin couldn't go outside the barbed-wire perimeter; they had to settle, or go back home (as each once threatened to do). It was like a think tank or military "problem-solving" exercise at some secluded lodge—applied to the real world.

Carter was comfortable with the format, and had the imagination to see the possibilities.

He failed to foresee one grave difficulty. He thought Begin had agreed to a moratorium on new Israeli settlements on the West Bank until the whole West Bank autonomy negotiation had been completed, which could take several years. Begin within hours was insisting he had agreed only to a moratorium during the Egypt-Israel treaty negotiation, which was to take three months. "I have an excellent memory," I heard him say at a breakfast in New York. Israel has been vigorously expanding the settlements ever since, perhaps as a base for outright annexation of the West Bank, and the West Bank autonomy negotiations have been virtually paralyzed.

Camp David did lead, however, to the Egyptian-Israeli peace treaty, following Carter's brave gamble in going to Jerusalem and Cairo in March 1979 and offering, once again, his brokerage services (and again he was skillfully supported by both Vance and Brzezinski).

After that, the "peace process" was losing momentum. And Carter began distancing himself from the Middle East. As the presidential election approached, he was not eager to be seen as leaning very hard on Israel, though he was privately furious. He talked very tough about Begin in White House meetings, to the occasional alarm of Mondale, Jordan and others especially sensitive to the Jewish vote.

The conflict between U.S. policy and politics was played out for the whole world to see, when in March 1980 our Ambassador to the UN supported a resolution condemning Israeli West Bank policies, then three days later was obliged to retract our vote. There was a pitifully lame public explanation about a mix-up in communications; Vance loyally took the blame. Meanwhile Carter was leaving much of the close-in work with Israeli's prickly Prime Minister to two Special Ambassadors, distinguished Jewish Democrats, first Robert Strauss, then the tireless Mr. Linowitz.

14

---●---

The Double Crisis:
Iran and Afghanistan

History sets up some striking juxtapositions. In 1979–80, the political fate of Jimmy Carter of Plains, Georgia, came to depend considerably on the physical and psychological condition of two Persians, the Shah Reza Pahlavi, and the Ayatollah Ruhollah Khomeini.

In the hostage crisis more was at risk, of course, than the career of one American politician or even the lives of the captives. The crisis involved—in debatable but important ways—the honor and credibility of the United States, and the political future of some very sensitive geography.

I doubt that anyone in the world could have foreseen on November 4, 1979, when the U.S. Embassy in Teheran was seized, that our people would be held hostage more than a year, never put on trial, finally set free and cleared from Iranian air space only a few minutes after a new President of the United States took the oath of office. A fantastic chronology. The captors themselves could not have predicted it. Nor could the Ayatollah or Jimmy Carter, the Secretary of State or any of the other eminences advising the President. Certainly not this one.

A few weeks after the seizure of the hostages, Lloyd Cutler and I proposed to the President that work begin on a "White Paper" to review the whole background of our relations with Iran. We were assuming a fairly early release of the hostages and then an instant demand in several congressional committees for a "full investigation." Carter shrewdly tabled the idea, on the grounds that any such paper, even in its most preliminary stages, would instantly become a "sup-

169

pressed report." Congress and the press would clamor for its release.*

After the hostages were finally freed, and by then our election campaign was over, there seemed to be no congressional appetite for a big investigation of "Who Lost Iran?" On Capitol Hill there was perhaps a tacit bipartisan consensus that there was enough blame to go around.

U.S. Presidents of both parties, all the way back to Harry Truman, had given strong support to the Shah. Under Nixon, Ford, and Kissinger, the U.S. made massive arms sales to Iran and treated the country as a major regional ally. The Shah was pro-West (and discreetly pro-Israel) and was seen as an enlightened autocrat who was using oil wealth to propel his people into the modern world. Carter in his first year and a half in office had not challenged these assumptions, though his Administration was perhaps more offended by SAVAK, the Iranian secret police, than his predecessors had been. At a state dinner in Tehran on December 31, 1977, Carter discarded a bland toast prepared by the U.S. Embassy and saluted Iran as "an island of stability" in a troubled region, a circumstance that was a great tribute to the Shah's leadership and to "the respect and the admiration and love" his people gave him. The Carter hyperbole even included this improbable bit of dialogue with Rosalynn: After the Shah's visit to Washington only a month earlier, "I asked my wife, 'With whom would you like to spend New Year's Eve?' And she said, 'Above all others, I think, with the Shah and Empress Farah.' "

The Carter Administration did not sense, any more than its predecessors had, the strength and nature of the revolutionary forces building up in Iran. Even in the late summer and fall of 1978, when the Shah's authority was disintegrating day by day, the general mind-set of Carter foreign policy was to look for "liberalizations" that might save the Shah's regime. But the reality was that he was being overthrown from both Left *and* Right. He was under attack by liberal-radical elements familiar to Western experience, but more important, and almost exotic to Washington, by clerical conservatives outraged by his years of modernizing, Westernizing "reforms." The U.S. response to the Shah's plight was muddled. Brzezinski from time to time urged that we press the Shah to get tough and if he wouldn't or couldn't, that we should

*When it became known that the complete files of the embassy had fallen into Iranian hands, Carter authorized the assembly of all State Department documents—there turned out to be more than 60,000—that might be pertinent for rebuttal of Iranian charges against the U.S. From this material some memoranda were later drafted not as a White Paper but as legal briefs if needed.

encourage a military coup. Vance tended to favor the reformist approach and retained confidence in the Shah, as did Carter, long after his personal weakness should have been apparent. When the Shah's police killed two hundred people in Jaleh Square on September 8, 1978, it was the beginning of the end for his regime. But Carter and Vance at that moment were at Camp David with Sadat and Begin, and utterly preoccupied with that demanding negotiation. The official U.S. line with the Shah was that it was up to him to decide how to handle the revolution. Unofficially, he could hear some conflicting signals. The Shah, prone to vacillation himself, was understandably confused.

And the President had understandably ambivalent feelings about the Shah. Though he had praised the monarch so extravagantly in his New Year's Eve toast in Tehran, there could scarcely have been two less congenial political types. By 1979, Carter had come to believe the Shah's ostentatious amassing of wealth and the indecisiveness masked by his imperious style had made his fall inevitable—which thesis made it possible largely to exonerate the Carter Administration from any responsibility for the "loss" of Iran.

Previous administrations, so ran the Carter rationale, could have done many things to change the character of the Shah's rule, or failing that, to reduce his role as a U.S. ally. By the time Carter took office it was too late. The architects of Iranian policy under previous administrations naturally dispute this, as indeed do some officials of the Carter Administration.

That earlier debate was still smoldering when the hostages were taken, and some of the debaters mentioned to me how right they had been all along. For at least the first six to eight weeks of the hostages' captivity, however, there was virtual unanimity within the Administration on the stance the U.S. should now take. We should pursue negotiations with the Iranians through any plausible channel, at the same time applying pressure through political and economic sanctions, seek the support of our allies and understanding in the Third World, and let it be known that any harm to the hostages would bring swift and stern reprisal.

Over the winter, this consensus unraveled. Relatively hard and soft positions began to emerge. Among the President's advisers most concerned with his domestic political standing, Jordan, Powell, and Rosalynn, a belief crystallized that he must be seen to do something bold if negotiations did not soon succeed. This was Brzezinski's view, for reasons of national honor and American credibility worldwide (though he was not uninterested in the President's ability to get reelected, which would have some bearing on his own future employment).

Cy Vance, supported by his able and selfless Deputy Secretary Warren Christopher, steadily counseled patience and restraint. That was his general philosophy in foreign policy, reinforced in the case of the hostages by the fact that they were employees of the State Department. He had the good officer's loyalty to "my people." The important thing was somehow eventually to have them home alive; spare him bluster about the national honor. In his memoirs, Brzezinski marvels that he, a native-born Pole, should be so jealous of American honor, while the WASP elite, Vance a prime example, seemed to have lost their nerve back in Viet Nam (p. 481).

The foreign policy establishment or elite, WASP and otherwise, had created and managed our Viet Nam policy, and they were right to be shaken by its failure. Private citizens who had urged support of the policy, myself included, were right to be chastened. (I have touched in earlier chapters on what I think I learned from Viet Nam.) Some lessons were doubtless overlearned. That can be seen in the eagerness of many high-minded Americans to spot "another Viet Nam" in unlikely places (e.g., El Salvador, possibly dangerous, but if so, in very different ways) and in their general reluctance to believe that force or the threat of force can ever serve worthy purposes. But these were not the attitudes of Cy Vance, and the Viet Nam syndrome had little or nothing to do with the Carter Administration's policy decisions about Iran.

Immediately after the Shah's flight from Iran in January 1979, Carter was willing to admit him to the U.S. But the Shah preferred to stay in the Moslem world, first in Egypt, then in Morocco. He had an instinct that he should not seem any sort of ward of the U.S. And he seriously thought he might be called back to his throne, as he had been after the Mossadegh episode twenty-five years before. (That time, the U.S. orchestrated the "calling.") When hope of the call faded, he was more attracted to asylum in the U.S., but the State Department was now advising against it, in part because of a mob's attack on the U.S. Embassy in February. When several of the Shah's highly placed friends, Henry Kissinger, David Rockefeller, and John McCloy, began interceding at the White House, Carter was vexed by this "campaign." The Shah had missed his chance. But then in October, Carter felt he had to relent on humanitarian grounds, when the plea was made that the Shah needed medical treatment available only in the U.S. Before the Shah was admitted to New York Hospital, it was known to the White House that he was terminally ill, and perhaps had only months or weeks to live. Carter's admission of the Shah to the U.S. became the pretext for the seizure of our embassy, and the return of the Shah to Iran the first condition laid down by the "students" for the release of the hostages.

There was never any question of handing the Shah over to the Iranians. I wondered whether he might decide himself, knowing he was soon to die anyway, that he should go home and face the firing squad, so the last chapter of his reign would not be his flight from Iran but a royal martyrdom. He might see it as a potent legacy to leave his son. When I speculated along these lines at one White House meeting, my colleagues looked at me as if I had been reading old storybooks about kings. Carter told me, realistically, I am sure, that nobody would believe the Shah was returning to Iran voluntarily.*

Even months after the poor man had died, the whole story of our dealings with the Shah remained very sensitive in the White House. Was it really true the treatment he needed could be had only at New York Hospital? When Carter decided to let him in, why weren't more precautions taken for the security of the embassy? If he hadn't been let into the U.S., would the embassy have been seized on some other pretext?

Nobody at the White House wanted to say we had blundered in letting the Shah in. And nobody in the White House felt very proud about it when he was negotiated back out of the U.S. We shunted him along to Panama in December. "A dividend from the Canal treaty," somebody said in the West Wing. Then the White House, through Hamilton Jordan and Counsel Lloyd Cutler, had to try to mediate the distasteful bickering between Panamanian and U.S. doctors, between the Shah's household and the Panamanian authorities, and cope with one Panamanian scheme for a facade of "extradition" proceedings which might mollify the Iranian revolutionaries without actually endangering the Shah. Carter could only brood with some bitterness that he and two of his most senior aides should be mired down in all this.

For many weeks a regular agenda item at White House meetings on the hostage crisis was a painful review of the dwindling list of countries that might conceivably be willing to receive the Shah. In the end the Shah insisted on clearing out of Panama, and Anwar Sadat coura-

---

*Barbara Walters subsequently asked the Shah on TV if he would consider going back and standing trial. His reply: "I have been called many things but I have never been called stupid."

geously let him come to Cairo to die. The U.S. was left looking a little shabby.

My first reaction to the seizure of the embassy in Tehran—and most of the foreign policy establishment reacted this way—was: Here is one more protest/demonstration/sit-in against a U.S. Embassy, outrageous but no major crisis. When the mob had broken into our Tehran embassy compound the previous February, they held some hostages for a few days; one Iranian employee had been killed before Iranian soldiers restored order. There had been a recent demonstration against the U.S. embassy in El Salvador, and in several other countries violence against the embassies of other Western nations. The demonstrators, "students" or whatever, made their point and after a few hours or a day or two went home (or their government made them).

People who later said the U.S. should have "gone in" right away, to bring the hostages out of Tehran, were talking nonsense. Gone in with what? Given the pattern of anti-Western embassy demonstrations up to then, no rational U.S. leadership in those first hours of the hostage crisis would have reacted more belligerently than Carter did.

Within days, however, it was clear that something new was going on—the Ayatollah was blessing the embassy seizure, a government was adopting as its own policy a seemingly spontaneous violation of diplomatic immunity by a few score of its own citizens. What was much less clear was whether the student captors would respond to orders from the Ayatollah, what the political profile of the students was, whether the Ayatollah was in fact the effective ruler of Iran, or was a front, and which other figures the U.S. could or should deal with.

Who was in charge over there? Much of the hindsight criticism of Carter's handling of the hostage problem fails to give enough weight to the sheer novelty of the situation. In 1933–45, we did at least know indisputably that Hitler was running Germany. When the Cold War began, we knew that Stalin was running Russia. The Tehran hostages were not World War II or Cold War or World War III, but they became a mid-rank crisis that stretched the nerves and emotions of the American people and the energies of the U.S. government, and uniquely, we were never absolutely certain whom we were dealing with. "Rational" pressures and threats, especially in the economic sphere, that might influence Western-educated leftist politicians, could be utterly uninteresting to clerical Puritans who could quite sincerely summon their followers to martyrdom against the forces of "the Great Satan" (who surely never had a more incongruous deputy than born-again Baptist Jimmy Carter).

The columnist Rowland Evans once phoned me to complain that in thirty years as a journalist "in this town" he had never known such a snafu in White House press relations as in the handling of the hostage situation. Never having liked the tinniness of "this town" as applied to Washington or New York, I couldn't refrain from a bit of upmanship, saying that I had started reporting in "this town" forty years ago, and couldn't remember any situation like the hostages, so perhaps it was appropriate that Evans couldn't remember press handling just like it.

It remained true throughout 1980 and even up to the diplomatic flurry in mid-January 1981, just before Reagan's inauguration, that our representatives, acting for the President of the United States, could never be entirely certain of the authority of the people they were negotiating with. Fortunately the U.S. had nothing to negotiate with the Iranians in President Reagan's first year, because there would still have been the question: who do you talk to? It has since become clear that the eighty-two-year-old Khomeini is the man to talk to, if you can get through his "court," by now fairly well identified. As of 1984, however, we still had nothing much to talk about.

The Painful Choices

With hindsight, I now think that as the hostage crisis began to solidify around late December, our two best choices, each very painful, were:

We could start downplaying the situation and demote it from "crisis" rank. American diplomats had been held captive after the Communists took over China, some for years. The *Pueblo* crew was held captive in North Korea for almost a year, and for days on end there would be no mention of them by the U.S. government or press. Not perfect parallels by any means, but drawing on those experiences, we might have been able to disabuse the Iranians of any idea that the hostages were a bargaining chip of vast value. We would let the U.S. government be seen as a very cool customer, negotiating quietly but quite ready to leave some of its employees at risk for a long time, leaving the Iranians to ponder the costs and dangers they had brought on themselves. This would have required a kind of hardness Jimmy Carter lacked and an almost superhuman willingness to separate the hostage situation from the upcoming presidential election.

The other painful course, if we wanted to treat the seizure of the hostages as a major offense against American interests, would have been to label it an act of war, which technically it was. We would have begun to deal much more severely with Iranian citizens and interests in the U.S. than we ever did, and we would have threatened Iran (somebody there) with dire punishment if the hostages were not released forthwith. The punishment could have been an attempt at seizure of the Iranian islands in the Persian Gulf, blockade, mining of the Gulf, punitive attack against Iranian oil fields and refining capacity, or some combination of these.

What we finally did do was painful enough, as the crisis dragged out for 444 days. Jimmy Carter found the worst of both worlds. He kept a great glare of publicity on the hostages but in the end was not perceived as doing anything effective about them. It was a policy of extreme forbearance, broken by the one spasm of the rescue attempt.

I continued through the first weeks of the hostage situation to admire the President's restraint, and to tell him so. He was superb in his first press conference after the seizure of the hostages, on the evening of November 28, a meeting perilous with opportunities to say the wrong thing. Carter was in full command of the nuances as well as the facts, and his combination of firmness and restraint was exactly right.* From this press conference performance of late November, through the evening of January 20, 1980, when he gave his tough State of the Union speech, following the Soviet invasion of Afghanistan, his presidential stature was higher than it was ever to be again in his last year in office.

In early December, I had briefly and uncharacteristically found myself more dovish than Carter on one point. I argued against the deployment of AWACS planes to the eastern Mediterranean as unconvincing saber-rattling. The Iranians had released thirteen black and female hostages just before Thanksgiving, and there was some hope they might release all or most of the other fifty-three at Christmas. The Shah was now out of the U.S. One experienced U.S. diplomat thought

---

*In one passage I had a faint seizure of pride of authorship, or brokership. I had asked him, relaying a suggestion from William Scranton, former governor of Pennsylvania, to be sure to praise the American people for *their* restraint and good sense. Carter did. He was so polite in receiving such suggestions you never knew whether he had already thought of the same point.

he saw daylight "for the first time in thirty-three days" (since November 4).

Alongside the December hope, there was in the White House an acute anxiety that the Iranians might hold back six or eight or twelve or fifteen hostages, proclaim these the most dangerous "spies," and put them on trial. And then there was a nightmare scenario—what if they executed one a day, saying they would not stop until the United States turned over the Shah's "billions" and otherwise confessed its sins? Privately, Carter had tried to make it clear—to everybody in Iran who might have some authority—that we would react punitively to any trial or any "sentence" of any hostage. But short of that it remained murky what we would do, if anything, to get them out.

As Christmas came and went, and the reconvening of Congress approached, I found myself moving toward the harder side in the Iran policy debate. In the White House terminology of those weeks I had been in favor of "holding" rather than "ratcheting." But now I questioned whether American public opinion could hold very much longer for Carter's policy of patience. I began, even without benefit of Polish blood, to fear damage to America's credibility in the world.

Dangers Intermingled

The Soviet military occupation of Afghanistan, begun on December 24, sharpened all apprehensions about the situation in Iran. The two crises intermingled. The Soviet move into Afghanistan could be interpreted in various ways—none flattering to U.S. power and foresight:

• That the U.S. had shown itself such a patsy in Tehran, it was ready to be pushed around some more.

• Or, quite the contrary, the U.S. would probably undertake some form of military action against Iran, so it was safe for the Soviets to move into Afghanistan; whatever they did there would look no worse to "world opinion" than the U.S. measures against Iran.

• And/or the U.S. didn't care about Afghanistan. By short-of-war steps, the Soviets for more than a year had been methodically consolidating their influence in Afghanistan. They might have concluded that the U.S. had simply conceded the country to them. The Carter Administration in fact had shown little concern, externally or internally. Afghanistan was barely mentioned at the White House foreign policy breakfasts of late summer and autumn 1979. Not until December 21 was there a substantial discussion—just three days before the Soviets lost patience with one set of Afghan puppets and moved in with troops.

• Or, never mind any of the above, there was now a power vacuum in Iran, post-Shah, and Soviet occupation of Afghanistan would position them for moves toward the Persian Gulf.

The Soviet move into Afghanistan narrowed our options in dealing with Iran. We could not desire chaos in Iran for fear of setting up a situation that the Soviet-backed Tudeh Party could exploit. There were great dangers in dabbling in anti-Khomeini politics inside Iran, lest that be used to justify Soviet meddling.

In 1981 and 1982, long after the American hostages were safely home, the Iranians were generating plenty of internal chaos on their own. I found it a luxury in those days to pick up the paper and see a story about ex-President Bani-Sadr in Paris or some Ayatollah in Tabriz and realize I didn't even have to read it, let alone try to understand it. But in the winter of 1979–80, every fragment of intelligence on the disputes and intrigues of the mullahs and the bazaars was a matter of urgent interest in the Carter White House, along with the scattered reports on the morale of the Shah's surviving military officers, the stirrings among the Kurdish rebels, the plottings of the exiles.

Those were somber days in the White House, dominated by the frustrations of Iran and Afghanistan. Washington is seldom really cold, but there can be a damp chill in the winter mornings as the U.S. government makes its way to the office. At the President's foreign policy breakfasts, I looked out from the Cabinet Room across the dormant Rose Garden to the bare oak and elm branches above the South Lawn. Carter would often be wearing his oyster-colored cardigan, the rest of us very proper in business suits—except Hamilton Jordan, who often showed up ten or fifteen minutes late in sports jacket and slacks and no necktie. The rest of us were all at our places before the President came in on the dot of 7:30; we stood and exchanged good mornings, then sat and inclined our heads at various angles of piety as he spoke a blessing. Once when Cy Vance was giving the blessing, he beseeched "wise judgments," and the President softly added: "Amen wise judgments."

Within minutes of the blessing there could be very blunt language: "There's a limit to how much we can kiss the Iranians' ass." The idiom, however, tended to be blunter than the action.

We talked, Friday after Friday for months, of the maddeningly meager progress in arriving at common measures with our allies for dealing with Iran and Afghanistan. Because of Afghanistan we were trying to lead a Western protest boycott of the July Olympics in Moscow. The Carter White House learned more about the politics of the Olympics bureaucracy than any White House has ever had to know before, and one hopes, forever. Lloyd Cutler and Warren Christopher did much of the work here; Carter lobbied the allied leaders by phone and note. We discussed the intricate structure of Iranian assets in the U.S. and Europe and the attendant legal technicalities, the proceedings in the World Court and the UN Security Council, the condition of the Iranian oil fields, the status of Iranian students and other nationals in the U.S., the astonishing difficulty in establishing just how many of these there were, and even the need to protect their "civil rights." I was amazed at the solicitude of the President, Secretary of State, and Attorney General on this latter point. We talked of the military-political situation inside Afghanistan—what little we knew of it, and of the various feuding elements in the resistance, and how we might get help to them.

There was continuous discussion of the internal Iranian political situation—who seemed to be up, who down, who might be reached through some intermediary. We rode a kind of roller-coaster of hope and discouragement. Between the seizure of the embassy and the U.S. election one year later, there were as many as six separate surges of hope in the White House. None could be dismissed at the time as totally wishful thinking; each arose from some apparent promise in a particular avenue of negotiation.

For a few days in late March it seemed that President Bani-Sadr had won approval from the Revolutionary Council for removal of the hostages from the embassy compound and transfer of their custody from the students to the Foreign Ministry. This had been seen all along as a necessary preliminary to release of the hostages. Bani-Sadr even made a public statement implying the transfer was about to take place, and Carter told the press this was a "positive step." A break seemed so close that Carter was kidding Harold Brown that it would be awfully embarrassing if the hostages came out and the Defense Department wasn't ready with an airplane and a hospital. Brown assured him there was a plane on hand and the medical facility in Wiesbaden, Germany, was ready. Within forty-eight hours the deal had fallen through. The disappointment in the White House was acute. Carter told Hamilton Jordan that Bani-Sadr was "gutless."* For Carter, of course, all this had excruciating relevance to his reelection prospects. (When Ted Kennedy, soon after entering the primary campaigns, made a violent denunciation of the Shah, there had been a fleeting fear in the Carter camp that Iran might choose to release the hostages *to* Kennedy.) Whatever his inner turmoil, Carter maintained a stoic and generally cheerful front.

From November through April there were almost daily meetings of the Special Coordination Committee, a standing subcommittee of the National Security Council for crisis management. The subject was Iran, and after December 24, Iran and Afghanistan. The SCC met at 9:00 AM in the Situation Room, a drably furnished, windowless space in the interior of the White House West Wing basement, shielded against any long-distance eavesdropping devices, one of the few totally secure rooms on the civilian side of the Potomac. Brzezinski chaired the meetings in a brisk and effective style. Up to twenty people might be there, crowding the room, representatives of State, Defense, the White House senior staff, and depending on the day's agenda, Treasury, Justice, sometimes Commerce and Agriculture. The diplomatic, economic, and legal aspects of Iran and Afghanistan policy were explored more exhaustively than at the President's Friday breakfasts, though some highly sensitive matters reserved for breakfast were left off the SCC agenda. One of Brzezinski's NSC people would take minutes and get those to the President within an hour or so of the end of our meeting. By the SCC meeting of the next morning the President's comments on the previous day's minutes would usually be available. These would indicate he liked some ideas, didn't like others, wanted to hold off on something else, and so on.

Whatever the substantive merits or otherwise of our Iran and Afghanistan policies during those months, the mechanism of decision making and follow-through was generally efficient. People knew what the other fellow was doing, and who was supposed to do what tomorrow.

I marveled in these meetings at the patience these senior officials could bring to the endlessly repetitive details that go into the execution of a policy—the process for deporting an alien, the legal and financial complexities of freezing assets, or of carrying out a grain embargo, as opposed to just talking about it. I was the only editor at the table, and editors get spoiled; if they tire of one subject, they can turn to another (especially if they are boss). Occasionally in those exhausting hours in the Situation Room some activist's temper would flare when some other

*Hamilton Jordan, *Crisis* (New York: G.P. Putnam's Sons, 1982), p. 246.

official (usually a lawyer) would seem to dwell too lovingly on the technicalities.

For all the tedium, there was an underlying tension. The hostages' lives were in peril. Carter discussed their plight with literally thousands of people in briefings and meetings in the White House, he assured the country he prayed for the hostages every night, he received delegations from their families, he allowed his personal schedule during an entire half year of his reelection campaign to be dominated by their captivity. It was an admirably humane reaction, and it weakened Carter's bargaining position vis-à-vis the Iranians and eventually hurt him with the U.S. electorate. Carter people began to accuse the media of overplaying the hostage story, especially ABC for its program "The Iran Crisis: America Held Hostage," which ran every week night for four months, and Walter Cronkite for his sign-off: "And that's how it was . . . [calendar date] . . . the 123rd day [etc.] of the hostages' captivity." CBS kept counting the days right up to 444. But Jimmy Carter himself did at least as much as the networks to keep the country—and his Administration —lacerated by the hostages.

Iran and Afghanistan intertwined had large implications for the U.S. world position. There was even, remotely, the danger of an armed clash with the Soviets in the Persian Gulf, leading on who knew where. Inside the Administration the people living with the double crisis for weeks and months on end were under continuous strain. There were some practiced poker faces around the table in the Situation Room and the Cabinet Room, and some faces were more transparent. In the privacy of my personal notes one evening I taxed one high diplomat with "dithering" over a ridiculous bit of fine print—but for all I knew, he could have been operating on two or three hours' sleep in the previous forty-eight.

There were a few light moments: One of the most dovish of Carter loyalists, after everybody agreed Afghanistan had brought back the Cold War: "At least we get one thing out of this—the Presidency is strengthened again." Carter looked a little pained. A Pentagon official, after we heard of some anti-Khomeini demonstration in the Iranian provinces, offering a sardonic "Congratulations, Stan" to Admiral Turner, chief of the CIA. Turner didn't even bother to look inscrutable.

I was marginally involved, in mid-February, in the drafting of a statement that Hamilton Jordan might offer the Iranians, in his backchannel negotiations, to respond to their demand for an apology for past U.S. support of the Shah. I was strongly opposed to any language constituting an apology, and proposed instead that the U.S. "understands that the Iranian people are critical of past policies of the U.S. toward Iran," and has consistently indicated willingness to have Iranian grievances against the U.S. expressed before an appropriate international forum. Various short-of-apology formulations, by various authors, circulated in the White House in those days. Carter was willing to go along with one cloudy formulation that Iranians might have interpreted as an implicit admission of past U.S. interference in their internal affairs, while still allowing the President to deny that any apology was being conveyed.* In the end, these literary exercises remained just that.

Despite my disinclination to be a speech writer, I came in one weekend to work on a possible presidential address on the hostages before the UN. I was quite eloquent. Carter decided not to make the appearance. I got a few words into the foreign policy passages of the 1980 State of the Union (and knocked a few out), and did occasional touches of editing for Vance and others.

I attracted, as everybody in the White House did, phone calls and mail from every old Middle East or Iranian hand you ever knew, and many you didn't know. (Some interesting, some crackpot.) I found myself the liaison between the White House and a group of Islamic and Arab-American scholars in American universities, and got Carter to appear before them, to stress that the U.S. had the greatest respect for the underlying tenets of Islam and indeed felt the Iranian revolutionaries were violating them.

In mid-March I argued that we should arrive within our own councils at a deadline for resolving the hostage crisis, not some arbitrary date out of the blue but a date tied to an event in the unfolding Iranian political process, such as the election and seating of the Majlis in mid-April. On their completing this important constitutional step, we could say to the Iranians: "Your new parliament is in place, we have been very patient, now we must have our people back." Some officials who back in November would have been horrified at any thought of a deadline now said it might have worked in those early days but at this point could only result in the hostages being harmed, or at least hidden.

Defeat in the Desert

Meanwhile, however, planning for the last-resort rescue mission had long been under way. The President invited me to a meeting on March 21 where rescue scenarios were to be reviewed, but I was due to leave earlier in the day with Ambassador Linowitz on one of his

*Pierre Salinger, *America Held Hostage* (New York: Doubleday, 1981), p. 166.

Middle East negotiating sessions and I stuck to that schedule. When the seemingly promising round of diplomacy with the Iranians collapsed in early April, the countdown for the rescue mission began in earnest. By bad luck or good, I was again out of the country, at a "Bilderberg Meeting" in Germany, a gathering of influential Atlanticists, when the decision was taken in the Cabinet Room on April 11, then reaffirmed in a final session on April 14.

In a curious conversation with Carter just before I left, dealing mainly with Western European attitudes toward his Administration, he expressed mild surprise I had not "postponed" my trip. Since the Bilderberg session was at a fixed date, I couldn't very well postpone my attendance. I could have called the trip off, but didn't catch his gentle signal. He shifted back to Europe: "Well, do the best you can for me with those people."

It was at the April 14 meeting that Cy Vance alone spoke up against the rescue venture. Vance (ironically, the only civilian at the table with combat experience, also a former Deputy Secretary of Defense) thought the military scenario was wildly impractical, that some of his embassy people would be killed, to say nothing of many Iranians, and that the international consequences, including a possible Soviet intervention, could be perilous. A week later he gave the President his resignation, to take effect after the mission even if it succeeded. Vance had been dispirited ever since the Soviet invasion of Afghanistan and the shelving of SALT II; the rescue scheme was just one thing too many.

Carter and the others saw the rescue operation as a "surgical" minimum, a daring attempt to rescue the hostages with the least possible harm to Iranians. Thus even as the rescue mission satisfied the urge to "do something," Carter could also see it almost as a continuance of his policy of moderation, as opposed to the warlike range of general reprisals that might have been hurled against Iran. This view of the mission may also have contributed to its fatal thinness. It should have been more heavily mounted, or not attempted at all. That of course is hindsight.

Vance reaped much praise for his principled resignation—and his soldier's hunch. He and I have a good many mutual friends in New York; some of them who knew I had not been at the White House meeting on April 14 agreeably assumed I would have sided with Cy. I had to say, No, I wouldn't have.

I thought Carter was right to try it. I don't know to what extent he was influenced by his declining public support, as measured by the polls and by the New York primary of March 25, when Kennedy overwhelmed Carter 59 to 41 percent. But politics aside, it would have been a great thing for the United States if the mission could have been pulled off.

In announcing for reelection on December 4, 1979, Carter had said he would stay at his post in the White House until the hostages were released. With the failure of the rescue mission, he abandoned the "Rose Garden strategy" and set out campaigning around the country. He said he could get out of Washington because the hostage situation was now "manageable." It was a tasteless word and a lame public explanation. But I knew what he meant. The diplomatic efforts to resolve the hostage crisis had absorbed a tremendous amount of presidential time; these were now stalemated. In the final phases of the rescue decision, there were punishing pressures on Carter, as there are on any President who may be sending men to their death. And before that, there had been for weeks the painful knowledge that such a decision might await him. Now that was behind the President. He did indeed have more time and strength for other things, including the campaign —not that he had ever neglected that subject.

Getting to Know the Russians

On the global scale, the long captivity of the hostages was less important than the Soviet invasion of Afghanistan—to the extent they could be separated. But the hostages had a far greater hold on American emotions. There were no Americans held prisoner in Afghanistan. There was almost no TV footage from inside Afghanistan, and there was little solid reporting of any kind.

The country that was outraging us in Afghanistan was the other superpower. Ever since we declined to do anything about the Hungarian freedom fighters in 1956 it had been clear we would not risk war against the Soviets within their own security perimeter as they saw it. (In the Cuba missile crisis of 1962 they were into our perimeter, as finally they tacitly conceded.)

But Iran was just a second- or third-rate regional power—if second-rate, only because of the oil resources the West had originally developed, and the political and military support the U.S. had been pumping in. To be thwarted by such a country, with its holy men and wild-eyed street mobs, was fundamentally more offensive to the American psyche, including the psyches in the White House, than to arrive at the prudent recognition that there just wasn't much we could do to get the Soviets out of Afghanistan if they insisted on being there.

The hostages did all eventually come home alive, but much of the world (including some Carter people) could conclude that it was the advent of Ronald Reagan rather than the patience of Jimmy Carter that had brought their release.* The U.S. suffered a considerderable international humiliation, though that kind of thing does tend to wear off. We didn't blunder into a war with the Soviets, and we have not seen (at least as of 1984) any serious Soviet penetration of Iran. Jimmy Carter is entitled to feel there could have been worse outcomes—for the country, whatever the effect on Candidate Carter.

The double crisis was perhaps educational for the U.S. in the long run. It brought further political and public support to the rebuilding of U.S. military strength, including the concept of the Rapid Deployment Force.

Afghanistan killed SALT II, if it was not already dead. It generally hardened U.S. attitudes toward the Soviet Union. In an ABC interview Carter said that Afghanistan in just a week had changed his whole thinking about the Russians. It was an honest confession that a good many other Americans might have made—after a decade of hopes for détente—but it was a deplorably naive thing for the President of the United States to say out loud. I told him I was distressed, and that some of his further comments—the nature of Soviet imperialism was "only now dawning on the world," even "former close friends of the Soviet Union" must face it—did not help matters. I said it also troubled me to have him assert the Russians would suffer "severe political consequences" when he couldn't yet say what. This created an unnecessary and quite uncomfortable resemblance between our stance toward the Russians and toward the Ayatollah.

Yet Carter didn't altogether mean that his view of the Soviets had been transformed. He was deeply ambivalent about the Soviets, and hence in the end about U.S. foreign policy. Less than six months after the invasion of Afghanistan, his two ranking Cabinet officers, Edmund Muskie, who had succeeded Vance at State, and Harold Brown, were arguing that Afghanistan made the ratification of SALT II "even more

*Within the Iranian regime, from August 1980 on, there was growing recognition that the hostages were a wasting asset. Those who now favored release still had to win over some bitter-enders, and found it useful to point to a deadline, first the U.S. election, when a deal was almost struck, then the Inauguration.

important." In a memorandum to the President on June 9, I said this reasoning left me "very uneasy . . .

"Would another Afghanistan somewhere else make SALT ratification still more important? How far would we carry this counter-linkage?

"The original Soviet invasion of Afghanistan was, as you said, a serious threat to world peace. If we seem to accept it, that is a second and perhaps more serious threat to peace.

"I don't argue that the Soviets want/need SALT more than we do. (I suspect we just don't know.) But it seems reasonable to assume they want it at least as much as we do, or they wouldn't have signed it, and that it matters more deeply to them than our grain or our absence from the Olympics."

For a few days, the President seemed to be accepting my argument. But I couldn't really believe I had turned the Administration around, and I hadn't. The general Administration line through the summer and right up to the election was to suggest that SALT was just temporarily derailed—to be sure because of Soviet misbehavior—but that after some unspecified interval, negotiations would be resumed regardless of Afghanistan.

Five years later, the Soviets still had about 100,000 troops in Afghanistan. They are content to control Kabul, the major highways and six or eight of the bigger towns; beyond these points they make little effort to subdue the fierce people and terrain. They continue to take several hundred casualties a month, but it is no "Viet Nam" for them. They may be modeling their tactics on the slow pacification and Sovietization of the Islamic republics within the U.S.S.R., a process that took some twenty to thirty years.

There have been no winners in Afghanistan, certainly not Jimmy Carter. He courageously maintained the grain embargo at some domestic political cost, as election year 1980 wore on, but it was no more than a mild inconvenience to the Soviets. The boycott of the Olympics was an admirable moral declaration by the U.S. and perhaps a propaganda embarrassment for the Soviets. Yet the difficulty of getting allied support on the embargo and the Olympics made all too vivid the strains and tensions within the West. Afghanistan and Iran together unquestionably contributed to the picture of ineffectuality that was so damaging to Carter in November 1980.

15

A Think Tank of My Own

In a talk about foreign policy one January afternoon in 1980, I asked Carter if he was satisfied there was enough contingency thinking in his Administration. He said No, and encouraged me to do some. I had already been writing myself occasional notes about this, and later that day I edited them into a list of fifteen or twenty possible developments around the world. My secretary typed it up and walked it down to the reception area outside the Oval Office. I thought of my list as for-instance stuff, just a postscript to an informal conversation, and I was a little embarrassed that the President promptly sent it on to Vance and Brzezinski, who perhaps found it an unnecessary piece of paper. My contingencies:

1) Hostages: held indefinitely (how long can we tolerate?)
   a hostage dies a natural death
   put on trial
   all released
   some released, some held
   one or more executed.
2) Invitation to the Soviets from Tudeh and/or some other Iranian faction to come in and "restore order."
3) Collapse of Afghan resistance.
4) Growing Afghan resistance, formation of a "Free Afghanistan Government," which appeals to the U.S. for aid.
5) Soviet military aid to dissident and separatist elements in Pakistan. Soviet strike at an Afghan refugee camp in Pakistan.
6) Upheaval in Saudi Arabia.

7) Death of: Khomeini
            Brezhnev
            Teng
            Tito
8) Assassination of: Sadat
                  Assad
                  Hussein
9) Fall of the Begin Government.
10) New or enlarged Cuban activity in Central America and Caribbean; or Africa; or Middle East.
11) Vietnamese pursuit of Pol Pot people into Thailand.

As the winter of 1980 wore on, seeing the President and his principal advisers so consumed by the day-to-day demands of Iran and Afghanistan, and the preoccupations of the coming election, I became more and more troubled that nobody was doing systematic thinking about U.S. foreign policy over the longer term. In a memo to the President on February 20, I suggested a high-level study of our foreign policy options and objectives, 1980–85 that is, the current year and the next Presidential term. I wrote:

> The underlying principles and premises of U.S. foreign policy should be re-examined, clothed in concrete detail, and ranked by priorities.
> There is considerable confusion today, among our Allies, probably in the Soviet leadership, and certainly in U.S. opinion, about the basic philosophy of your Administration in foreign policy. The confusion will be exploited and compounded as the election unfolds. But there is also genuine and legitimate confusion. It is not simple to answer the simple question: Has Carter's foreign policy changed? What is left of détente? How Allied are our Allies?
> I have been struck in my brief experience here with the difficulty that even the most thoughtful people have in finding time to think about the year after next . . . Even pre-Iran it was my impression that the top people in foreign policy, including the President, had little chance to stand off from immediate problems and think ahead.

I thought the proposed study would need "a few very good people detached from operational duties for a few months." I said they should work under "the general direction of Cy or Zbig (or somehow both?) with a firm understanding this study is expressly ordered by the President."

Carter shrugged off the "somehow both." While affably declining my previous advice about the two Secretaries of State, he did like the idea of a fresh look at the policy directions. I suggested various people, some of them in government, some in universities and think tanks, who could run such a study. Carter asked me to run it, to set up my own think tank. For the last four or five months I was in the White House I spent most of my time on the project.

The President announced and blessed the study at a Friday foreign policy breakfast. The eventual result was two big black books, total thickness about six inches, about the whole world. Chapters were done by State, Defense, NSC, CIA, and ICA (International Communications Agency). Zbig loaned me two of his part-time consultants, Professor Samuel Huntington of Harvard and Professor Michel Oksenberg of Michigan, to do the chapters on U.S.-Soviet relations, and U.S.-China relations. These were brilliant papers. Many a bureaucratic clearance had to be negotiated, as to who could be detached from his regular duties for how long. State's chapters were reviewed by NSC, NSC's by State. I edited and reedited. I told Carter I was "editing out" minor inconsistencies but the important disagreements between the agencies would be set forth, as well as my own dissents. He warmly approved this approach. The various Under Secretaries, Assistant Secretaries, "desk" experts who were my authors tended to be a bit late meeting their deadlines, rather like journalists, but professed to appreciate being edited.

Having set assignments in motion, I took two field trips, or refresher courses, of my own. The Middle East had baffled and fascinated me since a brief Navy call in World War II, and I had been back there on journalistic expeditions in the 1960s and 1970s. In March 1980, I jumped at an invitation from Sol Linowitz, then Special Ambassador for the Middle East "peace process," to come along on one of his negotiating trips (his fifth trip in that series, and he did two more). Linowitz made a few inches of progress, in Egypt and Israel. I relished again in Jerusalem the intensely fractious and intimate political life, where everybody knows, and often seems to disagree with, everybody else, and even a foreign visitor can sit in the Knesset dining room and in just a day or two talk with most of the principal figures in the government and opposition(s). It is a place of great political jokes and aphorisms. My favorite from that visit: "The Begin government is too weak to fall." But I wondered then, as I had before and have since, whether the Middle East, as a "problem," approaches the insoluble. I have occasionally felt the same about Northern Ireland. It comes hard to Americans to think such thoughts.

My other field trip was in April to a colloquium on the state of the Western Alliance, most appropriately held in Aachen, Charlemagne's Aix-la-Chapelle, a few kilometers from the German-Dutch-Belgian border juncture. It was the meeting (mentioned in the previous chapter) of the "Bilderberg" group, dating back to Marshall Plan days, generally pro-American Europeans and pro-Alliance Americans. It was painful to hear the Europeans' doubts, sometimes verging on contempt, about U.S. leadership. Stopovers in London and Rome did not yield much better readings.

As the work proceeded on my foreign policy study, some twenty-five to thirty people were involved in one phase or another. Given the general leakiness of Washington, I was relieved that the project never surfaced in the press. The "Secret/Sensitive" classification was intact when the only complete copy was delivered to the President's office on August 12, in my last week as his Senior Adviser.

I had written a foreword to the report, which has since been declassified, which expressed a much harder-line view than that of the Carter Administration. Since the Carter line wavered, I should say more precisely that my views were harder-line than an averaging-out of Carter positions. Whether my views would have had any serious influence in a second Carter term is doubtful. I hope my paper still has value, however, as the reflections of an editor with a long exposure to international affairs, after a year's involvement with U.S. foreign policy on the inside.

To write such a paper expressly for a President imposes its own discipline and opportunity. I was absolutely candid with my audience. I tried to avoid preachiness but was perhaps guilty of a touch or two of flag-waving. I tried to avoid the journalistic vice of "writing your way out of" hard questions. From ideas and impressions formed over many years, I tried to define a general view of the U.S. world position, from which policy priorities would flow. I quote most of my foreword below, and will let my 1980 views be judged by light of 1985. I do allow myself one footnote of clarification (*fn.* †, p. 191); editors can't quite stop editing. This, then, was my personal petition to President Jimmy Carter, August 1980, for a firmer and clearer course in U.S. foreign policy. Excerpts:

> As compared with the foreign policy objectives established in 1976–77 in the Carter campaign and the first year of the Carter Administration, I

would propose a considerable shift of strategy: heavier stress on the U.S.-Soviet relationship as the most important intersection in world politics. The corollary is a view that many Third and Fourth World situations and North-South relationships, though significant in terms of growing regional power, and also important to us for economic and humanitarian reasons, are at least equally important, and often more so, for their bearing on the U.S.-Soviet balance. There is no conflict here of morality vs. *realpolitik*. I assign very high moral worth to our ability to defend this country and our friends. And the only adversary capable of challenging that ability is the Soviet Union.

The first priority of U.S. foreign policy, 1980–1985, is to insure, both in reality and worldwide perceptions, the position of the United States as the preeminent superpower.

In other words, our first priority should be to make sure the President is right when he says the United States "is the strongest nation on earth, politically, economically and militarily." We must be certain that this is so, that it is seen to be so, and that we know how to keep it so. I am disturbed by the Cabinet-level attacks on the very notion of "superiority" as Reaganite recklessness when you have so often claimed precisely that for the U.S.

In terms of military power, my own impression, reluctantly arrived at, is that the Soviet Union is rapidly achieving, if it has not already done so, superiority over the U.S.* When our allies are added in, our "side" would seem still to have the military edge over the Warsaw Pact countries. And of course our side has overwhelming economic and technological superiority. But given the nature of alliances in general, and our own particular alliance of self-indulgent societies, strained by some genuine divergences of interest (amply demonstrated in recent months), the NATO vs. Warsaw military comparison is not entirely reassuring. We cannot be content with a situation in which the central force on the other side is moving toward military superiority over the main source of power and leadership on our side. Too many dangerous contingencies arise from that. We must try to establish a clear preeminence for the U.S.

I speak of preeminence rather than parity quite deliberately. Perfect parity could exist for only five minutes, and if it ever did, we wouldn't have known about it. Even "rough parity" is unlikely to last very long in a dynamic world.†

What we think of as the underlying strengths of a nation or coalition

*This view is of course at variance with the Department of Defense position, though the DOD paper in this report is rather more guarded about the U.S.-Soviet military balance than the public statements of the Department.

†If I were rewriting this memo today, I would stress that preponderant strength overall does not imply a need for nuclear superiority. We cannot regain the overwhelming nuclear superiority we enjoyed into the early 1960s. Short of that, a "rough parity" in nuclear strength is the least dangerous situation for the U.S. Admittedly it is almost as difficult to define rough nuclear parity as to maintain it.

—political, economic and military—are constantly being affected, short term or long term, by:

- Technological breakthroughs;
- The rhythmic character of economic activity—even socialist societies are not immune;
- The weather;
- Revolutions, assassinations, anywhere in the world;
- New political inventions and ideas;
- Unpredictable emergencies and failures of leadership;
- Unpredictable urges and moods of peoples;
- Demographic change.

Even if "parity" were a possibility, we need more than parity:

- As a margin against mistakes and bad luck;
- Because of the asymmetry between the Soviets and ourselves in the way we each use power. America has enormous long-range political advantage in the appeal of our principles and system to many peoples. Indeed it follows from our principles that the Soviets will tend to extract greater short-range advantage from a given level of power than we do. Alas, if they get away with too many of these short-range exploitations, it gives a certain appearance of momentum to their side, and that can dilute the appeal of our principles.

Whether we like it or not, one side or the other will be stronger. We surely must prefer it to be our side, and be prepared to meet the necessary costs.

For 15 to 20 years after World War II the U.S. enjoyed overwhelming military and economic preponderance. The question is not whether we can recapture that era—of course we can't—but whether we have allowed the decline in our relative power to go deeper than it needs to. Our response will depend in good part on the state of the national will. Last winter, as the public rallied behind this Administration's Iran and Afghanistan policies, it was widely commented that "the Viet Nam syndrome" was finally behind us. There will be many opportunities in 1980–85 to see whether this is a lasting change in the national temper.

Below, in my own rough ranking of priorities, are steps that can be taken right here in Washington to reinforce the world position of the United States. Some are entirely within the control of the Executive; the more difficult require Executive and Congressional agreement, and of course broad public support, which I believe the Executive and Congress could marshal.

(1) A vigorous and discriminating defense buildup. This effort should be highly publicized, including the fact that it requires sacrifices in civilian consumption, publicly funded and private.*

(2) Revitalization of the U.S. economy, and especially its technological and productive base. Some of the necessary and painful measures for a cyclical recovery are already taking hold. A long-term program is imperative. The eventual benefits will not be confined to our domestic life but will greatly strengthen our hand in world affairs. From our present level of economic activity we have a higher relative growth potential for 1980–85 than does the Soviet Union, and for that matter a higher relative potential than most of our Allies.

(3) An energy policy that will significantly reduce our dependence on foreign sources, especially the Persian Gulf. Considerable progress has finally been made. I continue to think we need a stiff tax on gasoline at the pump, to cut consumption further, to generate funds for Social Security tax relief and investment incentives, and to show the world we mean business.

(4) Presidential leadership must be seen to be more steadfast. I think this Administration talks too much about foreign policy; when several authoritative spokesmen generate thousands of words per week it is difficult to achieve total consistency. Sometimes we sound as if we are changing our policy when we really aren't. But when changing circumstances do dictate policy changes, these should be frankly acknowledged and explained. I find a certain capacity for self-deception even in our internal conversations about foreign policy—e.g., insistence that the Alliance is really in fine shape, that we have made great strides in our standing in the non-aligned world, etc. There are plenty of diplomatic problems that should not be spelled out in public, but the general tone about such matters should convey realism and a willingness to face the disagreeable.

(5) Related to the previous point—the "two Secretaries of State" situation must be ended. The confusion has been serious abroad, and considerable here, and directly affects world perceptions of the President. I have expressed myself on this before; as you know, my views in no way reflect on Zbig, for whom I have great respect. I had hoped the Ed Muskie ap-

---

*I favor the draft (contrary to DOD) primarily for reasons of equity but also to help overcome the deteriorating quality of our military manpower. Is it possible that the Russian peasant conscript, once synonymous with ignorant cannon-fodder, is today better educated than the average American soldier?

I am dismayed—this is not entirely a digression—by the present tendency of the unionized teachers, with this Administration's encouragement, to think of themselves as political activists and lobbyists for federal money.

Our educational system is in deep trouble, with immediate implications for the quality of military personnel and long-range implications for the technological lead the U.S. still holds.

pointment would resolve this situation, but now I am not so sure. (Apart from this glaring point, I have not tried in this report to address internal structure and relationships within the foreign policy and defense establishment.)

(6) Secretary Muskie has forcefully argued the general case for bigger U.S. aid programs in the coming years. This report points out specific opportunities in a number of countries (and dangers if we fail to respond). The aid recommendations scattered through this report probably imply a total increase of up to $1.5 billion in U.S. bilateral programs. I think an increase of that dimension would be an excellent investment.

*(7) We must enhance our intelligence capabilities.

*(8) We must improve our propaganda. At SCC meetings, it often seems no one really knows what the ICA is doing about some opportunity in the Iranian situation, Afghanistan, etc. Have we arrived at the right bureaucratic arrangements for this important arm of foreign policy, and does the ICA get enough State or NSC guidance on its major themes?

(9) In the broad concerns we project to the world, I wish we could once more put some stress on the fundamental conflict between our values and those of the Soviets. It is their *system* that generates an Afghanistan invasion or a Sakharov banishment. The system, armed with massive military power, is capable of much worse things.

I am afraid this Administration's emphasis on human rights as the over-riding moral theme of our foreign policy tends to obscure the unique character of the Soviet threat and the unique character of the U.S. responsibility. In some of our rhetoric the brute totalitarianism of the Soviets seems to get equated with a traditional Latin America military junta because they are both offenders against human rights.

The moral authority of U.S. foreign policy derives from our determination to defend the freedom of the U.S. and other countries which cherish individual rights. It does not depend on hectoring small and middle-size countries which have no capacity or desire to attack us or our allies, and in fact often wish to be friendly with us and helpful in our security arrangements. I would look mainly to history (helped perhaps by an occasional discreet nudge from the U.S.) to improve their human rights performances.

World politics today resembles, in at least one respect, a worldwide war. Everything seems to affect everything else—sometimes very fast. West Bank negotiations—Arab oil production levels—U.S./Europe relations—SALT—Afghanistan sanctions—Argentine grain. More than ever, senior policymakers need the resources to think six steps ahead, and keep

---

*The CIA and ICA papers in this report are in effect expositions of why they should have more money in 1980–85, and what they would do with it. I am generally persuaded.

all the continents and dozens of contingencies in view. In many situations policy necessarily will be "reactive," which should not be a pejorative word. The problem is not to get so busy reacting that there is no time to think through broad directions and options and major initiatives.

Moving away from the foreign policy choices within our domestic control, I now touch on various external relationships and regions of high importance to the U.S., 1980–85. Four in particular merit as much vigilance and imagination as USG can muster.

(1) "The Alliance." This anchor of our foreign policy truly requires a fresh appraisal. "Consultation" is permanently less perfect than it might be, but the fuss about consultation tends to obscure real collisions of attitudes and interests.

The American disappointment at the Allied response to Iran and Afghanistan takes on a special edge because the Europeans and Japanese seem to have more immediately at stake in that area than we do. Further divergences are probable—e.g., [on] the Palestinian issue.

We could see in Congress and the public in the early 1980s a growing impatience with Europe's inability or unwillingness "to defend itself." Western Europe, after all, has a greater population and GNP than the U.S. It is in many ways astonishing that there is still a large U.S. Army in Western Europe 35 years after World War II, and that so many Europeans seem to take it for granted that this is even more to our interest than theirs.

U.S. policymakers will have to counter neo-isolationist stirrings at home, and at the same time even use such sentiment to convince the allies we are not totally locked into the present deployments in Germany. A shift of some U.S. strength toward Middle East/S.W. Asia availability, with a corresponding increase in Allied commitments in Europe, would make the potential strength of the Alliance count more heavily in the world balance of power. But I don't think we can lecture the Allies too successfully until U.S. gasoline prices are closer to Europe's, and until we have the draft.

A larger Japanese defense effort is also clearly in our interest, and is attainable.

(2) Camp David remains a noble achievement, despite disappointments since. The search for Middle East peace must remain a very high priority of U.S. foreign policy.

(3) It should be a high-priority objective, 1980–85, to detach one or more countries from the Soviet orbit, or move one or two places from phoney non-aligned status to genuine non-aligned. Among the candidates: Cuba, Iraq, Syria, Angola, Libya, Ethiopia, South Yemen.

(4) From an improving U.S. power base, we should seek to improve

U.S.-Soviet relationships. It may be objected that the Soviets would not agree to restore détente* on such a "one-sided" basis. If so, the implication is that they will pursue détente only if they feel their own power base is growing vs. ours. (Unless they have completely abandoned Marxism, they could hardly believe in such a static concept as stable parity.)

When and as it becomes possible to improve U.S.-Soviet relations, we should make sure it is not at the expense of a productive U.S.-China relationship.

If the Soviets genuinely desire better relations, they must do something to defuse the Afghanistan issue. I do not agree with the arguments in other papers in this report (DOS, DOD, NSC) that SALT II is so advantageous to us we should press ahead for ratification regardless of Afghanistan. I am concerned, too, that an all-out drive for SALT II despite Afghanistan leads so easily to inflated rhetoric about the perils of non-ratification, with elements of self-fulfilling prophecy, especially as to the Alliance.

A period of serious international danger is upon us, and it could well last into the mid-1980s. It is brought about in part by the Soviet military buildup and the fact that much of the world *thinks* the balance of power has moved in favor of the Soviets.†

The Soviet threat to the West is intensified, paradoxically, by the internal weaknesses of the Soviet system, especially their declining economic growth rates and impending energy deficit. Soviet military power vis-à-vis the West will continue to grow in the early 1980s, and then crest in the mid-'80s.

To summarize, I believe we can come through this dangerous "window" period if:

- We are seen to be resolutely improving our military posture.
- We are making real progress toward the most important of the specific economic and diplomatic objectives set forth in this report—stronger U.S. productive base, greater self-reliance in energy, Middle East peace, strengthening of the Alliance.
- We are improving the coherence and consistency of our exposition of U.S. foreign policy, and projecting strong leadership qualities from the White House. The President's capital should not be squandered in a diffuse benevolence toward all nations, regions, problems, causes. Some of these are less important than others, and could benefit from no Presidential mention for weeks at a time. Your leadership should be sharply focused on the most important—and attainable—advancements of the national inter-

*You should award an in-house prize for some better word than détente to define a tolerable U.S.-Soviet relationship.

†The paper on the U.S.-Soviet Relationship speculates that the Soviet regime may be fragile in the 1990s. But we have to get from here to there.

est of the United States. Such advances serve the welfare of free people everywhere, and peoples aspiring to be free.

The Secret/Sensitive classification of my introduction remained intact, to my profound relief, throughout the 1980 election campaign. My blunt introduction drew on no military secrets, but it could have been politically explosive. My nightmare was: "EX-ADVISER BLASTS CARTER FOREIGN POLICY." But I had kept a very low profile during my year in the White House, I left very quietly, and I tried to stay out of the papers between my departure in mid-August and the election on November 4.

I thought Carter should be at least a little appreciative of my discretion, so I couldn't refrain from a small needle on October 6:

My dear Mr. President:

Knowing you as a clean In Box man, I have become increasingly curious as to your reaction to my "book" on U.S. Foreign Policy, submitted on August 12.

Respectfully yours,

In the midst of his campaign, poor man, he had to take time to reply. He wrote on October 23:

You shame me with your 'clean in-box' reference. I've gotten a little behind lately. The book is being very helpful to me ... There is a certain toughness about the analyses which are typical of your personal advice to me while you were here. The foreword is especially helpful and I will use it during the post-election period as a guide and reminder list in establishing my agenda for the future.

16

---◆►---

Domestic Doves and Hawks

The ambivalence in Carter foreign policy had its parallels in domestic policy, and here also Carter himself was both hard-line and soft-line. The engineer hated waste, duplication of services; the successful farmer and small businessman believed in plain living, hard work, and the profit motive. But the devout Christian humanitarian had a genuine compassion for the "disadvantaged" and a generous reluctance to differentiate very acutely the causes of disadvantage. The practical politician was also keenly aware of danger on the Democratic Left, i.e., Kennedy. And the rural southern populist had a genuine distrust of big corporations. One day he had just had lunch with "some of your friends"—sarcastic emphasis—referring to eight or ten heads of big banks and corporations; not his kind of folks. They all make speeches supporting the Carter economic program, he complained, but they always include at least one criticism and then, of course, the *Wall Street Journal* or *Business Week* or *Fortune* pick up the criticism and play that up.

The surrogate for the hard Carter was James McIntyre, Jr., director of the Office of Management and Budget. Jim was another frugal small-town Georgian with huge appetite for detail and an admirable perseverance. He had some successes against the spenders.

In the White House the leading domestic soft-liners were Vice-President Mondale and Stuart Eizenstat, counselor for domestic affairs. They of course had their victories, especially since such powerful spending constituencies were in place in Congress and the executive departments.

I was in the McIntyre camp, as the President knew. I once told him

198

that except for McIntyre I must be the most conservative fellow in his Administration. He claimed No, he was. His budget deficits, trifling by Reagan Administration standards, offended him deeply, and even in election year 1980, he would propose only a modest tax cut to take effect in 1981.

Carter was "absolutely correct," ex-Chairman Arthur Burns recalls, in his dealings with the Federal Reserve. His eyes "glittered with comprehension" as economic statistics were recited in front of him, though Burns didn't feel Carter drew the right conclusions from the figures.

The energy problem appealed intensely to Carter. The technological aspects keenly interested him, and he rather enjoyed the hair-shirt aspects—holding down on heating and air conditioning, encouraging people to walk to work, lowering speed limits, etc. Though his Synfuel scheme, heavily sweetened by Congress, was a wasteful failure, the Carter combination of conservation measures and graduated decontrol of oil and gas production in fact contributed to the stabilizing of energy prices (declining, in real dollars) in 1981–82, to the considerable benefit of Ronald Reagan.

Deregulation was generally congenial to the free-enterprise, anti-bureaucracy side of Carter, and regulation and over-regulation appealed to the moralistic defender of the people against the greed of big business. Thus he worked effectively for legislation loosening up the federal controls on trucking, airlines, banking, at the same time his Administration was tightening controls on industrial health and safety and the environment.

At Carter's request, I attended many of the budget review sessions in the Cabinet Room where he and McIntyre were hearing petitions from wounded departments or agencies as to why they needed more money than OMB was allowing them. Some of these meetings were put-up jobs, the President and McIntyre having already agreed that such and such department would get $95 million restored. But it was good for the morale of the appropriate Cabinet officer to get a chance in front of some of his subordinates to argue with the President and seem to prevail.

At one of these sessions, Henry Owen, formerly of the Brookings Institution, then with the NSC, was to argue for a bigger foreign aid request than McIntyre had approved. In the lull before the President came into the room, Owen pointed to the half dozen vacant seats around the Cabinet table between his delegation and the OMB team, and asked whether I would like to sit next to "the Forces of Light" or "the Forces of Darkness." I told Henry I was generally on the Dark side, but on this particular issue pro-Light, so I would sit next to him. At the end of the meeting the President, as I recall, came down about 55–45 Light.

I argued with the President, unsuccessfully, about inflation. Not only in speeches but in private conversation he tended to attribute it almost entirely to the surge in energy costs, and to take comfort in the fact that it was afflicting all the industrial countries and none of them, so he felt, could do much of anything about it.

I thought this defeatism was bad economics—and bad politics. For somebody fascinated by politics and elections for fifty years, it took stern self-discipline to honor my own intention not to get involved in the campaign. Once or twice I did violate my monastic vows not to discuss the election with the President. I tried to adduce some campaign reason for doing something I thought desirable on policy grounds. On the inflation issue I felt Carter was highly vulnerable to any Republican—who wouldn't even have to say what he would do about it. He could just point to 14 percent inflation in 1980 vs. the 4.8 percent Carter inherited from Ford. "Think what Jerry Ford himself would do with those numbers." At that time, February 1980, I thought Ford would be the candidate. Carter agreed that would be tough. I said if their roles were reversed, Carter would clobber Ford with those figures. Carter (almost with relish): Damn right. A couple of months later, when it had become almost certain Reagan would be his opponent, I couldn't resist saying that it would be ironic if Carter made Reagan look well informed and realistic about inflation while painting himself as simplistic and superficial. He managed a pained smile. His thank-you at the end of our conversation was a little on the stiff side.

I probably spent no more than a quarter of my White House year on domestic policy questions. There was more than enough to think about in the foreign policy sphere. Beyond that, I felt I made no dent in domestic policy areas, and that it became increasingly difficult, if not impossible, to separate the policy from the politics during an election year.

Carter only once asked me a head-on political question, and it was such an engaging one that I couldn't resist. I should take my time, but would I please think about why liberals didn't like him. (This was June 1980; he was looking past the nomination, which he then had sewn up, to the job of peacemaking with the Kennedy wing of the party.) Next time I saw him I said there were four reasons: Liberals are believers in the strong Presidency and hanker for a commanding figure in the FDR mold—Carter didn't come across that way; most liberals found his rural southern background uncongenial; ditto his born-again Christianity; and finally, liberals were more liberal than he was. He thought it was quite a good analysis.

Peering toward 1990

A richly instructive experience, early in my White House year, was the organizing of a presidential commission. In our first conversation after I came to work for Carter, I had said that his Administration was offering no vision for the future and that he as President was not publicly associated with any sense of long-range directions or purposes for the country. He had been thinking along the same lines, in part inspired by the "national malaise" findings of his pollster Patrick Caddell. He asked me to set up a commission to think about all this.

From previous experience I was skeptical of attempts to look into the far future. I had once served on a private Commission on the Year 2000, which held its meetings in 1966—much too soon. I think five years is about the maximum forecasting span. But a five-year study, announced in 1979, would have coincided exactly with what Carter hoped would be his second term. He had agreed the study should be bipartisan and nonpolitical, so we set the time frame as the decade of the 1980s, which would include at least two administrations.

I wanted to avoid any implication that the commission thought it could plan the ten-year future of the U.S. So we avoided talk of "goals," "blueprints," "program," and called the study the President's Commission on a National Agenda for the Eighties. In an internal memorandum for the White House senior staff I wrote:

> This project arises out of a conviction that America is not itself when it lacks faith in the future and lacks a vision of the future.
>
> The President has gone so far as to say the country is suffering a "crisis of confidence." Others have spoken of a "national malaise" or even "national despair."
>
> I myself think these characterizations are somewhat overdrawn, but there is no doubt that over the past 15 years *something has changed in the national spirit,* and the change is for the worse. The country rebounded well from Viet Nam and Watergate in many ways, but there are still residues of mistrust of institutions, including, perhaps especially, the Presi-

dency. The energy experience of the past half dozen years has been deeply unsettling to long-standing American habits and assumptions. The vicious rate of inflation can hardly fail to shake individual confidence in the future, and at the same time weakens the moral fibre of the country by discouraging saving and undermining many forms of contract.

Over the past 15 years we have also seen a decline in the relative strength of America in the world, not the fault of this Administration or any other but an inevitable historical development. Many Americans who compare 1979 with the early post World War II years of overwhelming U.S. dominance, military and economic, feel we are now being "pushed around." And it feels worse when the pushing-around also has painful consequences for the U.S. standard of living, as in the overthrow of the Shah.

Out of these factors, then, and doubtless others—many years of affluence; growth in the highly educated class (sophisticated, hard-to-please); the growing tension between egalitarianism and excellence; the disappointing or perverse consequences of many well-meant "reforms"—come the present currents of skepticism and irritability.

The Commission would address itself to the present national mood and to the very broad question of how some sense of common purpose and optimism might be restored. The Commission might conclude that the national mood will take care of itself if the specific problems of inflation, energy, productivity, etc., can be successfully dealt with. [I had told the President privately that a return to 5 percent inflation would mop up a lot of malaise.] Or the Commission might conclude that in addition to these crucial specifics, there is also a larger need that must be addressed. Here it might attempt to define a role for Presidential leadership, governmental leadership at all levels, and the many private centers of leadership in holding out a vision (and visions) as to where the nation could be going.

My chief contribution to the commission was to persuade William McGill, then in his last year as president of Columbia University, to become its chairman. But the credit for this stroke should go to my old friend John Gardner, who hunched McGill might be persuadable. McGill brought solid intellectual substance to the chairmanship and political skills honed over long years in dealing with faculties. He was perfect.

As McGill and I were lining up the fifty commission members, I was struck again by the magic of the White House. Here was a President at a sorry low in national esteem, here was a subject with considerable potential for boredom and platitude, and yet of all the busy and distinguished people we approached, only three declined. And there were many avid seekers of places on the commission, backed by heavy lobbying. Although Carter had casually told McGill and me just to go ahead and pick whoever we wanted, it was not that simple. We had to sacrifice some intellectual candlepower to White House senior staff pressures for more representation for this or that bloc. We drew the line in several cases, including one in which a visibly unhappy Carter (staring at one of those memo forms where the President must check "Agree" or "Disagree") had to support Bill and me against some of his most zealous political operatives.

The commission was to make public its report in December 1980, after the election, so nobody could charge that it was a think tank for the Democratic campaign. Stuart Eizenstat had the opposite concern —that during the election year there might be leaks of commission views divergent from Administration positions, permitting Republicans to say "even the President's own commission" disagrees with him. There were no leaks.

The study, presented to Carter in the Cabinet Room just four days before Reagan's inauguration, had cost the taxpayers $2.8 million. Was it worth it? It was a generally sensible document, addressing all the major domestic policy concerns and touching on the U.S. world position. The report was burdened with very few dissents, but was relatively free of the least-common-denominator pieties one might have feared. The report gave a very high priority to reducing inflation and acknowledged this might mean a short-term increase in unemployment. The country should not imagine the economy can be "fine-tuned," but should aim at long-term policies that would foster "a sustained increase in real output." The commission urged measures to stimulate savings and investment and restore productivity growth, and again noted there would be a "price tag." It recommended complete federalization of the welfare system, and a comprehensive national health insurance program.

For much less than $2.8 million, a team of academics or journalists could doubtless have come up with more original and provocative ideas. That is not really the point, however. Had Carter been reelected, he would have taken the report seriously, and the fact that all sensitive constituencies were represented or overrepresented in the commission's membership could have helped give the recommendations political support and credibility.

I doubt if President Reagan or his staff spent much time browsing in the report. (The American Heritage Foundation in 1980 had prepared a study of somewhat similar scope, for presentation to an incoming Republican Administration.)

The major publicity about the finished document focused on half a dozen pages out of 197; these contained a hard-boiled suggestion that maybe the beleaguered cities of the Northeast should be allowed to keep on contracting. Carter disavowed this thought; northern mayors, congressmen, senators were incensed. Stu Eizenstat told Senator Pat Moynihan: "I was never in favor of that commission anyway. Hedley Donovan filled it up with Republicans." Actually, there were about fifteen Republicans out of fifty commissioners, but that could look like a lot inside a Democratic White House.

Once the commissioners had all been politically cleared and presidentially approved, and the staff and structure of the study agreed upon, I phased myself out of the project, in early 1980. I kibitzed occasionally on the commission, but concentrated mainly on my foreign policy exercise.

I continued to attract the occasional orphan problem. Nature abhors a vacuum, and the presence in the West Wing of somebody with a big-sounding title and no visible duties was bound to bring in a certain amount of work that nobody else wanted, and that I didn't have the heart to refuse. I was told now and then about people whose feelings had been hurt, and I suggested little presidential gestures. I prevented one undeserving citizen from getting the presidential Medal of Freedom. I found myself, with no particular background, the chairman of an ad hoc interagency committee about Puerto Rico; we worried sporadically about the effects of amphibious landing exercises and offshore gunnery drills on Puerto Rican political tranquillity. Somehow I became the chief defender of the Asia Foundation against various bureaucratic and budget-cutting pressures that might have demolished it. There are lots of these orphan problems lying around the White House, lacking major domestic political ramifications and not big enough to be a desirable addition to anyone's turf.

Departing the White House

I knew I didn't want to be in the White House after the Republican and Democratic nominating conventions, when the "general" (as Hamilton Jordan called it, as opposed to the primaries) began. The primary season had been difficult enough for me, as an independent in a Democratic White House, but I had no problem in preferring Carter over Kennedy as the Democratic candidate. Versus Reagan and the Republicans, it would be a tough call. There was a lot that bothered me about Reagan (much still does) but I felt the Carter Administration was a disappointment, net. I didn't want to be in the West Wing of the White House during the twelve weeks of the "general" and be the only person there who wasn't knocking himself out to get Carter reelected. (Or, as one old Democratic friend put it, "You don't want to be the skunk at the Sunday School picnic.")

So I decided to make use of the happy coincidence, on August 15, 1980, of the first anniversary of my joining the White House staff, the end of the Democratic convention, and the completion of my foreign policy report (timing of the latter somewhat under my control). In July, I wrote Carter that I would like to leave on August 15.

In filling out one of the forms the White House serves on a departing official, I enjoyed fencing with some unknown bureaucrat. Under I RESIGN FOR THE FOLLOWING REASONS: I wrote by hand, "Reasons were given the President in a personal letter." After "Important note . . . generalized reasons, such as 'ill health' or 'personal reasons,' are not acceptable," I couldn't help writing, "To whom?"

Carter made only a perfunctory effort to dissuade me. He knew how far apart we were on many major issues. He understood the strain this would impose on me if I stayed on in the White House, and he perhaps whiffed a minor danger to his campaign. In our exchange of letters Carter was very gracious. I can't give such good marks to Jody Powell, who for days bottled up the announcement I was leaving, because he thought it would be damaging publicity for Carter on the eve of the nominating convention, and at a time when the Billy Carter business was severely embarrassing the Administration. I didn't think my departure would be much of a story, unless perhaps I announced it myself, which I finally threatened to do, which jarred a dignified little announcement out of Powell's office.

I had tried to stay out of the papers during my year in the White House. I declined all talk-show and "background breakfast" invitations and gave no press interviews on policy substance. On arrival I told my old colleague Robert Ajemian, head of the *Time* news bureau in Washington, that I aspired to be the worst source in the city; a few months later he told me I was succeeding famously. The press pretty much concluded it was a waste of time to talk to me, which suited me fine. My only governmental assignment was to give confidential advice to the President; the less I talked to reporters, the less chance of violating that relationship. I didn't want to be caught in interviews where I might have to air policy disagreements with the President—or be forced to defend policies contrary to my own views.

I stuck with my vows of silence from August 15, when I cleaned out my West Wing office and returned to New York, until after the election, when I felt free to begin some writing and speaking about my White House experience. I voted for Carter, chiefly as a matter of personal loyalty to a man I like very much, who had given me a quite extraordinary postgraduate year. As a citizen, however, I was not crushed at the outcome.

I have now supported the Democrat in seven presidential elections of my adult life, and six times the Republican. The box score:

> 1936-Living in England; failed to get absentee ballot, would have voted for Roosevelt.
> 1940-Roosevelt
> 1944-Roosevelt
> 1948-Dewey
> 1952-Eisenhower
> 1956-Eisenhower
> 1960-Nixon
> 1964-Johnson
> 1968-Nixon
> 1972-Nixon
> 1976-Carter
> 1980-Carter
> 1984-Mondale*

I suppose that table is one possible definition of an Independent, or in the good old usage, a mugwump. Or maybe (before anybody else says it), just a crazy mixed-up centrist.

*More on this choice in Chapter 20.

17

Advice to the Isolated

One of the gravest occupational hazards in the modern Presidency is isolation. Presidents are generally reluctant to recognize how isolated they can become, or if they do sense some problem here, reluctant to deal with it seriously.

The isolation has its agreeable aspects, of course. The President is spared the supermarket checkout line, the hunt for a parking place, all the routine vexations of everyday American life. His appointment calendar, in box, and telephone are beautifully protected. And though the President is indeed under pitiless scrutiny when he appears in public, he can often draw a cloak of deep privacy around the famous Goldfish Bowl.

Security is only the most obvious of the reasons for presidential isolation. In the Reagan Administration, the attempt on the President's life, only three months after he took office, led the White House staff and Secret Service to cut down sharply on his exposure to crowds. Nancy Reagan made no secret of her anxieties. The President, being a brave man (and a politician), chafed at the restrictions and perhaps occasionally overruled his security people. But security people generally get their way, and the precautions are pervasive.

A President doesn't overcome his isolation, of course, by waving to people outside a hotel door or along a motorcade route. But he does have a chance for useful contact with the country "out there" when he gets to the dinner, or convention, or church service, or town meeting, or theater party he is traveling to. If the security arrangements along the routes to these occasions and the screening at his destination get very much more elaborate than they are now (and they have been heavy for years), some of these events will simply seem more bother than they are worth.

Beyond the security requirement, however, the isolation of our Presidents has deeper causes. Even within a totally secure environment Presidents could do much more than they do to keep in touch. Why don't they? Presidential isolation can be brought about by temperament or health of the man himself, or external events, but it also grows out of the forces and pressures that have shaped the office as we know it today.

How much can a President's advisers, in-house and outside, help him overcome that isolation? In what ways might they actually intensify it?

Ideally, a President would come to office with a lifetime's accumulation of wise and honest friends from many fields of attainment, nicely distributed by geography. A few of these he might appoint to office, but most could be available for advice from the outside, one protection against the isolation that could otherwise settle so swiftly upon their old friend. Their advice would cost the government nothing. Their disagreements with Senators or Cabinet officers or foreign governments, expressed conversationally in the White House family dining room, would not get into the papers. And if the brilliant president of the most prestigious university in the President's home state turns out not to look so brilliant in the national policy context . . . well, no need to invite him back to dinner for quite a while. I did in fact think of this model now and then during my year in the Carter Administration, which in no way resembled that model. Nor does the Reagan Administration.

Reagan had more close personal friends from prepresidential days than Carter. The background of the Reagan Kitchen Cabinet did not, however, suggest much broadening of the President's perspectives. These intimates were mainly rich, self-made Southern California businessmen, and their informal advice could be pretty much what Reagan thought in the first place. But though they had considerable influence during Reagan's tenure as governor, and his campaigns for President, they seemed to have little input once he was in the White House.

Carter's only significant adviser from private life was the astute Mr. Kirbo of Atlanta, so astute indeed that his advice was seldom known to anyone but the President. Neither Carter nor Reagan had anywhere near so broad and varied a circle of prepresidential friends and connections as did Nixon, Johnson, and Eisenhower, though none of those Presidents drew on informal advice as much as they might have.

Friends of a President, it must also be noted, tend to relish that status, and are reluctant to tell him things he might not want to hear.

In their use of staff advice, there are fascinating contrasts—and ultimately some similarities—between Reagan and Carter. Reagan hasn't minded listening to quite a variety of advice, and has professed to benefit from and enjoy vigorous staff debate in his presence, even when one side was disputing what were thought to be the President's own views. Nixon hated that kind of encounter. (To be fair—so do many executives in private life. They are uncomfortable when subordinates go at each other very hard, in part because they don't want anybody to get hurt, in part because they know they will eventually have to adjudicate.)

Reagan's temperament is more open than that of Carter, Nixon, or Johnson, but his mind is less so. Though he would not seem to feel threatened or put down by a senior staff man or Cabinet officer questioning his views, his aides, including the ultra-loyal, have said the best way to get Reagan to change his mind is to convince him he is not actually changing his mind.

Carter could listen to head-on disagreement and even direct criticism with a tightly controlled calm (the effort was sometimes visible). I never would have dreamed of trying to convince Carter that some big shift of policy was really not a big shift of policy. Carter would not have been deceived in any case, and would have thought the worse of the adviser. He could deceive himself, however, by failing to spot change or inconsistency in his own positions, but this had less to do with his advisers than his own thinking process (as discussed in Chapter 19).

Perhaps only twice in the past half century have we had Presidents who did not become, in one way or another, cut off from the country. Those two, and they both had brief administrations, were John Kennedy and Gerald Ford, vigorous men, not backslappers but they liked to get around, fond of sports, parties—Kennedy cool but alive with intellectual curiosity, Ford stolid and very comfortable with all kinds of people. Both tapped in quite often on the judgment of friends outside the White House orbit.

All the other modern Presidents came to be seriously isolated within the White House. Franklin Roosevelt's mobility was restricted by his polio and then by wartime security. For Lyndon Johnson and Richard Nixon, political adversity, in the form of Viet Nam and Watergate, made it painful to move around much in the country. (Four decades earlier, Herbert Hoover had suffered similar imprisonment by the Depression; he was not much of a mixer even in good times.) Nixon and Jimmy Carter were more or less reclusive Presidents by temperament. Reagan's curiosity is well contained. Eisenhower was somewhat less gregarious than the famous grin suggested; age and illness also cut down his energy and perhaps his curiosity. Harry Truman was a parochial President in his friendships. The press critic Ben Bagdikian used to needle *Time* magazine because it had called the people President Truman played poker with "cronies," while the businessmen President Eisenhower played golf with were called "friends." Touché, though I got a little tired of the point when Ben kept bringing it up for fifteen or twenty years, three and four administrations later.

We have an image of American politicians as crowd-working, people-loving extroverts, but it takes a burning intensity of ambition and ego to seek the Presidency today, to undergo the brutally long campaigning season, the probing eye of the printed press and the TV cameras. There are surely tensions between the requirement for surface affability and calm, and the driving purpose inside the man. Jimmy Carter was something of a loner even when he had a thousand Georgians listening to Country and Western on the South Lawn of the White House. The Reagans, along with all their graceful entertaining and the President's old-shoe geniality, are said to be "very private people." The ability to tune out on many occasions, simply not to notice, not to listen, may be part of the armor that carries a presidential candidate through the campaigning. He may have been running for President twelve years, as Reagan had in 1980, four years as Carter had in 1976, and that experience had already given him at least a layer or two of insulation from his fellow Americans.

Living with the Football

Now he arrives in the Oval Office to take up the awesome responsibility he has so avidly sought. More insulation begins to envelop him at once. He assumes authority over the executive branch of the U.S. government, more than five million people—civilian and military—and a federal budget absorbing almost a quarter of our national product. Even a President who thinks the federal role is too large, as Reagan does, takes on a staggering administrative responsibility for fulfillment of his present role as mandated by law, and a formidable political campaign—and he has just finished one campaign—if he is to get some of the law changed.

He shares power over domestic policy with Congress, but the President has supremacy in foreign policy, and that supremacy has its terrors, or might have for people less endowed with the certitudes it takes to run for President. The "football," the briefcase with the coded command sequence for nuclear launch, goes with him everywhere, carried by a military aide. (Does he ever lighten his day by pretending the briefcase just contains the colonel's lunch?) But short of the finger on the button, a whole array of foreign policy and defense decisions comes before the President with an immense influence on all our lives.

To help the President cope with all this there has grown up the President's own internal government, a miniature government, still small by Washington standards but bigger than just a staff, maybe five hundred people, loosely known as "the White House." The White House staff really can't help the President much in opening himself out to the country. They are trying to represent the President's wishes to the giant bureaucracies—Defense, State, Treasury, Energy, Health and Human Services, Agriculture, and so on. They are trying to wheel and deal with Congress, which is generally better at it than they are. These White House staff people also have their own constituencies—business, labor, mayors and governors, minorities, "ethnics," Jews, women. The staffers try to keep unnecessary paper off the President's desk, but they generate their own paper and send plenty of it into the Oval Office. All of these advocates under his own roof also become a very intimate kind of human and political administrative problem for the President. They are family in a way, and they need care and feeding—all five hundred of them. There were just a few dozen in Hoover's day.

So a new President can be easily overwhelmed by all this, by the executive role and the executive apparatus. And he probably should be overwhelmed. But it leaves him little time or energy for personal efforts to be in touch with the country, with "out there."

When a President does circulate, if he has the strength for it and the interest, he runs into that principle of physics, the Heisenberg effect: a phenomenon changes by being observed.* The President of the United States dropping in on a PTA meeting does tend to affect the proceedings.

Yet it comes hard to a President to perceive that he could have an isolation problem. He did after all get elected—what better proof that

---

*In his column "On Language," William Safire has ruled that "Heisenberg Effect" became a journalistic cliché sometime during the 1984 campaign (*New York Times,* November 11, 1984). I first used "Heisenberg Effect" in 1967, however, in a speech at Mount Holyoke College, South Hadley, Mass., and I feel free to continue using it.

he is in tune with the country? He is subjected to vast quantities of free advice in our free press. He can command anyone in the country to his dinner table. He needn't even offer a meal. Singly or in groups, for a Coke or a Tab or coffee or nothing at all, he can summon bankers and corporation chairmen, Nobel laureates, publishers, union chieftains, clergymen, philanthropists.

A very appealing modesty in Jimmy Carter was to seem not quite to understand how easily he could bring important people to the White House. A very cool self-esteem in Jimmy Carter left him skeptical that he would learn much from these big shots that would be helpful in his work.

More important, the President's own top appointees, Cabinet officers and White House senior staff, do have a tendency to shield him from the unpleasant, and tell him what they think he wants to hear. The President halfway knows he is being sheltered but doesn't fully believe it—he wants to think he has appointed people of character and candor and that he is the kind of man who encourages his subordinates to tell it to him straight. For the subordinates, it's not entirely a matter of buttering up the boss. The senior officials themselves tend to become isolated. They work ferocious hours. They are quite sincerely prone to wishful thinking. They also have their own solicitous underlings protecting them from what the underlings think the Secretary wouldn't like to hear.

In many meetings during the year I was in the White House it would occur to me that I was perhaps the only person in the room who had no fervent desire to be there. (Possibly not the ideal attitude toward one's job.) If I had been six or eight years younger, hoping to hold my job through a second Carter term or maybe move up to a bigger job, I might have been less candid in my conversations with the President. I have to note, however, that some of the frankest of the President's men were among the youngest. Maybe the caution belt lies in the upper forties and the fifties.

At about the same time I was appointed Senior Adviser, the President brought two other "non-Georgians with gray hair" into the White House. These two had demanding operational duties, as I did not. Lloyd Cutler was a sage Washington lawyer, originally a New Yorker, silver-haired and sixty-two, and he replaced a Georgian as the President's chief legal counsel. Alonzo McDonald, sandy-haired but fifty-one, was brought in as deputy chief of staff. McDonald was a first-class administrator, which his boss Hamilton Jordan (one of the most thoroughly engaging people in the Carter Administration) was not, and did not pretend to be. McDonald happened to be a Georgian by birth, but had spent most of his career in the management consulting firm of McKinsey and Company in New York and Europe. (Cutler returned to his Washington law firm in 1981; McDonald became president of Bendix briefly, then chairman of a venture capital firm in Michigan.) The fact that the President brought in these three outsiders, McDonald, Cutler, and me, none previously close to him, was an admission that he did need an older, broader, more diversified staff. It was an admission that he did have an isolation problem, or at least that he should quiet down the people who were saying he had such a problem.

Carter and his staff had unfortunately neglected one very convenient source of information and wisdom about "out there"—the Congress. The Carter White House never recovered from its bad start in congressional relations. To the end it was too self-righteously preoccupied with the self-interestedness of various congressional positions (as though no White House positions were self-interested) to make an open-minded effort to listen and learn from what senators and representatives said they were hearing. A good many old Washington hands who had been following Congress for a long time thought the 95th Congress, in terms of individual talents, was the best Congress they had seen. It was also the most fractious and obnoxious from the standpoint of the leader in either house—or supposed leader—and the President. But the fifty or hundred best senators and representatives were probably more interesting to talk to than they had ever been before. If Carter —killing two birds with one stone—had done what he could for his legislation in meetings with these people, and also listened to them, it might have helped reduce his isolation.

There is a built-in tension, of course, between Congress and the White House staff under any President. Cabinet officers are confirmed by Congress and can be summoned up to the Hill for testimony at any time, whereas the White House senior staff is not. So far as executive-congressional relations are concerned, it is obviously better for a President to rely less on his own unexamined people, and show more confidence in the people who have to face some congressional scrutiny to get confirmed and to continue operations.

I am not sure I did anything to ameliorate President Carter's isolation problem. The President, courteous as always, insisted that I was very helpful to him during my year at the White House.

My advisory conversations had a curious rhythm. The agenda was mainly up to me. I would make some policy suggestion, or compliment or criticize the President on some recent deed or statement. His response was generally pleasant but did not necessarily invite further comment from me. I would usually press on, however, seeking to explore his thinking and elicit some argument on points where I knew or suspected he (or others in the Administration) must disagree with my position. His response to my elaboration tended to discourage further talk on that subject today: Yes, let me think about that. Or: That's very useful, thank you. A surprisingly long list of large topics could be disposed of in half an hour or so.

Sol Linowitz, wise in the ways of Washington, advised me early in my White House year to draw up a definition of my job much more explicit than the original announcement. I should specify the meetings I wanted to attend, the subjects I wanted to be involved with, get the President to agree and ask him to circulate the memo to senior people. Some combination of modesty and vanity kept me from doing that. I wasn't accustomed to pushing. The President had proposed the job; it was up to him to define it.

If you are an adviser dealing privately with the President, and especially such a polite President, you never know how many other people have already given him the same advice you are giving or whether he has already decided all by himself to do what you are now suggesting. If he goes against your advice, you don't necessarily know how much company you had on the losing side of the argument, or whether you came anywhere near affecting the result. If it is important to you that others should know what your advice was, and that you should know exactly how the President felt about it, then as a presidential adviser you are in the wrong line of work.

A presidential adviser obviously has more chance of having his advice accepted if it amounts to a modification, refinement, or extension of a presidential policy the adviser is in sympathy with, rather than a recommendation that some policy or tendency be totally reversed. The same phenomenon can be noticed in the offering and receiving of advice within a family.

Species of Advisers

Beyond that, it is clear that what I will call an organic adviser will have more influence than an artificially conceived adviser. One kind of organic adviser is the old friend like Kirbo, with whom Carter had had an intimate and trusting relationship for many years. Carter would phone Kirbo, or ask him up to the White House for the night, whenever he felt he was facing an especially difficult decision. The fact that Kirbo didn't want anything from Carter and didn't want to stay in Washington an hour longer than he had to enhanced the credibility of his advice.

The other kind of organic adviser is a White House senior staff official who has functional responsibilities that bring him constantly into the President's office. If the President comes to trust the judgments such people bring to their operational duties he will naturally tend to invite their views in other areas. This certainly applied to Jody Powell foremost, and then I would say to Hamilton Jordan, Stuart Eizenstat, and though he was there only sixteen months, to Lloyd Cutler. Brzezinski, of course, had significant influence in a very ample territory, national security policy, but was not encouraged, so far as I know, to enter other territories.

It was a staff of impressive individual competences. There was, as I think everybody ultimately agreed, some narrowness of experience. By the time Carter tried to correct it, it was perhaps too late in the day. Certainly the congressional attitudes toward the staff had hardened by then and were not going to be changed.

It was something of a puzzle why so many capable individuals didn't coalesce more effectively as a working body. If the White House staff was not really an effective arm of the Carter Presidency, it was in part, paradoxically, because most of them individually were *too* devoted to the President, without enough perspective on the country or even on Washington itself.

The two true "senior advisers" of the Carter Presidency were not identified as such in the organization charts. One, of course, was the Vice-President. Walter Mondale had a breadth of practical political experience the young Georgians couldn't match, and had his own constituencies that the Georgians were not always comfortable with. As Mondale later felt compelled to stress in his 1984 campaigning, he had had his differences with Carter: e.g., he had opposed the grain embargo and a sale of advanced F-15 gear to Saudi Arabia. But as VP, he never let any of his disagreements leak. Carter greatly valued Mondale's intelligence, discretion, and loyalty, though he could complain, a little perversely, that in the final crunches of a policy dispute, Fritz wouldn't fight hard enough for his own views.

Carter did not attempt to give the Vice-President any operating responsibilities, and Mondale wisely did not seek them. (Reagan and

Bush have experimented, I think misguidedly, with administrative roles for the Vice-President.) But Carter did make good on his promise that his Vice-President would be totally informed and "in the loop" on all major policy decisions. Mondale was the first Vice-President to have an office in the West Wing of the White House (as Bush did after him). The previous three or four VPs were across the street in the EOB when they were not in their ceremonial offices up on the Hill. During the long months of the Rose Garden strategy, Fritz Mondale carried much of the load of the campaigning against Ted Kennedy. Otherwise, Mondale filled his essential constitutional assignment of being there.

Mondale's irreverent wit was welcome relief in such an earnest and high-minded White House. From time to time he and I would go to lunch at Dominique's, his favorite nearby restaurant, and tell stories out of school. He was not a great admirer of pollster Pat Caddell,* and used very earthy language in arguing against the Caddell-Carter "crisis of confidence" speech. He felt you put up with certain afflictions in politics but didn't necessarily call attention to them. He once told Carter: "I sort of got this figured out. We're the nation's fire hydrant."

The other true senior adviser to the President—and ultimate example of the "organic adviser"—was the bright and spirited Rosalynn. In 1980, she also put in arduous days as a surrogate campaigner and intimate political counselor. Her husband never had cause to complain that she pulled any punches.

Adviser by Proclamation

My own White House role was not based on any deep-rooted personal association with the President or on any operational assignment. The President simply proclaimed that as of August 15, 1979, I would become his Senior Adviser.

In making this appointment, the President was going against a management theory he had often asserted in the past, that he didn't want any high-level advisers who had no responsibility for carrying out any of their advice. That's not a unique theory to Carter, of course. He may have imbibed some of that at the Naval Academy, and certainly there are many corporate managements that operate on that theory.

A further limitation was my status as a political independent. Dur-

---

*In the 1984 preliminaries, Caddell attached himself to Gary Hart. By September 1984, up against Ronald Reagan, the Mondale people were desperate enough to let Caddell part way into their councils.

ing the twelve months I was in the White House the election was a growing preoccupation of everybody there, except for me. I came to doubt that you can be an effective adviser within the White House in an election year if you are not the President's man in a partisan sense.

An election campaign, of course, puts the President in touch with the country in certain very practical ways. It also means that more and more of the conversation around the President takes on a fiercely partisan and protective quality. For at least some of his advisers, it's a fight not only to save his job but their own. Surrounded and sheltered by his loyalists, the President may travel tens of thousands of miles, shake tens of thousands of hands, and still end up as isolated as he began.

Even without an election, the role of "Senior Adviser" takes a lot of working out on the part of the adviser and on the part of the President; and the President has many more important things to think about. Carter and I were inventing the role as we went along; a different Senior Adviser or a different President might have arrived at some other invention.

Somebody set up strictly as an adviser, with no operating functions, at times will be in limbo. I had been on the other end of this relationship myself, as Editor in Chief of Time Inc., occasionally having consultants and advisers who did not have line responsibilities. Sometimes you had to remember: "Oh, I guess I better take so-and-so to lunch next week and ask him for some advice about something." The adviser can become a little bit of an administrative burden in himself.

There were two possible advantages in having no operational role. The arrangement left me more time to think beyond the day-to-day problems and brushfires that consume so much of the time of the line executives. Second, the fact that I had no operating authority meant that other officials would have no reason to think I was trying to muscle in on their turf. My only real product during my year in the White House was one-on-one advice to the President. So far as I know, nobody else in the government felt encroached upon by that advice. But it also is true that since others seldom saw any direct results of those conversations, which is the nature of that kind of confidential relationship, they could be puzzled as to what, if anything, the Senior Adviser did. That can lead to not being taken very seriously. If that becomes the general White House staff attitude, it can affect the attitude of the President, even though he is the one who created the job in the first place. These are rather complex relationships.

I ran into Art Buchwald at a party once in Washington and he thought it was odd that my private meetings with the President were always listed in the President's published appointment calendar. He had imagined I would just be ducking in and out of the Oval Office all the time. I pointed out that the President's weekly lunch with Rosalynn Carter was also listed in the published schedule. That was sort of a smoke-screen answer, but it held Art for a while.

One day early in 1980, a memo came around to White House senior staff from Hamilton Jordan and Alonzo McDonald appealing to us not to put through any more raises for our own staffs or subordinates and saying that they were trying to get through the rest of the fiscal year on the existing salary structure. I myself had chosen to work without salary.* The Jordan-McDonald memo said they had made a thorough study of existing White House salaries and they were convinced that people on the White House staff were being paid approximately what they were worth. I circled that sentence and sent it back to Hamilton and Al and said that in my own case I found this comment quite pointed. Al McDonald liked that, and I believe he had it up on his bulletin board for some weeks.

*I took a leave of absence from the Washington *Star* board on going to work in the White House, also from the Ford Foundation board. I resigned from the Merrill Lynch board, which I had joined on retiring from Time Inc., and from the Council on Foreign Relations Board of Directors. I remained on other nonprofit boards where there seemed no overlap with my White House concerns. I continued as a Time Inc. consultant at a reduced retainer, taking no part in any discussions involving government policy. Time Inc. contributed the services of my secretary Trudi Lanz to my White House office. I had a second secretary who was on the federal payroll; this was my total staff. I rented a room from Time Inc. in an apartment the company owned, and had on the market, at the Watergate.

18

——◆——

The White House and Press:
A Siege Mentality

When I first went to work in the White House, I found that conversations with old friends in the Washington press corps began with the question: "How does the press look from where you sit now? What kind of job do we do?" It surprised some of my White House colleagues to hear of this strain of humility in the press. Of course there were other questions from press friends: "Whatever came over you?" "What's a nice guy from Minnesota doing in with those Georgians?" ("Well, look at Mondale." "Yes, but he has to.") Etc.

Inside the government, new and old friends would ask essentially the same question, not humbly, however, but with a kind of relish: "Well, let's see, you've been here three weeks now—has the press started to look a little different to you?"

Since I had put in thirty-eight years as a professional journalist and then spent only one year as a White House official, my inside-outside view of the press–White House relationship lacks a certain symmetry. Much of my journalistic lifetime was in fact spent reporting, or editing, about government and politics. I also spent four years of World War II practicing a confidential quasi-journalism as an officer in Naval Intelligence, an experience that to this day has left me more sympathetic than many editors to the government side of secrecy arguments.

One-Day Secrets

Arthur Schlesinger, Jr., on the basis of his thousand days in the JFK Administration, said there was no resemblance between events as he saw them within the White House and contemporary press accounts.

My own impression (only 365 days, to be sure) was quite different. Maybe the Washington press corps is much better than it was in the early 1960s; maybe Schlesinger was wrong even then.

The press did a good job on big foreign policy stories that I knew about: the Soviet brigade in Cuba, the state of the Alliance, Iran, Afghanistan, the Middle East peace negotiations. On the inside, you knew some things sooner than the press did—for only a day or two in most cases—but the fact that the press lacked some momentarily secret item of information seldom led to egregiously misleading coverage. In the Iran hostage crisis there was some quiet diplomacy that was never blown. There were two other secrets—the presence of the six Americans in the Canadian Embassy, and the long buildup to the gallant attempt to rescue the other fifty-three. Both secrets were skillfully preserved by President Carter, Press Secretary Jody Powell, the State Department, Defense, CIA. The public didn't "need to know," and didn't.

This was remarkable, considering what an excessively talkative Administration it was. From November 4, 1979, through early May 1980, the President, Jody Powell, and Hodding Carter of State were speaking thousands of words per week on the subject of Iran. President Carter could be terse and highly disciplined in the tight format of a TV press conference. But in the long months of Rose Garden strategy, as he received countless delegations—ethnic, religious, professional, regional—he was a rambling and almost compulsive talker. On Iran, it was extraordinary how seldom he contradicted himself or other officials. When he did, and when the press zeroed in on it, he would of course consider such stories irresponsible.

Politics as Sport

On domestic politics, viewed as a sporting event, the Washington press corps does a generally good job. They did get one little detail wrong in 1980; they pronounced the election too close to call.

Through the long runup to the primaries, during the primaries, and on to the nominating conventions, I was repeatedly struck by how fast and perceptively the press reported the shifts in White House mood and strategy.

President Carter often complained that the correspondents covering political campaigns had no real interest in the substantive issues of domestic policy. More disinterested critics made the same point, but I am not much troubled by this charge that the press focuses too much on the personality of candidates, and on the horse-race aspect of elections. The nominating process and the general election do have aspects of a horse race, a very important one. I think *between* elections is the best time for serious coverage of issues—when the executive and legislature are really at work governing. In an election year what a candidate says about the issues is revealing of his intelligence, character, and judgment, all good things to know about. But it is not any sure guide to what he and his party would and could do in power.

The press does unquestionably enjoy the horse-race aspect of politics, in part because the tough domestic issues so often turn on economics, and that is a subject many reporters are still uncomfortable with. It was not President Carter's favorite either. He read the *New York Times* and Washington *Post,** the Washington *Star* and Atlanta *Constitution* and *Journal, Time* and *Newsweek,* but didn't spend much time with the *Wall Street Journal, Fortune, Business Week,* or the rest of the business press.

The View from the Bunker

The press, looking at the government, sees a colossus, rich in resources for evasion, disinformation, even intimidation, or at least the conferring of favor on a cooperative reporter and withholding of favor from a troublemaker. Bureaucrats will shade the truth to protect their jobs, make their boss look good, embarrass an enemy. Key officials are protected by massed ranks of underlings and PR people. The Oval Office is the most bristling citadel of all.

Within the Carter White House this picture looked almost ludicrous. Inside the "bunker" (a fairly common metaphor, especially during the six months Carter pursued the Rose Garden strategy) the officials looked out and saw an enormous press corps ready to pounce. There are now more than five thousand accredited newspaper, periodical, TV, and radio correspondents in Washington.

The fear of leaks, and the use of leaks, was pervasive. I thought I was reasonably sophisticated on this subject before arriving at the White House, but I had not realized how much bureaucratic warfare is conducted via the leak. It seemed to be taken for granted that, except for the most sensitive military and intelligence information, nothing

---

*He finished the morning papers by 6:30 A.M. or so. I once was struck by two outrageous samples of government waste, in front-page stories the same day in the *Times* and *Post,* and around 11:00 AM sent the President a note about it. His office told me the President had already cut out the same stories and sent a memo to James McIntyre, head of the Office of Management and Budget, several hours earlier.

could be kept secret more than twenty-four hours or so. It was astonishing in a meeting of only six or seven of the most senior officials, where I would have assumed everything was said in confidence, to hear the plea: "Now this *really* mustn't go outside this room."

Arrayed outside the bunker, some of the reporters were burning to be Woodward and Bernstein; all of them wanted to "break" something. Of course any sudden piece of good news would be broken by the government itself as soon as it happened, if not a little before. So anything broken by the press, almost by definition, would be negative. The best to be hoped for was that it would be negative about the Republicans, or heretical Democrats, as the Kennedy faction were regarded for some months.

The Carter White House saw the press as hopelessly addicted to stories of conflict, confusion, and scandal, and generally bored by anything "constructive." If 350,000 federal employees (civilian total in the Washington area) performed their work honestly yesterday, that wasn't news (in fact, if all 350,000 put in an honest day's work that *would* be news), but if one was caught with his hand in the till, that was news.

It is a familiar grievance of businessmen against the press, and a widespread complaint of ordinary readers and TV viewers: Why is there nothing but bad news? It is the exception, of course, that is one of the basic staples of news, in government, business, or people's daily lives. If the U.S. airlines safely complete their fourteen thousand scheduled flights today, that won't be news. In a reasonably orderly, honest, effective society, the exceptions will mainly be bad news.

But trends and movements are also news, and sometimes the change is for the better: personalities are news, sometimes attractive, even inspiring; "situations" are news, sometimes encouraging. The press in fact carried more of a good news–bad news mix about America than the Carter White House saw. But the White House naturally focused on coverage of the Carter Administration, and the net of that coverage was probably slightly negative. Those overworked future historians will have to decide whether that was a sound verdict.

Writing vs. Doing

So I told my journalistic friends: Yes, the Press–White House relationship does look different when you're sitting inside 1600 Pennsylvania Avenue, but more exactly, it *feels* different. It feels different, for instance, when a crisis bursts from out of nowhere. To the press, a crisis like the seizing of our Tehran embassy, was a professional challenge and excitement. For the White House it was a complex and cruel problem that demanded a response. Something had to be done about it, not just written about it.

Whether the taking of the hostages should have seemed to come "out of nowhere" became, for the press, a fascinating extra layer of the story. Was State at fault for not knowing the admission of the Shah to New York Hospital would produce this result, or was the CIA at fault, or Dr. Brzezinski, or the President? Did somebody in fact warn somebody else? Etc. Within the White House, this extra layer of the journalistic story was a very painful extra dimension of the policy problem. When the hostages were taken, I dare say Washington journalists had all the patriotic concerns of other Americans for the affront to national pride; they felt all the compassion of other decent people for the hostages and their families. But still it was a story, a very big one. TV and print news organizations began redeploying foreign correspondents; the foreign policy and defense beats suddenly became the hottest in Washington (replacing the state of the economy and the state of Ted Kennedy); newsmagazine editors were switching next week's cover. The journalistic adrenaline was pumping.

What often strikes the White House as recklessness in the press arises out of the extreme competitiveness of journalism. Unfortunately, when you get into the habit of calling all journalists "they" or "the media," it is easy to forget what a diversity of approach, opinion, ethics (and competence) is represented in the Washington press corps and their employers.

The profound difference between the White House—not just the Carter White House, anybody's—and the press is the difference between a story and a problem. And usually the tougher the problem, the better the story. Columnists and editorial writers, furthermore, could construct highly readable and convincing think pieces showing that if President Carter hadn't done A, and even Presidents Ford and Nixon B and C, this thing need never have happened. But within the White House, the problem was that A, B, and C, for better or worse, were done, and what do we do now? (If you start noticing, it is interesting how much punditry focuses on past folly rather than present solutions.)

A further unfairness, as felt from within the White House, was that you could go home drained and depressed, after a day or a week of no-progress, or setbacks, against problems like Iran, but the press had had a perfectly satisfying day or week reporting the no-progress or setbacks. (James Reston of the *New York Times* is one of the few Washington correspondents who conveys a consistently sympathetic interest in what it must be like in the maximum-pressure jobs, and what it must be like for the families of those officials.) When some minor but inflated one-day problem would arise, the press at least got a one-day story out of it. For the White House people who had to deal with it, it was a negative blip in the President's ratings and an irritating distraction from more serious work.

During the hostage crisis, ABC News neatly, and I am sure quite unconsciously, summed up the situation in a full-page ad celebrating the tenth anniversary of Roger Grimsby and Bill Beutel on "Eyewitness News": "After 10 years of international unrest, domestic crisis, and economic woes, the thrill still isn't gone. Happy 10th anniversary, Roger and Bill."

Unserious People

When Carter and others in the White House griped about the press in my presence, some of it was just friendly kidding around. "Your press won't pay attention, but . . ." "Hedley's media will undoubtedly say . . ." (Not a reference to the Time Inc. publications but to the whole industry.) Once half a dozen of us were discussing a foreign policy point that could stand more press attention, when the President said to one official: "Why don't you try to get together ten or fifteen responsible reporters—if there are that many . . ." I said: "*Watch* that." One Cabinet officer permitted himself a quick grin. Everybody else didn't hear.

Beyond the kidding, the President and his inner circle had a basically low opinion of the press, a mistrust of its motives and a misunderstanding of its role. When Bill Moyers, interviewing Carter midway through his term, asked what were his greatest disappointments, Carter thought about it "a good while" (he recalled later) and finally said, "The inertia of Congress and the irresponsibility of the press." He felt the same way at the end of his term. His view of journalists was not paranoiac but more that of a moralist, disapproving of people he saw as not serious and usually not serious in ways harmful to him.

Press Secretary Jody Powell shared and reinforced this attitude. This was not any sort of toadyism on Jody's part; he could argue with Carter very bluntly about other matters. The journalists knew he knew Carter's thinking, an indispensable credential for a press secretary. Under outrageous provocation he could handle himself beautifully in the bear-pit atmosphere that various journalistic boors had created in his daily briefing sessions. He was generally cool and often witty. He could be highly combative in behalf of his beleaguered President, but when stone-walling was called for, he had a remarkable repertoire of ways of saying nothing. The press generally respected him.

With the appearance of Powell's book *The Other Side of the Story,* * many journalists will now respect him less. He writes at the outset that he doesn't intend to be "balanced or fair," and he isn't. Along with some well-justified criticism of the coverage of the Carter White House, he indulges in an excess of score settling. Powell was in fact a much more effective press secretary than this vindictive—and readable—memoir might suggest.

A Running Skirmish

The President himself had a disarming willingness, in private, on occasion, to concede that if the situations were reversed, he'd be doing what he'd just denounced some other politician, or even a journalist, for doing. Episodes in the running skirmish with the press:

• Carter ridiculed John Anderson, the Republican-turned-Independent presidential candidate, as a "creation of the media," but would readily admit that he himself was in good part a media creation during the early stages of his 1976 campaign.

• In October 1979, the President complained at a Cabinet meeting that he had deplored high interest rates and high inflation rates in a speech in San Diego but the press stressed only his attack on high interest rates. At least six or eight times in the same Cabinet meeting, "the media" were presented as the leading cause, or perhaps the only cause, of some distressing situation they were reporting. But it wasn't news that any public figure in the United States was against high inflation. It was news, as I ventured to tell him later, if the President seemed to disagree with the monetary policies of his recent appointee as chairman of the Fed. Like presidents of corporations, universities, trade unions, the President of the U.S. bore a fundamental resentment that the press could declare which things were interesting or important in what he said.

• Hamilton Jordan and Dick Moe, of Mondale's staff, tried to get an unequivocal disavowal of any presidential ambitions from Secretary of State Muskie during the period when the Billy Carter furor seemed

*New York: William Morrow, 1984.

briefly to put the President's renomination in jeopardy. Muskie's statement was not entirely Shermanesque.

> Carter (wearily): The press of course pounced on the little openings.
> Donovan: The statement invited them to do that.
> Carter (reasonably): That's right.

• Dissension in the Atlantic Alliance was constantly being "blown
up by your friends in the media."

• After Carter made unintentionally revealing remarks about ex-
Secretary Cy Vance in Q and A after a speech in Philadelphia, there was
anger that the press was immediately interpreting it as a slap at Vance
and that this "news" overshadowed a serious foreign policy speech. I
ventured that the full Q and A transcript showed the press had interpreted the remarks about Vance the only way they could be interpreted. Carter unhappily agreed. I think he was genuinely surprised, and
unpleasantly so, to find himself saying those things out loud, topping his
own foreign policy story with a hot "people" story.

• Carter felt the press always tears down any new idea—like some
of his energy proposals. The press was always "trivializing" things. I
disagreed (Carter, pleasantly: I thought you would), and I could not
suppress a little lecture: The press does do some trivializing. But it is
a strange misunderstanding of the journalistic mind to assume it resists
new ideas. The press loves novelty—one of the synonyms for news. It
is also true that when people or ideas have been up on a pedestal for
a long time—the press maybe having had something to do with putting
them there in the first place—then the press sometimes does like to
knock them off.

A Medium Touchy President

As politicians go, Carter was not exceptionally thin-skinned about
the press.* Not having been on the inside in other Administrations, I
can only judge them from the press side of the fence. But the Nixon
White House was much more fearful of and hostile toward the press
than I saw Carter's to be. Johnson's White House, in his beleaguered
final year or two, was perhaps comparable to Carter's. JFK's was much
less embattled, though there was a narcissistic touchiness about his own

---

*And politicians are much less thin-skinned than journalists. Since I was trying to be
as little written about as possible during my year in Washington, I found myself patheti-
cally grateful when I was able to talk a reporter out of some item about me.

image. Ford was more relaxed about the press, and so, famously, was Ike. The General claimed his secret was not to read the papers, but this was an exaggeration.

There was a special edge to the Carter White House attitude toward the press because of the obvious if scientifically unprovable fact that the Washington press corps is heavily Democratic, and has been ever since the New Deal. It hurt that these liberal intellectuals (sort of) withheld any real measure of admiration or confidence from Carter. "They" were suspected of lingering Camelot allegiances and were accused of "building up" Ted Kennedy all through 1979; when he finally came out and started running, "they" admittedly did get pretty rough with him, but this was merely because they like to see a good fight.

I would speculate that in 1980 "they" voted about 50–30–20, Carter, Reagan, Anderson. Grudgingly.

The Uses of the Press

I dislike the notion of an "adversary relationship" between the press and the executive branch, the phrase that came into wide currency during the Nixon Administration. The press does of course have different purposes and perspectives from those of the White House. But the free press was in fact seen from the earliest days of the republic as charged with an indispensable role in our political system. It has unquestionably grown in power in the last quarter century, through the impact of TV and the emergence of a "national press" (network journalism, the four or five most widely read newspapers, the newsmagazines). The press has truly become one of the "powers" in the separation of powers, one of the "checks" in our system of checks and balances. Congress and the executive, and the courts and the executive, may often find themselves adversaries, but they are not locked into an adversary relationship. The press and White House need not be.

For all the differences between the Ronald Reagan White House and Jimmy Carter's, the pattern of press relationships did not change much. There was the predictable honeymoon. There were the familiar pledges of frequent press conferences and general "openness." The Washington press corps, apart from political preferences, is professionally biased in favor of a new administration. A party turnover brings new faces and new policies, at minimum half a year of fresh, rich subject matter. Then the rich new controversies begin to unfold.

In my days in the West Wing, I often wished that some administration some day would do itself and the country the favor of taking a somewhat relaxed view of the Washington press corps. It's not easy. But the tense view is dangerous. It can easily lead to the conviction that the press is a greater problem than the problems it reports, or indeed that there are few problems except as the press creates them. (Early in my year with Carter I told him the danger signal in his own attitude toward the press was "a reflex that blames the press first, and then asks only later—or maybe never—Was there some Administration mistake here, and is there something that needs correcting here?") This siege mentality can deprive an administration of valuable information about conditions and opinions "out there."

All administrations use the press in the sense of trying to influence its handling of the news. It would be refreshing to see high officials also use the press the way most readers and viewers do—to enlarge their understanding of what's going on.

I tried to follow my own advice during my year in the West Wing. Not counting my former Time Inc. and *Star* colleagues, there were at least two dozen Washington journalists whom I read (or watched) with some care. They were not infallible, but I thought of them as dedicated professionals who were frequently telling me something useful to know or think about. Two that I greatly admired, columnists Joseph Kraft and David Broder, get a heavy working-over in Jody Powell's book. Meg Greenfield's Washington *Post* editorial page and her own *Newsweek* column were often brilliant. I believe Carter and Powell regarded her as less hostile than they considered most of the *Post* people to be. After spending four days in Georgia just after the Democratic primary in March 1984, Greenfield wrote a column lamenting Carter's "unfair fate." She had heard some of Carter's former aides coolly discussing whether his support had hurt or helped Mondale *in Georgia.* "I was put in mind of the way some people talk about children or old people . . . in their presence, as if they can't hear or as if it doesn't matter if they do."

The personal chemistry between press and President matters, though not so much as some aggrieved Presidents imagine. Journalists not being totally alien creatures, their reactions to presidential personalities will differ only marginally from those of Americans in general. It plays out—to invent a statistic—to perhaps two or three percentage points in the President's public opinion poll ratings, maybe one or two points in an election, whether the President—issues aside—is liked as a man by journalists. Whether he likes them, or seems to, obviously enters into their feelings about him. To generalize: Kennedy was liked extravagantly by the press; Johnson began being liked warily, ended disliked; Nixon was never liked; Ford was liked; Carter was first seen as an interesting puzzle, ended disliked; Reagan has been liked. The latter fact, not surprisingly, strikes Jimmy Carter as one more proof of the incorrigible triviality of most journalists.

19

Something Enigmatic

Eleanor Randolph of the Chicago *Tribune,* who covered Jimmy Carter during the 1976 campaign, wrote that "he stretched the truth to the point where it becomes dishonest to call it exaggeration."* But she found that few of the reporters wanted to deal directly with the unattractive aspects of Carter; most settled for calling him "an enigma."

I prefer to think not that Carter was forever and immaculately truthful, but that there was indeed something enigmatic about the Carter mind and character. I remember once, age ten or so, asking my mother, a former high school teacher of English and Latin, to look at a story I had written, in which I described somebody as "very unique." She explained that a person could be unique or not unique, and that was it. (What a boon if this were known to all the toastmasters of the United States!) All Presidents must be unique, of course, not just in the literal sense that we have only one of them at a time, as Lyndon Johnson so often observed, but because it takes an extraordinary combination, never to be precisely duplicated, of personal qualities and historical circumstance to bring a man to the White House. But beyond that, and forgive me, Mother, I do think Jimmy Carter was *very* unique.

There were the surface paradoxes: the man of decency and compassion, of a deeply genuine goodness in all his instincts toward humanity in general, toward many groups, classes and particular individuals, yet also capable of petty and vindictive behavior. He had a long memory, and a tendency to impute unworthy motives to those who crossed him. The "mean streak" was real.

Esquire, November 1977.

Carter was a man of gentle modesty, almost meek in his public style; inside there was steely determination and a self-confidence bordering on arrogance. I remember hearing him as Governor of Georgia take questions from an audience of Atlanta college students, and thinking to myself that many American voters, especially the young, would be charmed by the soft voice and shy mannerisms after the hard-breathing belligerence of Nixon and the bombast of LBJ. But in the end the gentle persona hurt Carter—it seemed to convey a lack of force and contributed to the view that he wasn't "presidential."

The platform manner combined with the sheer virtuousness of the message created quite often an air of sanctimony. Many large audiences were left bored, though Carter could be highly effective with smaller groups, especially when he permitted his lively sense of humor to flash through. The humor could be a neat, even cruel putdown of somebody he was mad at, or just wanted to needle, but at least as often was directed at himself. He was far less earthy in private conversation than Nixon or LBJ, but still for a Southern Baptist Adult Bible Class teacher he came up with some pretty vivid stuff from time to time.

He had an incurable weakness for hyperbole. The United States, on countless occasions, was the greatest nation on earth "politically, economically, and militarily." (This did not prevent Carter Cabinet officers, as noted earlier, from attacking "reckless" Republicans for urging the military superiority the President was claiming we had.) The President returned from a summit meeting with allied leaders in Venice to escalate the usual claim—it was good to be back in the U.S., "the greatest nation by far on earth." So much for the friendly countries whose leaders he had just been conferring with.

A gathering of citizens in the Cabinet Room, sometimes for election-year stroking, sometimes to launch some worthy if not earthshaking project, easily became "one of the most important meetings ever held in this room." One friend of mine became a fellow-connoisseur of these Carter superlatives and once when we were both present at the coining of a new one, we had to avoid looking at each other, like giggly schoolboys.

Ted Kennedy, Carter's least favorite Democrat during many months of 1979–80, by the final days of the presidential campaign had become "one of the greatest people ever to live on this earth." Tip O'Neill, who did not conceal his low opinion of his President, which was fully reciprocated, was "someone who in such a short time can become one's closest friend." The *National Journal* compiled two arresting lists of people honored in more or less similar language.* My daughter Helen was startled, on first meeting Carter, to have him tell her I was his best friend.

Jody Powell, ever faithful, laughed off all the hyperbole: "If a South Georgia farmer has a mule, it's the best damned mule that ever existed."

Yet Jimmy Carter is a trained engineer, a clean-desk executive, fastidiously neat in his handwriting, punctual, precise. He has a very well-stocked vocabulary and a sharp eye for usage. He could take the trouble to make a sardonic marginal note on a memo from one unfortunate who thought to please the President by reporting "fulsome" support for one of his programs. He could be cold with the lower levels of White House staff people and, with all levels, stingy with thank-you's.

Maybe the Carter hyperbole was just a letting-off of steam for a highly disciplined man. But the habitual public resort to gross exaggeration can affect real thought processes, create appearances of insincerity, and sometimes paint the speaker into awkward corners.

Some of these contradictions in Carter were perhaps no more than normal complexities within a gifted individual, and normal contrasts between a man's previous being—any man's—and the circumstance of being President of the United States. But with Jimmy Carter there was a more profound contradiction, and it has baffled many who tried to understand him: How could a man be so very bright and still fail to get a good grip on the fundamentals of his job?

Portrait of a Mind

The fast answer would be that he was in the wrong job. Yet given Carter's brains, and the immense resources of the Presidency, the question must still be asked. It is almost impossible for any modern President to do less than a C+ or C job. He has working for him the mystique of the Presidency; the reverence for the Presidency; the whole vast executive support system, especially diplomatic and military, Treasury, OMB, Justice. A disastrous Presidency is impossible. (If some modern President manages to create a depression, preside over an erosion of our liberties, or get us devastated in a war, the previous assertion will

*August 5, 1978; December 30, 1978.

have been refuted.) The Carter Administration was not a disaster, but it came disappointingly close to the guaranteed minimum Presidency.

Again, given his intelligence, why? It was not because he was some dreamy theorist, or academic genius or caricature thereof, thinking brilliant thoughts and unable to change a light bulb. He was not off in an ivory tower. He was in many ways intensely practical, "handy around the house" (back in Plains, he promptly laid a new pine floor in the attic). He was also well informed in several advanced technologies and able to probe these areas in a knowing way, e.g., when the defense warning system was giving off false alarms of possible missile attacks in 1979–80, or when the U.S. government was trying to figure out a mysterious explosion over Atlantic waters off southern Africa in September 1979. He brought a powerful intellectual curiosity to such phenomena as Mount St. Helen's or, farther out, the black holes in the void.

He was less imaginative about human affairs. He was not a conceptualizer, except on such a broad and platitudinous scale as to give little specific direction to policy. Related to this was an odd lack of a sense of history. In Carter's immense storehouse of factual information there must be plenty of history packed away; yet it never seemed a steady presence in his thinking.

In twenty-five or thirty private conversations with him, and sitting in dozens of larger meetings with him, I almost never heard him mention any previous U.S. President, or World War II or I, or de Gaulle, Stalin, Hitler, Churchill, the Depression. (In his Camp David dealings with Begin and Sadat, he did bring a sense of history to the work at hand; it may have helped that some of the history was the Bible.) Joseph Califano, Health and Human Services Secretary until the Cabinet purge of July 1979, heard Carter refer occasionally to FDR and Johnson, and remembers that Carter once commended to the Cabinet Robert Donovan's biography of Truman.

If Carter felt he should have a favorite twentieth-century President, it would have to be a Democrat, of course, and it was interesting to note the ones he didn't choose: Ted Kennedy's brother Jack, for obvious reasons; the volcanic, larger-than-life LBJ, tainted with Viet Nam and withdrawal from the Presidency; the commanding figure of FDR—too commanding perhaps. The scholarly Woodrow Wilson put through important economic and social legislation, led the country in a successful war, was a world statesman and furthermore a southerner, but he wasn't chosen either—perhaps Wilson was just too long ago. (Interestingly, Wilson was Republican Richard Nixon's stated favorite.) Carter's proclaimed favorite was Truman, the feisty little man who surprised the pundits. He kept a bust of Truman in the Oval Office and an oil painting of Truman held the place of honor over the mantel in the Cabinet Room. Jefferson and Washington were at the other end of the room.*

Yet to work as much apart from history, outside of history, as Carter did meant that the "past" consisted largely of previous events and decisions of his own Administration. His term as governor of Georgia was also relevant history. When the Carter Administration normalized diplomatic relations with China, it was not just partisanship that made the President claim it as a brand-new, grand-scale foreign policy initiative. It was of course the logical outcome of the Nixon-Kissinger opening to China, but that had happened prior to Carter's inauguration on January 20, 1977.

My year on Carter's staff, more than any other experience in my life, caused me to wonder what we mean by "very intelligent." If a child seems very intelligent, the parents tend to assume he or she will get into a good college, make a good record there, and in due course do well in some profession. It usually works out that way, and there is no need to question what we meant by "very intelligent." In business and the professions, when a very intelligent individual fails to reach what seemed his or her potential, there are so many possible explanations (too much competition, bad luck, laziness, alcohol, poor health, disastrous marriage, etc.) that we have no particular reason to reexamine the meaning of intelligence. With Presidents it is different.

In profiles published just before and after the 1976 election, there were occasional gushes that Carter was a "near-genius" or at least "our most intelligent President of the twentieth century." Carter's academic ranking in his Annapolis class (No. 60 out of 820) was not spectacular, but suggestive of a very respectable I.Q.

Jimmy Carter has the mind of a very quick, keen student. He is a good listener and a fast reader—an extraordinarily efficient soaker-up of information. He could master masses of material, the more technical and statistical the better, and it would stay mastered. With his excellent memory, he could show a dazzling command of facts and figures in a press conference, town meeting, or a session with congressmen. He had a strong intuitive feel for where a question might be leading, but also the tact to let the question unfold, plus perhaps a shrewd sense that this

*President Reagan has Calvin Coolidge over the mantel. Lincoln and Washington are at the other end.

gave him more time to marshal his response. Few people could come away from one of these performances unimpressed.

What might be called the reconciling mechanism was less fully developed. Carter didn't seem to recognize instinctively when ideas are in collision, when two sets of facts cannot be equally pertinent, when desirable objectives are in conflict.* The heart of so many policy problems is how much will you give up of Good Thing A to realize how much of Good Thing B. I am not speaking of the horse-trading with senators or other governments. That comes later. I mean an intellectual process, a way of looking at things from the beginning, which recognizes that in public policy, and perhaps especially in foreign policy, there are very few completely self-contained situations. Carter did not always make the relevant connections between the information he had just absorbed about Country X and the information about Situation Y that he had so efficiently stored away a month ago.

I don't know whether the sheer bulk and detail of on-call information can interfere with a mind's ability to make such connections, but the time spent in acquiring masses of fact surely subtracts from the time available for thinking about the meaning of the facts. A former Pentagon official, reminiscing about top brass he had worked for, recalled James Schlesinger, Secretary of Defense for a time under Nixon and Ford, then Energy for Carter, as a big-picture man, "a forest man." Carter's Defense Secretary Brown was more of a "tree man." Carter himself? "My God, he was a leaf man!" I think Carter's joy in digging into the factual detail of a complex subject may have absorbed so much of his intellectual energy that he didn't always have the time or disposition to sit back and reflect on the implications of these facts, how they related to other facts he knew, which set of facts might be more important or, so to speak, more true.

This quality in Carter contributed to the zigzag tendency. This was the adaptation to the Presidency itself of the "fuzziness" that Carter was often charged with as a campaigner in 1976. Some policy zigs and zags are unavoidable as objective circumstances change, and as the inevitable compromises of political life are struck. But the Carter Administration had more than the normal quota of trimmings, lurchings, and retreats: on the deployment of the neutron bomb in Europe, on the Soviet brigade in Cuba, on our fundamental stance toward the Soviet

*I once wrote a note to myself to discuss this failing with him—not just a couple of particular cases that had come up. I didn't have the nerve. I discussed the particular cases but not the general difficulty.

Union, in our UN policy vis-à-vis the West Bank and Jerusalem, and in domestic economic policy. Some wobbles originated in the failure to spot conflicting purposes well enough in advance, reconcile them if that could be, or if not, give one or another priority and then stick to that. There was an urge to have it both ways up to the very last minute, in the hope that somehow doves and hawks, spenders and economizers, the saved and the damned, could all be kept happy. I think the President was often sincerely unaware of inconsistencies as they were building up, and was then aggrieved when he was accused of wobbling, waffling, expediency. He would complain that back in some of his fights with the Georgia legislature he used to be accused of being "stubborn," "stiff-necked," etc. A master politician might have gotten away with more. Carter's zigzags came out looking like zigzags.*

It could also happen, when various pieces of information were in conflict, that the President would simply opt for the most congenial interpretation rather than demanding a rigorous effort at reconciling the evidence. This led to a certain measure of self-deception: as to the health of the Western Alliance, the U.S. standing in the Third World, the state of the U.S. military, the progress of the various packages for dealing with inflation. The opportunities for self-deception grow, of course, during an election year. An administration can come to believe quite genuinely in the public claims it is making in its own behalf, and it will experience a declining interest in subjecting these claims to serious internal scrutiny.

In Carter's case, I think the capacity for self-deception was also related to, or supported by, his admirable calm. (Having been accused of calm myself, I tend to think well of it.) I saw him tired and tense at times. He aged, perhaps two years for one, as Presidents must (though ex-Presidents seem to reclaim some of the years). You could never forget there was a vulnerable human being inside this trim, contained figure. Some minor skin ailment could occasionally give him a splotchy complexion, and the effect was a little haggard or grim. But I never saw him rattled. He could discuss the most staggering concerns of state with the same low-keyed serenity he would bring to an account of his family doings last weekend at Camp David.

I never saw him really angry, or if he was I failed to catch the signals.

*Bruce Mazlish and Edwin Diamond in their "psychobiography" *Jimmy Carter: An Interpretive Biography* (Simon and Schuster, 1979), credit him with a considerable awareness of his inconsistencies, and even with a philosophical purpose or need to achieve a "fusion of contradictions." Maybe so. Mazlish and Diamond also quote Carter's old friend Charlie Kirbo: "I've seen him keep talking until people misunderstood him." (P. 16.)

But people who knew him more intimately than I found the exquisitely *controlled* nature of the anger, the "ice-blue laser" eyes and the unraised voice, quite formidable. Brzezinski writes of finding him one day in the Oval Office wearing "his nasty smile."*

Carter's religious faith no doubt contributed to his serenity (but is far from a total explanation, since everybody knows devout people who are not all that calm). The calm and the religious conviction and some indefinable something else, very appealing and almost innocent in Carter, all went into the gentle announcements of stupendous goals—like the abolition of nuclear weapons, in his inaugural—and the sweet presumption that the mere stating of the virtuous intention gets us halfway there.

Among all the professions, only two or three others can compare with political leadership in its demand that the individual be able to think one thing and yet *within certain ethical and practical boundaries* say something quite different. A doctor, perhaps, dealing with a dying patient; a diplomat, of course, but he is in a branch of politics; and in many situations a lawyer—which makes it no accident that so many of our politicians come from the law. Political leadership at the national level, and above all in the Presidency, steadily imposes a divergence between what is wise to say publicly, especially in times of danger, and what is said and thought privately. It takes a special kind of mind and character to handle this without damage to one's own intellectual and moral integrity, and with good results for the general welfare. The effort can be a strain on some personalities.

Carter did not handle this well. The repeated assertion in 1976 that he would never lie to us was a kind of embarrassment that should not be inflicted on the voters.† The voters know Presidents cannot always be totally truthful, but they are entitled to assume that presidential candidates have developed a workable ethic that rises above personal expediency and is based in the public interest. This should be implicit in their past performance and in their current policy positions, but is not served by a candidate's bald character testimony in his own behalf.

Carter came to office with a political philosophy that seemed to combine compassion for the unfortunate, a genuine concern for equity in the society, with a frugal concern for the taxpayer's dollar and a zealous commitment to efficiency in government. Along with his evident intelligence, his self-discipline and determination, and the fresh

---

*Power and Principle, p. 276.
†Though not so grotesque, of course, as Nixon's "I'm not a crook."

and interesting differentness of the man, he struck many political independents, including the author, as a hopeful figure. There seemed a promise of a kind of national reconciliation in a Deep South President who was not George Wallace. The populist tilt to Carter's rhetoric, the suspicion of any institutions that might come between "the people" and a government as good as the people themselves, could be taken as small-town canniness, or romantic nostalgia, or mildly sappy demagoguery. But it didn't really undercut the picture of a man from the conservative wing of the liberal party, hence a centrist in the national spectrum. Carter's thinking seemed to offer a sound philosophic and political base for a Presidency.

The difficulty came in moving from abstractly conceived "solutions" to the realities of execution, from general attitudes and goals to concrete objectives, in assigning priorities to the objectives, and then marshaling the resources of the Presidency behind the chosen objectives. Follow-through was feeble during the crucial first year when most of Congress and the public overwhelmingly want the new President to succeed. It had improved some by 1979–80, but by then too much skepticism about the Carter Administration had solidified.

Carter's failure to forge strong friendships and alliances in the Congress has been thoroughly documented. He had made no close friendships among congressmen even after he chaired a national committee to recruit Democratic candidates for Congress and for state office, an arrangement that enabled him to politick all over the country for eighteen months. He still had no close congressional friendships after he had won the Democratic nomination and then the election. This was curious enough, but far more revealing, he still had none four years later.[*] One former Democratic Senator summed it up: "There was no one up on the Hill who would go the last mile for him."

And this was an important aspect of the Carter enigma: how somebody so bright could fail to understand the full importance, like it or not, of Congress. He could be tireless on the phone with congressmen, and brilliant in informal briefing sessions with them, but he never made them feel he was entirely comfortable with them. He wasn't. One staffer who knew him very well simply says: "People can't be what they

---

[*]The late John Osborne, who was generally sympathetic to Carter, wrote in the *New Republic* (January 17, 1981), "Jimmy Carter leaves the presidency unknown and, in a narrow sense of the word, unloved by any in Washington beyond a tiny group composed of his wife, his daughter, his . . . sons and four of the several Georgians on his staff—his secretary, Susan Clough, and assistants Hamilton Jordan, Jody Powell, and Frank Moore. Respected and admired by others at the White House and elsewhere in Washington, yes. But known and loved in the warm and intimate meaning of the words, no."

aren't." But Carter in the course of his remarkable career had willed himself to be several things that didn't come naturally; this one he couldn't or wouldn't. I think it was more the latter. He felt morally superior to Congress. He was elected by all the people; he saw the individual representative or Senator as vulnerable to special interests, lobbies, selfish blocs back home, lacking the President's commitment to the welfare of the nation itself.

A more dynamic political leader might have been able to rally "the people" against the Congress on a few chosen battlefields, but that was not Carter's gift either. He could be very impressive in his televised press conferences but there was little uplift or eloquence in his set-piece speeches. Steven Weisman of the *New York Times* quoted an unnamed White House official (not me) in August 1980: "This Administration hasn't learned how to use the Presidency to lead the American people from one big place to another."

Some of the limitations of his leadership were evident also in the handling of his staff and Cabinet. He could be incisive in his comments on the paper that came across his desk—"I agree," "Not acceptable to me"—but was less crisp in meetings. Along with the southern good manners, there was a distaste for face-to-face disagreement.

The many impressive individual competences in the Carter Cabinet and White House staff somehow were not brought together as "an Administration." These were men and women who genuinely admired Carter (not just for appointing them) and believed in his capacity to be a successful President. He didn't fire them up as a leader.

With all his pride and self-confidence, Carter could be remarkably self-critical. In the summer of 1979 he often quoted the comment of a West Virginia woman who told him he was coming across just as the manager of the White House, not the leader of the country. He seemed to agree, or at least agree that it could look that way.

Perks and Parties

Jimmy Carter had a real zest for the Presidency, and notwithstanding his simple tastes, an honest enjoyment of the perks. Two years into his term, he would still confide to visitors he could hardly wait to get up in the morning and get at the job. Of Camp David he would say he didn't even want to know how much it cost. There are hundreds of rich Americans who have grander country establishments, but without the Navy's mess stewards, the helicopters in waiting, the Marines on the perimeter. (Some might prefer without.) Though he often felt ill used by the press and Congress, Carter never emitted the faintest suggestion that the Presidency was any sort of martyrdom.

The Carters gave every appearance of enjoying entertaining, which of course is the first law of entertaining. But I think they unselfishly enjoyed giving others the thrill of an evening in the White House, and for two people who were once quite shy (she longer than he) had themselves come to like the state dinners, the big populist parties on the South Lawn, the culture salutes. In any case, they were unfailingly attentive and considerate as hosts, and Carter had a very graceful touch in his toasts and the informal pleasantries.

The Washington *Star* calculated that the Carters, after three and a half years in the White House, had entertained no fewer than 32,650 guests at announced events, more per annum than in any previous administration, and that the guest lists were more politically oriented.* (The latter point could be the takeoff for an interesting Ph.D. thesis— history, political science, sociology?) Even at a state dinner for the visiting head of a major government you might be seated next to the wife of a Democratic fund raiser in a medium-size city in a state with an upcoming primary.

Plains, Georgia

Once everybody was accustomed to the idea of a President from Plains, Georgia, there was a tendency to forget how remarkable that was. When the press and Secret Service and some White House staff would troop along on a presidential visit, there was a sense that the White House for some odd reason was weekending in Plains, not that this was the President's real home. But Robert Ajemian of *Time* remembers standing in the two-block main street of Plains shortly before the 1976 election, and thinking, "this man spent *nine years* here, as an adult. This has to be part of him." Other twentieth-century Presidents were born in very small towns (Hoover's West Branch, Iowa, was even smaller than Plains), but none had spent mature years in that environment.

Carter was too free of prejudice, too eager to learn, too mobile to be fairly called provincial. Still less could he be called worldly or cosmopolitan. The North Carolina novelist Reynolds Price wrote that Carter was "from Plains but not of it" and noted that he didn't actually go there very often during his White House years.† It might also be said that

*June 15, 1980.
†*Time*, December 22, 1980.

Carter was from-but-not-of the Navy. He never, for instance, attempted to assemble his Annapolis classmates for any sort of party at the White House, a fact some of them noted. He was from but certainly not of the governors' fraternity, where he was considered a self-centered loner. Even in his fourth year as President, Carter seemed not a part of Washington, still the outsider. (Reagan in his fourth year as President was still "running against Washington," but this was political guile—nothing personal.) As to where was Carter truly *of*, I would say his church and his family.

Faith

I was surprised at how many people in Washington and New York, even allowing for the cynicism of those cities, would ask me whether Carter's evangelical faith was for real. It surely is. (Some of the cynics, wanting to have it both ways, would of course respond, "I was afraid of that.")

At the Friday morning Foreign Policy Breakfasts, grace was always said, usually by the President in a voice so soft he could hardly be heard two or three seats away. Sometimes he would call on Cy Vance or Fritz Mondale for the prayer, and once I was surprised (I don't know why) to hear him call on Brzezinski, who was not at a loss. I kept at the ready the grace that used to be spoken at the Donovan family table in Minneapolis at Easter, Christmas, and when the minister came to dinner. I never got asked.

Carter conveyed a joy in his own faith that was in no way oppressive or censorious toward those of less faith or no faith. I never heard him quote Scripture in private conversation or argue from religious tenets to some secular policy conclusion. His public references to the Deity were no more frequent than those of other Presidents less devout.

But I believe Carter's religious faith suffused his political being, contributing not only to the calm I have mentioned, but to his certitude that he stood for good and was in a kind of communion with the basic God-given goodness in the people. He often said he drew his strength from his personal relationship with the American people.

The Family

Religion fused with family in the spiritual and emotional grounding of the man. The closeness of his family bonds led Carter into a strangely royalist use of his family. Even while he was in his most populist mode, wearing the cardigan sweater on TV, taking away the black limousines from White House staffers, etc., he could dispatch son Chip, like a Prince of the Realm, to inspect blizzard damage in Buffalo. I thought it was a graceful gesture to send his mother Lillian to the funeral of the Indian President, Fakhruddin Ali Ahmed, since she had served in the Peace Corps in India, but not to send her to Marshal Tito's. Amy was sometimes present at White House state dinners, or at various half-social half-working meals, and not all guests were amused to draw her as a partner, especially if she were reading at the table.

Family love and sheer tastelessness accounted for Carter's long tolerance of the Billy excesses. At a time when it seemed all the people on the White House senior staff might have to recite each and every dealing they ever had with brother Billy, I was grateful I had never had occasion to speak to him. I did see him once. In my evening notes for March 19, 1980, a day that included a fairly weighty conversation with the President, I had written: "Billy, in vile rust-colored suede leisure suit, waiting to come in as I left."

The Court Chamberlain in charge of de-pomping the Imperial Presidency, so far as White House staff perks went, was, royally enough, Hugh Carter, Jr. He was an amiable man unjustly known as "Cousin Cheap"; he was simply carrying out the President's instructions.

Rosalynn

Carter would have said that, far from putting on any imperial airs, he was offering the taxpayers a real bargain. He had a view that the public was hiring the Carter family, and especially him and Rosalynn as a couple, when they elected him governor and then President.

It was in the Ford Administration that the White House for the first time began in staff memos and public announcements to speak of "The First Family," "Office of the First Lady," etc. What had once been harmless journalistic cliché became titles, odd usage in the republic. The Carters and Reagans, regrettably, continued the habit.*

Rosalynn Carter had an important voice in policy as well as politics. She attended Cabinet meetings, sitting quietly in the back-row seats used by the White House staff. Cabinet meetings sounded more impor-

---

*Jacqueline Kennedy early on told the Chief Usher of the White House: "Please, Mr. West, the one thing I do not want to be called is 'First Lady.' It sounds like a saddle horse" (J. B. West, *Upstairs at the White House* [New York: Coward, McCann & Geoghegan, 1973], p. 268). Later, alas, she came to like the term.

tant than they were, but Carter might have been smarter not to have her there. I was present at only one serious policy discussion where she sat in—four or five of us in rocking chairs on the West Balcony on a stifling August evening. She was cool and, in what little she said, very sensible. Their marriage was so close, and Carter so valued her judgment, that I am sure they talked about almost everything on his desk. He never quoted her to me, though I heard from others that her views were decidedly hawkish, toward the Iranians, Russians, Ted Kennedy, etc.

The Carters were unabashedly affectionate in public but not cloying about it. They did some pleasant kidding back and forth, his lines having a bit more edge. I once heard them discussing movies (the White House screening room was one of their favorite places), and Rosalynn was saying how much she disliked crime and war films, "all that violence and bloodshed." Her husband objected: "But you like Democratic Party politics."

I admired her greatly, and I admired their marriage. But I think Carter's Presidency was hurt by the widespread perception, in Congress among other places, that she had excessive influence, or even was the stronger.*

Rosalynn's memoir, *First Lady from Plains*† is a charming account of her girlhood in South Georgia, the years as a Navy wife, the hotly resisted return to Plains ("I argued. I cried. I even screamed at him"), and after Jimmy took over the family peanut enterprise, her growing confidence as a business and political partner to her husband. Her version of the White House years is implacably partisan, and she quotes without remorse her own comment during the evening of Election Day 1980, at a moment when Jimmy was professing to feel no bitterness: "I'm bitter enough for both of us."

Defeat

Jimmy Carter's capture of the Democratic nomination in 1976 must rank, perhaps permanently, as the greatest cavalry raid in the history of presidential campaigning. During his first year as Governor of Georgia, when he appeared on the TV program "What's My Line?" nobody guessed his line. Even after four years as governor he had a

---

*I also had a note to myself to speak to the President about this, but never did. Another failure of nerve as an Adviser.

†Boston: Houghton Mifflin, 1984.

national "recognition factor" of just 2 percent. In polls in December 1975, only seven months before his nomination, he was the choice of only 3 percent. But he and Hamilton Jordan had foreseen the effects of the McGovern-era reforms on the delegate selection process, the new significance of the Iowa caucus, preceding the New Hampshire primary, and the advantage of *not* being in office and being able to run full-time against assorted governors and senators. Ronald Reagan, four years later, showed a firm grasp of the latter point.

After Carter's loss to Reagan, and a few days before he was to leave Washington, the *New York Times* did a summary story on his accomplishments, quoting many politicians and professors who concluded that the chief one was his election. I think the nomination was more remarkable. Once nominated, he should have won big, as the candidate of the majority party (in registrations, at least), against our first appointed President, never even elected Vice-President, who furthermore had pardoned the disgraced Richard Nixon. Ford was certainly not inspiring or in any way charismatic. Yet Carter just barely beat him.

This should have been a signal even as he came to the White House that Carter had created no national constituency. He was not able to do so in the next four years; the best indicator of the 1980 election outcome, which could be picked up any time from mid-1979 on, was the extreme scarcity of people who had voted for Ford in 1976 who now said they were for Carter. He could have been saved only by colossal blunders of the opposition. Reagan and the Republicans refused to oblige. Carter could not even establish command of a regional constituency. One of the most crushing aspects of his 1980 defeat must have been the loss of all the South but Georgia.

Carter is now supporting the idea of a single six-year term for President. He argues that everything a new President does from Year 1 starts getting interpreted as buildup to a reelection campaign. This is an exaggeration; the next election begins to dominate in Year 3. Carter's proposal addresses not only the suspiciousness of others but also may reflect a certain guilt that the election loomed so large in his own thinking in 1979–80. This may have strained his conscience more than it would have troubled a less self-righteous politician, like Roosevelt or Kennedy.

The fact that Carter had come from out of nowhere to win in 1976 often seemed, at least to some of his younger lieutenants, to have conferred an aura of destiny. Hearing some bit of discouraging political news in 1980, they would say: "Don't forget, only five years ago people were saying, Jimmy Who?" One could also overhear a kind of macho refrain: "Well, maybe we don't know how to run the country, but we know how to run an election." Carter himself has said he was confident of winning—and in a sense implies he *was* winning—until, according to his pollster Pat Caddell, there was a sharp swing of undecided voters to Reagan the weekend before the election. The Carter campaign people attributed the swing to the new round of diplomatic activity on the hostage question, reminding the public once more of the humiliation Iran had inflicted on America.

It is a bearable disappointment for a politician to be told: "No, the Democratic/Republican Party is not going to nominate you for President." And the Democratic or Republican candidate can live with learning that the electorate has not called him to the White House. But the most shattering verdict our political system can deliver is to an incumbent President finishing his first term: "You have not been a successful President."

Since returning to Plains, Carter has said he hasn't missed Washington one minute. This is an extraordinary claim, but he is an extraordinary man. He threw himself into the writing of his memoirs with the taut self-discipline he brings to everything, and with a touch of the gadgetry he is so fond of—he composed on a video display terminal. He worked from five thousand pages of meticulously kept diaries and notes, and had access to twenty tractor-trailer loads of presidential documents, 25 million items in all.

Despite his meager interest in past Presidencies, Carter had taken the trouble to learn something about past presidential memoirs. As he put in his daily stint at his "trusty word processor," the competitive juices were flowing. He was aware that there had been no first-rate presidential memoirs for a century. Kennedy, Franklin Roosevelt, and Wilson might have written such, but never had the chance. Theodore Roosevelt, an accomplished writer and historian, for some reason included only six short chapters on his Presidency in his autobiography. Carter knew that Ulysses Grant had turned out to be a surprisingly good writer, and knew of the slander that Mark Twain was his ghostwriter.

No ghostwriter touched *Keeping Faith*. It is earnest and orderly, generally restrained about personalities, both those Carter admired and otherwise, and much less revealing of himself than his campaign autobiography, *Why Not the Best?** The focus is almost entirely on foreign policy, and even here is highly selective. Carter sails right past some of the most troubling questions about his diplomacy. But there is much of

*Nashville, Broadman Press, 1975.

historical value in the book, especially the absorbing narrative of Camp David. *Keeping Faith* is more interesting and rewarding than the official presidential memoirs of Ford and Johnson, less so than Nixon's, about on a level with Eisenhower's and Truman's (all ghosted). General Grant is still out in front.

Jimmy Carter remains elusive. In his fourth year out of office, he came one evening to the Woodrow Wilson Center in Washington, in the old Smithsonian Castle on the Mall, for a dialogue on the Presidency.* The performance was vintage Carter—open, confessional, and with such plentiful and various emotions and reactions confessed that it was almost as though a private man were trying to throw you off the trail. Simplicity, modesty, deep self-confidence: "I enjoyed being President. Even when I had my most disappointing days . . . I don't remember a single morning when I didn't look forward to getting to the Oval Office. I enjoyed the challenge of it—analyzing complicated issues, trying to put a plan into effect . . . overcoming a difficulty . . . In my judgment the Presidency is not an unmanageable office. (He had once written me —not necessarily a contradiction—"I don't guess anyone has ever claimed to master the job.") Then the wise perception burdened with one politically lethal word: "There are some problems in the world that [the U.S.] simply cannot handle. A certain reticence or even timidity ought therefore to prevail on the President." Would he have said "timidity" if he were still in politics? He might have. And then the sweetly barbed compliment: "One of the great things about President Reagan's personality is that he seems satisfied with the way the nation is doing . . . Popularity has to do with the way you present yourself, and I must say I have great admiration for President Reagan because he does it so well."

*Wilson Center Reports, June 1984.

PART VII

*The Communicator
in Chief*

20

---◆---

Ronald Reagan

Toward the end of a long conversation with Ronald Reagan, during the first year of his Presidency, I served him up a nice fat pitch:

"I take it you don't think this Administration is just a four-year blip off the long-term national direction?"

The President didn't swing for the fence. He contented himself with a single:

"I sure hope not. I feel that we did just about a hundred-eighty degree turn in the course of government, and I'd like to feel that it reflects what the people out there are thinking, that they now have recognized we've been on the wrong course."

It was pretty well settled on Election Day 1984 that Ronald Reagan will not go down in the history books as a blip. His landslide victory was not merely a reflection of his personal appeal, potent though that is. He had set the terms and tone of the national political dialogue for four years and dominated the political agenda—to the point indeed that he could suspend substantive discussion of the agenda during the twelve weeks leading up to November 6, 1984, and deal almost exclusively in themes. He was in part author and in part beneficiary of a palpable improvement in national mood and morale.

Just how strong a stamp he will leave on national policy will depend in good part on the 99th Congress, on the 100th, to be elected in November 1986, and on the course of the contention within the Republican Party for the next presidential nomination. But much finally depends on how much of Ronald Reagan, phenomenon that he is, is politically or philosophically transferable.

DeGaulle Next Door

In his fascinating biography of Walter Lippmann, Ronald Steel quoted Lippmann's acute perception about the leadership of Charles de Gaulle. It was not so much that he was a political leader within France—France was *inside him.**

Quite a lot of America is inside Ronald Reagan. He is two of America's favorite characters, the nice boy next door and the lovable, opinionated uncle, getting on but pretty damn lively for his age, cheerful, friendly, great storyteller (has been known to shade one to make a point), no big brain trust upstairs but plenty of common sense. Reagan comes from two quintessentially American places, the Middle Western small town and Golden California. The years as a movie actor, far from creating a stagy celebrity, seem to have merged role and reality—the good guy everybody (except maybe a few snobs and eggheads) wants to be, the American as seen by the American. This is a very different sort of leader from the aristocratic Franklin Roosevelt, the Hudson River squire, or the dashing young Jack Kennedy, the rich Irish-American nouveau Brahmin—two rare species. The many Americans who revered them did not for a moment imagine these romantic figures were simply themselves called to Washington. In his plain Americanness, Reagan is more like Ford or Truman or Eisenhower. But he is a better politician than Ford or Truman and he has had more of an idea of what he wanted to do with his Presidency than Eisenhower did.

As our fortieth President, the ninth of our modern Presidents, Ronald Reagan got off to quite a start. I explored Reagan's Washington for some weeks in the summer of 1981, and found it an intriguing place, verging on the exotic after all the years of Democrats and mainstream Republicans. I was now back as a reporter (on a *Fortune* assignment), an editor emeritus and an ex-Carter adviser, a credential that did not seem to inhibit Republican confidences. "*You'll* get a kick out of this one," I was often told, and often I did.

In those first months of his Presidency, Ronald Reagan, age seventy, neatly stood on its head a cherished assumption of most students of the Presidency. That was the assumption that vigorous, ebullient presidential leadership would just naturally be devoted to expanding the role of the federal government (and the Chief Magistrate) in our national life, and that any President of contrary outlook would necessarily be a cold,

---

**Walter Lippmann and the American Century* (Boston: Atlantic Monthly/Little Brown, 1980), p. 400.

crabbed type, or at best likably lazy. Franklin Roosevelt was the exemplar of the bold, joyous activist, Coolidge and Hoover the chill naysayers (so the academic stereotype went), Ike the lazy nice guy. So here came Reagan, not overworking himself but clearly relishing the job and the power, using it with great gusto and skill to shrink the role of government and indeed the President.

There were, furthermore, bright young and youngish Reaganite *believers* showing up all over Washington. These were articulate, attractive men and women in their thirties and forties excited by their work in the White House, the executive departments, the staff offices up on the Hill. Like their President, they were glorying in their jobs in a government they were dedicated to contracting. Their élan was perhaps comparable to that of Kennedy's New Frontiersmen. Some old-timers said there had been nothing like it since New Deal days. A blasphemy to alumni of those earlier dispensations, who, though they know better, still tend to think all youthful idealists have to be liberals.

Yet another blow, struck by Reagan and the Reaganites, was against the theory, quite fashionable in Washington in the mid- and latter 1970s, that the whole governmental process has been stalemated by the conflicts between Congress and White House. Many a thoughtful article and think-tank seminar pivoted on this theme—that in reaction against Viet Nam and Watergate, the Congress, press, and public had dangerously circumscribed the powers of the Presidency, while Congress, through an excess of internal reform, had become a kind of anarchy, incapable itself of leading, or of responding to presidential leadership. Could there be a responsible Congress again? Could there be strong presidential leadership again? Reagan in his first year made these questions sound a little dated. From a personal position well over on the right of the political spectrum, he was showing a remarkable gift for marshaling national majorities, in public opinion and in Congress. And he was prevailing over well-financed and highly sophisticated interest groups that fight the formation of national majorities.

"Not Since . . ."

All new Presidents have a lot going for them, of course. Reagan's performance rating in the public opinion polls of late summer 1981— about 60 percent said he was doing a generally good job—was actually about the same as all the Presidents of the previous twenty years had registered at that point in their first year.

In sheer personal popularity, however, Reagan probably stood higher than any President since Eisenhower. Journalists, "veteran Washington observers," etc., were outdoing themselves in "not since" comparisons. Following the historic victory on his tax bill, it was generally agreed that Reagan had established a mastery on Capitol Hill not seen since the prime of Lyndon Johnson. And the whole Reagan economic program, enacted just about as he wanted it, in just over six months, was the most formidable domestic initiative any President had driven through since the hundred days of Franklin Roosevelt. It was legislated faster than LBJ's Great Society programs, which it put a cap upon. Even FDR's famous hundred days were less a philosophic whole than a series of rapid-fire ad hoc assaults on a variety of problems strewn across the Depression landscape. The Reagan package represented, for better or worse, a much more coherent economic ideology than FDR brought to office.

So how did he bring it off?

To start with, there came the swift and overwhelming bipartisan recognition that he is a master "communicator." Ugly word, but it does convey something different from orator, spellbinder, eloquent, charismatic, etc. (Journalists are certainly in no position to object.)

But let other "communicators" note: Reagan deeply believes most of what he is communicating. There is plenty of hype and showmanship mingled with the message. He sees that as part of the work of communicating. FDR, whom Reagan sometimes quotes and in some things admires, would not have disagreed. But FDR, though he told the occasional lie, chiefly about his intentions, didn't bend and mangle verifiable fact with the frequency and versatility of Ronald Reagan. David Gergen, White House Director of Communications for Reagan's first three years, came up with the inspired explanation that his President talks in "parables."

Reagan is a Reaganite. He took his campaign promises seriously. He meant those things he had been saying all those years. Nobody was totally ready for that in Washington.

And an undernoticed point: Reagan considers himself thoroughly grounded in economics—and likes the subject! He took his degree in economics (Eureka College, Illinois, 1932). He ran a quite complicated trade union for six years. He delivered thousands of talks, chiefly on economic themes, to General Electric employees, to Republican banquets, on the radio. He ran a very sizable enterprise, the government of California, for eight years.

Along the way he acquired a circle of rich and very rich friends, and became a man of some affluence himself. He sees no harm in people enjoying their money; if the rich are going to have trouble getting into the Kingdom of Heaven, he doesn't seem to be brooding about it. But when he talks economics, Reagan is not just parroting the ideas of his California friends, nor of the various businessmen, bankers, economics Ph.D.s who came to work for him in Washington. He feels he's been working the territory longer than they have. He is comfortable with the vocabulary and with the big numbers (though he can simply disbelieve big numbers he doesn't like, e.g., $200 billion deficits).

So Reagan is a man of certitudes. "Not since" Harry Truman, very possibly, had a President been so confident he was right. There are plentiful hazards in that, but also many assets for a democratic leader. Reagan would not have chosen as one of his favorite messages the Reinhold Niebuhr line that Carter used to quote: "The sad duty of politics is to establish justice in a sinful world." Reagan is not a big ambiguity fan.

"No Gloating"

A senior official asked to characterize Reagan from close up said almost instantly, "Competitive." During the budget and tax battles of 1981 he was dedicated not only to winning his economic points but to *winning*. He pushed himself and his staff hard, and even some of the losing Democrats said the coordination between President, White House staff, and Republican leadership on the Hill was a beautiful thing to see.

After the big tax win, Reagan's first instruction to his staff was "No gloating." As everyone agreed, he was a nice guy, normal, fun to be with. (Most since . . . ?) This surely lubricated his relationships with Congress.

He and his advisers came to Washington with a powerful sense of priorities. They were determined to concentrate on their budget and tax objectives and so far as possible keep other issues off the front pages. They were convinced that the Carter Administration was constantly confusing the Congress and the public with too many problems and programs. This intentness, combined with the unique zeal and talent of the thirty-four-year-old David Stockman, Director of the Office of Management and Budget, equipped the Administration with comprehensive budget proposals and long-range economic projections within a month of Inauguration Day. Stockman was leadoff man in the running start, though it later transpired that he didn't believe his own numbers. The Reaganites were well aware of the perishable opportunities possessed by a new President in his first year, and perhaps the fact that their President was seventy lent a little extra urgency.

But finally, for all the coherence of purpose, all the communicating skills, all the charms and normality of Ronald Reagan, there had to be a receptive country "out there." Reagan through his long years of campaigning, for governor of California, three times for the Republican presidential nomination, then for the Presidency, was one of those who helped make conservatism respectable and even popular. He could be reassuringly down-home in behalf of daring ideas. In 1981 he made brilliant use of the "bully pulpit," as Teddy Roosevelt defined the Presidency. And the congregation was ready for the sermon.

He was of course fortunate in his opposition. The titular leader of the Democratic Party was in Plains, Georgia, virtually invisible. The most visible Democrat, Tip O'Neill, was the burly, cigar-chomping caricature of a machine pol. Chieftains of the party's battered liberal wing, e.g., Kennedy and Mo Udall, could rally only sad little skirmishing parties on some of the tax roll calls. The only possibility of stopping the Reagan tax bill, though it turned out to be no possibility at all, lay in a not especially liberal bill offered by the not especially charismatic leadership of the Speaker and West Side Chicago's Danny Rostenkowski.

A Choice in Packaging

There were ways of presenting the Reagan economic package that made it look like a rather modest restraint on previous trends in federal taxing and spending. It could be said, for instance, that the Reagan cuts in personal income taxes through mid-1984 would barely offset inflationary bracket creep and scheduled increases in Social Security taxes. It could also be pointed out that the Reagan budget cuts still left non-defense spending in fiscal 1982 higher in real dollars than in fiscal '81 (essentially a Carter budget), and therefore the total budget the highest in our peacetime history, not only in absolute dollars but as a percentage of GNP. Furthermore, even if everything in the Reagan economic scenario worked exactly according to plan, by fiscal year 1985 federal taxes as a percentage of national income would have been brought down only to the level where Jimmy Carter found them in 1977. And federal spending as a percentage of GNP would be back about to the levels of the early 1970s—about 19 percent. In the event, federal spending in Reagan's fourth year, in good part because of the defense buildup, was running at 24.5 percent of GNP.

As the figures looked to the Reaganites in their first year, however, they were tempted to work both sides of the street. They could come on as soothing gradualists, and sometimes they did. Or they could come on as the proponents of a profound change in the whole thrust of the U.S. political economy. In the final weeks before the showdown on the Kemp-Roth tax bill in the ostensibly Democratic House, the Administration seemed to settle on the more radical—and accurate—interpretation of its program.

Turning the Nimitz

It takes thousands of yards of ocean to turn the *Nimitz,* and it takes at least two fiscal years to turn the U.S. government. The Reagan program was intended as the beginning of a real turn. And just as LBJ's original Great Society programs had their own built-in multipliers—though nobody realized at the time how prolific—the Reagan program, unless interrupted by some counter-counterrevolution, would have much greater effects from the mid-1980s on than in 1982–83.

The Reagan economics program was indeed the first serious attempt in half a century to arrest the growth of government and return in substantial measure some choices and some dollars to the private sector. Or let the private sector keep more of what belonged to it in the first place, as Reagan would argue. Reagan of course would not say "private sector" but something more homely like "your own earnings." He was too shrewd, incidentally, to say "what you and I have earned," knowing that the public knew he enjoyed a very high standard of living at public expense. The public really doesn't mind that, but minds Presidents pretending otherwise.

"In my mashed potato tours," as Reagan recalled to me, "I have said many times that government doesn't tax to get the money it needs, government always finds a need for the money it gets." Or if you leave taxes where they are, wait for government to reduce spending, and only then distribute the benefits in tax cuts, you will have a very long wait.

So the great plunge of 1981 was taken. Senator Howard Baker had it about right: "What we are doing is really a riverboat gamble." He added that in his judgment it would work. The hunch that it could work rested on faith, hope, and a process of elimination—nothing else, by way of an overall economic program, had worked very well in recent administrations. Reagan-Stockman-Kemp-Roth was the only really new idea in town.

The Going Gets Tougher

Some of what I have written above was published in *Fortune* (September 21, 1981) under the title "Reagan's First Two Hundred Days." As things turned out, most of Reagan's first term did happen, ideologically, in those two hundred days. He was never able in that term to mount another initiative in domestic policy comparable to the tax-and-budget legislation of his first summer.

Reagan supported (with only one or two lapses) the rigorous tight money policy imposed through many months of 1981–82 by the Federal Reserve Board under the formidable Paul Volcker. (In playing the old journalistic game of who-is-the-second-most-powerful-man-in-Washington, I once nominated Ronald Reagan. My not entirely fanciful No. 1 was Chairman Volcker.) The Fed's policies were brilliantly successful in bringing down the rate of inflation. They also helped bring on the worst recession since the 1930s.

The severity of the recession and the monstrous swelling of the "out-year" deficits became grave embarrassments to most Reaganites. Especially those who had to run for reelection in November 1982.

It now takes an effort, after Reagan's triumph of November 1984, to remember what deep troubles afflicted his Presidency less than two years before. His reaction to his tough winter of 1982–83 might foreshadow how he would react to another such time, if it befell him, in his second term. In that earlier difficulty, the Reaganite-in-chief serenely counseled faith and patience: It would take time to overcome the follies of past administrations and Congresses.

Yet the President also knew that sooner or later in 1982 he would have to sacrifice some of what he had won in 1981, to preserve the main body of his program. In *Gambling with History** Laurence Barrett gives a richly detailed narrative of the White House and congressional maneuverings that eventually led to the tax increase of August 1982, repealing about a quarter of the massive tax cut Reagan had so proudly signed a year before. Barrett, *Time*'s senior Reaganologist, tells how the President as early as March 1982 had secretly given White House Chief of Staff James Baker the general outlines of the tax and budget deal he

*New York: Doubleday, 1983.

would be prepared to cut. (Baker is another of those second-most-powerful men in Washington. A very smart Texan, considered dangerously moderate by the more rigid Reaganites.) In the end Reagan had to sweeten his offer, then manfully went on prime-time TV to plead for passage of the compromise he had struck with the congressional moderates of both parties. OMB came up with "revenue enhancement" as a euphemism for tax increases.

Reagan even proposed a gimmicky contingent tax for October 1, 1985—an income tax surtax to be triggered if the projected 1986 deficit exceeded a certain percentage of projected GNP. It was hard to believe Reagan himself cared much for this complicated idea, and the Congress certainly didn't. (Ironically enough, as the numbers were looking in late 1984, the gimmick might have opened a beautiful escape hatch for Reagan from his campaign promises not to raise taxes: a statutory command that he do so.) The thing was in the budget for cosmetic purposes —an attempt to look fiscally sober without actually imposing new taxes before the 1984 election.

From the chronology it seems inescapable that Paul Volcker regarded the 1982 tax increase as the *quid pro quo* for cuts in the discount rate, which the Fed then knocked down two and a half points between August and December 1982. The stock and bond markets boomed, and the interest-sensitive auto and housing markets finally showed signs of life. It could be argued that the President prolonged the recession by two quarters by not agreeing to the tax increase at the beginning of 1982.

Despite his reputation for rigidity, however, it is doubtful whether any modern President compromised so often on so many major issues as Ronald Reagan did in the latter months of 1982. Along with the big tax bill, he accepted a gasoline tax increase linked to a public works jobs program. He had previously said it would take a palace coup to get any such bill past his desk. He was supporting a Social Security rescue plan that violated some of his longest cherished ideas about provision for the elderly, a plan acceptable not only to Tip O'Neill but to that wily lobbyist for the aged, Congressman Claude Pepper of Florida. (In the presence of federal funds, Pepper, 84, has the moves of a man half his age.) And the President signed his name—unhappily to be sure—to those staggering deficit estimates for the "out years." He backed down on his sanctions against the Soviet pipeline, and backed off the "dense pack" basing mode for the MX missile.

All this dismayed many of Reagan's earliest and most fervent admirers without earning him any very loud applause from the moderates who had so often called for just such "realism" and "flexibility." Some moderates in his own party were not sure but what he had been fatally wounded. They were not going to attack him, but they were keeping some daylight between themselves and the White House. Centrists, in any case, tend to be a little cool in their enthusiasms. Realism and pragmatism are not words to set the blood a-tingling. It could take the centrists time to get used to this newcomer in their midst. Centrists could also question whether Reagan would really stay in their midst.

The winter of 1982–83 was a grim season for the Reaganites, though their sunny President showed only an occasional flash of irritation. It was later evident that the recession had bottomed out by December, but conclusive evidence wouldn't quite jump out of the statistics for another two months or so. And even then unemployment remained painfully high. The mid-term elections, though not a disaster for Reagan, had been an unmistakable defeat. The complexion of the House changed in ways helpful to the orthodox Democratic opposition, and the Republicans suffered a grievous net loss of seven governorships.

A lame-duck session of Congress, which the President in a stunting way had insisted upon, was the fatuous event such sessions usually are. Public annoyance and bafflement at the proceedings may have focused more upon the Congress and the filibusterers than on the President, but the general reaction was not flattering to anybody in office in Washington.

Reagan's job-approval rating in the polls declined in November–January to a level below all the six previous Presidents at the same point in their presidencies. The Carter comparison (Reagan once behind a dozen points) must have been particularly galling to the President and his loyalists. Other polls soon began to show either Walter Mondale or John Glenn comfortably defeating Reagan.

Press coverage and commentary, often critical in 1982 but still respectful of the President's political resourcefulness, was turning increasingly hostile in January. The *New York Times* said, not without a touch of wishful thinking: "The stench of failure hangs over the Ronald Reagan White House."* The *Wall Street Journal,* which seldom agrees with the *Times,* detected "a whiff of panic at the White House."† Also from the Right, William Safire wrote wickedly of one of the President's

---

*January 9, 1983. Georgi Arbatov, the Kremlin's leading Americanologist, liked this formulation so much he repeated it, without crediting the *Times,* in an article for *Pravda.*
†Norman C. Miller, Washington Bureau Chief, January 13, 1983.

favorites, his National Security Adviser (later Secretary of the Interior), that "William Clark is living proof that still waters can run shallow."*

What was especially wounding in much of this wordage was the apparent ease with which journalists had found anonymous sources within the Administration to describe the struggles "across the mind of the President." This led the President to say he had "had it up to the keister with leaks." The repetition of this colorful language was in itself a leak, as the press happily noted, identifying the source as David Gergen. The notion that a President could prohibit leaking was promptly ridiculed within the Administration as well as the press.

These multiplying criticisms and pressures led to one of the most remarkable presidential press conferences in many years. Reagan on very short notice appeared in the White House press briefing room to assert that his Administration was *not* in "disarray." He said it was really the press that was in disarray. (How true. The press is always in disarray, and in a democracy is meant to be, speaking with many voices. A Presidency is different.)

Looking over this agitated political landscape, Richard Nixon offered an interesting metaphor. Perhaps in those winter weeks of 1982–83, Nixon mused, Reagan was having his "second Iowa"—a reference to Reagan's sharp setback at the beginning of the 1980 primaries season, which led him to shake up his staff and pull his campaign act together.

Fighting Over the Figures

There was ample disarray among the President's economic advisers. Treasury Secretary Donald Regan admitted to strenuous "wrangling" with OMB Director David Stockman and Martin Feldstein, then chairman of the Council of Economic Advisers, since returned to Harvard, over the cautious recovery projections built into the President's 1983 budget. Regan had been burned earlier when he predicted the economy would "come roaring back" in the spring of 1982. Stockman was not burned as much (like at the stake) as many Republicans thought he should be when his disbelief in his own optimistic 1982–83 projections was revealed in the famous *Atlantic Monthly* article.†

The reasoning that finally prevailed in the White House was that the Administration couldn't stand another major miscalculation on the optimistic side, while nobody would be mad if 1983 turned out better

New York Times, November 29, 1982.
†December 1981.

than predicted. It was also true that Feldstein and other nonpolitical types saw virtue in a slow acceleration, as less likely to reignite inflation and set us up for another recession in 1985 or so. In the event, Don Regan was much more nearly right about the speed of the recovery than Professor Feldstein. Through 1983 and the first half of 1984, the economy consistently outperformed the CEA expectations.

The vigor of the recovery permitted the Administration to argue that the 5-10-10 tax cut was "working," though initially it was stimulating consumer spending far more than business investment, and the rate of personal saving even declined. The tax increase of 1982 had been mainly a take-back from business; for consumers the Reagan tax cuts of 1981–83 more than offset the 1981–83 increases in Social Security taxes. For most people, there was indeed more after-taxes money around.

But philosophically the whole basis of Reaganomics was shifting. The monstrous deficits had to be accommodated within the theology. The recession accounted for about half the 1982 and 1983 deficits, by increasing unemployment benefit payments, interest on the public debt, and farm price subsidies, and by shrinking tax receipts. This was the "cyclical" deficit, chargeable to hard times. The rest was the "structural" deficit, the underlying mechanisms and urges that lead our polity, even in good times, to spend more than we are willing to tax ourselves to pay for. "Entitlements" in the broadest sense—including the entitlement of politicians to be reelected. It was easy to make fun of Reagan's belated discovery of "cyclical" vs. "structural" red ink, a distinction he had not previously mentioned in two or three decades of deficit-denouncing. The distinction, in fact, is a valid one.

Along with this insight, Reaganomics was invaded by a potent strain of Keynesianism. The deficit for 1983, the first fiscal year Reagan controlled the full cycle of budget writing, was $195 billion. The figure was numbing. The President was quick to point out that Congress had a large say in what the final deficit figures looked like—and he went on that if his Administration made a mistake, it was in underestimating what a fiscal mess previous Presidents (apparently including at least a couple of Republicans) and Democratic-controlled Congresses had created. (Senate Majority Leader Robert Dole, former chairman of the Senate Finance Committee, wistfully recalled "some experts from HEW coming up here around 1968 or 1969 and warning us if we didn't watch this medicare thing, it could get up to $9 billion in 1990." It was recently projected to hit $120 billion in 1990.)

But the Reagan Administration was tacitly accepting the view of most private economists, conservative as well as liberal, that the vast deficit of fiscal 1983 was a good stimulus for a flat economy. The vast deficit of 1984 might not be a totally bad thing either.

It was after that the picture began to terrify. If a fully recovered economy still couldn't come within $200–300 billion of balancing the budget, if booming private demand for credit had to compete with government debt financing on that scale, interest rates could zoom up again and we could have the makings of an even more severe recession than 1981–82.

About a B in Economics

As the fourth year of Reagan's Presidency was ending, I thought the old economics major deserved about a B for his handling of economic issues (better than the grades he used to get at Eureka):

• For the recovery from the recession, and the boom of 1983–84, Reagan, Paul Volcker and the business cycle could share the credit. Reagan's salient contributions were his tax cuts and the massive federal deficits that accompanied them. His firm handling of the air traffic controllers' strike in 1981 doubtless had something to do with the relative moderation in union negotiating positions over the next three years. His general friendliness to enterprise and optimism about America helped improve the business climate and the country's confidence in the economy.

• The spectacular reduction in inflation enhanced the sense of well-being. Again, credit the business cycle, Volcker, and Reagan, plus the worldwide softening of oil prices. But real interest rates, the spread between 4 percent inflation (fourth quarter 1984) and nominal rates (such as 11.25 percent prime, 13 percent mortgage), were the highest in American history, reflecting low confidence by lenders in the future of the dollar.

• Among the most free of the free markets Reagan so devoutly believes in are the stock and bond markets, where tens of thousands of independent judgments are rendered daily on the future of the dollar and the economy. During 1984 neither the bond market nor the stock market (despite generally strong corporate profits) was giving Reagan much better than a C+. His deficits frightened the financial markets. And years of imprudent overseas lending by Western banks to ill-governed countries heavily dependent on a few export commodities had created a precarious world debt structure. The banks' lofty interest rates were in part a judgment on their own past policies. These rates were a potential political embarrassment to Reagan in 1983–84, and he tried now and then to talk the rates down—a case of "government" trying to tell a "market" what to do. Meanwhile the U.S., remarkably, was becoming one of the biggest debtors in the world, as our high interest rates drew in floods of foreign money, while we ran the highest international trade deficits in our history. To an uncomfortable degree, the world was financing Reagan's red ink, making possible—for the time being—very low U. S. inflation rates despite the massive budget deficits. This figured in the financial markets' nervousness.

• The President, in line with good laissez-faire doctrine, stuck fairly firmly to his free-trade principles. He did some compromising during the Presidential campaign year, but earlier, during the recession, he had shown considerable political courage. He had pretty much handed the Toyota issue to the Democrats, and Mondale made some flagrant use of it. (Of the 219 representatives who backed the "local content" legislation of 1983, 187 were Democrats. An odd historical reversal for the Democrats to evolve into the party of protectionism.)

• A major theme in Reaganomics was deregulation. The Administration did some good work here and, out of dozens of little bits and pieces, there should be a payoff in enhanced industrial productivity. There had been an excess of consumerism and environmentalism in the Carter years—under the general motif of Washington Knows Best. In attacking some of the excesses of OSHA, EPA, FTC, etc., etc., the Reaganauts committed excesses of their own. Some sort of balance finally set in. James Watt, with his seemingly inexhaustible store of indiscretions, was eventually replaced at Interior by Judge Bill Clark, who began to undo some of the Watts policies. At EPA, the hard-right ideologue Anne Gorsuch Burford gave way to the temperate William Ruckelshaus.

• Reagan did succeed in arresting the growth in non-defense programs overall. That was a notable accomplishment, though it arguably included some economies that cut too deep. Harsh restrictions on aid to the disabled were later undone by Congress and the courts. Tighter eligibility requirements for various federal benefits generally bore more heavily on the working poor than on the nonworking poor. Reagan was providing at least one outrageously swollen subsidy—farm price supports were running about twice as high as in any previous administration. Even so, farmers were in considerable distress, in part because of high interest rates and the super-strong dollar, which was devastating their export markets. The farm supports, like other middle-class entitlements, were left untouched in election year 1984, but these were among the few remaining non-defense areas where worthwhile budget cuts were possible.

• The big monster out there was still the federal budget. I was one of those who thought the gamble of 1981 might just work. It didn't. The tax cuts were too generous, the buildup in defense spending was too fast. According to the Administration's original projections on taking office, the budget was to show a surplus in fiscal 1984 and again in fiscal 1985. Instead the government was in the red by $175 billion in 1984. For 1985, the Administration projected a deficit of $172 billion, then upped it to $190 billion, then a few days after the Presidential election said it looked more like $210 billion. Any of these stupefying figures would be more (in real dollars) than Jimmy Carter's four deficits combined. The conservative columnist George Will, a personal friend and long-time supporter of Reagan, wrote: "The new budget is the Republicans' 'Chapter 11,' a declaration of bankruptcy of political will and intellectual integrity."* As far out as 1988, the Administration could see the deficits still running as high as $100 billion, while the Congressional Office of the Budget, whose predictions had usually been more realistic, foresaw much larger numbers through the rest of the 1980s. Even by the Administration's numbers, the piling up of public debt and the interest charges on the debt (already more than half the deficit in the 1985 budget) became a kind of perpetual-motion inflationary engine.

Meanwhile the Administration and congressional leaders of both parties in 1984 negotiated a symbolic "down payment" on the deficit, a combination of creative bookkeeping, modest budget cuts and modest "revenue enhancements." The political jockeying was similar to that in 1982, with all players seeking to look "responsible" without accepting the onus for anything painful to any large bloc of voters. Ronald Reagan was of course a master of that sort of maneuver. And he was mightily helped by the perception that the Democrats had historically been the free-spending party, and the Republicans the party of fiscal orthodoxy. He could run deficits that would ruin a Democrat, for somewhat the same reason that Nixon could negotiate with China and Russia more freely than Hubert Humphrey could have.

*Washington *Post,* February 12, 1984.

The Big Silence

On this same general principle, one might have speculated that Ronald Reagan could pursue détente more boldly than Jimmy Carter would have dared, that he might even have dreamed of being the Peacemaker President. If he had such a dream, however, it was one that could be fulfilled, as he saw it, only after U. S. policy had been rigorously purged of false hopes about détente and powerfully fortified by a military buildup. This outlook was concisely summarized when he adopted the name Peacekeeper for the MX missile.

U. S.-Soviet relationships through most of 1984 were worse than they had been for two decades. But the superpowers were locked in no confrontation comparable to the Berlin and Cuba missile crises of the early 1960s. They simply were barely speaking to each other. For this state of affairs, the bigger blame belonged to the Soviets. Yet the larger question for Americans was whether our country, with a presumed advantage over the Soviets in enlightenment, and even morality, was managing our end of the relationship as wisely as we might.

The central subject that was not being talked about, in any serious way, was arms control. The whole SALT process had perhaps played itself out. But arms control was never the sine qua non of peace, as some overeager U. S. negotiators of the 1970s tended to assume. The profound philosophical difference between our system and the Soviet system breeds the understandable fears that breed the hellish weapons. The weapons systems now have such a hair-trigger jumpiness (if you were President, would you "launch on warning" of incoming missiles?) that they are indeed a danger in themselves. But even if military technology were still back in the age of tanks, armored flight decks and iron bombs, we would have the potential of fighting a long and terrible World War III against the Soviet Union, for reasons each country would find sufficient. The mushroom cloud may have prevented just that. If tomorrow you could cut U. S. and Soviet nuclear firepower by 75 percent—more than any rational arms controller would dream possible in ten years—each country would still have the power to devastate the earth. I have felt the problem was less the weapons themselves than the reasons we and the Russians want them.

The Kremlin must occasionally speculate on whether the U. S. would respond with nuclear weapons to a Soviet attack on the West. Reagan's rhetoric, more than any President's since Kennedy, could have led the Soviet leaders to think: "He just might . . ." I preferred that, at least in the world of 1984, to: "He never would." There were horrifying dangers, of course, in each surmise. And the Reagan Administration had done little sustained thinking as to whether, along with the maintenance of MAD—Mutual Assured Destruction— there could be other approaches to our mutual fears. Reagan's Strategic Defense Initiative came closest to being a fresh approach, and though the derisive "Star Wars" tag was unjust, there were grave technological and political doubts about the value of S.D.I.

Reagan in four years had confronted three Soviet leaders: the dying Leonid Brezhnev, the dying Yuri Andropov, then the frail Konstantin Chernenko, 73. Perhaps the chief elements of leadership continuity were Foreign Minister Andrei Gromyko, 75, and Defense Minister Dimitri Ustinov, who died at 76 late in 1984. It was a hard-line stand-pat leadership.

The Soviet leadership, as Lawrence Caldwell and Robert Legvold wrote in the journal *Foreign Policy* (Fall 1983), "by its own peculiar criteria . . . takes the Reagan Administration very seriously . . . While capable of picking out elements of restraint, they tend to focus on what they view as the more ominous aspects of policy, and this approach inevitably makes the rhetoric seem more important . . . No one gets ahead in Moscow these days by looking for reasons to give the Reagan Administration the benefit of the doubt."

The President did make at least two personal appeals across the chasm. While he was recovering from the Hinckley assassination attempt in 1981, he sent a handwritten letter to Leonid Brezhnev recalling that when they met ten years earlier, at Nixon's San Clemente house, "You took my hand in both of yours and assured me . . . you were dedicated, with all your heart and soul and mind to fulfilling [the] hopes and dreams of world peace." Reagan went on to a more conventional critique of Soviet policy, and it was this part of the letter that Brezhnev chose to answer—coldly.

In a speech in January 1984, Reagan sketched out a scene starring Ivan and Anya, Jim and Sally, Soviet and American couples, somehow thrown together in a rainstorm, discovering they were just regular people with—yes—children, jobs, bosses, etc., liking each other in spite of their respective forms of government. Reagan's corny vignette was much ridiculed by American critics of his foreign policy. Imagine the hope and enthusiasm of the same people if Andropov or Chernenko had told such a friendly little fable over Soviet TV.

The Soviets found the Ivan-Jim story childish and insulting, and perhaps detected a sly advantage Reagan was taking. Reagan had been campaigning against the United States government for thirty years, and still did in 1984, notwithstanding being President of the United States. It came easy to him to suggest that governments might somehow be interfering with the natural urge of people to be friends. That suggestion would not come easy to a Soviet leader.

Danger and Opportunity

In foreign policy the President of the United States is playing from a strong hand, even a President who isn't fascinated by the game. Since the Truman-Eisenhower era, however, when America's relative power was so much greater than now, no administration has made a broadly successful use in world affairs of our still formidable assets. Nixon and Kissinger came closest, though the pointless prolonging of the Viet Nam war was a sorry mistake. We have survived this and other mistakes and humiliations that seemed more monstrous at the time than they do now. In the powerful Britain of the eighteenth century, Adam Smith wrote to John Sinclair: "Be assured, my young friend, that there is a great deal of ruin in a nation."

Reagan took office in years bristling with danger to America—and bright with opportunity. The mix was not new, but the possible penalties and rewards had multiplied. It is a fragile world out there. There are nearly fifty thousand nuclear warheads deployed in the Northern Hemisphere. Things will probably come out all right, but sometimes it takes strong nerves just to watch.

U. S. foreign policy did not change as much with the party turnover of 1980 as the election-year oratory would have suggested. The nation's fundamental interests remain, and the ways that reasonably intelligent men seek to advance them can't vary widely from one administration to the next. The diplomatic and military bureaucracies and the "foreign policy community" out in the universities, banks, law offices, press, foundations, and think tanks all contribute to the continuity.

There have been hard-liners and softer-liners in the Reagan Administration, as there were in the Carter Administration, though the debate takes place further over toward the hard end of the spectrum. It was interesting that two Carter officials from the "hard" side of that house, Dr. Brzezinski of Columbia and Dr. Huntington of Harvard (sometimes known as Zbig's Zbig), both spoke well from time to time

of Reagan foreign policy. From the softer wing of the Carter Administration, Cy Vance attacked a decision to sell arms to China as "needlessly provocative" and found the Reagan Administration generally
engaged in "posture" rather than policy.

Reagan's rhetoric has been very different from Carter's, of course
—and rhetoric is not unimportant. But an even bigger change was in
the degree of presidential involvement in foreign policy. The foreign
policy process, always a bit messy in our democracy, became the subject
of a novel experiment: Could the machinery work in the 1980s without
the deep and consistent engagement of the President? While in domestic affairs the Congress theoretically can fashion national policy, and
sometimes does, our system assumes the President at the heart of foreign policy-making. The President needs to do more than just speak the
final Yes or No. Few students of foreign policy think it necessary or even
desirable for a President to immerse himself so deeply in the minutiae
of foreign policy decision-making as Jimmy Carter sometimes did. Reagan represented a swing of the pendulum all the way out of the clock.

Reagan's courage, calm, and perseverance could be invaluable
qualities in the conduct of foreign policy. But the genial offhandedness
and the detachment from the details—including very large details—
could be breathtaking. Among the occupants of the modern Presidency, Presidents of a superpower but also a vulnerable America, several were relatively innocent of foreign policy experience. But none of
them managed or chose to stay so far out of it as Reagan did in his first
two years. The President's strong tilt toward domestic policy reflected
not only his own interests but a calculated decision that foreign issues
should not distract attention from his economic package.

Editorial writers, columnists, TV commentators asked: Do we have
a foreign policy? There were zigzags, bobbles, and a considerable bab-
ble of conflicting voices. If we had a foreign policy, it seemed at times
to consist of "The Haig Question"—would General Alexander Haig be
able to hang on as Secretary of State or would "they" (White House staff,
possibly even the Pentagon) get him? They did undermine him, but it
was the President who finally got him, in June 1982, accepting a resignation that Haig offered once too often.

In *Caveat: Realism, Reagan and Foreign Policy,** Haig tells a fascinating if not entirely disinterested story of the West Wing palace guard
sealing him off from access to the President. But he didn't seem to
realize, or wasn't willing to admit, that Reagan really didn't want much

*New York: Macmillan, 1984.

time alone with his Secretary of State. This was partly for reasons of personal chemistry, partly for lack of deep interest in the Secretary's work.

So Haig and various of his appointees were often publicly debating other Administration officials, via speeches, TV talk shows, and newspaper leaks, on the meaning of Reagan foreign policy, especially in Central America and the Middle East. In a conversation in the West Wing, Edwin Meese, then White House Counselor, later nominated as Attorney General, pleasantly acknowledged that the Administration contained "multiple sources of comment" on foreign policy. But the sources fell into line, he insisted to me, once a decision had been reached at the presidential level. They sometimes did, as things worked, but not always. And while the debating and leaking went on, it was a serious question whether the U.S. foreign policy establishment knew how to get its work done, and whether foreign governments were needlessly confused, or even felt encouraged to play to whatever factions or rival schools of thought they decided they had detected in Washington.

The managerial failure here was twofold. The President was unable or unwilling to recognize the harm done his Administration and the country by the debating society he was hosting. And some of the strong-willed men in his employ would have had less to debate about if the President had worked his way through to clear foreign policy views of his own.

It was in some ways refreshing to have a President who did *not* feel a deep pull toward foreign policy, who would settle for changing the United States. But alas, the world out there could also transform the United States, not necessarily for the better.

In 1983–84, Reagan became more engaged in foreign policy, in part under the pressure of external events, especially Lebanon, the shooting down of KAL 007, and the antinuclear movements in Western Europe. The President and his advisers also saw foreign policy as a major arena of the 1984 election. And perhaps he had concluded—this is sheer speculation—that some of the problems were fairly interesting after all.

George Shultz had made a difference. Reagan found him more congenial company than Haig, and this in itself led him to give more time to foreign policy. The two Secretaries of State did not greatly differ in their policy views, but the (almost) imperturbable, Shultz was a more effective advocate than his excitable predecessor. The built-in tension between the State Department and White House staff was still there, but less acute. Shultz also had his policy disputes with Weinberger—the fact that both men had been executives of the Bechtel Construction Company did not seem a particular bond.

Reagan and Shultz could count some foreign policy successes, and one grievous defeat.

The Alliance: Strained but Standing

An important success for Reagan foreign policy was something that didn't happen: The NATO Alliance did not come apart. It did undergo severe strain.

The Reagan Administration in its early days frightened the Allies, and on into 1983–84 it could still make Western Europe very nervous from time to time. The President casually speculated one day in 1981 that a nuclear exchange might be confined to Europe. A Pentagon document implied that a nuclear war was in some sense winnable. Reagan and Haig both openly suggested the Soviet Empire was on its last legs. But that line was toned down, perhaps in recognition that it might not be helpful in the Polish situation, perhaps for fear that it might undercut the case for the U.S. defense buildup. The President's fervent insistence on Soviet evil could lead to the inference that the system must be forcibly overthrown. Indeed in 1983 he told a gathering of evangelical clergy in Orlando, Florida, "We are enjoined by Scripture and the Lord Jesus to oppose it [the Soviet evil] with all our might."

But the fiery rhetoric, as the Alliance finally began to notice, was accompanied by policies of considerable restraint. In 1981, in fulfillment of his political campaign pledge to U.S. farmers, Reagan lifted Jimmy Carter's courageous embargo on grain shipments to the Soviets. In 1982, in punishment for the imposition of martial law by the puppet regime of Poland, Reagan attempted to persuade Western Europe to cut down on industrial sales to the Soviets and cancel the Siberian gas pipeline deal. The Administration even tried to prohibit Western European subsidiaries of U.S. firms from taking any of the pipeline business. George Shultz eventually helped the President down off this position. As German Chancellor Helmut Schmidt had coolly noted, "Technology is our grain."

The East-West trade dispute was only one of the economic strains within the Alliance. The Allies were complaining in 1981–82 that the U.S. was exporting unemployment and recession with our brutally high interest rates and high-priced dollar; the fact that many Americans, starting with Ronald Reagan, devoutly wished the rates would come down did not make the Allies feel any better. Western Europe has to pay for its Middle East oil in dollars. Germany blamed U.S. interest rates in cutting back on its NATO defense spending commitment.

In 1983, as the U.S. economic recovery took hold, and in 1984, as the U.S. economy boomed, it supplied a powerful stimulus to Western Europe. There was still complaint about U.S. interest rates and growing anxiety about Reagan's budget deficits, but the immediate effects of U.S. prosperity, including the flourishing market for Western European exports, were mainly pleasing. When Reagan in June 1984 met in London with the leaders of the other major industrial nations, it was probably the least contentious of the four economic summits he had endured.

But the health of the Alliance depended finally on our partners' perceptions of U.S. competence and sobriety in the face of the great war-and-peace issues. (It could become equally dependent on Americans' perceptions as to whether Western Europe was doing its share in the common defense, but for thirty years U.S. administrations of both parties had been remarkably patient on this point.) The key test of U.S. sobriety, in the Allies' view, was that the U.S. should be engaging in good-faith negotiations with the Soviets on arms control.

It was to meet this condition that the Reagan Administration had continued the Carter Administration's two-track approach to the deployment of Intermediate-range Nuclear Forces. The placement of these weapons had been requested by the Allies, to counter Soviet deployment of their SS-20s, and Reagan was following through on his predecessor's promise to deploy. At the same time the Reagan Administration offered the Soviets a "zero option"—we would not deploy the Pershing II's and cruise missiles if the Soviets would dismantle the SS-20s. Paul Nitze in 1982 explored with his Soviet counterpart in Geneva a compromise which would have allowed each side 75 intermediate range missiles in Europe, instead of the 572 we intended to deploy and the 600-odd the Soviets already had in place. Then the White House and the Kremlin each threw cold water on the idea. The White House apparently threw first. There was no movement in INF negotiations in the next two years.

The U.S. deployments began in late 1983, despite widespread demonstrations against them and despite a massive Soviet propaganda campaign, designed to break NATO apart. The British, West German, and Italian governments received the missiles as they had agreed; the Dutch delayed. The Soviets walked out of the Geneva negotiations. The long silence ensued.

In *Deadly Gambits,** Strobe Talbott of *Time* gives a brilliant account of these events and of the whole play-by-play of arms control policy in Reagan's first term. He presents a devastating portrait of the President's misconceptions of some of the rudimentary facts about U.S. and Soviet weapons and his cheerful permissiveness toward the philosophic disorder in his own Administration. (For balance, it would be good to know the inside story of Soviet arms control policy during the same period, but alas, no chronicler is likely to tell us.) The bureaucratic warfare between Defense and State involved principle as well as pettiness (as bureaucratic warfare often does). The Pentagon hard-liners, led by Richard Perle, Assistant Secretary for International Security Policy, won more often than they lost, and their case was constantly strengthened by Soviet intransigence. Negotiations on long-range missiles, as well as the medium-range, were frozen.

Back to Geneva

Yet even as U.S.-Soviet relations reached this low point, the Presidential election was introducing a new dynamic. Reagan and his handlers wanted to deprive the Democrats of any trigger-happy accusation. In January 1984, Reagan said the U.S. "must and will engage the Soviets in a dialogue as serious and constructive as possible." In May, Reagan said the U.S. remained ready to negotiate with the Soviets "fairly and flexibly without preconditions." The conciliatory statements started coming closer together, despite an utter lack of any Soviet encouragement. In June, Reagan said he would be willing to discuss a joint Soviet-NATO renunciation of the use of force. In a speech in September before the UN General Assembly, he called again for "a better working relationship" and "constructive negotiations."

The Soviet Foreign Minister did not applaud that day in New York, but his government in fact had begun to budge. The Soviets presented the President with a nice campaign goodie: A visit to the White House by Andrei Gromyko six weeks before the election, deflating the Democratic charge that Reagan was the first President since Hoover who had failed to meet with the top Soviet leadership. During the attendant

*New York: Alfred A. Knopf, 1984.

"photo opportunity" in the Oval Office, Gromyko managed a smile of sorts.

The Soviets had clearly reconciled themselves to Reagan's reelection, and after the event they did some further reconciling. They agreed to a meeting of Gromyko and Secretary Shultz in Geneva in early January 1985 to talk about talking—how to discuss a whole "umbrella" of arms control questions.

President Reagan, for his part, was said to feel that now the time was ripe, as he thought it was not in 1981, for a real breakthrough. The President saw arms control, one of his officials said, as being something like "what China was to Richard Nixon." He could "make a deal with the Russians that very few people can quibble with because nobody's going to accuse him of going soft on the Soviets." It was worth remembering, however, that Ronald Reagan himself did accuse Nixon of just that—couching it as an attack on Kissinger—when he was trying to wrest the Republican nomination away from Gerald Ford in 1976. How much this weighed on his memory or conscience in late 1984 was hard to say, but there could be no doubt that Reagan felt an urge to be remembered for something even bigger than getting reelected in a landslide. Failing an arms control agreement that would suit both Reagan and the Russians—a large order—it is possible the President would see the startup on a comprehensive strategic defense system as a splendid legacy to his people.

The Turbulent Backyard

Another of President Reagan's second-term ambitions must surely be to find vindication for his controversial Central American policies. In his first months in office his Administration inflated the importance of El Salvador as a major U.S.-Soviet test of will. Then there was a decision to downplay it and imply "the media" were making too much of it. It was brought back with a vengeance in 1983–84.

One of the few real parallels between Viet Nam and Central America was that we could so easily talk up the stakes. In Viet Nam, ultimately, the commitment became the commitment.

The Administration and its critics were both exaggerating the importance of El Salvador and its Marxist neighbor Nicaragua. Victory for the Salvadoran rebels would have represented only a very modest and indirect danger to the United States. The Reagan Administration's military and economic assistance to the Salvadoran government was likewise modest, and Congress in 1984 seemed grudgingly to go along. The Salvadoran government was making a little military progress against the rebels, but the most hopeful developments were the victory of the moderate Jose Napoleon Duarte in the presidential election of March 1984, and his courageous initiative in opening talks in October with the guerrilla leaders. A decent result—for the U.S. and Ronald Reagan, but more important, for the long-suffering people of El Salvador—began to be conceivable.

Nicaragua looked less promising. Mexico and other Latin American states had opposed Reagan's not very covert aid to the *contras* who were seeking to overthrow the Sandinista regime. So did the U.S. House of Representatives, so did much of Western European opinion, which indeed seemed romantically preoccupied with Central America, far more than with, say, Poland. Safer perhaps.

Nicaragua's Soviet friends could of course read the U.S. election returns of November 6, 1984, but it was not clear that the young militants in the Managua junta—their careers, perhaps lives, on the line—were going to turn pragmatic. From the U.S. point of view, it would be desirable, if not essential, to have an open democracy emerge in Nicaragua. But the Reagan Administration had not figured out how to promote such an outcome at a sensible price.

Reagan's most spectacular intervention to the south was, of course, Grenada (also not well received in Western Europe). I thought he made the right decision. The ability of U.S. Marines, Rangers, and Airborne to occupy a small Caribbean island and overwhelm a few hundred Cuban construction workers and militia scarcely needed demonstrating. But the willingness to use force, promptly and amply, in an ambiguous but arguably legitimate cause, did make a salutary point.

Beyond the backyard, there was important change in South America: a trend toward civilian democratic rule. Military regimes peaceably stepped aside as free elections were held in 1983 and 1984 in Argentina, Uruguay and Brazil. Jimmy Carter and some of his officials see this as a payoff from the human rights emphasis in his foreign policy. Reagan people think the friendlier and less censorious line his Administration took with the military rulers made it easier for them to step down. Still another possibility is that these countries, regardless of the noises out of Washington, move pretty much according to their own music. In the case of Argentina, of course, Margaret Thatcher from London administered a powerful stimulant to the democratic impulses. The military junta never recovered from their debacle in the Falklands.

The Middle East Morass

The harshest defeat for Reagan's foreign policy came in Lebanon, a climax to three years of frustration and failure in the Middle East. When Reagan took office he inherited the Camp David agreements and a nominal state of peace between Israel and Egypt. The other issues remained intractable: the status of Jerusalem, the Golan Heights (Syrian territory conquered by Israel in the 1967 and 1973 wars), Palestinian aspirations for a homeland, Arab recognition of Israel's "right to exist."

Haig tried off and on to apply an East-West lens to the Middle East, seeking to form a "strategic consensus" among Israel and the moderate Arab states that the Soviets were the chief threat to stability in the region. It was a valid enough perception for the U.S. The difficulty was that the Arab nations perceived Israel as a greater menace than the Soviet Union. All the Third World countries, behind their shield of weakness, supported the Arabs on this, in the United Nations and wherever else it was convenient to assail the U.S.

The world oil glut mercifully brought a cresting to the flow of money and political influence to the OPEC countries. But the Arabs were not notably more conciliatory at $28 a barrel than they had been at $32. And God knows (the expression is not used lightly) that our Old Testament mentor, client, and ally Menachem Begin did not make things easy. Yitzhak Shamir, who succeeded him in 1983, was a little less formidable, and the curious Shamir/Perez rotational government which took over in September 1984 was another notch less difficult. But these successor governments have not forsworn further Israeli colonizing of the West Bank of the Jordan, a Begin policy that had created a new issue as bristling as any of the old grievances.

On September 1, 1982, Reagan made his first major speech on the Middle East, proposing self-rule for West Bank Palestinians "in association with Jordan." Shultz had a large hand in this carefully balanced statement, more admired in U.S. editorial pages, however, than by the Middle East antagonists. Shultz and Reagan were soon drawn in deeper. The U.S. brokered the May 1983 agreement between Israel and Lebanese President Amin Gemayel, calling for withdrawal of Israeli and Syrian forces from Lebanon. The U.S. Marines, having been sent to Lebanon a year before to help chaperone the defeated PLO out of the country, were now sent back to help stabilize the Gemayel regime. But

Lebanon was a far more fragile and complicated place than the Reagan Administration seemed to grasp. And Syria, contrary to optimistic State Department assumptions, had no intention of getting out of Lebanon even if Israel did. (Israel unilaterally withdrew to the border area chiefly because of the domestic unpopularity of the Lebanon war.) There followed the tragic bombing of the Marine barracks at the Beirut airport, then a painful sequence of White House bluster, "redeployment" of the Marines to ships offshore in February 1984, then within weeks the quiet departure of the naval task force. The cost in U.S. lives was 264. The cost in U.S. credibility was heavy, at least in the short run, and Syria and the Soviets were the winners.

Cap's World

Beirut notwithstanding, Reagan was soon using the line: "America is back and standing tall." There was a whiff of Grenada here, to say nothing of Hollywood. This was not the language of the foreign-policy intellectuals, but Reagan might have figured cowboys and sheriffs are better box office than professors.

There was something to it. What the Soviets call the correlation of forces did shift some in 1981–84. The U.S. defense buildup was an important element. I have argued earlier in this chapter that the ballooning of Pentagon budgets was too fast for the good of the economy. But some significant growth in defense spending (larger than likely in a Carter second term) was essential to worldwide perceptions of American seriousness. The perceptions by 1984 had perhaps outrun real increases in military effectiveness. But in the 1985–89 period, even assuming some slowdown by Congress of the spending schedules, there would be a real improvement in relative strength vis-à-vis the Soviets. Not nuclear superiority, neither attainable nor desirable, but a thoroughly believable nuclear deterrent and greater conventional capabilities.

For this some credit would be due Caspar Weinberger, notwithstanding his budget-busting and his turf-feuding with Secretaries of State. The line between State and Defense jurisdictions is never easy to draw—especially where arms sales, training missions, or negotiations over foreign bases are involved. Weinberger regularly crossed the line, about as often as Robert McNamara in the Kennedy Administration. Weinberger could say disarmingly, "Oh dear, have I committed foreign policy again?"

Weinberger was generally less solicitous of the NATO Alliance than

Haig or Shultz. In one of the Pentagon's annual "Posture" statements, Weinberger included a sharp little lecture on the follies of Western economic support for Soviet military development. He favored throwing Poland into default. Some State Department officials thought they saw strains of Fortress America thinking in the Pentagon. Weinberger denied being any sort of isolationist, or even a "global unilateralist" (a coinage by multilateralist Helmut Sonnenfeldt, former Counselor to the State Department). In fact, Cap noted, he is a *Tri*lateralist, a daring reference to his past membership in the private U.S.-European-Japanese commission that has alarmed various Far-Right kooks.

He and his President were very comfortable with each other. Lou Cannon of the Washington *Post,* in his excellent biography *Reagan** tells of a moment when Weinberger got out a Denver *Post* cartoon showing Uncle Sam playing a shell game with a Russian. He was inviting the Russian to guess which shell concealed the MX missile, in the race-track basing mode which Cap opposed. "The Russian in the cartoon takes out his hammer and destroys all the shells. Reagan chuckled and approved the Weinberger plan" (p. 392).

Though hard-liners are generally all-out supporters of Israel, as an anti-Soviet bastion, Weinberger tended to be sterner than the State Department when Israel misbehaved, and has angered Israel by arms-selling trips to Saudi Arabia and Jordan. On Central America, Weinberger was less hawkish than State, perhaps reflecting the caution of his Generals. In his vast E-ring office in the Pentagon, Cap Weinberger could create a curiously restful atmosphere for discussing the unimaginable—$1.6 trillion of defense spending. He would sit with head tilted back, fingertips touching, eyes often closed, perhaps because the questions were so familiar, perhaps for relief from all the reading matter running across his desk.

If the Soviets were to get a little more receptive to serious arms reduction talks, Weinberger thought it would be because they recognized that the U.S. had made a serious start on rebuilding its defenses and had the will to follow through. "They had considerable reason to think in 1980 they were opening a gap." The U.S. margin for error was still "extremely small." "But the Soviets must have thought all along we could inflict unacceptable damage," I ventured, "or wouldn't they have attacked us by now?" "I don't know if they believe that or not. I cannot afford to be wrong."

Weinberger back in his days as OMB Director under Nixon came

*New York: G. P. Putnam's Sons, 1982, p. 392

to be known as "Cap the Knife." As Defense Secretary he said he still liked to think of himself as a "fiscal Puritan." Lucky for the bond market he was not a fiscal spendthrift.

He thought of Reagan as "very deeply a man of peace." This President, you know, "just wishes everybody could be out at the ranch." Pedants might object that not everybody had a ranch, but it was an appealing idea.

On Leadership

The political and journalistic battlefields are strewn with the unfortunates who underestimated Ronald Reagan. When I saw him occasionally from 1968 through the 1970s, while he was governor of California, and taking two runs at the Republican presidential nomination, I thought he was a likable lightweight, probably a bit lazy, obviously a good politician but nowhere near presidential.

The first year of his Presidency powerfully impressed me, not just because my expectations had been so modest. He got a lot done. The second year was less impressive, but still nobody was reviving the old "B-movie actor" clichés.

By December 1982, writing in *Time,* I ventured that in the presidential campaign of 1984 many citizens of this populous republic would be wondering "if Reagan-Mondale, for instance, is the best we can come up with." My for-instance was a pretty safe prediction, even two years ahead of the event, and so was the reaction of a sizable part of the electorate: How did the system present us with these two people? "This is not to deny the several estimable qualities of the President," I wrote, "or the former Vice President. We could do worse; arguably we have, quite possibly we will again."

Off and on through the third and fourth years of Reagan's first term, I had speculated that there could be an element of vulnerability in the man's charm. Broadway hits do not run forever, and the hottest TV sitcoms eventually drop in the ratings. Could Ronald Reagan suddenly seem dated, even tiresome? He had enjoyed some remarkable immunities from popular indignation. This was in part because of his fabulous skill in walking away from losing situations, contriving to suggest the mess was somebody else's, in part because people (even journalists) didn't think he *really* could mean what he just said. But could there come one big gaffe or blooper or insensitivity (blacks, women) too many? If it came in foreign policy, where his minimal homework made him especially gaffe-prone, it could be especially damaging.

But the giant gaffe didn't happen, and Reagan's personal appeal—for the many susceptible to it—was in fact more compelling in 1984 than ever before. His campaign for reelection was magnificent theater: from the DMZ in Korea, to the Great Wall of China, Utah Beach in Normandy, the XXIII Olympiad (USA! USA!) in Los Angeles.* On to the balloons of Dallas, all the red-white-and-blue rallies in the strategic states, then a cocky ride through the golden Ohio countryside in Harry Truman's old whistle-stop Pullman car.† At the last minute a bold little foray into Mondale's Minnesota—about the only thing that didn't work, though poor Fritz carried his own state by only 4,000 votes out of 2 million.

"The Gipper as Sun King," Lance Morrow wrote in *Time.*‡ The King's age, far from being a weakness, seemed to have become a facet of his strength, especially and remarkably among the youngest voters. The King defers to his consort perhaps as much as Jimmy Carter did to Rosalynn, especially for judgments about people. Yet such is Reagan's whole style and bearing (physical size matters, too) that any suggestion of wimpishness would be unthinkable. Reagan had perfected the projection of presidential leadership, in four years of *being* President, and the projection is an important part of the real thing. Thus despite the many millions, perhaps a majority of adult Americans, who thought Reagan-Mondale a sorry choice, Reagan had built by Election Day an unassailable command of the political terrain of 1984. And Mondale, as Sidney Blumenthal wrote in the *New Republic,* served as the indispensable symbol of the system that Reagan always runs against, "a pole of negative energy that gives Reagan his magnetism." For 1984, Walter Mondale was "the best of all possible Mondales."¶

I voted, on November 6, 1984, not from the pocketbook nerve but

*Jimmy Carter just couldn't seem to stop being useful to Ronald Reagan. Carter's boycott of the 1980 Olympics in Moscow (to rebuke the Russians, remember, for Afghanistan) doubtless figured in the Soviet-bloc boycott of the 1984 Games, which certainly figured in the U.S. sweep of Olympic Gold. The national surge of pride in our showing in Los Angeles blended beautifully with Reagan's campaign theme music. His campaign, to be sure, had several other things going for it.

†Reagan kept invoking Truman in the Middle West, Kennedy in New England, FDR wherever convenient, Scoop Jackson on foreign policy, and even occasionally Hubert Humphrey. For some reason, he seldom mentioned Eisenhower, or even Lincoln (controversial?). Lou Cannon observes that Reagan, though he started voting Republican more than thirty years ago, "remains a cultural Democrat" (Washington *Post* Weekly, October 1, 1984).

‡November 9, 1984.
¶October 22, 1984.

from the viscera. Being almost as old as Reagan, I am entitled now and then to rise above strictly rational analysis and indulge a crotchet. In the rational mode, I think Reagan overall is a better President, or a less unsatisfactory President, than Mondale would have been. Mondale during the campaign was much more honest and sensible about the danger of the deficits (though demagogic in his solutions). On most other issues, domestic and foreign, I prefer Reagan's record and approaches to Mondale's.

So I voted for Fritz. It had been a frightful fall for Minnesota. Every weekend the Vikings and the University of Minnesota were being clobbered, and every time you picked up the paper you saw Fritz, B.A. '51, Law '56, being clobbered in some poll by 15 to 20 points. I felt it was time to show a little school spirit.

There was something more, of course. I couldn't stomach Reagan's shameless exploitation of religion and patriotism—they matter too much to be used in that way. I must confess to a special allergy to the Jerry Falwell types whom Reagan used (and is used by). My reaction perhaps traces back to my devoutly Christian (and devoutly Republican) parents, who were intellectually serious about their religion, and had small use for the backwoods, brimstone fundamentalist sects. Nor did they have much tolerance for Catholic prelates playing politics. The jollying-up between Reagan and the Bishops offended me, and I think their stand on the cruel question of abortion is finally less compassionate than that of the Supreme Court.*

I was able to keep my vote slightly open, my mind a little ajar, until the last week of October. Then Reagan went to El Hillel, a Jewish congregation on Long Island, put on a yarmulke (his advance men had given out skull caps with the presidential seal inside) and gave a completely preposterous explanation of why he sent the U.S. Marines to Beirut. They were there to help defend Israel, because he knew "the lesson of the Holocaust." In fact he had sent them there the first time to prevent the Israeli Army from destroying the PLO. When he sent them back in again it was to help (how was never clear, and the Corps paid dearly) prop up the frail Lebanese government. It was hard to know whether the Commander in Chief believed what he said at El Hillel, and hard to know whether to hope he did or didn't.

*In Roe v. Wade, 1973, the Court gave legal protection to abortions through the second trimester of pregnancy. In the light of subsequent medical findings it may be that the fetus' "right to live" should take precedence over the mother's "right of choice" sooner than the sixth month of pregnancy. But if President Reagan gets a chance to appoint two or three more justices, the Court might reverse *Roe* altogether.

On the "social issues," I thought there was a distinct aroma of hypocrisy in the Reagan positions. It is a fair inference from the Reagans' Hollywood background, the lifestyle of some of their friends and family, that the President himself is not exactly Puritanical. That is fine by me; I wished he wouldn't pretend to be somebody he isn't.

I remain respectful of Ronald Reagan's political acumen and extraordinary talent as a salesman. He is shrewd, intuitive, tough (except about firing people). It is not always clear how much he is being manipulated by senior White House staff and the major Cabinet officers, and how much he is the manipulator. There is a cold side to him. But his voice can catch and his eyes moisten, as Bob Ajemian noticed, even when he is not on camera. He is "sentimental about sentiment," Eric Sevareid once noted. After four years in the White House, Ronald Reagan was widely ignorant and not about to exert himself to learn much new. And he was unmistakably a leader. Something to think about.

PART VIII

---

*At the Mercy
of History*

21

---◆---

The Fall and Rise
of Presidential Reputations

Jimmy Carter, within twenty-four hours of his defeat by Ronald Reagan, was telling reporters he was confident "history" would rate his Presidency more highly than the election returns might momentarily suggest. It is a theme Carter has pursued with many of his visitors in Plains, and it is the implicit thesis of his memoirs.

No President defeated for reelection, so far as is known, has ever felt differently. President William Howard Taft, even before he lost in 1912, put it well: "By and by, people will see who is right and who is wrong."

Presidents who win reelection care just as deeply about their place in history. For them it is not a matter of vindication—they have no reason to question the good judgment of the electorate—but rather a reach for the ultimate goal of greatness.

There are some difficulties about a President's appeal to history. There is the unfortunate probability that he will not live long enough to hear what history has to say. But his children will, and his grandchildren, and the nation, and that is something—depending on what history finally has to say.

On the day he leaves office, a President's place in history depends heavily on some history that hasn't happened yet. In midsummer of 1981, for instance, when Reagan had just won his dazzling legislative victories on taxes and the budget, Jimmy Carter—if anybody was thinking about him at all—probably seemed an even more ineffectual President than so many voters had thought in 1980. Within a few months, however, Reagan was beginning to get mussed up on his economic program, on AWACS, on his defense proposals, and Jimmy Carter was looking a bit better. And so it would go all through Reagan's years and on into one or two of his successors' administrations. As these Presidents do well or badly with the economy, the Soviets, etc., Carter's rating will fluctuate, not all the way off the chart, but somewhere between "Unsuccessful" and "So-so but Who's Done Better Lately?"

Jimmy Carter's repute was subjected to interesting shoving and hauling in the 1984 election. To the extent that Mondale's role as VP in the previous Administration enabled Reagan to run against Carter all over again, Carter was once more repudiated. But Jimmy Carter could scarcely fail to notice that he, the outsider, odd-ball, etc., had done much better against Super Ron in 1980 than Fritz Mondale, consummate Democratic insider, experienced national politician, etc., did in 1984.*

Longer-term, Jimmy Carter's historical standing could be improved by any of the following:

• During Reagan's second term a collapse of his economic policies, leading to high inflation, another severe recession, or both. The patriot side of ex-President Carter can scarcely wish for such a national affliction, but the human side is, well, human.
• A reinvigoration of the Camp David "peace process."
• A strategic arms limitation treaty building on SALT II.
• Publication of memoirs by foreign leaders, opening of foreign archives, showing that Carter was taken more seriously as a world statesman than contemporary journalistic accounts suggested.

For outgoing Presidents an important part of the history that has yet to happen is the future intellectual climate of the country and in particular the temper of the book-writing classes. Conservatism has greater intellectual respectability today than at any time in the past half century. This is bound to affect academic appraisals of past Presidents, liberal as well as conservative.

When told that Calvin Coolidge was dead, Dorothy Parker said, "How do they know?" Now the historian Thomas Silver (writing in the Phi Beta Kappa quarterly *The American Scholar*†) can praise Coolidge as "a statesman" who presided over a time of "peace, national calm, unprecedented inflation-free prosperity and rigid executive integrity."

---

*Carter carried six states and the D.C. in 1980, Mondale one state and D.C. in 1984. Without the John Anderson Independent candidacy in 1980, mainly draining votes from the Democrats, Carter might have carried as many as sixteen states.
†Autumn, 1981.

I became something of a Coolidge revisionist myself on a visit to his birthplace at Plymouth, Vermont, a very moving place. The displays include many reminders of how well the man wrote, better than any President since. I told the Time Inc. managing editors this austere Yankee shrine was worth a slight detour from Route 100. I believe they were shocked.

History struck an extraordinary long-range blow at Andrew Jackson, President from 1829 to 1837, when in 1975 a Berkeley political scientist named Michael Rogin published a book *Fathers and Children: Andrew Jackson and the Subjugation of the American Indian.* * Rogin said that he was writing under "the sway of the Viet Nam War." He saw Jackson as little more than a vicious Indian hater, "presiding over American expansion and Indian destruction," presaging general American attitudes toward "native peoples" everywhere. Andy Jackson in fact was quite an Indian fighter, but long before Professor Rogin, Jackson was already one of the most volatile of Presidents in his historical repute. The dominant historians of the nineteenth century, mainly proper New Englanders and other eastern gentry, sniffed at Jackson as an uncouth frontiersman, author of the spoils system, and a dangerous demagogue about money and banking. Then the "progressive" historians of the early twentieth century, led by Frederick Jackson Turner, Charles Beard, and Vernon Parrington, began to celebrate him as a democratic hero, come out of the West to fight the moneyed eastern interests. Arthur Schlesinger, Jr., carried the celebration a large step further in his classic, *The Age of Jackson,* dewesternizing the man and nationalizing him, finding under his leadership an almost New Deal–like coalescence of West and South and eastern workingman.†

Jefferson has undergone even wider swings in the historical standings, perhaps the greatest for any President. He is one of several Presidents (Madison, Grant, some would say Eisenhower) whose previous accomplishments were greater than anything he did as President. He had savage critics while he was in office; "mad Tom" was one of their epithets for him. (Washington was called "a tyrant" and Lincoln "a baboon." Lyndon Johnson, touchingly, took comfort in those contemporary misjudgments.) The conservative northeast historians of the nineteenth century held essentially to the Hamiltonian belief in a strong central government and saw Jefferson as the exponent of weak government and of an excessive trust in the people. Jefferson did not fare much

*New York: Alfred A. Knopf, 1975.
†Boston: Little Brown, 1945.

better with progressives, who loved the people all right, but thought a powerful government, wrested away from the interests, was the only sure protector of the people. (Teddy Roosevelt a hundred years later was still angry about Jefferson's foreign policy: "a discredit to my country.") Woodrow Wilson made some scholarly attempts to rescue Jefferson from the presidential scrap heap. President Warren Harding struck back in 1923 by dedicating a statue to Hamilton in front of the Treasury. It was left to Franklin Roosevelt, no scholar but a superb manager of political stage effects, to elevate Jefferson to the presidential pantheon. Pantheon quite literally, for that Roman dome was the architectural inspiration for Jefferson's Monticello and for the great marble memorial on Washington's Tidal Basin that Roosevelt dedicated to Jefferson in 1943. The intellectual sleight-of-hand was simple enough: the New Deal was the modern embodiment of the Jeffersonian "spirit," in which government, depending on its purposes, was either "a threat and a danger" or "a refuge and help" to the people. And to this day the Democrats hold Jefferson-Jackson day dinners.

Franklin Roosevelt himself, for such a large and bold figure, has held remarkably consistent ratings among the scholars, though in popular memory he diminishes some as he recedes. When he died in 1945, many Americans felt orphaned: What will become of us now? Harry Truman's original surge of popularity came from the delighted discovery, by many of the same stricken Americans: By God, this little guy can do it. Most of the original Roosevelt "haters" have now died off, though some younger people have taken up the work. There are still fatuous idolators, original and second generation. In between, there is a broad scholarly consensus that here was an extraordinary political leader, not matched since. Ronald Reagan, in at least some aspects of leadership, comes close, and his record in his second term may indeed come to have some bearing on Roosevelt's place in history.

Meanwhile, in giving FDR his steady ranking just behind Lincoln and Washington, the scholars are placing a heavy load on him. Washington and Lincoln, after all, are prime form-giver of the Republic and savior of the Union. Roosevelt's greatest achievements, though more diverse, were not quite of that order, and some of them, for the general public, have come to suffer a declining relevance. His social and economic reforms are easily taken for granted by the vast majority of citizens who never knew the previous America. This must explain in part the startling survey results of 1983 (already cited, in chapter 7), in which Jack Kennedy so far outdistanced FDR in popular esteem.

Among our postwar Presidents, both Harry Truman and Dwight Eisenhower stand significantly higher today than when they left the White House. Eisenhower probably could have been elected on any platform he chose in 1952, but he and his Republican handlers relished running against the Truman "mess in Washington"—and poor Adlai Stevenson, from Springfield, Illinois, was not allowed to change the subject. Today that mess ("Communism, Corruption, Korea") is largely forgotten; we have seen worse. And Harry Truman is now a kind of Democratic legend. He is seen as a statesman, one of the founders of the international order (approximate) built after World War II. Most scholars (the left excepted) now rate him a strong and generally successful President. In the popular memory, the "yellow dog" Democrat has been transfigured. Truman is the endearingly plain-spoken and gutsy common man undaunted by awesome responsibility he never sought.

History has its various authors, custodians, and constituencies. Sometimes the broadest constituency of all, "the people," is more perceptive than the professional historians. Thus Eisenhower retained an immense national popularity throughout an Administration that the academy (largely Democratic) disdained, and that some thoughtful Republicans found disappointingly passive. The caricature was the amiable old fellow out on the golf course. (Except for Gerald Ford, no incumbent President has dared play much golf since.) Ike could doubtless have been reelected to a third term in 1960 if the Twenty-second Amendment had not prohibited it. John Kennedy was among those who thought Ike's personal political strength would have been unassailable. But Kennedy defeated Ike's Vice-President (just barely) by running against Nixon the man and against the "passive" record of the Eisenhower Administration. "Let's get America moving again," said Kennedy. So Eisenhower left office to mixed notices. The same electorate that liked the man enough to elect him forever didn't think all that well of his Presidency.

The fact that Eisenhower's Presidency is so much more highly regarded today is mainly because of the intervening history. Ike himself was well aware of the ways a leader's reputation is hostage to the future. Showing visitors around Gettysburg, he would ask not the obvious question about Lincoln's reputation, but a much more subtle question: What would be the historical standing of *George Washington* if the South had won that battle?

Liberals who once would have ridiculed Ike for lethargy now see considerable virtue in an eight-year Presidency in which nothing really bad took place. The two most important things that didn't happen during Eisenhower's years in the White House were that the U. S. didn't get into any war, anywhere, and that inflation was barely a topic of conversation. It has taken six more administrations, Kennedy through Reagan, for these blessings to be sufficiently appreciated.

The liberal *New York Review of Books* in 1981 discussed half a dozen new Eisenhower books under the headline "Two Cheers for Ike."* Some of the new Eisenhower literature goes much beyond a claim that he did nothing harmful. In his fascinating study *Eisenhower the President,* William Ewald, Jr., one of his speech writers, contends that Ike was an astute administrator and a subtle protector of presidential authority and options, with a sure instinct for when finally to commit. He also argues that the legislative record of the Eisenhower years was at least as constructive as that of various "activist" administrations of the recent past. All in all, says Ewald, "eight good years—I believe the best in modern memory" (p. 324).

A veritable festival of Eisenhower revisionism was mounted at Hofstra College, Long Island, in March 1984. More than sixty historians, political scientists, journalists, and Eisenhower Administration alumni assembled to celebrate his Presidency, though at least a few of the scholars still had their reservations.

John Kennedy is going to be a puzzling President for the historians. His foreign policy record is so mixed, his domestic policy record so scanty, that appraisals of his Presidency become in good part speculation on what he would have done had he lived. If Eisenhower's historical standing has benefited from events in subsequent administrations, Kennedy's has suffered. Viet Nam is a heavy burden on the Kennedy record because of the tragedy it became under Johnson and Nixon. Yet if the U. S. had somehow "won" in Viet Nam, Kennedy would get credit for farsightedness in putting all those advisers out there.

"Camelot" may seem a somewhat embarrassing metaphor today (Sam Giancanna doesn't play too well as a Knight of the Round Table). But the Kennedy legend still has great vitality, as shown in the polls cited earlier and as we saw in November 1983 in the outpouring of affectionate reminiscence, in print and on TV, on the twentieth anniversary of his death. The legend is powerful enough to have sustained Ted Kennedy for years as a major political figure, despite rather modest abilities and some difficult personal baggage. It has sustained Jacqueline Kennedy Onassis, despite the unromantic second marriage, as interna-

*September 24, 1981.

tional Goddess of Celebrity. In the 1984 Democratic primaries, Senator Gary Hart was accused by his rivals of an unfair campaign tactic—speaking with his left hand in his jacket pocket, while chopping the air with his right. He denied that he was consciously imitating John Kennedy.

Lyndon Johnson is not looking any healthier in history than he was in the public opinion polls of 1967–68. There are stirrings in the country of a revisionist attitude toward the war in Viet Nam—President Reagan is willing to say out loud that we should not be ashamed of having fought there—but the corollary of that view, for Reagan and others, is that we should have gone all out to win. LBJ loses both ways, with the hardliners for the defeat, with everybody else for getting into Viet Nam in such a big way.

The other landmark of the LBJ Administration was his Great Society legislation. These programs were slowed down by the Reagan Administration, amidst a congressional and popular consensus that they had gone out of control. Most of them will continue to get substantial funding, but they are no longer invested with the hope and idealism of the 1960s.

Finally, LBJ has his personal vulnerabilities, and the biographers and memoirists are not likely to ignore them. In his study of Johnson's "Path to Power," Robert Caro pictures a wheeler-dealer with a mania for secrecy and duplicity. His 882-page work takes LBJ only to his late thirties—over the next few years, two more Caro volumes will be detonating.

Richard Nixon, having left the Presidency in disgrace, can't very well fall any lower in history's regard. Diligent journalists and archivists will doubtless keep mining the transcripts of the famous tapes. (Four thousand hours' worth have not yet been published; only twelve hours and thirty minutes were released by the Watergate special prosecutor's office in 1974.) For unreconstructed Nixon haters it must have seemed like old times when the *New York Times*—seven years after he resigned—ran a front-page story quoting Nixon and H. R. Haldeman as planning to use thugs from the Teamsters Union to beat up on student antiwar demonstrators.* There was the further bonus in the article of a flagrantly anti-Semitic innuendo from Nixon.

It is doubtful that historians will ever take a more tolerant view of Watergate than Congress and the public did in 1974. But the sheer passage of time is helping Nixon change the subject, from Watergate to

*September 24, 1981.

foreign policy. The *Times* invites Nixon these days to appear on its Op-Ed page. A brief volume he brought out in 1983, *A Strategy for Real Peace,** was widely and quite respectfully reviewed. He urged "hard-headed détente." In the spring of 1984 he was paid $500,000 by CBS, once his least favorite network, for 90 minutes of prime-time interviews. He said Watergate was "a very, very stupid thing to do." But in his writing and interviews, he generally keeps the focus on the strongest aspect of his Presidency. He does not deliver lectures on Ethics in Government.†

Aging was wonderful medicine for one President who left office widely despised: Herbert Hoover. He was fifty-nine in 1933; the Depression shantytowns all over America were called "Hoovervilles." By the time he died at ninety he was a Grand Old Man, the oldest ex-President since John Adams. Harry Truman, for all his fierce partisanship, had done much to rehabilitate Hoover, by appointing him chairman of a well-publicized commission on reorganization of the Executive Branch. Historians would never come to credit Hoover with effective measures against the Depression, but people had long since stopped thinking he caused it. On into his eighties, pink-cheeked and bright-eyed, he gave stout Republican speeches at Republican conventions, puffed on his pipe, and wrote some rather mellow reminiscences, including a volume on trout fishing.

Professor Henry Graff of Columbia points out that in the nineteenth century most Americans didn't even know what their President looked like. Today everyone can "see" the President, practically every day. We now know so much about the man while he is in office, and about his career before he got there, that it might seem there was nothing left for history to say.

But the sheer volume of fact and opinion about a sitting President opens up whole realms for later discovery of further fact, and later revision of once dominant opinion. The impact and immediacy of electronic communication inject another uncertainty. Can a newly enfranchised eighteen-year-old or even a fifty-year-old political scientist

*Boston: Little Brown.
†I don't agree with the proposal that the country should make use of the ex-Presidents in some systematic institutional way. We are blessed with three at the moment, and their views are readily available to us. They are all sought after for books, articles, interviews, speeches. Ford and Carter have arrived at a pleasant rapport, coauthoring some articles and exchanging guest appearances at each other's "Center," Carter to Ann Arbor, Michigan, Ford to Emory University in Atlanta. The ex-Presidents are handsomely supported by the taxpayers, as they should be, while they work on their "place in history." The one who seems least concerned with that, and seems also to be having the most fun, is Ford.

watch an old newsreel clip of FDR and fully understand the force in that voice and presence at that time? Will a film segment of John Kennedy, or even the master communicator Ronald Reagan, some day leave people marveling, as though watching a snatch of some ancient TV hit: What was *that* all about?

So history has its work cut out for it. And in this age of paper, government and its officials are generating documentation at a prodigious and accelerating rate. The Franklin Roosevelt Library in Hyde Park holds 10 million pages on a twelve-year Presidency. In the Gerald Ford Library in Ann Arbor, dedicated in 1981, there are 12 million pages dealing with a thirty-month Presidency. As historians and biographers mine all this material (some of it under security restrictions for twenty years or more), as reminiscences of presidential intimates become available, as diaries and letters come to light, presidential ratings will continue to fluctuate.

Above all, new events, new conditions, will impose new judgments. Professor Donald McCoy, of the University of Kansas, says that Presidents who do well handling small crises that could have turned into large ones "will get the ho-hum from historians." But perhaps the public, even including historians, is developing greater awareness of the stubbornness of some of the national problems, of the tendency of so many solutions to breed new problems. This can lead to a kindly view of those Presidents who, all in all, leave things slightly better or at least no worse than they found them. But it takes a decade or two before it can be certified this was indeed the effect of somebody's Presidency.

An increasingly informed and sophisticated country may be less ready to grant greatness than it once was. This throws a certain light on present Presidents, but could also beam back. What would we have thought of Lincoln during his Presidency? Could the Civil War have survived the 7:00 P.M. news? (Could Valley Forge?) What would the *New York Times* and the Washington *Post* have said about Lincoln's suspension of habeas corpus? (Maybe nothing; they didn't object when FDR forcibly relocated the Japanese-Americans in World War II.) Presidents present and past may come to seem more like the rest of us, though their ability to get nominated and elected will always, to say the least, set them somewhat apart. Though war and crisis have been the traditional backdrops for greatness in the White House, we seem to live now, if not in permanent crisis, at least permanently on the edge. The late-twentieth-century Presidents are adequately challenged.

PART IX

---

*Can We
Do Better?*

22

———◆———

Job Specs for the Oval Office

In 1984—as in 1976 and 1980—a good many Americans thought neither Presidential candidate was really equipped for the job. Few of the 37 million people who voted for Walter Mondale, outside of his immediate family, did so with deep enthusiasm.* His votes came from the hardest of hard-core Democrats and/or people offended or frightened by Reagan. Among Reagan's 53 million voters, there were plenty of fervent admirers, but also critics who thought he was merely the lesser evil. And among the other 83 million voting-age Americans who didn't bother with the election, it must be assumed that a fair number didn't think either candidate was worth the trouble.

How did the machinery for identifying potential Presidents, nominating candidates and choosing winners come to be so seriously out of sync with what the electorate itself sees as the modern requirements of the office? From this literate democratic society of some 236 million people, compare the political leadership we are now producing with the leadership of the thirteen colonies in the late eighteenth century. For all its familiarity, the point is still a painful one. From 3 million people living on the edge of a wilderness: Washington, Jefferson, Hamilton, Madison, Franklin, the Adamses. But perhaps, out of all the mysterious historical chemistries that can produce a Golden Age—the Athens of Pericles, Renaissance Florence, Elizabethan England—the America of two centuries ago was a Golden Age for political thought and political leadership. Perhaps we should simply be grateful for the Founders, not haunted by them.

*His gallant quip on leaving the polling place with his wife and three children: "I think maybe I got three out of five [Mondales]." The *New York Times,* November 7, 1984.

If so, we could better be bothered by a comparison from our own time. The modern Presidency begins with Franklin Roosevelt, and nine men (as of December 1984) have held the job. In the twenty-eight years from 1933 to 1961, we had one great President, FDR, one very good President, Dwight Eisenhower, and by my ranking, one good-to-very-good President, Harry Truman. None of the next four Presidents could be put in any of those categories. The short Presidencies of John Kennedy and Gerald Ford, for all the differences of philosophy and style, were the best, or perhaps the least unsuccessful, of the 1960s and 1970s. Lyndon Johnson's Great Society legislation was a noble achievement but his Presidency is forever blighted by the tragic failure in Viet Nam. Richard Nixon was our best President of foreign policy since Eisenhower, not just because he had the wit to employ Dr. Kissinger. And he presided over Watergate. The full returns are not yet in on Jimmy Carter, nor, of course, on Ronald Reagan.

It is not an inspiring roll call. William Leuchtenberg of the University of North Carolina, author of a number of notable studies of FDR and the New Deal, suggested in 1983 that the country might simply be in a fallow period in political thought. "We cannot expect our Presidents to rise very far above the level of thought in the political culture." Leuchtenburg is so fervent a Roosevelt admirer that it may have come hard to him to recognize that Reagan's ideas, like them or not, are indeed ideas.

Yet the gap between electability and the capacity to govern is indisputably growing. No American under forty has adult experience of a broadly successful Presidency. The considerable achievements of Reagan's first term were contingent achievements; his first term is now hostage to his second. A more cautious seventy-three-year-old might have decided to go back to the ranch, and let his successor dodge some of the land-mines waiting out there in 1985–88. But if Reagan can now tame the deficits (without bringing on a major recession), improve our tax system, and achieve something worthwhile in foreign policy, his Administration would be the most successful since Eisenhower's, though his management methods might defy emulation by future Presidents.

Meanwhile we have no up-to-date working standard to measure presidential candidates against. The country and the world have changed profoundly since the successful Presidencies of the 1940s and 1950s. The job has surely grown more difficult and more important, even as the quality of the incumbents has fallen off. Since the mid-1960s, as the U. S. has declined in relative military power, we have also declined in political and economic muscle vis-à-vis our allies. We have lost something in cohesiveness and social discipline within the U.S. The economy can no longer generate steadily higher after-taxes living standards for the private sector and steadily growing tax-funded entitlements. The choices in tax and budget policies grow harsher. We are still, all in all, the strongest nation and society, but it is a tough time to be President.

Those Beautiful Watchworks

There are thoughtful students of government who believe the job —as presently constituted, in the country we have become—is almost hopeless. They think our problem is less the inherent quality of the recent Presidents than the state and structure of our governmental system and the whole temper of our society.

The central structural question is whether those beautiful checks and balances, beloved of political scientists no less than patriotic orators, have become a formula for paralysis. Or more exactly, whether the system devised in Philadelphia in 1787, after all that has happened over two centuries, including the decline in the last generation of political parties and party discipline, both among the electorate and in Congress, makes it too hard for the President, any President, to lead. Nobody is proposing to pack up the whole Philadelphia contraption and put it in a museum of eighteenth-century watchworks. But several searching studies of possible changes are being undertaken, inspired in part by the approach of the bicentennial of the Constitution in 1987.

Alexander Heard, political scientist and Chancellor Emeritus of Vanderbilt University, believes we must ask whether the nation in some respects has simply become ungovernable. Heard is conducting a study (on a $1-million grant from the Sloan Foundation) of the presidential selection process. He has two dozen scholars at work and hopes to bring in his report by 1985 or 1986, on the eve of the bicentennial. The report will examine the specifics and mechanics of picking Presidents, and also seek to place the process "in the larger contemporary universe of American political arrangements," including the interplay with foreign policy.

In a *Foreign Affairs* article (Fall 1980), Jimmy Carter's counsel

Lloyd Cutler advocated "a set of modest changes that would make our structure work somewhat more in the manner of a parliamentary system, with somewhat less separation between the executive and the legislature than now exists." (Cutler experienced the White House–Congress deadlock at its worst in 1979–80 but scrupulously insisted his views were "formed in large part" before he went to work for Carter.) Cutler has suggested that Presidents might be permitted (or required) to fill up to half the Cabinet posts with sitting members of Congress. Cutler and Douglas Dillon, Under Secretary of State under Eisenhower and Secretary of the Treasury under Kennedy, are cochairmen of the Committee on the Constitutional System, which intends to offer some structural recommendations by 1987. They will consider, among many ideas, the proposal of former Representative Jonathan Bingham of New York that members of the House should serve for four years and run as part of a ticket with the presidential and vice-presidential candidates of their party.

Also inspired by the bicentennial, the American Political Science Association and the American Historical Association are undertaking a joint constitutional review, to be completed by 1987. And the Committee for a Single Six-Year Presidential Term is pressing that familiar proposal, which indeed was seriously considered at Philadelphia in 1787. (Backers include Ike's brother Milton, Cyrus Vance, former Attorney General Griffin Bell, former Treasury Secretary William Simon.) I am skeptical about the single six-year term; six years is too long for a poor President, as Harry Truman argued, and not long enough for a good one. James MacGregor Burns, Williams College political scientist and Democratic activist, argues passionately against the single term: "For hundreds of years men and women have fought for the sacred right to *fire* as well as to hire their leaders . . . To be governed by an endless, uninterrupted series of lame-duck Presidents—is this the culmination of the democratic dream in America?"*

In his forceful book *None of the Above,* Robert Shogan, a Washington correspondent for the Los Angeles *Times,* argues that our political system has produced "a substantial enlargement of presidential responsibility, both explicit and implied . . . without a corresponding increase in presidential power". We must "shift the burden of national leadership from the personality of the president to the collective authority of the executive and the legislature, bound together by clear policy goals and

The Power to Lead (New York: Simon and Schuster, 1984), pp. 12–13.

a vigorous majority party". The subtitle of Shogan's book is *Why Presidents Fail—And What Can Be Done About It.* *

Along with all the other checks and balances, the Constitution permits itself to be amended but doesn't particularly encourage the process. Since the ten Amendments composing the Bill of Rights were adopted in 1791, the Constitution has been amended just sixteen times in 194 years. Ten of these sixteen Amendments affected the Presidency —who can vote, how long a President may serve, disability, and succession. None touched the distribution of power between President and Congress.

It will be extremely difficult to arrive at more effective Presidencies via constitutional reform. It may be a little less difficult, by no means easy, to get better people into the running for President. Our democracy cannot allow the failed Presidencies of the 1960s and 1970s and the bristling difficulties of the 1980s to foster a defeatist view that the job has become impossible. If we can arrive at a better understanding of what the job requires today—and what it doesn't—we may arrive at ways of finding better candidates. If structural reforms can also help highly qualified Presidents operate up to their full potential, so much the better.

Lion or Prisoner?

The abiding paradox of the U. S. Presidency is that it is the most powerful political office in the world—hedged about by a mighty host of contending powers: Not just Congress, but the bureaucracy, the press, business, the courts, lobbies, the great American electorate itself, and then all the other countries on earth, at last count 167.

Through several decades of scholarship, students of the modern Presidency have tended to stress either the powers of the office or its limitations. The living, changing amalgam of authority and constraints is perhaps too subtle to capture in any theoretical model. Bryce Harlow, a wise counselor to all the recent Republican Presidents, saw the powers of the office as so great, even in the hands of the prudent Ike, as to leave him in "almost fearful awe." Among academics, Clinton Rossiter of Cornell took an equally sweeping view of the power, but rejoiced in it with a romantic fervor. He saw the President as "the American people's one authentic trumpet." Also: "A kind of magnificent lion who

*New York: New American Library, 1982, pp. 13, 24.

can roam widely and do great deeds so long as he does not try to break loose from his broad reservation."*

The heroic view of the Presidency is powerfully fortified by modern U. S. journalism, with its insatiable demand for personalities, action, and movement, and its swift and versatile technology. TV, in particular, gives new dimensions and intensities of exposure which are a priceless opportunity—and ever present danger—to a President. The heroic view of the Presidency of course includes the possibility of failure on a grand scale.

Richard Neustadt of Harvard, in his classic *Presidential Power*, stressed the limitations: all the constitutional authority conferred upon the President amounted to less than his opportunity "to persuade." But of course the power to persuade derives in large part from who the President is, under the Constitution, and what the office has become over two centuries. Neustadt was writing toward the end of the Eisenhower Presidency, which he did not admire. He later came to see more power in the Presidency, for good (he worked for JFK) or evil (the latter-day LBJ, Nixon).

The most concise presidential summary of the "limited" view came from Harry Truman, a strong President who didn't always get his way. He said: "The principal power that the President has is to bring people in and try to persuade them to do what they ought to do without persuasion." But Truman frequently did get his way, particularly in foreign policy, where his powers ran well beyond "bringing people in" for persuasion.

Lyndon Johnson, when the self-pity was running strong, could say, "Power? The only power I've got is nuclear—and I can't use that."† This was silly, and Johnson's record didn't suggest he believed it.

Rossiter was closer to the truth, but the danger in the heroic view of the Presidency is that it can lead to vastly inflated public expectations. Two generations of historians and their readers were prepared to be disappointed with anything less than a Roosevelt, Franklin or Theodore. In *The Age of Roosevelt*, Arthur Schlesinger, Jr., saw FDR in an exalted light,‡ and he later found enough activist electricity around JFK to want to work for him. It was only during the Nixon Administration

*The American Presidency, (New York: Harcourt Brace and World, 1960), pp, 23, 68.

†Hugh Sidey, A Very Personal Presidency (New York: Atheneum, 1968), p. 260.

‡Boston: Houghton Mifflin, 1957.

that Schlesinger began to worry about the excesses of an "Imperial Presidency." James S. Young, of the University of Virginia, argues that there must be a "retrenching" of presidential power "in order to save the presidency for the things that only it can do." The President himself can and should restrain public expectations of his office, "regaining the ability, within the presidency at least, to distinguish between true and pseudo-crises, real alarms and false ones, threats to the Republic and mere problems for the Administration."* Bruce Miroff, of the State University of New York, thinks the President occupies far too much of "the public space," especially on TV.† The irreverent Senator Eugene McCarthy used to promise that if elected he would turn the White House and its eighteen-acre grounds into a public park and museum and do the President's irreducible business from an ordinary government office. In the spirit of a smaller Presidency, McCarthy and Professors Young and Miroff might have relished a comment in the White House the morning after a bad Carter primary in 1980: "I understand," confided one of the young Georgians, "that the Leader of the Free World took quite a chewing-out from his wife last night."

Even without war or depression the times are sufficiently difficult to test Presidents as severely as ever in our history. To be a good President in the 1980s may be as hard, maybe harder, than to be a great President in the days of Antietam or Pearl Harbor.

Ideally:

So what are we looking for? An appealing formulation has been offered by Mrs. Debbie Wernersbach, a school administrator in Milltown, New Jersey: The honesty of Abraham Lincoln, the intelligence of Henry Kissinger, and the soothing TV personality of Marcus Welby/- Robert Young.‡ John Rhodes, the former Arizona congressman who knew several Presidents very well, names a few of the obvious desiderata, and then offers an epigram: "The President should like his fellow man—and he should have read Machiavelli."

In a President we are looking always for enough of a good quality, but not too much. In almost every presidential virtue, a little too much becomes a defect, even a danger. The President must be "a good politi-

*The *New York Times,* December 7, 1978.
†*Rethinking the Presidency,* ed. Thomas Cronin (Boston: Little Brown, 1982) pp. 218–232.
‡The *New York Times,* October 9, 1983.

cian" but not "too political." The President should be decent but not
"too nice." Etc. To start at the easy end of the checklist—

The Body. We prefer our Presidents to look like the President: FDR
did (supremely so), also Ike, JFK, Reagan. Other recent incumbents,
through no fault of their own, didn't. Carter's sweaters didn't cast a
presidential aura (nor did his insistence on Jimmy as the official name).

A President needs tremendous stamina and resilience, although
George Reedy (the LBJ press secretary) has noted that "no President
ever died of overwork."* The 25-primary, 26-caucus campaign, whatever else may be said of it, is a rigorous physical exam. We at least know
that anybody who can get nominated and elected is in good shape.

How old should the President be? Thirty-five is old enough, the
Constitution says, and when JFK was running at forty-four, he liked to
point out that the average age of the members of the Constitutional
Convention was forty-three. Today, with people staying alive and vigorous much longer, the optimum experience/energy mix might come in
the mid-fifties to early sixties. As we saw in 1980, however, a sixty-nine-
year-old could whip a fifty-six-year-old, and in 1984 the same senior
citizen, now seventy-three, whipped still another fifty-six-year-old. (I
found Reagan's election and reelection reassuring in at least one respect; other things being anywhere near equal, I prefer the President
to be older than I am. This gets increasingly difficult to arrange.)

The President ought to be an athlete (Ford, JFK, Ike), or at least an
outdoorsman (Reagan), not just because it appeals to voters but because
it helps make a rounded man, capable of relaxing. FDR, almost never
photographed in his wheelchair, was often photographed at sea, on the
bridge of a warship, at the helm of a sailboat; he did love blue water.
As did Kennedy. Carter was good at softball (as President he was entitled to pitch), fair at tennis, very serious about running. After the frightful front-page photo of his buckling in a mini-marathon, he shifted some
of his competitive urges to the science of trout fishing. LBJ poured all
his volcanic energies into politics; his was the youngest natural death (at
sixty-four)—of any postwar President. Nixon is an essentially sedentary
man. Truman's sports were walking, poker, and bourbon.

Character and Temperament. The presidential bedrock must be
integrity, perceived and real. "Integrity," says Bryce Harlow, "is numbers One through Ten." There is an unavoidable tension between this
necessity and the political necessities of maneuver, indirection, and the

The Twilight of the Presidency (Cleveland, Ohio: New American Library, 1970).

calculated ambiguity. Of the three masterful political operators among the modern Presidents, FDR was frequently dancing along the ethical borderline, LBJ was often well across it, and Ronald Reagan projects a genial astonishment that anyone could think he could be anywhere near any such line.

Presidents need "drive but not drivenness," as Richard Neustadt puts it. LBJ, Nixon, and Carter were all driven. Jack Valenti credited his boss LBJ with "extra glands" (and Jack also slept better, he said, knowing Johnson was President). When Walter Mondale dropped out of the running for the 1976 nomination, he confessed to a lack of "fire in the belly"; in 1984 he told voters the requisite flames were there. The President needs perseverance, and personal ambition within healthy limits. Henry Graff of Columbia notes that we like a presidential candidate to look "called," but it's hard for him to create this effect while selling himself on TV. A fashionable cynicism is that anybody so ambitious that he would put up with what it takes to get nominated and elected is morally disqualified for the Presidency. Actually, what seems such an "ordeal" to the lay observers of a campaign—the crazy hours, bad food, overscheduling of flights and speeches, intrusiveness of the press, endless handshaking and backslapping—is not all that distasteful, and even has its excitements, for the professional politician.

A President should look fair and be fair, be magnanimous, willing to give trust, compassionate. No very high marks for any recent President. Roosevelt relished his enemies excessively, and taunted and incited them: "I welcome their hatred." Reagan gives the impression of insensitivity to the poor. More liberal politicians—LBJ and Carter come to mind—can be highly compassionate about "the people" and for some reason insensitive to individuals.

The President needs presence, dignity, a certain touch of distance and even mystery; he is also expected to be "human." FDR and Ike set a high standard, as does Reagan. The aloofness of a de Gaulle would not sit well here.

He needs courage, physical (just to go outdoors) and moral. He must be tough, even ruthless, but not find sick enjoyment in ruthlessness. He needs the nerve to fire people—and the discrimination to know who should be fired. All the recent Presidents have been weak in this department, Reagan pitifully so, though he did finally accept Al Haig's third or fourth resignation, to Haig's surprise. The mild-mannered Jimmy Carter dropped five Cabinet members in his clumsy purge of 1979, though earlier he had stuck by OMB Director Bert Lance much longer than he should have. Some of the presidential tenderness is a misplaced loyalty to old friends, some is a stubborn defense of the President's original judgment of an individual, some is simply a shrinking from the unpleasant.

The President needs a deep self-confidence—stopping short of a grandiose sense of destiny. FDR and Ike both had it in full measure—a bit over-full in Roosevelt's case. Reagan has it and so, though he didn't project it, did Carter. Truman grew it, JFK and Ford were doing so. Neither LBJ nor Nixon ever quite overcame his own doubts that he belonged in the White House.

The President must be steady and stable, housing his exceptional combination of gifts within a personality approximately "normal." Among the modern Presidents the most nearly normal personalities are probably Truman, Ike, Ford, Reagan. It may be significant that Ford and Truman had not aspired to the Presidency, and Ike began to think of it only in his late fifties when he had already won world fame in a job about as big as President. Reagan had had two satisfying careers in the public eye, as actor and after-dinner free-enterprise speaker, before turning to politics.

The President should be "from" somewhere: Hyde Park, Independence, the Pedernales. The place can be less literal, almost metaphor, if it seems descriptive of the man: a sailboat off Cape Cod, the Plain at West Point. Nixon did not convey rootedness.

Brains. Justice Holmes called Franklin Roosevelt "a second-class intellect but a first-class temperament." The President needs superior intelligence (at least a B from Holmes), but needn't be brilliant, deep, or blindingly original. He needs common sense—Ike and Truman had more of it than the great FDR. It would be good if he found relief from all the official paper in reading a book now and then. He needn't be an intellectual, and we haven't been threatened with one any time lately. He needs to be able to communicate with the intellectuals, however; he needs to hear their ideas, and they can confer a kind of legitimacy on an administration, much as "business" or "Wall Street" did in a distant era. JFK was the most fluent of the modern Presidents at this dialogue. A controversial nomination for second-best: Ronald Reagan, not in all-round rapport with the whole intellectual world, of course, but for his serious use of the ideas of conservative and neoconservative academics and writers.

The President needs the ability to reduce complex issues to the essentials, to guide his own decision making and his appeals for public

support. He must be a wise simplifier. Reagan is rightly criticized when
he oversimplifies, which is often, but some of his simplifying is just right,
not unlike good teaching or preaching, not unlike FDR.

In abstract intelligence it could be that LBJ, Nixon, and Carter
would rate highest among the modern Presidents. All suffered from
some lack of judgment and proportion, which doesn't show up in IQ
tests.

A President needs a sense of history, including a feel for the situations where history doesn't apply. Jimmy Carter, despite his speed-
reading studiousness and remarkable memory, was, as I have noted,
strangely deficient here. Reagan seems relatively innocent in the field.
Truman and JFK were well steeped in history. From a sense of history
(preferably not just American) flows an informed patriotism, a feel for
the powers of an office unique in the world, the restraints upon it, and
the tempo of a presidential term, including the special opportunities of
the first twelve to eighteen months and the special learning-curve problems of these same months.

This might seem elementary, but a President must understand our
history well enough to understand the Congress, or at least not misun-
derstand it. Those 535 men and women up there on the Hill are a
co-equal branch of government. It is not necessary to love them, or
their 300-odd committees and subcommittees. The President must understand the situations in which the members of Congress want the
President in effect to legislate, reserving to themselves the veto power.
He should be gratified, and only slightly suspicious, when some of his
appointees make their own independent alliances on the Hill.

A President must offer the country vision, and he must animate his
administration with purposes larger than the enjoyment of office. A
visible zest for the job is perfectly legal, even desirable. But the love of
the job can contribute to a certain blurring of the national interest and
the personal interest. FDR was doubtless genuinely convinced in 1940
that it was for the good of the nation and the world that he should be
the first three-term President. It would be refreshing sometime—but
not auspicious—to hear a politician admit he wanted to be President
because it's the top job in his line of work. This was essentially the
motivation of JFK, Nixon, and Carter, though of course they did not say
so out loud. Once in office, being men of ability and goodwill, they
began to develop their public agendas. To be reelected, to be known
as a good or even great President, is still for such men a test of competitive prowess, but these personal motivations are now thoroughly min-

gled with public purposes. It still remains a handicap to begin a first term without a coherent political philosophy and an idealistic urge to put it to work. A successful President needs a secure relationship in his own head and heart with some settled convictions and purposes. Thus Nixon, in a touching passage of a memo written nine years after he had to resign: "A President cannot be a great leader unless he is motivated by a great idea. He must want the Presidency not to be somebody but to do something." Reagan and LBJ, whatever their shortcomings, must be credited with a vision of using the Presidency for the country.

The President's political philosophy needs to be earned, hammered out in some detail, tested intellectually and in experience. It is good for the stability of the country that the American center—which is essentially where we want our Presidents to be—is so spacious. But there are drawbacks in this vast and vague consensus; presidential candidates and even Presidents can evade the hard work of thinking out policy specifics and confronting the harsh choice between two good things.

As to the roots of a President's philosophy—a religious affiliation is of course necessary for a major-party candidate, but is religious conviction necessary for a President? Certified historians and political scientists shy away from such an embarrassing "value judgment." But the voters know they wouldn't want a non-believer President, and their instinct is correct. Somewhere, however, there is a line between belief and the politicizing of belief, which I believe we saw crossed, by Ronald Reagan, in 1984. It has been settled that a Roman Catholic may be President. The droll Bob Strauss likes to ask whether the country is grown-up enough for "a Texas Jew."

The President must be a communicator. Reagan of course is the best since FDR. Indeed, in 1981, when he had Congress eating out of his hand, it seemed as though mastery of TV and one-on-one charm had become the very key to the Presidency. As his first term unfolded, events and realities suggested some limits on what a President can accomplish by communicating. His second term, won so spectacularly, will tell us more. TV is still a major resource for a President—at least as important in governing as in getting elected. The three previous victors—Carter, Nixon, LBJ—all won elections (two of them landslides) without being compelling TV personalities. Nixon was excellent on radio. LBJ was an all-enveloping persuader close-in, a gripper of elbows, clutcher of lapels. We have not had high presidential eloquence since Ted Sorensen was writing for JFK. Ford (speech writer Robert Hartmann) came close at times, and Reagan, a heavy contributor to his own speeches, can be forceful and moving. The arts of presidential communicating should also include a sense of when to keep quiet. No recent outstanding examples.

For his own sanity, a President needs a sense of humor. Reagan and JFK get high marks here, Ford so-so. Carter and Nixon each had a lively wit, on the biting side, but never developed an attractive way of showing it—just the right amount—in public. LBJ had little public humor and in private leaned heavily on the set-piece joke. ("There was this colored boy once up in front of this old judge in Panola County . . .")

The President needs to be an optimist. Ford: "You can't just sit back and say this is wrong, it is terrible, that is wrong and I can't do anything about it." But the President shouldn't be so optimistic that he can't face unpleasant facts—and spot them early. Reagan has not shown much of a built-in early-warning system, and neither did Carter.

A President must be capable of thinking in contingencies: What if? Some of the biggest contingencies—what if the Soviet Union did A or B—get reasonably steady attention at the White House. But many scarcely less important possibilities, non-Soviet in origin, some of which might stimulate Soviet reaction C or D, don't get seriously thought about.

A President needs an ever fresh curiosity about this big and complicated country. It changes—from the last time he campaigned across it. He can help overcome his isolation by seeking and taking advice from a broad circle. But many otherwise forthright people will simply not talk candidly to a President. He gets out of the habit of face-to-face give and take. He may be an excellent listener, as Carter was, and still be incapable of any real exchange except with a very few intimates. Reagan is more open as a personality but not notably open to "new" facts.

We want the President to be flexible, pragmatic, capable of compromise—but also firm, decisive, principled. Carter was hurt by policy zigzags. Reagan advisers once were said to worry about their man being "Carter-ized" if he compromised too readily. But many Republicans on Capitol Hill also worried about his being "mulish." This is a tough one to win. The President should be capable of admitting error to himself—and once in a while out loud. Theoretically, the public confessions could become too frequent, but that is not a real-life danger.

A crucial quality for any executive, above all for the Chief Executive of the United States, is perceptiveness about people. This will bear heavily on the caliber of the President's appointments and his ability to mold his people into an effective administration. He must be shrewd enough to see when infighting is unavoidable, even useful, and when it is destructive. FDR, Truman, Ike, JFK, and for a time LBJ were good managers and motivators of people. Nixon's management methods brought us Watergate. Ford and Carter were weak as people managers. Reagan has presided over some famous feuds and outlandish administrative arrangements. He has straightened things out from time to time, but things don't stay straightened out in his heavily overdelegated Presidency. When a President fills many of the top White House jobs with people from "the campaign," which has been the recent tendency, the staff then reinforces whatever is parochial in him. An awareness of the larger gaps in his own knowledge and concerns should enter the President's criteria for his immediate staff appointments. Self-knowledge without self-doubt is admittedly a lot to ask.

The President must manage more than people. The fearfully complex systems and institutions in his care need executive oversight and control. It is not enough to say a President "can hire managers"; as he delegates, he must know how to keep track of the delegated work; he must understand what his managers are managing. Of our postwar Presidents, Ike may have had the best grasp of this. He was the last of them with a good intellectual purchase on the Pentagon, an easier place to comprehend then than now. The Pentagon remains the most severe test of the Commander in Chief's instinct for what can be delegated and what must not be.

A President needs a strong sense of priorities, for the country and in the use of his own time. Reagan has this ability to concentrate his energies and the country's attention. Detractors might say this was because he has less energy to deploy. Carter had prodigious energy and diffused it too widely. Presidents should have the knack for keeping three or four balls in the air, but not the urge to toss up ten or fifteen.

Related to a sense of priorities is a recognition that the Presidency in some ways resembles a naval "watch." Some issues will demand action; in other matters it is enough, though not easy, to keep the government—not to be confused with the nation—running on course. Philosophically, this concept comes more readily to Republicans than Democrats. JFK had a weakness for speaking of "the unfinished public business"—as though it might all be cleaned up some day!

Well, I have proposed no fewer than thirty-one attributes of presidential leadership. Stephen Hess, White House alumnus and Brookings scholar of the Presidency, looking over the list above, proposed a thirty-second: Luck. "I always thought of Dwight Eisenhower as a uniquely lucky man," he said. "At the other extreme, the second President I worked for was Richard Nixon, who never struck me as lucky. He always seemed to have to work harder than anyone else for anything he wanted." Napoleon would have agreed with Hess. "Has he luck?" he would ask about a general.

Some of the thirty-two qualities are clearly more necessary than others, and some will be more pertinent to one era than another. Justice Abe Fortas, a sensitive Washington insider for over forty years, semipro violinist, almost Chief Justice, had a valuable perspective. Fortas, interviewed by Emmet Hughes, thought Eisenhower was a pretty good President for his time (Abe was not a raging revisionist), while in another period, Ike might have been "a catastrophe."* Yet "this leads to a further speculation: That different times might have induced Dwight Eisenhower himself to be different." Harry Truman, above all, "had a clear conception of *the point in history* at which he operated." Then there is "the crisis President." He "must not only know and respect the outer limits of the feasible, he must also have the courage and resourcefulness to exploit the range of feasible action in the national interest and not to undershoot it. And if he is a very great leader, he can shape and expand the dimensions of the feasible. The master in this area was Franklin Roosevelt."

Keeping handy the Fortas lens, we can also agree that there could be longer or much shorter lists of presidential virtues than the one I have constructed above. But all such lists would have this in common: no one of the cited qualities is by itself rare, and indeed we all know people who possess a number of them. The problem is to find somebody with all these qualities, or all but a very few, who is willing and able to seek a major-party nomination. Better yet, to find a dozen such people, so each party can choose from among first-class candidates before presenting the electorate the final decision in November.

The Résumé

Just from reading the résumés of the modern Presidents, you would have had a hard time predicting their effectiveness in office. The only fairly safe guess would be that one term as governor of Georgia is not ideal preparation. This is a retroactive guess; in 1976 the writer was among the 40 million voters who didn't think the point mattered that

---

*The Living Presidency, (New York: Coward, McCann & Geoghegan, 1973) p. 331.

much. A might-have-been: Carter, as a well-respected Georgia state senator, had a good chance for a seat in Congress in 1966, when he decided instead on his unsuccessful first run for governor. I suspect he would have been a more effective President if he had put in four years in Congress before becoming governor in 1970—but maybe he wouldn't have become governor running from Washington.

Two of the modern Presidents were two-term governors of our two biggest states—FDR and Reagan. Many students of politics think the governor's job in a big complicated state is the closest thing there is, though nothing is very close, to the Presidency.

The résumé of the now-legendary Harry Truman was modest indeed. He came out of the seamy politics of Kansas City and went to the White House from two terms, one very quiet, one effective, as a "machine" senator.

When Ike was elected some of his critics were genuinely worried about a "military mind" in the White House. Admirers who understood Ike's extraordinary kind of command success, at least as much political and diplomatic as military, expected a presidential greatness he didn't quite achieve.

One might have expected less—or more—than we got from Kennedy and Ford. JFK had served fourteen years on Capitol Hill, though he was not particularly diligent or influential there. Ford called himself "a child of the House," where he had spent twenty-four years, always in the minority; he served eight months as our first appointed Vice-President.

Probably the best résumés of all the modern Presidents were Johnson's (federal bureaucrat, congressman, Navy, Senator, Majority Leader, three years as Vice-President) and Nixon's (federal bureaucrat, Navy, congressman, Senator, eight years as Vice-President). One of the best résumés in two centuries included state legislator, congressman, Senator, Ambassador to Russia, Ambassador to Britain, Secretary of State. The possessor of these superb credentials was the ineffectual President James Buchanan.

Jimmy Carter, interestingly enough, was the only one of the modern Presidents with significant business experience. He successfully expanded the family's peanut enterprises; he "met a payroll." Harry Truman was a failed haberdasher. Roosevelt dabbled in some business ventures, not very successfully, while he was out of office, and was not too fastidious about the use of his political connections. Neither Roosevelt nor Kennedy managed his inherited wealth; FDR's mother wouldn't let him near the family money. Lyndon Johnson showed considerable entrepreneurial flair—in office.

Eight of the nine were college graduates, and the list of their institutions evokes the American dream. Harvard, Yale Law, and Michigan are there, and the senior service academies. But a young man from Southwest Texas State Teachers can grow up to be President (and boast of all the Ivy Leaguers working for him). So can a young man from Whittier, or from—perfect name—Eureka. Truman studied some law at night school in Kansas City; he earned no degree.

The academic performances are not very revealing. The best was Nixon's: No. 3 out of 25 at Duke University Law School. FDR tended to the "gentleman's C." Carter, as previously noted, was No. 60 out of 820 at Annapolis, Ike an unostentatious 61 out of 164 at West Point. Only three of the nine had law degrees (Ford and FDR as well as Nixon), a much lower proportion than in the membership of Congress (still about 50 percent lawyers). Apart from the lawyers, none of our modern Presidents has held an advanced degree. Only Carter had any technological background; he took postgraduate training in nuclear engineering for the submarine service (in some of his speeches he became a "nuclear scientist").

Lateral Entry. It will be interesting to see whether a Ph.D. can be elected again (Woodrow Wilson was the first and only), before a woman or a black. Possibly a black female professor of economics who has become a university president—we could really use some good economics—in 1996. Meanwhile, not even counting lawyers, the country's advanced-degree holders—the M.A.s, M.B.A.s, Ph.D.s, etc.—now number some 3 million men and women, and they are a formidable talent pool.

This brings us to the perennial question: Isn't there some way to get good people from "outside" politics into politics—at the level where they might be considered for the Presidency? The answer remains Probably Not. Wendell Willkie in 1940 was the last major-party nominee from outside politics. Ike had never run for elective office but had been very high in government, the armed branch.

"New Places to Look for Presidents" was the subject of a *Time* Essay in 1975.* Out of voluminous reports from the *Time* news bureaus around the country, more than 150 names made the working lists. The printed Essay narrowed this down to 38. All 38 have since pursued their worthy careers in business, academia, law, labor, philanthropy; some

*December 15, 1975.

have now retired. Only two, Cyrus Vance and George Shultz, then cited as a highly capable businessman who also had governmental and academic experience, came anywhere near the presidential orbit.

In 1982, *Time* again asked its news bureaus for regional lists of people outside politics who might be presidential. This time the exercise yielded a national total of only twenty-one names. Among them: two former astronauts, Frank Borman, President and Chairman of the Board of Eastern Airlines, and Neil Armstrong, oil equipment executive; Chairman Robert Anderson of Arco, Lee Iacocca of Chrysler, James Beré of Borg-Warner, and President Thomas Wyman of CBS; Presidents Hannah Gray of the University of Chicago, Marvin Goldberger of Cal Tech, Bartlett Giamatti of Yale.

TV had clearly been at work. The two former astronauts owed their high "name recognition" in good part to TV, and Borman helped keep his alive with TV commercials. Iacocca also gave himself heavy exposure as a TV pitchman; it's an expressive face, an appealing tough-guy personality and, who knows, having pulled Chrysler out of the hole, saved American jobs . . . ? (There was actually a brief flurry of Iacocca-for-VP talk among the Democrats in 1984.) The President of CBS was of course an unknown face, but any heir apparent who could avoid being fired by Bill Paley—Wyman has now safely ascended to chairman —has undeniable political talents. And the list included, inevitably, Walter Cronkite.

"It's lists like this," says Jonathan Moore of Harvard, "that make you think the people inside politics aren't so bad after all." Nothing personal, he hastens to add, but the outside types tend to be "one-dimensional in experience."

How to give them another dimension? Most private institutions are proud when one of their people is offered a prestigious appointive job in Washington. Depending on the man's age and length of absence in Washington, the organization is glad to welcome him back, sometimes to a higher job than he left; and if that can't be done, the individual will usually be snapped up elsewhere. There is no taint to Cabinet or sub-Cabinet experience under either party; it is highly marketable.

What is needed is for some courageous corporations, universities, foundations to give "electoral sabbaticals." A promising forty-year-old corporation VP or university dean could try for a nomination to Congress (or indeed the state legislature). If he wins, he's now in politics, and if he has the talents that would have made him an impressive figure in private life, at fifty-five say, he might at fifty-five be a governor, senator, or Cabinet officer with a shot at President. If he loses, he gets his old job back and his organization learns not to be embarrassed that one of its people is an openly confessed Republican or Democrat. One of the reasons that Congress and the state legislatures are so loaded with lawyers is that they can run and, lose or win, benefit from the publicity and contacts.

Why Not the Best?

More urgent than the "outside" talent question, however, is the inside talent question: Do the best people in politics, dedicated for most of their careers to politics, get to the top?

As compared with the six Presidents from Kennedy through Reagan, you can draw up a list of defeated candidates and defeated contenders for nomination that may well include some better presidential material than what we actually got. On the Democratic side: Edmund Muskie, Hubert Humphrey, Scoop Jackson, Adlai Stevenson (still a factor in 1960). Republican: Nelson Rockefeller, William Scranton, Howard Baker, George Bush, John Connally.

For the Republicans, Bush and Baker are still very much available for 1988, likewise Senator Majority Leader Robert Dole, steadily positioning himself toward the center, and Congressman Jack Kemp, steadily holding to the right. Also Senator (and former Governor) Dan Evans of Washington; Governors Richard Thornburgh of Pennsylvania, Thomas Kean of New Jersey, George Deukmejian of California; Lew Lehrman, the very bright and conservative businessman who almost got himself elected governor of New York in 1982.

The Republican party is well stocked with women of national stature, better stocked, ironically, than the Democrats, whose views on "women's issues" have been so much more congenial to feminist groups. The Republican roll call would include Anne Armstrong of Texas, former co-Chairman of the Republican Party and Ambassador to the U.K.; Senator Nancy Kassebaum of Kansas; Jeane Kirkpatrick, Ambassador to the UN; Supreme Court Justice Sandra Day O'Connor; and Elizabeth Dole, Secretary of Transportation. Liddy's fond husband, Senator Robert, says if there is a Dole and Dole ticket in 1988, he isn't sure which gets to be VP.

Among the Democrats, Gary Hart and perhaps others of the disappointed 1984 contenders will surface again. More will perhaps be heard from Geraldine Ferraro, less, probably, from Walter Mondale.* Ted Kennedy, in taking himself out of the 1984 running, indicated he might like to be asked another time. The pros (including at least one rather experienced Republican, Richard Nixon) consider New York's Governor Mario Cuomo a very hot item. Senator Bill Bradley, the most impressive Democratic winner of 1984, swept New Jersey by 65-35 while Reagan was carrying it 60-40. Bradley's "modified flat tax" ideas will keep him in the news. Also attractive and able: Senators Sam Nunn of Georgia (80-20), Joseph Biden of Delaware (60-40), and two freshman Senators, Albert Gore, Jr., of Tennessee (61-34) and Jay Rockefeller of West Virginia (52–48)—all prevailing against the Reagan tide in their states. The highly respected Senator Dale Bumpers of Arkansas will make some of the 1988 lists, as will Governors Robert Graham of Florida, Bruce Babbitt of Arizona, Richard Lamm of Colorado, and Michael Dukakis of Massachusetts. The veteran Indiana congressman and former Majority Whip, John Brademas, now President of New York University, has probably not forsworn politics for all time.

These are strong lists, for both parties. Many of these people will end up being "merely" vice-presidential, but remember that four of the nine modern Presidents came from V.P.

Henry Graff points out that we've had no ex-mayor as President since Grover Cleveland (Buffalo). It must be because "mayors deal with garbage and it rubs off on them." Hubert Humphrey (Minneapolis) came close, however, and Senator Richard Lugar (Indianapolis), one of the biggest Republican winners in 1982, now Chairman of the Senate Foreign Relations Committee, gets talked about.

Reform and Unreform

There are several changes that would help the best of these people get serious consideration for the Presidency:

The Democrats in their McGovern era reforms tried to convert their nominating conventions into a faithful profile of the Democratic voting population and the party's major target groups. They achieved

*Jesse Jackson, whether or not he runs again, will continue as a major force in Democratic politics. He may have opened the way for less flamboyant black leaders, e.g., Mayor Andrew Young of Atlanta, Mayor Wilson Goode of Philadelphia, Vernon Jordan, former head of the Urban League, or Franklin Thomas, president of the Ford Foundation. However, so long as Democrats feel the black vote is locked up (it went 91-9 for Mondale), they are unlikely to see any need for a black on the national ticket.

weird results: in 1980, 10 percent of the delegates in Madison Square Garden were members of NEA, the ravenous teachers' union, and only 2 percent were government officeholders. The party has now partially unreformed itself—about 22 percent of the 1984 delegates were elected officeholders and party leaders. But almost everybody—except the blocs and pressure groups—agrees the judgment of people already in government should weigh more heavily in the choice of a presidential candidate. Tom Wicker of the *New York Times* has proposed* that 40 percent of the delegates should go to the conventions—Republican as well as Democratic—uncommitted.† Bring back the bosses, part way. But also make it possible for a figure highly regarded by the professionals, such as ex-President Gerald Ford in 1980, to get serious consideration at the convention even though he has not gone through the primaries mill.

James MacGregor Burns would like to see the primaries reduced to a purely "advisory" role, with the real nominating process moving forward through party caucuses and conventions, state by state, climaxing in national conventions with real power. He urges revitalization of the parties as the only path to effective national leadership. Candidates for President and Congress would be powerfully motivated to develop coherent party positions in their campaigning and to follow through if they got to Washington. The restoration of party must begin in the nominating process, Burns believes; along with that, some of the structural proposals for binding President and Congress may be useful, but without strong parties, these would be meaningless tinkering.

Shortening and simplifying the marathon campaign for the nominations would reduce the numbing effect on the electorate, perhaps lead to higher voter turnout and, conceivably, more thoughtful voting. The Democrats have taken some preliminary steps in this direction. Shorter campaigns would be somewhat less expensive and might help the working officeholder get as much attention as the full-time presidential candidate. Howard Baker has complained of the difficulty of running against an "unemployed millionaire." In 1980, while he was busy as Senate Majority Leader, he was up against three of them: Reagan, Bush, Connally. Carter in 1976 was approximately a millionaire, and had been running full-time for two years; all his rivals had demanding jobs.

Speaking of money, the game is still heavily stacked toward those

*August 14, 1980.

†Most Democratic delegates in 1984 were effectively committed, though technically free to switch before the first ballot.

who have some of it, or whose policies (on the subject of unionism, insurance, Israel, oil, whatever) attract plentiful contributions. Once a candidate is rated as having a serious chance, the money tends to flow, but some first-class people never get sufficiently funded to be seen as "serious."

Mainly because of the price of TV ads, it can cost millions to run for governor or senator in a sizable state, a serious constriction on the size of the pool from which presidential possibilities are drawn. In 1982, Lew Lehrman spent about $7 million of his own money running for governor of New York. Democrat Mark Dayton of the department store Daytons spent about the same—but four times as much per voter—in his run for senator from Minnesota. Both lost, to be sure, and in Dayton's campaign in stolid Minnesota, the lavish spending may have hurt him. Dayton is married, somewhat superfluously from a financial point of view, to a Rockefeller, sister of Jay, who in getting reelected West Virginia Governor in 1980 spent some $12 million in that small but hungry state, or almost $29 for each vote he got. In the thirty-three Senate races of 1982, twenty-seven of the winners outspent their opponents. Total spending on the 1982 congressional races exceeded $300 million.

In 1984, the North Carolina Senate race in which Jesse Helms beat Governor James Hunt cost $22 million—a national record. Neither is a rich man; their candidacies attracted torrents of out-of-state money. In Illinois, Charles Percy spent about $6 million, some of it his own, in losing his Senate seat to Paul Simon ($5 million). In West Virginia, Jay Rockefeller retrenched a little: he spent about $9.3 million in moving from Governor to Senator.

The total cost of the 1984 elections, presidential and congressional, may have reached $1 billion. This is not an excessive advertising budget for the most important act a democracy performs (Procter & Gamble spends $600 million a year on ads). The question is whether the money is fairly distributed, and whether contributors in effect can buy a politician's loyalty. But campaign financing is a very complicated thing to regulate. Freedom of speech is involved, also the law of unintended consequences: past "reforms" have often created whole new sets of problems.

Perhaps the greatest stroke in behalf of better Presidents would be for the incumbent President to consider as one of his major responsibilities the identification and grooming of possible successors. A corporate

Chief Executive Officer would be considered shamefully derelict if he did as little about his successor as the President of the United States does. To be sure, the CEO has more power over his company than the President has over his party. We don't want the President decreeing his successor. The last time it was tried was in 1908, when Teddy Roosevelt handpicked William Howard Taft. By 1912, the two were running against each other, splitting the Republican Party and presenting the Presidency to Woodrow Wilson.

While a President can't and shouldn't anoint his successor, he should see to it that strong people are in the right places to get serious consideration. Ike gave fitful attention to the problem, and kept lists. He thought Robert Anderson—Texas businessman, his Secretary of the Navy, then Treasury—was best qualified to succeed him. But when Anderson wasn't interested, Ike seemed to lose interest in the whole question. He was not a great Nixon fan, but wouldn't move against his Vice-President. Nixon as President came to think John Connally would be his best successor, toyed with the thought of moving Spiro Agnew to the Supreme Court (!) and making Connally his running mate in 1972. He could have commanded that, but backed off; then when Agnew had to quit in disgrace in 1973, Nixon was in enough trouble himself that he didn't want to risk a congressional fight over the controversial Connally. He chose the safe and well-liked Jerry Ford.

Not only in the choice for VP, but in his major Cabinet appointments, a President has the chance to put good people into the running for the future. In his dealings with senators, representatives, governors, mayors, he can give discreet encouragement to careers that deserve it. He can bring strong people into government from the "outside." The President needs to be big enough, of course, not to feel threatened or upstaged by big people around him.

The President can fight the idea that the Presidency is unmanageable, for the sake of his own place in history but also for the sake of the office and the appeal it could hold for others in the future. He should liberate himself from what Stephen Hess calls the "overblown" staff, which "has become counter-productive to the purposes of Presidents." It "increasingly draws no-win problems into the Oval Office; this in turn contributes to undermining public trust in Presidents."* There has been far too much lamentation about the President's helplessness vis-à-vis the bureaucracy. JFK called the State Department "a foreign power." Charles Dawes, Vice-President under Hoover, liked to say that

*Stephen Hess, *Organizing the Presidency* (The Brookings Institution, 1976), p. 179.

the members of the Cabinet "are the President's natural enemies." This was half-true in the days when Cabinet officers tended to be the leaders of major factions within the President's party. But few Cabinet officers in recent administrations have had powerful constituencies of their own. A John Kennedy could not very well complain that it was impossible to control a Dean Rusk. So Presidents use the power of the permanent bureaucracy as an alibi for their own nonfeasance in the managerial role, and this encourages their Cabinet officers to adopt the same attitude within their departments. When a candidate runs "against Washington," as Carter and Reagan did, this mindset continues long after the candidate has himself become Washington. He is not an autocrat, of course, but he is far the most powerful person in government. Plenty of people will always seek the Presidency, but we may be losing some principled people who have been persuaded by Presidents themselves that the job is just about impossible. No one, however, could accuse the incorrigibly cheerful Ronald Reagan of consciously conveying such an impression.

Refining Expectations

Finally, along with thinking of the Presidency as manageable, we need to learn not to expect too much of the President. This is a difficult balance, but justly so, because we want equally delicate balance within the mind and temperament of the President: just enough of this or that quality, but not too much.

We Americans can be quite inconsistent in the ways we look at that mortal man in the White House. A part of the original American suspicion of central authority still survives. To that old strain of cranky skepticism about political leaders is now added the fact that at least five or ten million citizens are at least as well educated as anybody likely to be running for President. America can be a very tough audience. But we are also deeply susceptible to heroes and leaders. We doubt that the President always knows best, but we wish he did. A part of us resists strong leadership, a part of us hankers after it.

TV does not make matters easier. It has not supplanted the political parties, but it enables candidates and voters to bypass the parties. It can be harsh, as it was with Reagan when he faltered for a few minutes in the first debate with Mondale, and as it consistently was with Mondale, who came across as boring. TV can confer and enhance a celebrity that may be confused with leadership quality. But at the same time it has become one of the major tests of political leadership whether a candidate understands the medium and knows how to use it. (And has the sense to appoint staff people who know TV.) In the immediate aftermath of November 6, 1984, there was some gabble to the effect that our electoral process has gone totally Hollywood. I think this underestimates the ways in which substantive issues—prosperity and peace—favored Reagan. Mondale failed to mount an effective argument that these large and happy circumstances were illusory. That he was dull on TV was important but not crucial.

In his morning-after press conference, Mondale had some rueful things to say about TV:

> Modern politics today requires a mastery of television. I've never really warmed up to television and, in fairness to television, it's never warmed up to me. By instinct and tradition I don't like these things [TV mikes] . . . American politics is losing its substance . . . It's losing the depth . . . Tough problems require discussion. . . . I hope we don't lose in America this demand that those of us who want this office must be serious people of substance and depth and must be prepared not to handle the 10-second gimmick that deals, say, with little things like war and peace.*

But Mondale and Reagan had both had hours and years to develop and expound their political identities and appeals; it is not unreasonable now and then for the electorate to welcome a brisk summary. I will be more receptive to the Mondale grievance when we see one of the Hollywood ultraliberals—Paul Newman, Robert Redford, Warren Beatty, Jane Fonda—better actors and bigger box-office than Reagan ever was, get to Congress, let alone the White House. The content of the message does matter.

TV also contributes, in these dragged-out campaigns, to the steady inflation of political promises. As the talking goes on and on, presidential candidates seem drawn to grander and grander claims of what they are going to do. You could cry or laugh or both on rereading some of the promises of Reagan, Carter, Nixon, Kennedy. The apparent necessity of talking such nonsense is one of the things that keep some good people out of politics. A presidential candidate who won on reasonably sober rhetoric might encourage good people for the future, and along the way save himself some trouble in office. For that to happen, the voters—the audience—would have to want it that way.

Thomas Cronin of Colorado College, one of the most perceptive of

*The *New York Times*, November 8, 1984.

the new generation of presidential scholars, puts it well: "We must refine our expectations of the President and raise our expectations of ourselves."*

Some Inauguration Day morning—1989, 1993, whenever—a citizen with a long memory and a faith in America might be musing over breakfast:

> The country is confronted by a very long list of problems, foreign and domestic. Several are so pressing they must be mastered in the next four years, by the new President and Congress, with the help of the people. In some of the other situations, it would be good to make some progress, and that is entirely possible. But some of the old problems, to tell the truth, will look just as tough four years from now as they do today. Many are not problems for government at all but for society. Fortunately, our society works well in most respects, and we should take pains not to interfere with those workings. (They deserve celebration.) May the new President have the wisdom to know which problems are which.
>
> But meanwhile it is absolutely predictable that new problems will begin to appear, and that some previously trivial problems will become important. It is always jarring to have familiar agendas rearranged, and this new Administration will do well if it grants legitimacy to the new problems, and passes them along, defined, sorted by possible solutions, to future administrations. But it is also likely that in foreign affairs new challenges will arise that cannot be passed along. They will be met, or not met. God willing, this government and people will meet them.

If that hypothetical citizen thinking these thoughts on Inauguration Day morning were the President-elect, I would think the voters had been offered a good choice on the recent Election Day, and had made a good choice. I would even hope for an Inaugural Address infused with an exalted modesty.

*The State of the Presidency (Boston: Little Brown, 1980), p. 379.

Index

About the Author

Hedley Donovan confesses to a liking for American politicians, and an intense curiosity (and sneaking optimism) as to what they will do next. He grew up in Minneapolis, was graduated from the University of Minnesota and studied at Oxford as a Rhodes Scholar.

"I once planned to be a history professor," he recalls, "but got diverted into journalism for forty years or so." When he recently accepted a Harvard appointment as Fellow of the Faculty of Government, the Dean of the Kennedy School, Graham Allison, greeted him: "Better late than never."

Donovan was a reporter on the Washington *Post* during Franklin Roosevelt's second term and the first year of his third. He served four years in Naval Intelligence during World War II. He was a writer for *Fortune* magazine for five years, then Associate Managing Editor, and in 1953 became Managing Editor. Six years later Henry Luce appointed him his deputy, as Editorial Director of Time Inc., and in 1964 he succeeded Luce as Editor in Chief. A few weeks after retiring from Time Inc. in 1979, he accepted Jimmy Carter's invitation to become Senior Adviser to the President. "I stayed one year, door-to-door. I'm not sure how much I was able to help Carter, but it was educational for me."

A number of colleges and universities have given Donovan honorary degrees, and he is an Honorary Fellow of his old (quite old—700 years) Oxford College, Hertford. He has seved as a trustee for various educational and philanthropic bodies including the Ford Foundation, New York University, and the National Humanities Center.